Sounds Delicious!

PUBLISHED BY THE
VOLUNTEER COUNCIL OF
THE TULSA PHILHARMONIC SOCIETY, INC.
TULSA, OKLAHOMA

THE VOLUNTEER COUNCIL OF THE TULSA PHILHARMONIC SOCIETY, INC. WAS FOUNDED IN 1948 AS THE WOMEN'S ASSOCIATION OF THE TULSA PHILHARMONIC. THE PURPOSE OF THE COUNCIL IS TO HELP SUPPORT AND PROMOTE THE GROWTH OF THE TULSA PHILHARMONIC ORCHESTRA THROUGH COUNTLESS HOURS OF VOLUNTEER TIME AND FINANCIAL SUPPORT WITH A SERIES OF FUNDRAISING ACTIVITIES, THE MOST RECENT BEING *SOUNDS DELICIOUS*.

ISBN 0-9617004-0-8
LIBRARY OF CONGRESS CATALOG CARD NUMBER 86-60337
FIRST PRINTING OCTOBER 1986 15,000 COPIES

ADDITIONAL COPIES MAY BE OBTAINED BY ADDRESSING:

Sounds Delicious!

VOLUNTEER COUNCIL OF THE
TULSA PHILHARMONIC SOCIETY, INC.
8177 S. HARVARD
SUITE 431
TULSA, OKLAHOMA 74137

FOR YOUR CONVENIENCE, ORDER FORMS ARE PROVIDED IN THE BACK OF THE BOOK. COST PER BOOK IS $14.95 PLUS $2.00 POSTAGE AND HANDLING. OKLAHOMA RESIDENTS PLEASE ADD $.94 PER COPY SALES TAX.

PRINTED BY HART GRAPHICS, INC.
AUSTIN, TEXAS

Introduction

From its inception to its fruition, **Sounds Delicious** was carefully shaped into a single object. The criteria for our cookbook was to produce a book which would be of interest to experienced cooks as well as a tool for beginners. Hence, the techniques and charts for measurements and substitutions came into being. We strived to bring into our book a new generation of recipes and presentations. Not for us the same old recipes seen in every cookbook.

Our deLIGHTful section was painstakingly researched and compiled into a cookbook within a cookbook. The treatment of this section takes into account the need for lighter, healthier meal planning.

The creative touches and thoughtful details which we believe make **Sounds Delicious** superior are all designed with you, the reader, in mind. It is our fervent hope that **Sounds Delicious** will earn a favored spot in your kitchen, not only for its beauty, but also as a well used resource.

Recipes which consistently received high ratings during testing have been designated with this symbol for excellence.

Recipes which are more complex and require some cooking expertise have been designated with this symbol.

It is with sincere appreciation and special thanks that the cookbook committee recognizes the contributions of those who helped make **Sounds Delicious** so extraordinary. Especially we wish to thank Gene Johnson whose stunning photographs so enhance and carry out the theme of our book.

Color photography by

Gene Johnson, Owner
Bob Hawks Photography
Tulsa, Oklahoma

Cover Shot on Location
Doubletree Hotel
Tulsa, Oklahoma

Props Furnished By
Sanger Harris
Tulsa, Oklahoma

Photograph Ideas and Food Preparation by
Claudia Hawn   Donna Muscovalley   Barbara Naugle

Book Title by
Barbara Horn

Special Thanks to:
Nan Mulvaney, Hart Graphics

Patrons

The Cookbook Committee gratefully acknowledges our special friends who have supported our endeavors.

Mrs. Charles H. Adams (Jacquelyn C.)

American Bank & Trust Co.

Arthur Young and Company

Mr. and Mrs. Richard L. Boerger

Mr. and Mrs. Latham L. Brundred, Jr.

Mr. and Mrs. Joseph F. Clark

Mary Lou Daniel

Margaret Dean

Tom and Chris Herrmann

Kidder Peabody & Co., Inc.

Raymond F. Kravis

Mr. and Mrs. Robert Lorton (Tulsa World)

Mr. and Mrs. Richard H. Kristinik

Main Hurdman

Mapco, Inc.

Miss Jackson's

Nick and Donna Muscovalley

Tom and Barbara Naugle

Mrs. H.E. Pickhardt

Sooner Federal Savings and Loan Association

Texaco Refining & Marketing, Inc.

Richard and Nora Walworth

Barbara J. Wilson, Inc.

Sounds Delicious *Cookbook Committee*

	1983 – 1985	1985 – 1986	1986 – 1987
Advisor		Bobbie Kristinik	Donna Muscovalley
Chairman	Bobbie Kristinik	Donna Muscovalley	Barbara Naugle
Co-Chairman	Donna Muscovalley	Barbara Naugle	Loretta Pickhardt

Section Committees

Appetizers

Barbara Naugle, Co-Chairman
Debbie Turner, Co-Chairman

Beverages

Lee Ann Wortham, Chairman

Breads

Natalie Brundred, Co-Chairman
Millie Millspaugh, Co-Chairman

deLIGHTful

Melonnie Dauben, Co-Chairman
Pat Payton, Co-Chairman

Desserts

Loretta Boerger, Chairman
Monica Bryant, Co-Chairman
Margaret Dean, Co-Chairman

Eggs, Cheese & Pasta

Judi Klein, Chairman

Fish & Shellfish

Polly Hamilton, Co-Chairman
Susan Huffman, Co-Chairman

Meats

Barbara Naugle, Chairman

Poultry

Margaret S. Rutter, Chairman
Chris Herrmann, Co-Chairman
Sally Rice, Co-Chairman

Salads & Dressings

Loma Lavell, Co-Chairman
Jean Risser, Co-Chairman

Sauces & Accompaniments

Anne Steelman, Chairman

Soups & Sandwiches

Claudia Hawn, Co-Chairman
Carolyn Savage, Co-Chairman

Vegetables

Judy Miller, Co-Chairman
Jean Gannon, Co-Chairman

Other Committees

Editing

Donna Muscovalley, Chairman

Publicity

Nancy Evans, Co-Chairman
Patti Fehrle, Co-Chairman
Jan Jones
Susan Postier
Dianne Renkes

Promotions

Diane Michael, Chairman
Chris Davies
Dorothy Frisson
Maureen Hyde
Kate Lalonde
Jane Lankie
Jan Menger
Keir Morrison
Lynn Reynolds
Denise Selke
Johnnye Vinson

Proofreading

JoAnn Allen
M. J. Barbere
Nancy Caudell
Margaret Dean
Melissa Fell
Laurie Fiocchi
Polly Hamilton
Claudia Hawn
Tina Melton
Pricilla Moore
Donna Muscovalley
Pat Payton
Margaret S. Rutter
Anne Steelman
Tina Townsend

Sales

Bonnie Epstein, Chairman
Debbie Dill, Co-Chairman
Lin Kobsey, Co-Chairman

Special Events

Mary Lou Bianchi, 1985 – 86
Margaret S. Rutter, 1986 – 87

Staffing

Karla Campbell, Co-Chairman

Treasurers

Tina Melton, 1985 – 86
Laurie Fiocchi, 1986 – 1987

Assistant Treasurer
Sherril Sibley, 1986 – 1987

Typing

Francis Campbell
Jean Spears

Contributors

The Cookbook Committee would like to thank all Volunteer Council members and friends who contributed recipes to *Sounds Delicious*. Each recipe has been multi-tested for taste and accuracy. Recipes have been edited to conform to style and guidelines and some modifications made by the committee. We regret that we were unable to include all recipes which were submitted due to availability of space.

Joann Allen
Loretta Allen
Betty Anderson
Jo Layne Antry
Bea Arend
Elizabeth Ashley
Wendy Auten
Linda Baker
Sharon Bartlet
Judy Bebernes
Rita Bell
Paula Berry
Mary Lou Bianchi
Patsy Bobek
Loretta D. Boerger
Susie Bolthin
Julie Brown
James W. Brownlee
Natalie Brundred
Monica Bryant
Linda Bump
K. Caldwell
Frances Campbell
Karla Campbell
Jo Ann Carlson
Edna Cheatham
Marilyn Chenoweth
Rosie Childs
Betty Clark
Joanne Claussen
Shirley Coffin
Faye Conklin
Harry O. Cramton
Flo Crawford
Ginny Creveling
Fran Crosby
Francoise Dauben
Melonnie Dauben
Frances Dauteuil
Grace Davis
Margaret Dean
Mary Beth Dolan
Beth Dunkin
Margaret Dunlop
Laura Dunson
Rose Ellzey
Nancy Evans
Elizabeth Failing
Clara Flinn
Karen Fraser
Sally Frasier
Janis Fritz
Carolyn Fulton
Jean Gannon
Jo Ann Garrison
Catherine Gawey
Charlene Gibson
Linda Goldsmith
Dian Gosswiller
Mary Graham
Jimmie Haggard

Vicky Hale
Hazel Hall
Kathryn Hall
Polly Hamilton
Claudia Hawn
Suzanne Hebertson
Bee Helgeson
Beverly Hembree
Lowena Henshaw
Chris Herrmann
Jody Hitt
Judy Hoberock
Virginia Hocutt
Sandi Hodges
Norma Hollinger
Lorene Hopkins
Barbara Horn
Elizabeth Horne
Kathy Hoyt
Susan Huffman
Sylvia Joanedis
Jan Jones
Charlotte Jordan
Lorraine Kelley
Dianne Kesinger
Nancy Kirby
Judi Klein
Sharon Kramer
Cathy Kranz
Bobbie Kristinik
Loma Lavell
Maralyn Lavenstein
Sayde LeVine
Julia Lee
Charlene Long
Donald G. Long
Phyllis Long
Marguerite Lovell
Gertrude Lovoi
Alexa Maples
Mary Ann Marberry
Darlene Martin
Martha A. Mattes
Carolyn McClure
Evelyn McDonald
Doris McGrath
Bettie Meissner
Andrew Melton
Tina W. Melton
Judy Miller
Millie Millspaugh
Inez Milstead
Annette Morey
Becky Murphy
Donna Muscovalley
Rose Muscovalley
Sheila Muscovalley
Barbara A. Naugle
Thomas E. Naugle
Nancy Neale

Betty Neeley
Romney Nesbitt
Elizabeth Newman
Almeta Norfleet
Jan Nunn
Mary Ann Orr
La Verne Osborn
Dottie Parker
Jan Pastor
Pamela Payne
Pat Payton
Patty Perryman
Teri Peters
Loretta Pickhardt
Sandi Pitman
Jackie Poe
Jonene Pruitt
Linda Rackley
Jan Reinhart
Jean Risser
Audrey Robison
Marcella Rollins
Joyce Roodman
Margaret S. Rutter
Carolyn Savage
Beverly Schafer
Lawton Scott
Diane Seebass
Dee Sloan
Betty Jane Smith
Iris Smith
Mary Kathryn Smith
Nan Smith
Rosetta Smith
Lonnie Snyder
Carmen Spencer
Anne Steelman
Sadie Stephens
Nan Stevens
Sally Stewart
Judy Stout
Lois Stratton
Cathy Swadener
Byrdie Thompson
Patricia Tomer
Paula Torrence
Sandy Tyler
Cinda Viles
Virginia Watkins
Mark Watson
Nan Weisrock
Midge West
Marian Whitehead
Margaret Willhour
Jerry Willits
Kathy Winslow
Sheryl Wiruth
Diane Word
Lee Ann Wortham
Ann Youngdahl

TABLE OF CONTENTS

Techniques

To conserve space and make serving easier, place an assortment of hors d'oeuvres on a tray rather than separate trays for each. A variety of shapes and colors makes garnishing unnecessary.

To avoid ragged edges when cutting bread for canapes or sandwiches, choose firmly textured bread and use a serrated knife.

Dip hands in cold water frequently when making meatballs. The meatballs will stay firm and will stick to hands less.

Scoop out lemon shells, green or red peppers or tomatoes to make attractive containers for dips, mayonnaise, etc.

Use a small palette knife to stuff artichokes, tomatoes and other awkward to fill vegetables.

To "frost" a glass, bury it in shaved ice long enough to give it a white, ice cold look and feel.

To quickly chill wine, beer or champagne, add 1 cup of salt to ice bucket or fill with water. Both reduce temperature of ice.

Prepare ice ring for punch by freezing a portion of punch in mold, or fill heavy gauge rubber balloons with water and freeze. Punch will not become diluted. Muffin tins make excellent jumbo ice cubes.

To serve hot spiced wine or similar drinks, keep at an ideal temperature by using a crockpot set on low temperature.

Use a blender to make cappuccino. Put hot milk and flavorings into blender, set on high for 2 to 3 seconds and pour over coffee.

To remove a stubborn cork, wrap a cloth dipped in boiling water around the neck of the bottle for a few minutes.

Use half as much sugar for tea by adding it to the brewed tea. This also keeps tea from clouding when refrigerated.

Black and green olives will keep longer if a few tablespoons of vodka are added to jar. Vodka will not change flavor of olives.

ESCARGOT AND PROSCIUTTO HAM

YIELD: 72 SERVINGS

PREPARATION TIME: 20 MINUTES

72 COUNT CANNED FRENCH SNAILS
72 WAFER THIN SLICES PROSCIUTTO HAM
2 CUPS BUTTER
1 TABLESPOON FINELY MINCED GARLIC
2 TABLESPOONS FRESH LEMON JUICE
2 TABLESPOONS DRY WHITE WINE
1/4 TEASPOON WHITE PEPPER
1 TABLESPOON CHOPPED FRESH PARSLEY

ROLL UP SNAILS IN HAM AND SECURE WITH TOOTHPICKS. PLACE IN CHAFING DISH AND WARM.

MEANWHILE, MELT BUTTER WITH GARLIC IN 1 1/2 QUART SAUCEPAN. LET BOIL UNTIL FOAMY AND CONTINUE TO BOIL ABOUT 30 SECONDS. REMOVE FROM HEAT AND BEAT WITH FINE WIRE WHISK ABOUT 1 MINUTE. WHILE CONTINUING TO BEAT, GRADUALLY ADD LEMON JUICE, WINE, PEPPER AND PARSLEY. POUR BUTTER MIXTURE OVER SNAILS AND KEEP WARM. AVOID HIGH HEAT WHICH WILL BREAK DOWN SAUCE.

EXECUTIVE CHEF DONAL WEAVING
SOUTHERN HILLS COUNTRY CLUB

ARTICHOKE HEART PUFF

YIELD: 6 TO 8 SERVINGS
PREHEAT OVEN: 375°

PREPARATION TIME: 20 MINUTES

28 OUNCES CANNED ARTICHOKE HEARTS, DRAINED
8 OUNCES CREAM CHEESE, SOFTENED
2 TABLESPOONS BUTTER, SOFTENED
2 EGGS
JUICE OF 3 LEMONS, OR TO TASTE
1 CUP GRATED AMERICAN OR MOZZARELLA CHEESE
SALT AND FRESHLY GROUND PEPPER, TO TASTE
1 TEASPOON GARLIC POWDER
GRATED PARMESAN CHEESE
DRY BREAD CRUMBS

IN FOOD PROCESSOR, CHOP ARTICHOKE HEARTS UNTIL ALMOST PUREED. IN MEDIUM BOWL COMBINE CREAM CHEESE, BUTTER, EGGS, LEMON JUICE, CHEESE, SALT, PEPPER AND GARLIC POWDER. ADD ARTICHOKES AND BLEND WELL. POUR INTO SHALLOW BAKING DISH; TOP WITH PARMESAN CHEESE AND BREAD CRUMBS. BAKE UNTIL BUBBLY, APPROXIMATELY 20 TO 30 MINUTES.

PANACHE

Farm Style Chili Con Queso

Preparation Time: 25 minutes

Yield: 2½ cups

2 slices bacon, chopped
1 small onion, finely chopped
1 medium tomato, peeled, seeded and chopped
½ cup finely chopped celery
7 ounces green chili salsa
¼ teaspoon salt
2 cups grated Monterey Jack cheese
Tortilla chips

In medium skillet, cook bacon until most of fat is rendered. Add onion, tomato and celery. Stirring occasionally, cook over medium heat until onion is tender. Stir in salsa and salt. Over low heat, stir in cheese until melted; do not boil. Pour into small fondue pot or small bowl on hot tray. Serve with tortilla chips for dipping.

Reprinted with permission from *Appetizers*, H. P. Books, Inc.

HINT: Additional cheese may be added for thicker queso.

Artichoke Hideaways

Preparation Time: 15 minutes

Yield: 25 to 30 pieces
Preheat Oven: 350°

1 cup shredded cheddar cheese
1¼ cups mayonnaise
2 to 4 tablespoons minced green onions
1 teaspoon minced fresh parsley
½ teaspoon lemon pepper
Dash cayenne pepper
8 ounces sliced cocktail rye bread
14 ounces canned artichoke hearts, drained and squeezed dry

Mix together cheese, mayonnaise, green onions, parsley and peppers. Cut crusts from bread, if desired. Quarter large artichoke hearts and halve small ones. Place bread on cookie sheet, top with piece of artichoke heart and cover with 1 tablespoon of mayonnaise mixture. Bake 5 to 10 minutes until hot and bubbly.

HOT CRISPED ARTICHOKE HEARTS

WONDERFUL ALTERNATIVE TO ARTICHOKE SPREADS.

YIELD: 8 SERVINGS *PREPARATION TIME: 25 MINUTES*

- **3/4 CUP BUTTERMILK**
- **3 TABLESPOONS ALL-PURPOSE FLOUR**
- **1/2 TEASPOON BEAU MONDE SEASONING**
- **9 OUNCES FROZEN ARTICHOKE HEARTS, THAWED, WELL DRAINED AND QUARTERED**
- **1/2 CUP ITALIAN BREAD CRUMBS**
- **1/2 CUP GRATED PARMESAN CHEESE**
- **VEGETABLE OIL FOR DEEP FRYING**

COMBINE BUTTERMILK WITH FLOUR AND BEAU MONDE; MIX THOROUGHLY. DIP ARTICHOKES IN BATTER AND COAT WITH BREADCRUMBS. DEEP FRY IN HOT OIL AT 350° UNTIL GOLDEN. DRAIN ON PAPER TOWELS AND SPRINKLE WITH PARMESAN CHEESE. SERVE WITH GARLIC HOLLANDAISE SAUCE FOR DIPPING.

*VARIATION: SUBSTITUTE **MUSHROOMS** FOR ARTICHOKES.*

QUICK GARLIC HOLLANDAISE:

- **1/2 CUP BUTTER**
- **1 CLOVE GARLIC, MINCED**
- **3 EGG YOLKS**
- **1 1/2 TABLESPOONS FRESH LEMON JUICE**
- **1/4 TEASPOON DRY MUSTARD**
- **4 TABLESPOONS COLD BUTTER, CUT INTO SMALL PIECES**

IN SMALL SKILLET OVER LOW HEAT, MELT BUTTER AND ADD GARLIC; COOK UNTIL SOFTENED. IN BLENDER OR FOOD PROCESSOR, BLEND YOLKS, LEMON JUICE AND MUSTARD AT HIGH SPEED. WITH MOTOR RUNNING, ADD MELTED BUTTER IN SLOW STEADY STREAM UNTIL SAUCE IS SMOOTH AND THICKENS SLIGHTLY. ADD COLD BUTTER ONE PIECE AT A TIME, BLENDING WELL AFTER EACH ADDITION. SAUCE CAN BE SERVED AS IS, OR WARMED IN DOUBLE BOILER.

SKEWERED BEEF TERIYAKI

YIELD: 75 PIECES *PREPARATION TIME: 40 MINUTES*

- **4 POUNDS SIRLOIN TIP ROAST, SLICED IN 1/8 × 3 INCH STRIPS**
- **12 OUNCES SOY SAUCE**
- **3 TABLESPOONS BOURBON OR SAKI**
- **1 TABLESPOON SUGAR**
- **1 TEASPOON GROUND GINGER**
- **2 TEASPOONS JANE'S KRAZY MIXED UP PEPPER**

AFTER SLICING BEEF, MIX REMAINING INGREDIENTS. MARINATE MEAT IN SAUCE AT LEAST 4 HOURS. THREAD MEAT ONTO 7 OR 8 INCH WOODEN SKEWERS. BROWN ON GRILL OR BROIL UNTIL DESIRED DONENESS, APPROXIMATELY 5 TO 8 MINUTES. IF HOLDING IN CHAFING DISH, ADD HEATED MARINADE TO DISH TO KEEP BEEF FROM DRYING OUT.

HINT: SEVERAL HOURS BEFORE COOKING, SOAK SKEWERS IN ICE WATER TO PREVENT BURNING.

CROUSTADES WITH TWO FILLINGS

PREPARATION TIME: 25 MINUTES

YIELD: 36 PIECES
PREHEAT OVEN: 400°

MELTED BUTTER
36 SLICES PEPPERIDGE FARM WHITE SANDWICH BREAD

BRUSH MELTED BUTTER IN MINI MUFFIN TINS. WITH 3 INCH ROUND COOKIE CUTTER, CUT BREAD INTO ROUNDS. FIT INTO MUFFIN TINS, MOLDING GENTLY AGAINST BOTTOMS AND SIDES. BAKE 10 TO 12 MINUTES.

PREPARE ONE OF THE FILLINGS. FILL EACH CUP WITH TEASPOON OF FILLING MIXTURE. REDUCE HEAT TO 375° AND BAKE APPROXIMATELY 8 TO 10 MINUTES OR UNTIL PUFFY AND LIGHTLY BROWNED. SERVE WARM.

SWISS CHEESE FILLING:
1 CUP MAYONNAISE
1 CUP FRESHLY GRATED PARMESAN CHEESE
1 CUP GRATED SWISS CHEESE
DASH TABASCO
1 TABLESPOON FINELY MINCED GREEN ONIONS

COMBINE ALL INGREDIENTS.

CRAB AND SWISS FILLING:
6 OUNCES FRESH OR FROZEN ALASKAN KING CRABMEAT, SHREDDED
1½ TABLESPOONS MINCED GREEN ONIONS
1 CUP SHREDDED SWISS CHEESE
½ CUP SOUR CREAM
1 TEASPOON FRESH LEMON JUICE
½ TEASPOON WORCESTERSHIRE SAUCE
¼ TEASPOON SALT

COMBINE ALL INGREDIENTS.

HINT: CROUSTADES ACCOMMODATE VARIETY OF FILLINGS, SO EXPERIMENT WITH YOUR FAVORITE.

CRAB STUFFED MUSHROOMS

YIELD: 25 TO 30 PIECES
PREHEAT OVEN: 375°

PREPARATION TIME: 20 MINUTES

REMOVE STEMS FROM MUSHROOMS AND RESERVE FOR ANOTHER USE.

MIX REMAINING INGREDIENTS AND PRESS INTO MUSHROOM CAPS, MOUNDING SLIGHTLY. PLACE IN JELLYROLL PAN AND ADD 1/4 CUP HOT WATER TO BOTTOM OF PAN. BAKE 15 TO 20 MINUTES.

1 POUND FRESH MUSHROOMS
3 TABLESPOONS FRESHLY GRATED PARMESAN CHEESE
3 OUNCES FRESH ALASKAN KING CRABMEAT, SHREDDED
1 TEASPOON DRIED PARSLEY, CRUMBLED
1 TABLESPOON ITALIAN BREAD CRUMBS
1 TEASPOON DRIED TARRAGON, CRUMBLED
3 TO 4 DASHES GARLIC POWDER
1/2 TEASPOON SALT
1/4 TEASPOON PEPPER
1 1/2 TEASPOONS MINCED GREEN ONIONS
4 TABLESPOONS BUTTER, MELTED
1/2 TEASPOON DIJON MUSTARD
1 TEASPOON SHERRY

SAVORY STUFFED MUSHROOMS

A HIT AT THE "A FEW OF OUR FAVORITE THINGS" COCKTAIL PARTY.

YIELD: 25 TO 30 PIECES
PREHEAT OVEN: 375°

PREPARATION TIME: 30 MINUTES

REMOVE STEMS FROM MUSHROOMS; CHOP. SAUTÉ BACON UNTIL PARTIALLY COOKED. ADD ONION, BELL PEPPER, SALT, PEPPER AND STEMS. COOK UNTIL TENDER; COOL. REMOVE TO BOWL; ADD CREAM CHEESE AND MIX WELL. PRESS INTO MUSHROOM CAPS, MOUNDING SLIGHTLY. PLACE IN JELLYROLL PAN; ADD 1/4 CUP HOT WATER TO BOTTOM OF PAN AND BAKE 20 MINUTES.

1 POUND FRESH MUSHROOMS
4 SLICES BACON, DICED
3/4 CUP CHOPPED ONION
2 TABLESPOONS MINCED GREEN BELL PEPPER
1 TEASPOON SALT
DASH FRESHLY GROUND PEPPER
3 OUNCES CREAM CHEESE, SOFTENED

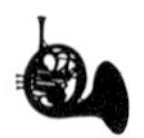

Tortellini with Pepperoni Pesto

Have plenty of cocktail picks on hand when you serve this dish!

Preparation Time: 45 minutes | *Yield: 8 to 10 servings*

- 1/2 pound each of spinach and egg tortellini
- 2 tablespoons sliced shallots
- 1/4 pound sliced pepperoni
- 1 cup drained sun-dried tomatoes packed in oil
- 1 tablespoon green peppercorn or Dijon mustard
- 2 cloves garlic, chopped
- 1 tablespoon fresh lemon juice
- 2 tablespoons white wine vinegar
- 2 tablespoons vermouth
- 1/4 teaspoon red pepper flakes, or to taste
- 1/2 cup extra virgin olive oil
- 3 tablespoons minced onion
- Shredded lettuce
- Grated Parmesan cheese

Cook tortellini al dente; drain and rinse under cold water. Set aside. In processor or blender, coarsely chop shallots, pepperoni, tomatoes, mustard, garlic, lemon juice, vinegar, vermouth and red pepper flakes. With motor running, add olive oil in steady stream; blend until combined well.

In large bowl toss onion and tortellini with sauce until pasta is well coated. Arrange on lettuce for first course or place in large attractive bowl with cocktail picks inserted in top layer for buffet. Serve at room temperature. Sprinkle with Parmesan cheese.

Spicy Cheese Truffles

This recipe was requested by several tasters!!

Preparation Time: 45 minutes | *Yield: 4 dozen*

- 12 ounces Bonchampi cheese, rind discarded, softened
- 1/2 cup butter, softened
- 5 ounces cream cheese, softened
- 2 teaspoons fines herbes
- 1/2 teaspoon dried thyme, crumbled
- 8 drops Tabasco
- Salt and white pepper, to taste
- 5 ounces dense dark pumpernickel bread, cubed

Combine all ingredients except bread in mixing bowl; beat until smooth. Chill overnight. Process bread cubes finely in processor or blender. Form cheese mixture into 1 inch balls. Roll in bread crumbs, coating completely; refrigerate. Bring to room temperature 15 minutes before serving.

CALIFORNIA CHEESE BALLS

THESE HAVE A MILD FLAVOR AND WILL BE A POPULAR ADDITION TO ANY MENU.

YIELD: 15 PIECES | *PREPARATION TIME: 20 MINUTES*

COMBINE ALL INGREDIENTS EXCEPT PECANS. CHILL UNTIL ALMOST FIRM. FORM INTO BITE-SIZE BALLS AND ROLL IN PECANS. REFRIGERATE UNTIL READY TO SERVE.

8 OUNCES CREAM CHEESE, SOFTENED
2 OUNCES BLUE OR ROQUEFORT CHEESE, SOFTENED
1 TABLESPOON FINELY CHOPPED ONION
1 TABLESPOON FINELY CHOPPED CELERY
DASH CAYENNE PEPPER
GROUND PECANS

HONEY YOGURT FRUIT DRESSING

DRESSING CAN BE POURED OVER FRUIT OR USED AS DIP FOR FRUIT PLATTER APPETIZER.

YIELD: 1 1/2 CUPS | *PREPARATION TIME: 10 MINUTES*

COMBINE YOGURTS, VANILLA, LEMON JUICE AND HONEY. SPRINKLE WITH GINGER.

8 OUNCES PLAIN YOGURT
3 OUNCES LEMON YOGURT
1 TEASPOON VANILLA
1 TABLESPOON FRESH LEMON JUICE
1 TO 2 TABLESPOONS HONEY
GROUND GINGER

NOTE: TO PREPARE DELICATE WHITE **COCONUT BANANAS** *FOUND IN SECTION PHOTOGRAPH, PLACE SLICED BANANAS IN LEMON JUICE, DRAIN, SMEAR WITH SOUR CREAM AND ROLL IN FLAKED COCONUT.*

SALMON DELIGHTS

TRULY A MELT-IN-YOUR-MOUTH APPETIZER OR FIRST COURSE.

PREPARATION TIME: 20 MINUTES *YIELD: 20 PIECES*

- **8 OUNCES SMOKED ALASKAN SALMON (LOX), THINLY SLICED, DIVIDED**
- **3 TABLESPOONS SOUR CREAM**
- **2 DASHES TABASCO**
- **1/4 TEASPOON DRIED DILL WEED**
- **1 1/2 TEASPOONS FRESH LEMON JUICE**
- **20 THIN SLICES PARTY PUMPERNICKEL OR FRENCH BAGUETTE BREAD**
- **20 SMALL PAPER-THIN SLICES ONION**
- **DRAINED CAPERS**

IN BLENDER, PURÉE HALF OF SALMON WITH SOUR CREAM, TABASCO, DILL WEED AND LEMON JUICE, SCRAPING DOWN SIDES OF CONTAINER AS NEEDED. REMOVE AND SET ASIDE.

CUT CRUSTS FROM BREAD, IF DESIRED. CUT REMAINING SALMON INTO 1 × 2 INCH STRIPS AND SET ASIDE. SPREAD EACH BREAD SLICE WITH PURÉED SALMON. DIVIDE SALMON STRIPS EVENLY AND PLACE ON TOP OF PURÉED SALMON. TOP EACH WITH ONION SLICE AND CAPERS. COVER AND REFRIGERATE UNTIL READY TO SERVE.

MEXICAN HATS

PREPARATION TIME: 20 MINUTES *YIELD: 70 PIECES*

- **2 CUPS RIPE MASHED AVOCADO, PEELS OR SEEDS RESERVED**
- **JUICE OF 1 LEMON**
- **1 TO 2 TABLESPOONS FINELY MINCED ONION**
- **2 TO 3 TABLESPOONS PICANTE SAUCE**
- **1/8 TEASPOON GARLIC POWDER**
- **1/8 TEASPOON WHITE PEPPER**
- **ROUND TORTILLA CHIPS**
- **35 FRESH MEDIUM SHRIMP, COOKED, PEELED AND DEVEINED (1/2 POUND)**
- **1/4 POUND THINLY SLICED PROSCUITTO HAM, TRIMMED AND CUT INTO SQUARES**
- **PARSLEY SPRIGS**

SPRINKLE MASHED AVOCADO WITH LEMON JUICE; ADD ONION, PICANTE SAUCE, GARLIC POWDER AND PEPPER. COVER GUACAMOLE WITH RESERVED PEELS OR PLACE SEED IN CENTER TO PREVENT BROWNING. COVER TIGHTLY WITH PLASTIC WRAP AND REFRIGERATE. MAKES 2 CUPS. GUACAMOLE WILL HOLD ABOUT 8 HOURS WITHOUT BROWNING.

PLACE 2 TEASPOONS OF GUACAMOLE ON EACH CHIP. TOP EACH WITH 1 SHRIMP OR HAM SQUARE AND GARNISH WITH SPRIG OF PARSLEY.

*HINT: **GUACOMOLE** MAY ALSO BE SERVED AS IS WITH TORTILLA CHIPS.*

GARLIC TOAST ROUNDS

A THOUSAND TIMES BETTER THAN PACKAGED ONES!

YIELD: 65 SLICES
PREHEAT OVEN: 325°
PREPARATION TIME: 45 MINUTES

- **3** MINI LOAVES FRENCH BREAD OR 1 24 × 2 INCH FRENCH BAGUETTE LOAF
- **1/2** CUP BUTTER (NO SUBSTITUTIONS)
- **1/2** CUP MARGARINE
- **1/4 TO 1/2** TEASPOON GARLIC POWDER

CUT BREAD INTO 1/4 INCH SLICES. MELT BUTTER AND MARGARINE AND STIR IN GARLIC POWDER. BRUSH BOTH SIDES OF BREAD WITH BUTTER MIXTURE AND PLACE ON COOKIE SHEETS. BAKE 10 TO 13 MINUTES OR UNTIL CRUNCHY AND LIGHT BROWN. COOL AND STORE IN AIRTIGHT CONTAINER. WILL KEEP SEVERAL WEEKS.

VARIATIONS: TO BUTTER MIXTURE ADD ONE OF THE FOLLOWING:
1) 1 TO 2 TEASPOONS TARRAGON, GROUND ROSEMARY OR GROUND THYME;
2) 1 TABLESPOON GREEN PEPPERCORN MUSTARD AND 1 TABLESPOON WORCESTERSHIRE SAUCE. LIGHTLY GRIND BLACK PEPPER ON TOPS OF BUTTERED ROUNDS BEFORE BAKING.

HINT: BAGUETTE WILL MAKE APPROXIMATELY 100 1/4 INCH SLICES. ADDITIONAL BUTTER MIXTURE MAY BE NEEDED.

OYSTER CRACKER SNAX

YIELD: 3 CUPS
PREPARATION TIME: 20 MINUTES

- **1** CUP VEGETABLE OIL
- **16** OUNCES ORIGINAL HIDDEN VALLEY RANCH DRESSING MIX
- **2** TEASPOONS DILL WEED
- **1 TO 2** TEASPOONS LEMON PEPPER
- **1 TO 1 1/2** TEASPOONS GARLIC POWDER
- **24** OUNCES MINIATURE OYSTER CRACKERS

COMBINE WELL OIL, DRESSING MIX, DILL WEED, LEMON PEPPER AND GARLIC POWDER. POUR OVER CRACKERS AND MIX WELL. SET ASIDE AND STIR OCCASIONALLY UNTIL OIL IS ABSORBED, ABOUT TWO HOURS. IF CRACKERS DO NOT ABSORB ALL OIL MIXTURE, RUB IT INTO THEM WITH YOUR FINGERS.

DELTA SHRIMP

PREPARATION TIME: 40 MINUTES

YIELD: 10 SERVINGS

- 1/2 CUP FINELY CHOPPED GREEN ONIONS, TOPS INCLUDED
- 1/2 CUP FINELY CHOPPED CELERY, LEAVES AND STALK
- 1/2 CUP FINELY CHOPPED FRESH PARSLEY
- 4 CLOVES GARLIC, CRUSHED
- 1 CUP EXTRA VIRGIN SPANISH OLIVE OIL
- 1 CUP TARRAGON VINEGAR
- JUICE OF 3 LEMONS, OR TO TASTE
- 1 TABLESPOON SALT
- 1 TABLESPOON FRESHLY GROUND PEPPER
- 2 POUNDS LARGE FRESH SHRIMP, COOKED, PEELED AND DEVEINED

COMBINE ALL INGREDIENTS EXCEPT SHRIMP AND MIX WELL. COVER AND LET STAND AT ROOM TEMPERATURE 48 HOURS.

ARRANGE SHRIMP ON LARGE PLATTER. SPOON MARINADE OVER SHRIMP AND LET STAND 30 MINUTES BEFORE SERVING.

CRAB CLAWS MAY BE SUBSTITUTED FOR SHRIMP.

HINT: DIP CRUSTY FRENCH BREAD IN MARINADE AND EAT WITH SHRIMP.

CLAM DIP

PREPARATION TIME: 20 MINUTES

YIELD: 4 CUPS
PREHEAT OVEN: 225°

- 1 LOAF SHEPHERD'S BREAD
- 19 1/2 OUNCES CANNED MINCED CLAMS, DRAINED (RESERVE 1/3 OF LIQUID)
- 16 OUNCES CREAM CHEESE, SOFTENED
- 2 TEASPOONS GRATED ONION
- 2 TEASPOONS WORCESTERSHIRE SAUCE
- 6 DROPS TABASCO
- 2 TEASPOONS FRESH LEMON JUICE
- CHOPPED FRESH PARSLEY
- FRENCH BREAD, THINLY SLICED

SLICE TOP OFF BREAD TO FORM LID. PULL OUT CENTER OF BREAD, BREAK INTO BITE-SIZE PIECES AND STORE IN AIRTIGHT CONTAINER. RESERVE FOR DIPPING.

MIX TOGETHER CLAMS, RESERVED LIQUID, CREAM CHEESE, ONION, WORCESTERSHIRE, TABASCO AND LEMON JUICE. POUR INTO HOLLOWED BREAD; SPRINKLE WITH PARSLEY. PLACE LID ON BREAD AND WRAP IN HEAVY FOIL. BAKE 3 TO 4 HOURS. REMOVE LID AND USE RESERVED BREAD PIECES FOR DIPPING. FOR LARGE CROWD, HAVE EXTRA FRENCH BREAD AVAILABLE.

Hot Nacho Supreme

An instant hit at any party.

Yield: 18 to 20 servings
Preheat Oven: 400°
Preparation Time: 25 minutes

- **1½ pounds lean ground beef**
- **1 cup chopped onion**
- **1 tablespoon chili powder**
- **1 teaspoon ground cumin**
- **16 ounces refried beans**
- **4 ounces chopped green chiles**
- **Garlic salt and freshly ground pepper, to taste**
- **4 cups shredded Cheddar cheese**
- **8 ounces medium taco sauce**
- **Chopped black olives**
- **Chopped green onions**
- **Guacamole or chopped avocado**
- **Sour cream**
- **Tortilla chips**

In large skillet over medium-high heat, brown beef; add onion, chili powder, cumin, refried beans and green chiles. Cook 3 minutes and season with garlic salt and pepper. Spread mixture in greased 2 quart flat casserole. Top with shredded cheese. Sprinkle taco sauce over cheese. (May be frozen or refrigerated at this point.) Bake 25 to 30 minutes.

Garnish with olives, green onions, guacamole and sour cream; serve with tortilla chips.

Prairie Fire

Excellent do-ahead dish for cocktail party.

Yield: 30 servings
Preheat Oven: 250° to 275°
Preparation Time: 15 minutes

- **48 ounces Wolf Brand chili, no beans**
- **8 ounces chopped green chiles, drained**
- **2 pounds Velveeta cheese, thickly sliced**
- **2 bunches chopped green onions**
- **Tortilla chips**

Spread chili in bottom of large flat casserole. Sprinkle green chiles over chili and place cheese on top. Top with green onions. Bake 1 hour. Serve with tortilla chips.

HERBED GARLIC CHEESE

PREPARATION TIME: 15 MINUTES

YIELD: 1 1/2 CUPS

- 8 OUNCES CREAM CHEESE, SOFTENED
- 1/2 CUP UNSALTED BUTTER, SOFTENED
- 1/2 TEASPOON MINCED GARLIC
- 1/4 CUP FINELY CHOPPED GREEN ONIONS
- 1/2 TEASPOON DRIED OREGANO
- 1/4 TEASPOON DRIED THYME
- 1/4 TEASPOON DRIED MARJORAM
- 1/4 TEASPOON DRIED BASIL
- 1/8 TEASPOON DRIED DILL WEED
- 1/4 TEASPOON DRIED CHIVES
- 1/8 TEASPOON FRESHLY GROUND PEPPER
- 6 DASHES TABASCO
- ASSORTED CRACKERS

COMBINE ALL INGREDIENTS IN FOOD PROCESSOR EQUIPPED WITH STEEL BLADE. TRANSFER TO SERVING DISH; COVER AND CHILL. SOFTEN 30 MINUTES BEFORE SERVING AND STIR UNTIL SMOOTH. SERVE WITH CRACKERS.

JALAPEÑO CHEESE SPREAD

PREPARATION TIME: 15 MINUTES

YIELD: 1 1/2 QUARTS

- 10 TO 12 SLICES CANNED JALAPEÑO PEPPER SLICES, DRAINED
- 1 LARGE ONION, CUT INTO WEDGES
- 1 1/2 CUPS MAYONNAISE
- 1 POUND VELVEETA CHEESE, CUT INTO CHUNKS
- 1/2 TEASPOON GARLIC POWDER
- CRACKERS OR TOAST ROUNDS

IN FOOD PROCESSOR, FINELY CHOP JALAPEÑO PEPPER AND ONION; REMOVE AND SET ASIDE. PROCESS MAYONNAISE AND CHEESE UNTIL SMOOTH. ADD GARLIC POWDER AND JALAPEÑO MIXTURE; PROCESS UNTIL EVENLY MIXED. CHILL AND SERVE WITH CRACKERS OR GARLIC TOAST ROUNDS (SEE INDEX).

HINT: THIS SPREAD IS EQUALLY GOOD MADE WITH REDUCED CALORIE MAYONNAISE AND WILL KEEP FOR WEEKS IN REFRIGERATOR.

STEAK TARTARE

ALSO ATTRACTIVE AND ELEGANT SERVED IN FRESH MUSHROOM CAPS.

YIELD: 6 SERVINGS

PREPARATION TIME: 20 MINUTES

- 1 POUND BEEF TENDERLOIN, FINELY GROUND
- 1 LARGE EGG YOLK
- 2 TABLESPOONS EXTRA VIRGIN OLIVE OIL
- 1 TEASPOON RED WINE VINEGAR
- 2 TABLESPOONS FRESH LEMON JUICE
- 1 TEASPOON WORCESTERSHIRE SAUCE
- 1/4 TEASPOON DRY MUSTARD
- 1/4 CUP FINELY MINCED ONION
- 2 TEASPOONS DRAINED AND MINCED CAPERS
- 1 TABLESPOON CHOPPED FRESH PARSLEY
- 2 ANCHOVY FILETS, MASHED
- 2 TABLESPOONS COGNAC
- SALT AND PEPPER, TO TASTE
- CORNICHONS
- FRENCH BREAD OR MELBA TOAST

COMBINE LIGHTLY BEEF, EGG YOLK, OIL, VINEGAR, LEMON JUICE, WORCESTERSHIRE, MUSTARD, ONION, CAPERS, PARSLEY, ANCHOVIES, COGNAC, SALT AND PEPPER. MOLD ONTO SERVING PLATTER. SURROUND WITH CORNICHONS AND SLICED FRENCH BREAD OR MELBA TOAST.

GREEN PEPPERCORN SPICED HAM

YIELD: 12 CUPS

PREPARATION TIME: 20 MINUTES

- 2 TABLESPOONS DRAINED GREEN PEPPERCORNS
- 1 TEASPOON GARLIC POWDER
- 2 TEASPOONS CINNAMON
- 3/4 CUP UNSALTED BUTTER, SOFTENED
- 12 CUPS MINCED BAKED HAM (APPROXIMATELY 6 POUNDS)
- 1/2 CUP DIJON MUSTARD
- 3/4 CUP MAYONNAISE, APPROXIMATELY
- SALT, TO TASTE
- PARSLEY
- FRENCH BREAD OR CRACKERS

MASH GREEN PEPPERCORNS WELL WITH GARLIC POWDER AND CINNAMON. COMBINE WITH BUTTER UNTIL THOROUGHLY BLENDED. CHOP HAM IN FOOD PROCESSOR. MIX HAM, BUTTER MIXTURE, MUSTARD AND ENOUGH MAYONNAISE TO BIND TOGETHER. ADD SALT IF NEEDED. PACK INTO 3 LIGHTLY OILED FOUR-CUP MOLDS. CHILL UNTIL FIRM. UNMOLD ON BED OF PARSLEY. SERVE WITH SMALL FRENCH BREAD SLICES, CRACKERS OR TINY HOT BISCUITS.

HERBED WHITE PATÉ

PREPARATION TIME: 30 MINUTES

YIELD: 18 TO 20 SERVINGS
PREHEAT OVEN: 350°

- **6 TABLESPOONS BUTTER (NO SUBSTITUTIONS)**
- **2/3 CUP THINLY SLICED GREEN ONIONS**
- **4 TABLESPOONS THINLY SLICED SHALLOTS**
- **2 POUNDS SKINNED, BONED CHICKEN BREAST, CUT INTO 1 INCH PIECES (DIVIDED)**
- **2 LARGE EGG WHITES (DIVIDED)**
- **1 1/2 TEASPOONS SALT (DIVIDED)**
- **1/4 TEASPOON FRESHLY GROUND PEPPER (DIVIDED)**
- **1/4 TEASPOON FINES HERBES (DIVIDED)**
- **2 CUPS WHIPPING CREAM (DIVIDED)**

MELT BUTTER AND SAUTÉ GREEN ONIONS AND SHALLOTS UNTIL TENDER; COOL. IN FOOD PROCESSOR, PURÉE HALF OF CHICKEN TO SMOOTH PASTE. ADD 1 EGG WHITE, 3/4 TEASPOON SALT, 1/8 TEASPOON PEPPER, 1/8 TEASPOON FINES HERBES AND HALF OF ONION MIXTURE; MIX WELL. WITH MOTOR RUNNING, POUR IN 1 CUP CREAM; PROCESS UNTIL BLENDED. REMOVE MIXTURE TO BOWL. REPEAT PROCESS WITH REMAINING CHICKEN, EGG WHITE, SEASONINGS, ONION MIXTURE AND CREAM. COMBINE BOTH MIXTURES IN BOWL.

LINE 9 × 5 INCH LOAF PAN WITH FOIL, LEAVING ENOUGH OVERHANG TO SEAL. SPOON CHICKEN MIXTURE INTO LOAF PAN, PRESSING TO FORM SMOOTH TOP. FOLD FOIL OVER AND SEAL. PLACE LOAF PAN IN ROASTING PAN. POUR WATER INTO ROASTING PAN TO COME 2/3 UP SIDES OF LOAF PAN. BAKE 1 1/4 HOURS. REMOVE; UNSEAL AND POUR JUICE INTO LARGE NON-STICK SKILLET. SET PATÉ ASIDE. PREPARE SAUCE. CUT PATÉ INTO THIN SLICES; ARRANGE ON SERVING DISHES. DRIZZLE SAUCE LENGTHWISE OVER CENTER OF EACH SLICE. SERVE WARM OR AT ROOM TEMPERATURE.

BASIL TOMATO SAUCE:

- **RESERVED JUICE**
- **6 CUPS PEELED, SEEDED AND CHOPPED FRESH TOMATOES**
- **6 LARGE CLOVES GARLIC, MINCED**
- **6 TEASPOONS DRIED PARSLEY, CRUMBLED**
- **4 1/2 TEASPOONS DRIED BASIL, CRUMBLED**

TO SKILLET WITH JUICE, ADD TOMATOES, GARLIC, PARSLEY AND BASIL. COOK OVER MEDIUM-HIGH HEAT UNTIL LIQUID HAS EVAPORATED AND SAUCE IS REDUCED TO A PASTE, ABOUT 10 TO 15 MINUTES.

Royal Dilled Meatballs 

Yield: 75 meatballs | *Preparation Time: 1 hour*
Preheat Oven: 375°

Combine beef, veal, pork, salt, pepper, eggs, onion and cream in large bowl and mix until well blended. With wet hands, shape mixture into 1 inch balls. Roll balls in bread crumbs and place in shallow baking pan. Cover and chill. Prepare dill sauce. About 40 minutes before serving time, melt butter and drizzle over meatballs. Bake 35 minutes turning occasionally for even browning. Reheat sauce until bubbly, add meatballs and keep warm in chafing dish.

- **1 pound ground beef**
- **1/2 pound ground veal**
- **1/2 pound ground pork**
- **2 teaspoons salt**
- **1/4 teaspoon freshly ground pepper**
- **2 eggs, beaten well**
- **1/3 cup finely chopped onion**
- **1/2 cup heavy cream**
- **Dry bread crumbs**
- **1/2 cup butter**

Melt butter in large saucepan. Stir in flour and cook 1 to 2 minutes. Gradually stir in hot chicken broth. Cook over low heat, stirring constantly, until sauce bubbles and thickens. Stir in sour cream and dill weed; cool. Cover and refrigerate. Makes 4 cups.

Dill Sauce:
- **1/2 cup butter**
- **1/4 cup all-purpose flour**
- **2 cups hot chicken broth**
- **2 cups sour cream**
- **1 1/2 tablespoons dried dill weed**

Crispy Chicken Drummettes

Yield: 18 servings | *Preparation Time: 15 minutes*
Preheat Oven: 350°

Mix together bread crumbs, cheese, marjoram, thyme and oregano. Dip drummettes into melted butter and roll in crumb mixture. Place on cookie sheet and bake 30 to 35 minutes, turning to brown evenly.

- **1/2 cup Italian bread crumbs**
- **1/4 cup Parmesan cheese**
- **1/8 teaspoon ground marjoram**
- **1/8 teaspoon ground thyme**
- **1/2 teaspoon dried oregano, crumbled**
- **1 1/2 pounds chicken drummettes**
- **1/4 cup butter, melted**

HINT: Drummettes are meaty first joint of chicken wing; meat and skin are pushed down to look like drumsticks.

DIJON SHRIMP ON CORN BREAD ROUNDS

PREPARATION TIME: 1 HOUR 10 MINUTES

YIELD: 10 SERVINGS
PREHEAT OVEN: 450°

CORN BREAD ROUNDS:
1 CUP ALL-PURPOSE FLOUR
1 CUP WHITE CORNMEAL
1 TEASPOON BAKING SODA
2 TEASPOONS BAKING POWDER
1 TEASPOON SALT
2 CUPS BUTTERMILK
2 EGGS
2 TABLESPOONS UNSALTED BUTTER, MELTED

GENEROUSLY BUTTER 11×17 INCH JELLY-ROLL PAN. COMBINE WELL FLOUR, CORNMEAL, SODA, BAKING POWDER AND SALT. ADD BUTTERMILK AND COMBINE. BLEND IN EGGS AND BUTTER. POUR BATTER INTO PREPARED PAN, SMOOTHING TOP. BAKE UNTIL BREAD SHRINKS AWAY FROM SIDES OF PAN AND SPRINGS BACK WHEN LIGHTLY TOUCHED, ABOUT 10 TO 14 MINUTES. IF CORNBREAD IS NOT LIGHTLY BROWNED, TURN BROILER ON DURING LAST 2 TO 3 MINUTES OF BAKING TIME. COOL IN PAN; CUT IN ROUNDS WITH BISCUIT CUTTER. MAKES 15 2½ TO 3 INCH ROUNDS.

SHRIMP SAUCE:
2 TABLESPOONS VEGETABLE OIL
1 POUND FRESH MEDIUM SHRIMP, PEELED AND DEVEINED
¼ CUP MINCED SHALLOTS
1 CUP RHINE WINE
1½ CUPS OLD FASHIONED EXTRA HEAVY CREAM (NO SUBSTITUTIONS)
½ CUP FINELY CHOPPED GREEN ONIONS, WITH TOPS
¼ TEASPOON SALT
¼ TEASPOON FRESHLY GROUND PEPPER
3 TABLESPOONS DIJON MUSTARD
2 TEASPOONS FRESH LEMON JUICE
½ CUP BUTTER CUT INTO SMALL PIECES (NO SUBSTITUTIONS)
CHOPPED PARSLEY OR MINCED CHIVES

HEAT OIL IN LARGE NON-STICK SKILLET UNTIL VERY HOT. ADD SHRIMP IN BATCHES; STIR-FRY 1 TO 2 MINUTES (SHRIMP SHOULD BE SLIGHTLY UNDERCOOKED). REMOVE WITH SLOTTED SPOON AND SET ASIDE. REDUCE HEAT TO MEDIUM. ADD MORE OIL, IF NECESSARY, AND SAUTÉ SHALLOTS 1 MINUTE, BEING CAREFUL NOT TO BROWN. POUR IN WINE; COOK UNTIL REDUCED BY HALF. SCRAPE SIDES OF SKILLET; ADD CREAM AND GREEN ONIONS. REDUCE UNTIL MIXTURE THICKLY COATS BACK OF SPOON, 5 MINUTES OR LONGER. IF USING REGULAR WHIPPING CREAM, USE MORE; REDUCE LONGER. WHISK IN SALT, PEPPER, MUSTARD AND LEMON JUICE. REDUCE HEAT TO LOW. ADD SHRIMP; HEAT 2 MINUTES. REMOVE; GRADUALLY WHISK IN BUTTER PIECES UNTIL INCORPORATED (DO NOT BOIL). TO SERVE, PLACE CORNBREAD ROUND ON PLATE; TOP WITH ABOUT 6 SHRIMP. NAP WITH SAUCE; SPRINKLE WITH CHOPPED PARSLEY. FOR BUFFET SERVING, KEEP WARM IN CHAFING DISH (SAUCE WILL THIN).

(CONTINUED ON NEXT PAGE)

(CONTINUED FROM PREVIOUS PAGE)

VARIATION: OMIT SHRIMP. SUBSTITUTE 1 POUND BONELESS, SKINNED CHICKEN BREASTS CUT INTO STRIPS 1/2 INCH WIDE BY 1 INCH LONG. STIR-FRY 2 MINUTES. LOWER HEAT; COVER AND STEAM UNTIL TENDER.

HINT: FOR MAIN DISH, PLACE SHRIMP SAUCE OVER 3 CUPS COOKED RICE AND BAKE UNCOVERED 30 MINUTES AT 350°.

AUNT HELEN'S SPECIAL MEATBALLS

YIELD: 100 SMALL MEATBALLS
PREHEAT OVEN: 350°
PREPARATION TIME: 30 MINUTES

- 3 POUNDS GROUND CHUCK
- 1 POUND GROUND SAUSAGE
- 2 EGGS, BEATEN WELL
- 1 1/2 CUPS QUICK OATS
- 1 TEASPOON SALT
- 1 TEASPOON GARLIC SALT
- 1 TEASPOON FRESHLY GROUND PEPPER
- 1/2 TEASPOON CRUMBLED SAGE
- 4 TABLESPOONS MILK
- 1/2 CUP MINCED ONION

COMBINE CHUCK, SAUSAGE, EGGS, OATS, SALTS, PEPPER, SAGE, MILK AND ONION IN LARGE BOWL. FORM INTO 1 INCH BALLS. PLACE IN BAKING PAN AND BAKE 20 TO 25 MINUTES, TURNING MEATBALLS FOR EVEN BROWNING. DRAIN AND PLACE IN LARGE ROASTING PAN OR SLOW COOKER. PREPARE SAUCE AND POUR OVER MEATBALLS. BAKE IN 300° OVEN OR SIMMER IN CROCKPOT 3 TO 4 HOURS.

SAUCE:

- 46 OUNCES CATSUP
- 4 TABLESPOONS FRESH LEMON JUICE
- 4 TABLESPOONS WORCESTERSHIRE SAUCE
- 4 TABLESPOONS SOY SAUCE
- 1 TEASPOON GARLIC SALT
- 1 1/2 CUPS BROWN SUGAR, FIRMLY PACKED

COMBINE ALL INGREDIENTS AND SIMMER 15 MINUTES.

HINT: WITH A LARGE HEAVY DUTY MIXER, THE MEATBALL MIXTURE CAN BE COMBINED EFFORTLESSLY.

STRAWBERRY LEMONADE

PREPARATION TIME: 20 MINUTES *YIELD: 8 SERVINGS*

- 4 CUPS FRESH STRAWBERRIES, CLEANED AND HULLED
- 1 1/2 CUPS SUGAR
- 3 CUPS WATER
- 1 1/2 CUPS FRESH LEMON JUICE

PROCESS STRAWBERRIES IN FOOD PROCESSOR UNTIL SMOOTH. COOK SUGAR AND WATER IN SAUCEPAN UNTIL SUGAR DISSOLVES. COMBINE SUGAR MIXTURE, STRAWBERRIES AND LEMON JUICE; CHILL. SERVE OVER ICE.

VARIATION: ***STRAWBERRY LEMONADE SPRITZER*** *- OMIT 2 CUPS OF WATER. ADD 16 OUNCES CHILLED SELTZER TO COLD STRAWBERRY MIXTURE; COMBINE WELL. SERVE OVER ICE.*

SNAPPY TOMATO SIPPER

UNUSUAL COMBINATION OF INGREDIENTS FOR A GREAT TASTE!

PREPARATION TIME: 15 MINUTES *YIELD: 16 SERVINGS*

- 32 OUNCES MAJOR PETERS' BLOODY MARY MIX
- 20 OUNCES SNAP • E • TOM TOMATO AND CHILE COCKTAIL
- 46 OUNCES TOMATO JUICE
- 1/2 CUP FRESH LEMON JUICE
- 17 OUNCES TOM COLLINS MIX
- LEAFY CELERY RIBS

MIX ALL LIQUID INGREDIENTS TOGETHER AND REFRIGERATE UNTIL READY TO SERVE. GARNISH EACH SERVING WITH CELERY RIB.

GRAPE PUNCH

PREPARATION TIME: 15 MINUTES *YIELD: 32 4-OUNCE SERVINGS*

- 1 CUP WATER
- 2 CINNAMON STICKS
- 1/4 TEASPOON WHOLE CLOVES
- 18 OUNCES FROZEN GRAPE JUICE, THAWED AND UNDILUTED
- 1/2 CUP LIME JUICE
- 3 QUARTS GINGER ALE, CHILLED

BRING WATER AND SPICES TO BOIL. REMOVE FROM HEAT AND LET STAND 5 MINUTES. MIX SPICE MIXTURE WITH JUICES. ADD GINGER ALE JUST BEFORE SERVING. SERVE OVER ICE.

HOT APPLE CIDER NOG

THIS RECIPE GIVES EGGNOG A NEW TWIST!

YIELD: 6 SERVINGS

PREPARATION TIME: 10 MINUTES

IN MEDIUM SAUCEPAN COMBINE WELL EGGS, SUGAR, CIDER, SALT, CINNAMON AND ALLSPICE. GRADUALLY ADD SCALDED MILK, STIRRING CONSTANTLY WITH WHISK. CONTINUE STIRRING AND COOK OVER LOW HEAT UNTIL HOT. BE CAREFUL NOT TO BOIL AS EGGS WILL CURDLE. LADLE INTO MUGS. TOP WITH DOLLOP OF WHIPPED CREAM AND GRATING OF FRESH NUTMEG. SERVE HOT. MAKES 4½ CUPS.

2 EGGS, BEATEN WELL
½ CUP SUGAR
1 CUP APPLE CIDER OR JUICE
¼ TEASPOON SALT
¼ TEASPOON GROUND CINNAMON
¼ TEASPOON GROUND ALLSPICE
3 CUPS MILK, SCALDED
½ CUP WHIPPING CREAM, WHIPPED
GRATED FRESH NUTMEG

JOHNNY APPLESEED MIX

YIELD: 42 SERVINGS

PREPARATION TIME: 5 MINUTES

IN A LARGE BOWL, MIX ALL INGREDIENTS WELL. STORE IN AIRTIGHT CONTAINER.

TO SERVE: PLACE 1 TABLESPOON PLUS 1 TEASPOON MIX IN CUP AND ADD 8 OUNCES BOILING WATER. SERVE HOT. GARNISH WITH LEMON OR ORANGE SLICES.

1 CUP ORANGE-FLAVORED DRINK MIX
1 CUP SWEETENED APPLE-FLAVORED DRINK MIX
½ CUP BROWN SUGAR, FIRMLY PACKED
½ CUP SUGAR
½ CUP INSTANT TEA
6 OUNCES SWEETENED LEMONADE-FLAVORED DRINK MIX
1 TEASPOON GROUND CINNAMON
¼ TEASPOON GROUND CLOVES
LEMON OR ORANGE SLICES

HINT: IF USING SMALLER CUPS, ADD 1 TABLESPOON MIX AND 6 OUNCES BOILING WATER.

HOMES FOR THE HOLIDAYS SPICED TEA

PREPARATION TIME: 15 MINUTES

YIELD: 20 SERVINGS

1 GALLON STRONG BREWED TEA
1 CUP SUGAR
12 OUNCES FROZEN LEMONADE, UNDILUTED
3 OR 4 CINNAMON STICKS

IN LARGE STOCK POT COMBINE TEA, SUGAR, LEMONADE AND CINNAMON STICKS. HEAT AND POUR INTO PUNCH BOWL TO SERVE.

PINK ICE

PREPARATION TIME: 10 MINUTES

YIELD: 6 SERVINGS

6 OUNCES FROZEN PINK LEMONADE, UNDILUTED
1/3 CUP GIN OR VODKA
3 TABLESPOONS CREAM OF COCONUT
3 TABLESPOONS MARASCHINO CHERRY JUICE
20 ICE CUBES
MARASCHINO CHERRIES

COMBINE ALL INGREDIENTS EXCEPT MARASCHINO CHERRIES IN BLENDER. BLEND ON HIGH SPEED UNTIL FROTHY. POUR INTO STEMMED GLASSES AND GARNISH EACH WITH MARASCHINO CHERRY.

STRAWBERRY CHAMPAGNE PUNCH

PREPARATION TIME: 10 MINUTES

YIELD: 25 SERVINGS

3 CUPS SUGAR
2 CUPS FRESH LEMON JUICE
ICE RING
1 1/2 QUARTS CLUB SODA, CHILLED
1 QUART SAUTERNE WINE, CHILLED
2 BOTTLES CHAMPAGNE, CHILLED
20 OUNCES FROZEN SLICED SWEETENED STRAWBERRIES

IN MEDIUM BOWL, DISSOLVE SUGAR IN LEMON JUICE. PLACE ICE RING IN 6 QUART PUNCH BOWL. ADD SUGAR MIXTURE AND REMAINING INGREDIENTS. STIR GENTLY TO COMBINE.

Frosted Egg Nog

Yield: 25 servings — *Preparation Time: 20 minutes*

- **8 eggs**
- **1 cup sugar (reserve 1/4 cup)**
- **1/2 teaspoon salt**
- **2 teaspoons pure vanilla extract (reserve 1 teaspoon)**
- **4 cups milk**
- **2 1/2 cups whipping cream (reserve 1 cup)**
- **3 tablespoons sugar**
- **1 teaspoon pure vanilla extract**
- **6 ounces bourbon**
- **2 ounces rum**
- **Whipped cream**
- **Grated nutmeg**

In large bowl, beat eggs to fullest volume. Gradually add 3/4 cup sugar, salt and 1 teaspoon vanilla. Beat until sugar is dissolved. Add milk and 1/2 cup whipping cream. Set aside. In large bowl whip 1 cup whipping cream; gradually add 1/4 cup sugar and 1 teaspoon vanilla. Fold into egg mixture. Chill overnight.

Just before serving, whip reserved cup of cream; add 3 tablespoons sugar and vanilla. In large punch bowl combine chilled egg mixture, whipped cream, bourbon and rum. Garnish with whipped cream and sprinkle with nutmeg.

HINT: Use pastry bag fitted with star tip to pipe whipped cream into rosettes.

Gin Punch

Tangy, tart and terrific.

Yield: 24 servings — *Preparation Time: 15 minutes*

- **6 cups water**
- **2 cups sugar**
- **48 ounces canned pineapple juice**
- **48 ounces canned grapefruit juice**
- **8 ounces maraschino cherries, undrained**
- **Ice ring**
- **2 cups gin, chilled**
- **32 ounces ginger ale, chilled**

Combine water and sugar in large saucepan; bring to boil and stir until dissolved. Let cool. Combine sugar mixture, juices and cherries; chill. Place ice ring in punch bowl. Add juice mixture, gin and ginger ale.

MARGARITA PUNCH

AN INTERESTING CHANGE FROM COMMON PARTY PUNCHES.

PREPARATION TIME: 15 MINUTES *YIELD: 32 4-OUNCE SERVINGS*

1½ QUARTS TEQUILA
1 PINT TRIPLE SEC
1 CUP FRESH LEMON JUICE
1 CUP FRESH LIME JUICE
COARSE SALT
FRESH LIME WEDGES
ICE RING
1 QUART CLUB SODA, CHILLED

COMBINE TEQUILA, TRIPLE SEC, AND JUICES IN GALLON JAR. BLEND WELL AND CHILL. POUR SALT INTO SMALL DISH. RUB RIMS OF PUNCH CUPS WITH LIME WEDGES. PRESS RIMS INTO SALT. SET ASIDE. JUST BEFORE SERVING, PLACE ICE RING IN PUNCH BOWL. ADD TEQUILA MIXTURE AND CLUB SODA. COMBINE GENTLY. LADLE PUNCH INTO PREPARED CUPS AND SERVE.

SPARKLING MELON SANGRIA

PREPARATION TIME: 10 MINUTES *YIELD: 15 SERVINGS*

2 CUPS WHITE WINE
2 LITERS CLUB SODA
4 OUNCES ROSES LIME JUICE
6 OUNCES MIDORI LIQUEUR
1 TABLESPOON HONEY
2 TABLESPOONS COINTREAU LIQUEUR
STRAWBERRIES
THINLY SLICED KIWI

COMBINE ALL LIQUID INGREDIENTS AND CHILL. POUR OVER ICE INTO STEMMED GLASSES. GARNISH WITH STRAWBERRIES OR KIWI.

HINT: A FEW DROPS OF GREEN FOOD COLORING MAY BE ADDED TO INTENSIFY COLOR.

ALOHA RUM SPRITZER

PREPARATION TIME: 5 MINUTES *YIELD: 1 SERVING*

1½ OUNCES WHITE RUM
3 OUNCES UNSWEETENED PINEAPPLE JUICE
1 TABLESPOON FRESH LEMON JUICE
5 OUNCES CHILLED CLUB SODA
LEMON SLICE

IN TALL GLASS COMBINE RUM AND JUICES WITH ICE. ADD CLUB SODA AND STIR TO BLEND. GARNISH WITH LEMON SLICE.

Hot Buttered Rum Mix

Beating the mix until fluffy will take some time, but it is well worth the effort!

Yield: 25 to 30 servings | *Preparation Time: 15 minutes*

Base:
- **2 cups butter**
- **4 cups brown sugar, firmly packed**
- **3 eggs**
- **1 teaspoon allspice**
- **1 teaspoon cinnamon**
- **1 teaspoon ground cloves**
- **1 teaspoon nutmeg**

Combine butter, brown sugar, eggs, allspice, cinnamon, cloves and nutmeg in mixing bowl and beat until light and fluffy, about 10 to 15 minutes. Store mix in air-tight container in freezer.

- **1 ounce rum**
- **6 ounces boiling water**

For each serving place one rounded tablespoon of mix in mug, add 1 ounce rum and fill with boiling water.

Café Diablo

The devil's coffee.

Yield: 8 servings | *Preparation Time: 20 minutes*

- **50 ounces brewed coffee**
- **3 cinnamon sticks**
- **12 tablespoons Kahlua (divided)**
- **6 tablespoons brandy (divided)**
- **6 teaspoons chocolate syrup (divided)**
- **Whipped cream**
- **Cinnamon sticks**
- **Grated sweet chocolate**

Combine brewed coffee and 3 cinnamon sticks; let stand 15 minutes to blend flavors. For each 8 ounce coffee mug, add 2 tablespoons Kahlua, 1 tablespoon brandy and 1 teaspoon chocolate syrup. Fill with coffee and top with dollop of whipped cream, cinnamon stick and sprinkle of grated chocolate.

Hint: For easier serving, measure capacity of cups to be used and calculate number of teaspoons of premixed Kahlua, brandy and chocolate syrup per cup. Mixture may also be measured and added to party-size percolator after brewing.

Irish Mocha Coffee

Preparation Time: 10 minutes *Yield: 6 to 8 servings*

1 tablespoon unsweetened cocoa
1 tablespoon sugar
3 tablespoons whipping cream
5 cups brewed coffee
1/4 cup Kaluha
1 cup Bailey's Irish Cream

Combine cocoa, sugar and cream in saucepan over medium heat, stirring to combine. Add coffee and heat through. Stir in Kaluha and Irish Cream; heat until hot (do not boil). Pour into cups and serve immediately.

Velvet Hot Chocolate

Preparation Time: 15 minutes *Yield: 6 servings*

1/2 cup semi-sweet chocolate chips
3 cups milk
1 cup half and half
1/2 cup sugar
1/2 cup light rum
1/2 cup Frangelico or Amaretto liqueur
Whipped cream
Cinnamon sticks

Melt chocolate chips in top of double boiler over hot (not boiling) water. In large saucepan scald milk, half and half and sugar. Add 1 cup of milk mixture to melted chocolate mixture and combine well. Stir chocolate mixture into remaining milk mixture. Add rum and liqueur. Divide into six cups. Top with whipped cream and cinnamon stick.

HINT: Sprinkle whipped cream with grated chocolate or mini-chocolate chips.

Hot Spiked Cider

Your home will be redolent with wonderful spices.

Preparation Time: 20 minutes *Yield: 16 to 18 servings*

1/2 cup brown sugar, firmly packed
1 gallon apple cider
1 1/2 teaspoons whole allspice
1 1/2 teaspoons whole cloves
3 cinnamon sticks
1/8 teaspoon nutmeg
1/2 cup apple brandy
Orange or lemon slices

In large pan combine brown sugar and cider. Tie spices in cheese cloth and add to cider. Slowly bring to boil. Lower heat; cover and simmer 20 minutes. Add brandy; pour into cups and garnish with orange or lemon slices.

Techniques

To crisp freshly washed spinach and lettuce, spread on clean, dry towel, roll up and refrigerate.

Make your own delicious croutons. Cut leftover bread into cubes with a pizza cutter. Pour 2 tablespoons melted butter over each cup of cubes and add seasonings such as paprika, salt, freshly ground pepper, garlic powder or other herbs. Microwave on high power 3 to 4 minutes until golden brown and crisp.

Salad greens should be torn, not cut. Cutting bruises lettuce and turns it brown where knife touches surface.

To serve tossed salad on picnic, place lettuce in zip-lock plastic bag and dressing in jar. Pour dressing into bag, seal top and work dressing over lettuce. Serve directly from bag and throw it away.

If preparing tossed salad ahead of time, do not add salt until ready to serve as it causes lettuce to wilt.

One envelope of unflavored gelatin will support 2 cups liquid. If adding solids, reduce liquid by 1/4 cup. Lemon juice, vinegar, wine and other acids make gelatin mold softer and more fragile; 1 to 2 tablespoons of an acid per cup of liquid is all that should be added.

To core iceberg lettuce, hit stem end sharply on countertop; core will easily twist out.

Cucumbers are easily peeled with swivel-bladed vegetable peeler. Alternate peeled and unpeeled strips. When sliced, cucumbers will look like pinwheels.

Substitution for fines herbs seasoning: 1/2 teaspoon each thyme, rosemary, sage, basil, marjoram and oregano.

Save vegetable parings (carrots, potatoes, onions, etc.); freeze in airtight plastic bag and add to liquid when making stock.

When making creamed or puréed soups, grate raw vegetables in blender or food processor and add during last 30 minutes of cooking time. Vegetables will cook into pulp and straining will not be necessary.

Strain clear soups through coffee filter to improve clarity and for no-mess cleanup.

Place fresh chopped parsley in ice cube tray sections, fill with water and freeze. Drop cubes into soups, stews, etc. when needed.

Caesar Salad

Yield: 2 servings

Preparation Time: 20 minutes

- **1 large clove garlic, sliced**
- **6 anchovies (reserve 2)**
- **1/4 teaspoon dry mustard**
- **Juice of 1 lemon, or to taste**
- **1/4 teaspoon freshly ground pepper**
- **2 1/2 to 3 ounces extra virgin olive oil**
- **4 cups romaine lettuce, chilled and torn into pieces**
- **1 coddled egg**
- **2 tablespoons Parmesan cheese**
- **4 tablespoons garlic flavored croutons**

Rub garlic over inside of large wooden bowl, using large spoon to press garlic into bowl. Remove any uncrushed garlic pieces. Place 4 anchovies in bowl and slice into small pieces. Add dry mustard, lemon juice and pepper. Mix together and add olive oil. Add lettuce and toss lightly. Add egg and break yoke. Toss until lightly coated. Add Parmesan; toss and transfer to chilled salad bowls. Top each salad with 1 anchovy filet and 2 tablespoons croutons.

Executive Chef Donal Weaving
Southern Hills Country Club

HINT: To prepare coddled egg, simmer in water for 1 1/2 minutes.

Curried Duck Salad

Yield: 8 to 10 servings

Preparation Time: 30 minutes

- **Meat from 2 roasted ducks, cut into chunks**
- **1/2 cup mayonnaise**
- **1/3 cup fresh lemon juice**
- **2 teaspoons curry powder**
- **17 ounces Major Grey's Chutney**
- **1 tablespoon salt**
- **1 tablespoon freshly ground pepper**
- **1 cup walnuts, chopped (reserve 1/4 cup)**

Refrigerate meat overnight. Mix together mayonnaise, lemon juice, curry powder, chutney, salt, pepper and 3/4 cup walnuts. Pour over meat and combine well. Sprinkle with reserved walnuts.

Executive Chef Louis Krupka
Doubletree Hotel, Tulsa

Duck Salad

Preparation Time: 20 minutes

Yield: 1 serving

1 duck breast, cut into julienne strips
2 ounces sesame oil
2 ounces rice wine vinegar
1 ounce julienned celery
1 ounce plus 2 tablespoons cranberries (reserve 2 tablespoons)
1/2 cup cooked wild rice
2 ounces mango chutney

Combine duck, sesame oil, vinegar, celery, 1 ounce cranberries, rice and chutney. Chill 30 minutes before serving. Top with reserved cranberries.

Executive Chef Louis Krupka
Doubletree Hotel, Tulsa

White Bean Salad

Preparation Time: 30 minutes

Yield: 8 to 10 servings

1 pound dried small navy or great northern beans
7 cups cold water
1 tablespoon salt (reserve 2 teaspoons)
1 cup finely chopped onion
1/2 cup coarsely chopped fresh parsley
1/2 cup vegetable oil
2 tablespoons Dijon mustard
1 tablespoon red wine vinegar
Freshly ground pepper, to taste

Rinse, sort and soak beans 1 hour in cold water. Drain; transfer to large pan. Add 7 cups water and 1 teaspoon salt. Bring to boil. Reduce heat and simmer 1 to 1 1/2 hours, or until just tender. Do not overcook or salad will be starchy. Drain beans well and pour into large mixing bowl.

To the warm beans, add onion, parsley, oil, mustard and vinegar. Add pepper and remaining salt, to taste. Toss well; serve at room temperature.

Reprinted with permission from
Hors d'Oeuvre Varies Cooking Demonstration
Jacques Pepin

HINT: Beans in white bean family do not need to be soaked longer than 1 hour.

APRICOT MOLD 

YIELD: 6 TO 8 SERVINGS

PREPARATION TIME: 30 MINUTES

- **6** OUNCES LEMON GELATIN
- **1** CUP BOILING WATER
- **8** OUNCES APRICOT NECTAR (RESERVE 2 OUNCES)
- **17** OUNCES PEELED APRICOTS, DRAINED AND PURÉED
- **8** OUNCES CREAM CHEESE, SOFTENED (RESERVE 1/3)
- **1/2** CUP CHOPPED NUTS
- **17** OUNCES WHOLE PEELED APRICOTS, DRAINED

DISSOLVE GELATIN IN BOILING WATER. ADD 6 OUNCES APRICOT NECTAR AND PURÉED APRICOTS; STIR WELL AND POUR INTO 8 INCH SQUARE DISH. CHILL UNTIL SLIGHTLY FIRM.

MIX 2/3 OF CREAM CHEESE WITH NUTS; STUFF EACH WHOLE APRICOT WITH CHEESE MIXTURE. ADD STUFFED APRICOTS TO GELATIN. CHILL UNTIL FIRM. COMBINE RESERVED CREAM CHEESE WITH SMALL AMOUNT OF RESERVED APRICOT NECTAR TO MAKE SPREADABLE. FROST TOP OF SALAD WITH CHEESE AND CHILL UNTIL SERVING TIME.

CINNAMON SWIRL SALAD

VERY SWEET AND PRETTY

YIELD: 9 SERVINGS

PREPARATION TIME: 45 MINUTES

- **6** OUNCES LEMON GELATIN
- **1/2** CUP RED HOTS (CINNAMON CANDY)
- **3** CUPS BOILING WATER
- **2** CUPS APPLESAUCE
- **1** TABLESPOON FRESH LEMON JUICE
- DASH SALT
- **1/2** CUP COARSELY CHOPPED NUTS
- **8** OUNCES CREAM CHEESE, SOFTENED
- **1/4** CUP MILK
- **2** TABLESPOONS MAYONNAISE

DISSOLVE GELATIN AND CANDY IN BOILING WATER. STIR IN APPLESAUCE, LEMON JUICE AND SALT. CHILL UNTIL PARTIALLY SET. FOLD IN NUTS. POUR INTO 8 INCH SQUARE PAN.

BEAT TOGETHER CREAM CHEESE, MILK AND MAYONNAISE. SPOON ON TOP OF SALAD AND SWIRL TO MARBLE. CHILL UNTIL SET.

Molded Tuna Salad

Preparation Time: 30 minutes

Yield: 4 to 6 servings

- **1 ounce unflavored gelatin**
- **1/4 cup cold water**
- **1/4 cup hot water**
- **2/3 cup mayonnaise**
- **1 1/2 teaspoons prepared mustard**
- **2 tablespoons fresh lemon juice**
- **9 3/4 ounces canned tuna, drained**
- **3/4 cup minced celery**
- **2 tablespoons minced onion**
- **2 tablespoons minced pimiento**
- **1 teaspoon salt**
- **1 hard boiled egg, chopped**
- **1/2 cup canned peas, drained**

Soften gelatin in cold water and dissolve in hot water. Combine mayonnaise, mustard and lemon juice in large mixing bowl. Add gelatin mixture and set aside.

In medium bowl mix together tuna, celery, onion, pimiento, salt and egg. Combine with mayonnaise mixture. Gently fold in peas. Pour into 9 inch square pan that has been rinsed with cold water. Refrigerate until firm. Cut into squares and serve on lettuce leaves.

HINT: Salmon or crabmeat may be substituted for tuna.

Spanish Vegetable Salad

Pretty for a summer buffet.

Preparation Time: 45 minutes

Yield: 10 to 12 servings

- **6 ounces lemon-flavored gelatin**
- **1 1/2 cups boiling water**
- **1 1/2 cups vegetable juice cocktail**
- **1/4 cup Italian salad dressing**
- **3 tablespoons wine vinegar**
- **8 ounces canned kidney beans, rinsed and drained**
- **3/4 cup tiny caulifloweret s**
- **1/2 cup chopped celery**
- **1 tomato, seeded and chopped**
- **1/3 cup green bell pepper, chopped**

In large bowl, dissolve gelatin in boiling water. Stir in vegetable juice, salad dressing and vinegar. Chill until partially set. Fold in remaining ingredients. Turn into oiled 6 1/2 cup mold. Chill until firm.

CHINESE CHICKEN SALAD

YIELD: 6 SERVINGS *PREPARATION TIME: 1 HOUR*

- 1/2 CUP VEGETABLE OIL
- 4 OUNCES RICE STICKS
- 4 CHICKEN BREASTS, POACHED WITH 1/2 INCH PIECE GINGER ROOT
- 1 HEAD ICEBURG LETTUCE, SHREDDED
- 6 GREEN ONIONS, SLICED
- 1/2 CUP SLIVERED ALMONDS, TOASTED
- 1/4 CUP SESAME SEEDS, TOASTED

HEAT OIL IN LARGE SKILLET AND COOK RICE STICKS UNTIL PUFFED. REMOVE RICE STICKS AND DRAIN ON PAPER TOWEL. BONE AND SHRED CHICKEN. COMBINE CHICKEN, LETTUCE, ONIONS, ALMONDS AND SESAME SEEDS. ADD RICE STICKS AND TOSS. PREPARE DRESSING, POUR OVER SALAD AND TOSS AGAIN. (DO NOT ADD DRESSING UNTIL READY TO SERVE OR RICE STICKS WILL BECOME SOGGY.)

DRESSING:

- 4 TABLESPOONS VINEGAR
- 4 TABLESPOONS SUGAR
- 1 TEASPOON SALT
- 1/2 TEASPOON FRESHLY GROUND PEPPER
- 1 TEASPOON ACCENT

TO OIL IN SKILLET, ADD VINEGAR, SUGAR, SALT, PEPPER AND ACCENT; COOK OVER LOW HEAT UNTIL DISSOLVED.

ORIENTAL TUNA SALAD

YIELD: 6 TO 8 SERVINGS *PREPARATION TIME: 20 MINUTES*

- 1 CUP MAYONNAISE
- 1 TABLESPOON FRESH LEMON JUICE
- 1 TEASPOON SOY SAUCE
- 1/4 TEASPOON CURRY POWDER
- 13 OUNCES CANNED TUNA, DRAINED
- 1/2 CUP CHOPPED GREEN ONIONS
- 1 CUP CHOPPED CELERY
- 10 OUNCES FROZEN PEAS, THAWED
- 8 OUNCES CANNED SLICED WATER CHESTNUTS, DRAINED
- 3 OUNCES CANNED CHOW MEIN NOODLES
- RED LEAF LETTUCE

MIX TOGETHER MAYONNAISE, LEMON JUICE, SOY SAUCE AND CURRY POWDER. STIR IN TUNA, ONIONS, CELERY, PEAS AND WATER CHESTNUTS. WHEN READY TO SERVE, ADD NOODLES AND STIR WELL. SERVE ON LETTUCE LEAVES.

Turkey Salad Normande

Preparation Time: 30 minutes — *Yield: 6 servings*

- 2 tablespoons fresh lemon juice
- 1 tablespoon Dijon mustard
- 1 egg yolk
- 1 teaspoon sugar
- 1/2 cup extra virgin olive oil
- 1/2 cup vegetable oil
- 1 pound smoked turkey breast, skinned and cut into julienne strips
- 2 medium Granny Smith or other tart apples, cored and diced
- 1 1/2 cups diagonally sliced celery
- 4 ounces smoked cheddar cheese, cut into cubes
- 1 cup broken walnuts or pecans (reserve 1/4 cup)
- Red leaf lettuce, torn in large pieces

In blender or food processor, combine lemon juice, mustard, yolk and sugar. With machine running, add oils in slow steady stream until all is incorporated and dressing is thick. Set aside.

Combine turkey, apple, celery, cheese and 3/4 cup walnuts in large bowl. Add dressing and toss well. Cover and refrigerate 3 hours.

To serve, line platter with red leaf lettuce. Mound salad on platter, allowing red lettuce to show around edges. Sprinkle reserved walnuts on top.

HINT: Cut cheese into triangles, circles, etc. for visual appeal.

Summer Rice And Ham Salad

Preparation Time: 40 minutes — *Yield: 6 servings*

- 3/4 cup chopped celery
- 3/4 cup chopped green onions
- 1/2 cup sliced carrot
- 2 cups cooked cubed ham
- 11 ounces canned mandarin oranges, drained
- 2 cups cooked rice, cooled
- 1 teaspoon onion salt
- 1/8 teaspoon freshly ground pepper
- 3/4 cup mayonnaise

Combine all ingredients and mix well. Chill several hours.

DILLED SCALLOP SALAD

YIELD: 4 SERVINGS *PREPARATION TIME: 30 MINUTES*

- 1 CUP WATER
- 1 TEASPOON SALT
- 1/2 POUND FRESH BAY SCALLOPS
- 1 MEDIUM TOMATO, DICED
- 1/2 CUP SLICED CELERY
- 2 TABLESPOONS CHOPPED GREEN ONIONS
- 1 TABLESPOON FRESH DILL (OR 1 TEASPOON DRIED)

BOIL WATER AND SALT. REDUCE HEAT; ADD SCALLOPS. SIMMER ONE MINUTE; DRAIN. COMBINE SCALLOPS, TOMATO, CELERY, GREEN ONIONS AND DILL. PREPARE DRESSING, POUR OVER SCALLOPS AND MIX WELL. CHILL SEVERAL HOURS OR OVERNIGHT.

DRESSING:

- 2 TABLESPOONS WHITE WINE
- 2 TABLESPOONS FRESH LEMON JUICE
- 2 TABLESPOONS VEGETABLE OIL
- 1 TEASPOON SUGAR
- 1/2 TEASPOON SALT
- DASH FRESHLY GROUND PEPPER

COMBINE WINE, LEMON JUICE, OIL, SUGAR, SALT AND PEPPER IN JAR WITH TIGHT FITTING LID. SHAKE WELL. LIME JUCE MAY BE SUBSTITUTED FOR LEMON JUICE.

CRAB RICE SALAD

YIELD: 6 TO 8 SERVINGS *PREPARATION TIME: 1 HOUR*

- 3 CUPS COOKED RICE, COOLED
- 1 TEASPOON CURRY POWDER
- 1/2 CUP CHOPPED FRESH PARSLEY
- 3 TABLESPOONS FRENCH DRESSING
- 1 CUP SLICED RIPE OLIVES
- 1/2 CUP DICED CELERY
- 12 OUNCES FRESH OR FROZEN ALASKAN KING CRABMEAT, DRAINED AND CUT INTO 1/2 INCH PIECES
- 1/3 CUP MAYONNAISE
- 1 LARGE RIPE PINEAPPLE

TOSS TOGETHER RICE, CURRY AND PARSLEY. DRIZZLE WITH FRENCH DRESSING AND TOSS WELL. FOLD IN OLIVES, CELERY, CRABMEAT AND MAYONNAISE; REFRIGERATE.

CUT PINEAPPLE IN HALF LENGTHWISE THROUGH LEAFY TOP. HOLLOW OUT EACH HALF USING CURVED GRAPEFRUIT KNIFE. REFRIGERATE SHELLS. CORE AND CUT PINEAPPLE INTO SMALL PIECES TO MAKE 1 CUP. RESERVE REMAINING PINEAPPLE FOR ANOTHER USE. STIR PINEAPPLE PIECES INTO SALAD MIXTURE. TO SERVE, LIGHTLY SPOON MIXTURE INTO EACH PINEAPPLE HALF.

HINT: FOR VARIETY AND LESS EXPENSE, SUBSTITUTE CUBED COOKED CHICKEN FOR CRABMEAT.

SEASHELL PASTA SALADE

VERY SPECIAL WHEN SERVED IN LARGE NATURAL SCALLOP SHELLS

PREPARATION TIME: 1 HOUR

YIELD: 12 TO 15 SERVINGS

- 1/2 CUP EXTRA VIRGIN OLIVE OIL, DIVIDED
- 1 SMALL EGGPLANT, CUBED
- 1/2 POUND MUSHROOMS, SLICED
- 1 GREEN BELL PEPPER, CUT INTO STRIPS
- 1 RED BELL PEPPER, CUT INTO STRIPS
- 1 ZUCCHINI, QUARTERED AND CUT INTO 1/2 INCH SLICES
- 2 LARGE TOMATOES, PEELED, SEEDED AND CUBED
- 1 RED ONION, CUT INTO STRIPS
- 3 CLOVES GARLIC, MINCED
- 3 TABLESPOONS CHOPPED FRESH BASIL (OR 1 TEASPOON DRIED, CRUMBLED)
- 1 1/2 CUPS SMALL SEASHELL PASTA
- 1 CUP SHREDDED MOZZARELLA CHEESE
- 1/4 CUP GRATED PARMESAN CHEESE
- 20 OIL-CURED ITALIAN OLIVES, PITTED AND HALVED
- 1/2 CUP TOASTED PINE NUTS
- FRESH BASIL LEAVES
- TOMATO STRIP ROSE

IN LARGE SKILLET OVER MEDIUM-HIGH HEAT, SAUTÉ EACH OF FOLLOWING SEPARATELY UNTIL CRISP-TENDER IN 1 TABLESPOON OLIVE OIL: EGGPLANT, MUSHROOMS, GREEN BELL PEPPER, RED BELL PEPPER, ZUCCHINI, TOMATOES, ONION AND GARLIC. COOL. IN LARGE BOWL COMBINE VEGETABLES WITH CHOPPED BASIL.

COOK AND DRAIN PASTA; ADD TO VEGETABLES. BLEND IN MOZZARELLA, PARMESAN, OLIVES AND PINE NUTS. TOSS GENTLY AND DECORATE WITH WHOLE BASIL LEAVES AND TOMATO ROSE.

Zesty Herbed Pasta Salad

Yield: 10 to 12 servings *Preparation Time: 1 hour*

In large bowl, mix together broccoli, cauliflower, tomato, carrot, zucchini, squash, artichoke hearts and mushrooms. Prepare dressing, pour over vegetables and mix well. Gently fold in pastas. Marinate in refrigerator 5 to 6 hours.

- **1 cup fresh broccoli flowerets, cooked and drained**
- **1/2 cup cauliflowerets, cooked and drained**
- **1 cup diced tomato, drained**
- **1/2 cup thinly sliced carrot**
- **1/2 cup thinly sliced zucchini**
- **1/2 cup thinly sliced yellow squash**
- **6 ounces artichoke hearts, leaves separated**
- **1 cup sliced fresh mushrooms**
- **6 ounces rotini pasta (corkscrew), cooked and drained**
- **6 ounces spinach noodles, cooked and drained**

Dressing:

Place all ingredients in jar with tight-fitting lid and shake well.

- **.6 ounces Good Seasons Zesty Italian salad dressing mix**
- **1/4 cup red wine vinegar**
- **2 tablespoons water**
- **2/3 cup vegetable oil**
- **1 teaspoon dried parsley, crumbled**
- **1 teaspoon dried oregano, crumbled**
- **1/2 teaspoon whole fennel seeds**
- **1/2 teaspoon dried basil, crumbled**
- **1/2 teaspoon dried rosemary, crushed**
- **1/2 teaspoon garlic juice, (equivalent of 2 cloves garlic)**

HINT: Variety of ingredients may be added or substituted — sliced black olives, peas, bay shrimp, chicken.

CURRIED COLESLAW

PREPARATION TIME: 20 MINUTES *YIELD: 6 SERVINGS*

3½ CUPS SHREDDED CABBAGE
¼ CUP SHREDDED CARROT
2 TABLESPOONS CHOPPED GREEN BELL PEPPER
2 TABLESPOONS CHOPPED ONION
½ CUP MAYONNAISE
1 TABLESPOON CIDER VINEGAR
1 TEASPOON SUGAR
½ TEASPOON CURRY POWDER
6 SLICES BACON, COOKED AND CRUMBLED

COMBINE CABBAGE, CARROT, BELL PEPPER AND ONION IN LARGE BOWL; SET ASIDE. MIX MAYONNAISE, VINEGAR, SUGAR AND CURRY. SPOON OVER CABBAGE MIXTURE AND TOSS. COVER AND CHILL. SPRINKLE BACON OVER SLAW JUST BEFORE SERVING.

KOREAN SALAD

PREPARATION TIME: 20 MINUTES *YIELD: 6 TO 8 SERVINGS*

1 POUND FRESH SPINACH, TORN
8 OUNCES CANNED SLICED WATER CHESTNUTS, DRAINED
2 HARD BOILED EGGS, SLICED
2 CUPS FRESH BEAN SPROUTS
8 STRIPS COOKED BACON

COMBINE SPINACH, WATER CHESTNUTS, EGGS, AND BEAN SPROUTS. PREPARE DRESSING AND POUR OVER SALAD. CRUMBLE BACON AND SPRINKLE OVER SALAD. SERVE IMMEDIATELY.

DRESSING:
¾ CUP SUGAR
1 CUP VEGETABLE OIL
⅓ CUP CATSUP
¼ CUP VINEGAR
1 TABLESPOON WORCESTERSHIRE SAUCE
½ CUP CHOPPED ONION
SALT, TO TASTE

COMBINE IN JAR WITH TIGHT FITTING LID AND SHAKE WELL.

HINT: TO THOROUGHLY MIX DRESSING, COMBINE ALL INGREDIENTS EXCEPT ONION IN BLENDER. STIR IN ONION.

Fruited Spinach Salad

Yield: 6 servings — *Preparation Time: 30 minutes*

- 1 grapefruit
- 4 slices bacon
- 3 tablespoons pine nuts
- 1 pound spinach, torn
- 1/2 cup red onion slivers
- 16 ounces canned sliced pears, drained (reserve 1/4 cup juice)
- 1/4 cup diagonally sliced celery

Peel and remove membrane from grapefruit; section and set aside. Cook bacon; drain and crumble. Toast pine nuts. Combine spinach, grapefruit, onion, pears and celery. Toss well. Prepare dressing and pour over salad; toss gently. Sprinkle salad with bacon and pine nuts and serve immediately.

Dressing:

- 1/4 cup reserved pear juice
- 2 tablespoons white wine vinegar
- 2 tablespoons fresh lime juice
- 1/4 teaspoon grated lime rind
- 1/4 teaspoon celery salt
- 1/4 teaspoon salt
- 1/8 teaspoon cayenne pepper
- Dash onion powder
- 1/4 cup vegetable oil

Combine reserved pear juice, vinegar, lime juice, lime rind, both salts, cayenne pepper, onion powder and vegetable oil in jar with tight fitting lid. Cover and shake vigorously until well blended.

Hearts of Palm Salad

Yield: 4 servings — *Preparation Time: 45 minutes*

- 1 tablespoon white wine vinegar
- 1 tablespoon dry white wine
- 1/2 teaspoon salt
- Freshly ground pepper, to taste
- 1 tablespoon minced shallots
- 2 tablespoons minced red onion
- 1 small clove garlic, sliced
- 2 tablespoons chopped fresh parsley
- 1 tablespoon drained capers
- 1/2 cup safflower oil
- 16 ounces hearts of palm
- 4 tomatoes, peeled and seeded
- 2 large hard boiled eggs

In food processor or blender, combine vinegar, wine, salt, pepper, shallots, onion, garlic, parsley and capers. With motor running, add oil in stream and blend dressing until smooth.

Drain hearts of palm; rinse and cut crosswise into 1/2 inch slices. Cut tomatoes into julienne strips. Separate egg yolks from whites and put through ricer separately.

Arrange hearts of palm on platter; sprinkle with tomatoes and egg whites, and garnish top with egg yolks. Drizzle dressing over salad.

WALNUT AND SPANISH ONION SALAD WITH WALNUT VINAIGRETTE

DISTINCTIVE IN TASTE, AND ATTRACTIVE IN APPEARANCE.

PREPARATION TIME: 20 MINUTES *YIELD: 8 SERVINGS*

- 1/4 CUP TARRAGON WINE VINEGAR
- 2 TEASPOONS GREEN PEPPERCORN MUSTARD
- 1/2 CUP VEGETABLE OIL
- 1/4 CUP WALNUT OIL
- 1/2 POUND RED LEAF LETTUCE
- 1/2 POUND BUTTER LETTUCE
- 1/4 CUP RED ONION SLIVERS
- 4 OUNCES REGULAR OR SMOKED GOUDA CHEESE, CUT IN 1/4 INCH CUBES
- 1/4 CUP SHREDDED CARROT
- 1 CUP WALNUTS, TOASTED AND BROKEN INTO LARGE PIECES

COMBINE VINEGAR AND MUSTARD IN BLENDER OR PROCESSOR. WITH MACHINE RUNNING, SLOWLY POUR OILS THROUGH FEED TUBE. COMBINE UNTIL EMULSIFIED. SET ASIDE.

TEAR LETTUCE INTO BITE-SIZE PIECES. COMBINE WITH ONION, GOUDA AND CARROT IN SALAD BOWL. ADD NUTS AND DRESSING. TOSS AND SERVE IMMEDIATELY.

ROSEMARY POTATO SALAD

PREPARATION TIME: 1 HOUR *YIELD: 8 SERVINGS*

- 2 POUNDS SMALL RED POTATOES
- 4 OUNCES RONDELE CHEESE WITH PEPPER
- 1/4 CUP SOUR CREAM
- 1/4 CUP EXTRA VIRGIN OLIVE OIL
- 2 TABLESPOONS WHITE WINE VINEGAR
- 1 TABLESPOON DIJON MUSTARD
- 1 1/2 TEASPOONS FRESH ROSEMARY, CHOPPED (OR 1/2 TEASPOON DRIED, CRUSHED)
- ADDITIONAL ROSEMARY

IN LARGE SAUCEPAN, BOIL POTATOES UNTIL TENDER. IN MEDIUM BOWL, COMBINE CHEESE, SOUR CREAM, OIL, VINEGAR, MUSTARD AND ROSEMARY; BEAT WELL. DRAIN POTATOES AND SLICE THICKLY. POUR SAUCE OVER WARM POTATOES AND COMBINE. GARNISH WITH ADDITIONAL ROSEMARY. SERVE AT ROOM TEMPERATURE.

*VARIATION: **DILLED POTATO SALAD.** OMIT MUSTARD AND ROSEMARY. ADD 2 TABLESPOONS FRESH CHOPPED DILL OR 2 TEASPOONS DRIED.*

Sweet Pickle Potato Salad

Yield: 12 servings *Preparation Time: 50 minutes*

Lightly combine potatoes, eggs, pickles, pimiento, olives and green onions; set aside. Mix together sour cream, mayonnaise, pickle juice, celery seed, paprika, salt and pepper. Pour over potato mixture and stir well. Chill several hours or overnight.

- 6 cups cooked, cubed potatoes
- 4 hard boiled eggs, chopped
- 1 cup sweet pickles, chopped
- 2 ounces canned diced pimiento, drained
- 1/4 cup chopped pimiento-stuffed green olives
- 1/4 cup finely chopped green onions
- 1/4 cup sour cream
- 3/4 cup mayonnaise
- 2 tablespoons sweet pickle juice
- 1/2 teaspoon celery seed
- 1/4 teaspoon paprika
- Salt and pepper, to taste

Grande Fruit Bowl 

Yield: 8 to 10 servings *Preparation Time: 30 minutes*

Cut cantaloupe, honeydew and pineapple into 3/4 inch cubes. Combine with watermelon, oranges and strawberries. In small bowl, combine wine, Grand Marnier and sugar; stir until sugar dissolves. Add to fruit mixture and stir to coat. Cover and chill 3 hours, stirring occasionally. Add kiwis when ready to serve. Make dish shortly before serving as fruit doesn't hold well.

- 1 small cantaloupe, peeled
- 1 small honeydew, peeled
- 1 pineapple, rind and woody core removed
- 2 cups cubed watermelon
- 11 ounces canned mandarin oranges, drained
- 2 cups strawberries, hulled
- 1/2 cup Rhine wine
- 1/2 cup Grand Marnier liqueur
- 1/4 cup sugar
- 6 kiwis, peeled and cut in 1/2 inch cubes

MOHAVE FRUIT SALAD

PREPARATION TIME: 30 MINUTES

YIELD: 6 SERVINGS

- 2 CUPS CORED, CUBED RED DELICIOUS APPLES
- 1½ CUPS CHOPPED DATES
- ½ CUP CUBED SHARP CHEDDAR CHEESE
- 1 CUP FRESH ORANGE SECTIONS
- ½ CUP CHOPPED WALNUTS OR PECANS
- ½ CUP MIRACLE WHIP SALAD DRESSING
- 1 TEASPOON GRATED ORANGE RIND

COMBINE APPLES, DATES, CHEESE, ORANGE SECTIONS, WALNUTS, DRESSING AND ORANGE RIND. CHILL BEFORE SERVING.

HINT: MAY BE PREPARED ONE DAY IN ADVANCE.

SUMMER FRUIT SALAD

PERFECT FOR BRUNCH.

PREPARATION TIME: 30 TO 45 MINUTES

YIELD: 16 SERVINGS

- 1 CANTALOUPE, PEELED AND CUT INTO ¾ INCH CUBES
- 20 OUNCES CANNED PINEAPPLE CHUNKS, UNDRAINED
- 2 UNPEELED APPLES, CORED AND CUBED
- 3 TO 4 PEACHES, PEELED AND CUT INTO WEDGES
- 2 BANANAS, PEELED AND CUT INTO ¼ INCH SLICES
- 1 QUART STRAWBERRIES, HULLED AND HALVED
- 12 OUNCES FROZEN ORANGE JUICE, THAWED AND UNDILUTED

IN LARGE BOWL, LAYER CANTALOUPE, PINEAPPLE, APPLES, PEACHES, BANANAS AND STRAWBERRIES. SPOON ORANGE JUICE OVER FRUIT. COVER AND CHILL 6 TO 8 HOURS.

Camembert Dressing

Yield: 2 1/4 cups — *Preparation Time: 20 minutes*

In blender or processor combine vinegar, cheese, salt, lemon juice, wine, garlic, egg, pepper, parsley, chives and Worcestershire until smooth. With motor running, add oils in steady stream, blending until smooth. Cover and chill at least 1 hour or overnight.

- **1/4 cup white wine vinegar**
- **1 1/4 ounces Camembert cheese, softened and rind removed**
- **3/8 teaspoon salt**
- **1 tablespoon fresh lemon juice**
- **1/4 cup dry white wine**
- **1 small clove garlic, crushed**
- **1 large egg**
- **Dash white pepper**
- **1 tablespoon chopped fresh parsley**
- **1 tablespoon dried chives**
- **1/2 teaspoon Worcestershire sauce**
- **1 cup vegetable oil**
- **3/4 cup extra virgin olive oil**

HINT: Try this dressing on shredded cabbage, tomatoes or fruit salad.

Chantilly Cheese Dressing

Distinctive flavor, but not over-powering.

Yield: 1 1/2 cups — *Preparation Time: 10 minutes*

In food processor or blender combine mayonnaise, sour cream, buttermilk, lemon juice, salt and garlic. Process until smooth. Pour into storage container and stir in cheese. Refrigerate overnight before serving.

VARIATION: Substitute 2 tablespoons freshly grated ***Parmesan cheese*** *for Roquefort.*

- **1 cup mayonnaise**
- **1 cup sour cream**
- **1/2 cup buttermilk**
- **2 teaspoons fresh lemon juice**
- **1/4 teaspoon salt**
- **1 clove garlic, chopped**
- **3 ounces Roquefort cheese, finely crumbled**

FARMHOUSE DRESSING

PREPARATION TIME: 10 MINUTES

YIELD: 1 CUP

- 1/2 CUP COTTAGE CHEESE
- 2 TABLESPOONS FRESH LEMON JUICE, OR TO TASTE
- 2 TABLESPOONS MILK
- 1/2 TEASPOON DRIED TARRAGON
- 1/4 TEASPOON COARSELY GROUND PEPPER
- 1/4 TEASPOON DRIED THYME
- 1/8 TEASPOON CELERY SALT
- 1/2 CUP VEGETABLE OIL

IN BLENDER OR FOOD PROCESSOR, COMBINE COTTAGE CHEESE, LEMON JUICE, MILK, TARRAGON, PEPPER, THYME AND CELERY SALT. WITH MOTOR RUNNING, ADD OIL IN STEADY STREAM AND BLEND WELL, STOPPING ONCE TO SCRAPE DOWN SIDES OF CONTAINER. CHILL BEFORE SERVING.

HINT: VERY GOOD TOPPING FOR BAKED POTATOES.

HONEY DILL DRESSING

THIS IS A SWEET-TART DRESSING.

PREPARATION TIME: 15 MINUTES

YIELD: 1 1/4 CUPS

- 1/2 CUP VEGETABLE OIL
- 1/4 CUP WATER
- 1 TABLESPOON HONEY
- 1 TABLESPOON FRESH LEMON JUICE
- 2 TEASPOONS WHITE WINE VINEGAR
- 2 TEASPOONS DRIED DILL WEED
- 1 TEASPOON LIGHT SOY SAUCE
- 1 TEASPOON CHOPPED FRESH CHIVES
- 2 CLOVES GARLIC, SLICED

MIX ALL INGREDIENTS IN BLENDER UNTIL SMOOTH. STORE IN REFRIGERATOR.

PARISIENNE DRESSING 

YIELD: 2 CUPS *PREPARATION TIME: 10 MINUTES*

COMBINE ALL INGREDIENTS IN GLASS JAR WITH TIGHT FITTING LID. SHAKE WELL.

- 1/2 CUP RED WINE VINEGAR
- 1/2 CUP EXTRA VIRGIN OLIVE OIL
- 1 CUP VEGETABLE OIL
- 1 TEASPOON SALT
- 1/2 TEASPOON FRESHLY GROUND PEPPER
- 1/2 TEASPOON DRIED TARRAGON, CRUMBLED
- 1/4 TEASPOON DRIED BASIL, CRUMBLED
- 1/4 TEASPOON GARLIC POWDER
- 2 CLOVES GARLIC, CRUSHED
- 1 TEASPOON GREEN PEPPERCORN OR DIJON MUSTARD
- 1/4 TEASPOON DRIED MARJORAM, CRUMBLED
- 3/4 TEASPOON DRIED CHIVES

HINT: TARRAGON WINE VINEGAR MAY BE SUBSTITUTED FOR RED WINE VINEGAR.

SWEET ONION DRESSING

YIELD: 1 CUP *PREPARATION TIME: 10 MINUTES*

COMBINE ONION, VINEGAR, SUGAR, SALT, MUSTARD AND CELERY SEED IN BLENDER AND MIX WELL, STOPPING TO SCRAPE SIDES OF CONTAINER AS NEEDED. WITH MOTOR RUNNING, GRADUALLY POUR IN OIL AND BLEND UNTIL CREAMY. TRANSFER TO JAR WITH TIGHT FITTING LID AND REFRIGERATE.

- 1/2 CUP MINCED RED ONION
- 1/4 CUP TARRAGON VINEGAR
- 2 TABLESPOONS SUGAR
- 1/2 TEASPOON SALT
- 1/2 TEASPOON DRY MUSTARD
- 1/4 TEASPOON CELERY SEED
- 1/2 CUP VEGETABLE OIL

HINT: SHAKE DRESSING IF IT SEPARATES AFTER STANDING.

Cuban Black Bean Soup

Preparation Time: 1½ hours

Yield: 10 servings

- 1 pound dried black beans
- ⅓ cup diced salt pork or bacon
- ½ cup diced cooked ham
- ½ cup extra virgin olive oil (reserve 6 tablespoons)
- ¾ pound onions, chopped (reserve 1 small whole onion and stud with 2 cloves)
- ½ pound green bell peppers, chopped
- 5 cloves garlic, peeled
- ½ tablespoon cumin seeds
- ½ tablespoon dried oregano
- ¼ cup white wine vinegar (reserve 3 tablespoons plus 1 teaspoon)
- 2 quarts beef stock
- 1 quart water
- 1 large bay leaf
- ⅛ teaspoon Tabasco
- Salt and freshly ground pepper, to taste
- 2 tablespoons dry sherry
- 2 cups hot cooked rice
- ¼ cup finely chopped green onions
- ½ cup sour cream
- 2 hard-boiled eggs, chopped

Soak beans overnight in cold water; drain. Boil salt pork 5 minutes; drain and pat dry. In large skillet over medium heat, sauté salt pork and ham in 2 tablespoons oil. Add chopped onions and bell peppers; cook 5 minutes. Crush together garlic, cumin, oregano and 2 teaspoons vinegar. Add mixture when onions are lightly browned, frying slowly.

In heavy 6 quart saucepan, add beans, beef stock, water, bay leaf and whole onion studded with cloves. Add chopped onion mixture. Bring to boil and simmer, covered, 1 hour or until beans are tender. Remove and purée two-thirds of beans. Return to soup. Discard whole onion and bay leaf. Season to taste with Tabasco, salt and pepper. Add sherry and cook 20 to 30 minutes longer.

Marinate rice and green onions in reserved oil and vinegar. Add 1 soup spoon of rice mixture to each serving of soup. Top with dollop of sour cream and chopped egg.

Bernard Rubenstein
Conductor

KEY LIME AVOCADO TROPICAL SOUP

YIELD: 8 SERVINGS *PREPARATION TIME: 30 MINUTES*

- 3 3/4 CUPS CHOPPED AVOCADO
- 1 CUP CHOPPED PAPAYA
- 1 CUP CHOPPED MANGO
- 1/2 CUP CHOPPED KIWI
- 1/4 CUP PINEAPPLE JUICE
- 1/4 CUP ORANGE JUICE
- 1/4 CUP FRESH KEY LIME JUICE
- 1/4 CUP FRESH LEMON JUICE
- 1/4 CUP DARK RUM
- 1/4 CUP DARK BROWN SUGAR, FIRMLY PACKED
- 2 TABLESPOONS FINELY CHOPPED CANDIED GINGER
- 2 TABLESPOONS FINELY CHOPPED FRESH CILANTRO
- DASH BITTERS
- 1/2 CUP WHIPPING CREAM
- 8 THIN WEDGES AVOCADO
- 1 TABLESPOON GRATED LIME PEEL

COMBINE AVOCADO, PAPAYA, MANGO, KIWI, JUICES, RUM AND BROWN SUGAR IN LARGE SAUCEPAN. HEAT 5 MINUTES OR UNTIL SUGAR DISSOLVES. PURÉE TWO-THIRDS OF MIXTURE IN BLENDER OR FOOD PROCESSOR UNTIL VERY SMOOTH. IN LARGE BOWL COMBINE PURÉE AND REMAINING MIXTURE. ADD GINGER, CILANTRO AND BITTERS; STIR TO BLEND. CHILL SEVERAL HOURS.

IN SMALL CHILLED BOWL WHIP CREAM UNTIL VERY STIFF. SERVE SOUP IN CHILLED BOWLS. GARNISH WITH WHIPPED CREAM, AVOCADO WEDGES AND GRATED LIME PEEL.

HINT: SOUP IS BEST WHEN ALL FRUITS AND JUICES USED ARE FRESH. IF KEY LIMES ARE NOT AVAILABLE USE REGULAR LIMES.

PEACH VICHYSSOISE

THIS COLORFUL SOUP HAS SURPRISE TASTE AND SMOOTH VELVETY TEXTURE.

YIELD: 4 SERVINGS *PREPARATION TIME: 45 MINUTES*

- 1/2 CUP FINELY CHOPPED ONION
- 1/2 CUP CHOPPED LEEKS
- 1 TEASPOON UNSALTED BUTTER
- 1 1/2 CUPS PEELED, DICED POTATO
- 4 CUPS PEELED, PITTED, CHOPPED PEACHES
- 2 CUPS CHICKEN BROTH
- 1 TEASPOON CORIANDER
- SALT AND FRESHLY GROUND PEPPER, TO TASTE
- 2 CUPS HEAVY CREAM
- 1 TABLESPOON CHUTNEY
- MINT LEAVES

IN LARGE SAUCEPAN OVER LOW HEAT, SAUTÉ ONION AND LEEKS IN BUTTER UNTIL TENDER. ADD POTATO, PEACHES, BROTH AND SEASONINGS. BRING TO BOIL. REDUCE HEAT AND SIMMER 25 TO 30 MINUTES. ADD CREAM. SIMMER 15 MINUTES.

PURÉE SOUP IN SMALL BATCHES IN BLENDER OR PROCESSOR UNTIL SMOOTH. CHILL. SERVE COLD GARNISHED WITH CHUTNEY OR MINT LEAVES.

Fire and Ice Mango Senegalese

Preparation Time: 35 minutes *Yield: 6 servings*

- 2 tablespoons unsalted butter
- 2 tablespoons minced shallots
- 1/2 teaspoon curry powder
- 1 1/2 tablespoons all-purpose flour
- 3 cups chicken broth
- 1/2 teaspoon cayenne pepper (reserve 1/4 teaspoon)
- 2 tablespoons minced, preserved ginger
- 2 egg yolks, beaten lightly
- 1 cup heavy cream
- 1/2 cup cooked slivered chicken breast
- 1 cup sour cream (reserve 6 tablespoons)
- 3/4 cup mango chutney (reserve 6 tablespoons)
- 2 tablespoons chopped fresh chives

In large saucepan melt butter and sauté shallots over low heat. Stir in curry powder and flour until blended. Slowly add chicken broth, stirring constantly. Bring soup to boil. Season with 1/4 teaspoon cayenne pepper and ginger. Reduce heat to low. When soup is no longer boiling stir in egg yolks and cream. Continue stirring, until slightly thickened. Do not boil. Remove from heat. Add chicken, 1/2 cup plus 2 tablespoons sour cream and 1/4 cup plus 2 tablespoons chutney.

Refrigerate until chilled. Serve in iced bowls and top individual servings with 1 tablespoon each of reserved sour cream and chutney. Sprinkle each with 1 teaspoon chives and reserved cayenne pepper.

Broccoli Bisque

Preparation Time: 20 minutes *Yield: 6 servings*

- 20 ounces frozen chopped broccoli, thawed
- 2 cups chicken broth
- 1/4 cup chopped onion
- 2 tablespoons unsalted butter
- 2 tablespoons all-purpose flour
- 1/2 teaspoon salt, or to taste
- 1/4 teaspoon freshly ground pepper
- 1/8 teaspoon mace
- 2 cups half and half
- 1/3 cup grated Cheddar cheese

Combine broccoli, broth and onion in medium saucepan; bring to boil. Simmer 10 minutes or until broccoli is tender. Purée broccoli mixture until very smooth. Melt butter in large saucepan. Add flour, salt, pepper and mace, stirring until smooth. Slowly add half and half, blending well. Add broccoli mixture; cook over medium heat, stirring frequently, until soup boils. Add cheese and stir just until melted; serve immediately.

AUTUMN HARVEST BISQUE

A WONDERFUL, SLIGHTLY SWEET-TASTING SOUP.

YIELD: 10 SERVINGS

PREPARATION TIME: 1 HOUR 10 MINUTES

- 1/2 CUP CHOPPED ONION
- 2 LEEKS INCLUDING 2 INCHES OF GREEN TOPS, WASHED WELL AND CHOPPED
- 1/4 CUP CHOPPED SHALLOTS
- 1/2 CUP CHOPPED CELERY
- 9 TABLESPOONS UNSALTED BUTTER (RESERVE 6 TABLESPOONS)
- 1/2 CUP CHOPPED CARROT
- 1 POUND BUTTERNUT SQUASH, PEELED, SEEDED AND CHOPPED
- 1 CUP RUTABAGA OR PARSNIPS, PEELED AND CHOPPED
- 1 CUP PEELED, CORED AND CHOPPED TART COOKING APPLE
- 6 CUPS CHICKEN STOCK OR BROTH
- 6 TABLESPOONS ALL-PURPOSE FLOUR
- 1 CUP UNPASTEURIZED APPLE CIDER
- 1/4 TEASPOON NUTMEG
- 1/4 TEASPOON ROSEMARY, CRUSHED
- 1/4 TEASPOON SAGE, CRUMBLED
- 1/2 CUP HEAVY CREAM
- SALT AND FRESHLY GROUND PEPPER, TO TASTE
- 1/2 CUP GRATED GRUYERE CHEESE
- CROUTONS

IN LARGE SAUCEPAN OVER MEDIUM HEAT COOK ONION, LEEKS, SHALLOTS AND CELERY IN 3 TABLESPOONS BUTTER 5 MINUTES OR UNTIL VEGETABLES ARE SOFT. ADD CARROT, SQUASH, RUTABAGA, APPLE AND STOCK. BRING TO BOIL AND SIMMER 45 MINUTES.

IN SMALL SAUCEPAN MELT REMAINING BUTTER OVER MODERATE HEAT. ADD FLOUR AND COOK 3 MINUTES, STIRRING CONSTANTLY. REMOVE FROM HEAT. GRADUALLY STIR IN 1 CUP OF LIQUID FROM VEGETABLE MIXTURE; ADD CIDER, NUTMEG, ROSEMARY AND SAGE. COOK UNTIL SLIGHTLY THICKENED. ADD CREAM AND HEAT THROUGH. RETURN CREAM MIXTURE TO VEGETABLE MIXTURE AND STIR UNTIL BLENDED. ADD SALT AND PEPPER. TOP WITH GRATED CHEESE AND CROUTONS BEFORE SERVING.

ICED ZUCCHINI SOUP

YIELD: 4 TO 6 SERVINGS

PREPARATION TIME: 25 MINUTES

- 1 TABLESPOON VEGETABLE OIL
- 2 MEDIUM ZUCCHINI, SLICED
- 1 MEDIUM ONION, SLICED
- 2 CLOVES GARLIC, CRUSHED
- 1 3/4 CUPS CHICKEN STOCK
- 1 TEASPOON SALT
- 1/2 TEASPOON CURRY POWDER

HEAT OIL IN LARGE SAUCEPAN. ADD ZUCCHINI, ONION AND GARLIC; SAUTÉ 2 MINUTES. ADD REMAINING INGREDIENTS; COVER AND SIMMER 10 MINUTES. PURÉE IN BLENDER OR PROCESSOR UNTIL SMOOTH. CHILL. (MAY ALSO BE SERVED HOT.)

Savory Celery Soup

Preparation Time: 30 minutes *Yield: 12 servings*

- 2 1/2 quarts rich chicken stock
- 4 1/2 cups finely diced celery (reserve 2 1/2 cups)
- 1/4 cup dry vermouth
- 1 tablespoon snipped fresh dill (or 1 teaspoon dried)
- 2 teaspoons chopped fresh savory (or 1/2 teaspoon dried, crumbled)
- 1 1/2 teaspoons fresh thyme (or 1/2 teaspoon dried, crumbled)
- 1/2 cup unsalted butter
- 1 1/2 cups finely diced onion
- 2 tablespoons minced shallots
- 1 cup finely julienned carrot
- 2 bay leaves
- 2 cloves garlic, minced
- 3/4 cup all-purpose flour
- 1 1/2 cups whipping cream
- 2 pinches fresh grated nutmeg
- Salt and freshly ground pepper, to taste
- Celery leaves

Bring stock to boil in 6 quart saucepan. Add 2 cups celery, vermouth, dill, savory and thyme. Reduce heat and simmer 5 minutes. Cool completely. Transfer mixture to blender and purée 30 seconds. Strain through fine sieve and set aside.

In same saucepan, melt butter over medium heat. Add remaining celery, onion, shallots, carrot and bay leaves; cook until onions are transparent, stirring frequently, about 10 minutes. Add garlic and cook 1 minute. Reduce heat to low. Add flour and stir 5 minutes; do not brown.

Discard bay leaves. Stir in stock mixture. Slowly bring soup almost to boil. Stir in cream and heat through; do not boil. Season with nutmeg, salt and pepper. Garnish with celery leaves.

Carrot Soup

Preparation Time: 30 minutes *Yield: 6 servings*

- 2 slices bacon
- 1/4 cup chopped onion
- 1 clove garlic, chopped
- 2 cups chopped carrot
- 1 cup diced potato
- 1 medium tomato, chopped
- 21 ounces condensed chicken broth
- 1 teaspoon salt
- Dash pepper
- 1 cup water
- Sour cream

In large skillet sauté bacon, onion and garlic. Add carrot, potato, broth, salt, pepper and water; simmer 20 minutes, or until vegetables are tender. Cool; purée in blender in two batches. Thin with additional water, if desired. Return to skillet and heat through; ladle into bowls and top with dollop of sour cream.

Corn and Cheese Chowder 

Yield: 10 servings *Preparation Time: 35 minutes*

- 2 cups water
- 2 cups diced potato
- 1/2 cup chopped onion
- 1/2 cup diced celery
- 2 tablespoons butter or margarine
- 1/2 teaspoon dried basil, crumbled
- 1 bay leaf
- 17 ounces canned cream-style corn
- 2 cups milk
- 1 cup canned tomatoes, chopped
- 2 teaspoons salt
- 1/8 teaspoon freshly ground pepper
- 1/2 cup cheddar cheese
- 1 tablespoon minced fresh parsley

Combine water, potato, onion, celery, butter, basil and bay leaf in 4 quart saucepan. Bring to boil. Reduce heat and simmer 10 minutes or until potato is tender. Discard bay leaf.

Stir in corn, milk, tomatoes, salt and pepper. Heat thoroughly. Add cheese. Cook over low heat, stirring constantly, until cheese melts. Garnish with parsley.

Mexican Maize Olé

Yield: 8 servings *Preparation Time: 35 minutes*

- 4 cups frozen whole-kernel corn, thawed
- 1/4 cup thinly sliced onion
- 1 clove garlic
- 2 cups water
- 2 tablespoons butter
- 2 tablespoons all-purpose flour
- 2 cups milk
- 1 teaspoon chili powder
- 1/4 teaspoon ground cumin
- Salt and freshly ground pepper, to taste
- 1/4 cup chopped black olives
- 1/2 cup grated cheddar cheese
- 16 tortilla chips, crushed

Combine corn, onion, garlic and water in medium saucepan. Simmer covered 5 minutes, or until corn is tender. Discard garlic. Melt butter in heavy skillet. Blend in flour and stir over low heat 5 minutes. Do not brown. Add corn mixture and blend in batches in blender or processor. Return to saucepan and add milk, chili powder and cumin. Reheat but do not boil. Add salt and pepper. Garnish each serving with chopped olives, cheese and chips.

CREME AU CRABE

PREPARATION TIME: 35 MINUTES *YIELD: 12 SERVINGS*

3 TABLESPOONS UNSALTED BUTTER
1/2 CUP CHOPPED ONION
1/2 CUP CHOPPED CELERY
3 CUPS MILK
10 3/4 OUNCES CANNED CREAM OF POTATO SOUP
8 OUNCES CANNED CREAM-STYLE CORN
7 OUNCES FRESH OR FROZEN CRABMEAT, DRAINED
1 BAY LEAF
1/4 TEASPOON DRIED THYME, CRUMBLED
1/4 TEASPOON SALT
1/4 CUP DRY SHERRY
1/4 CUP CHOPPED FRESH PARSLEY
CAYENNE PEPPER, TO TASTE

MELT BUTTER IN LARGE SAUCEPAN OVER MEDIUM HEAT. ADD ONION AND CELERY. SAUTÉ UNTIL TENDER, ABOUT 15 MINUTES. ADD MILK, SOUP, CORN, CRABMEAT, BAY LEAF, THYME AND SALT. CONTINUE COOKING UNTIL HEATED THROUGH, STIRRING FREQUENTLY, ABOUT 15 MINUTES. STIR IN SHERRY AND HEAT 2 MINUTES. DISCARD BAY LEAF. GARNISH EACH SERVING WITH PARSLEY AND DASH OF CAYENNE PEPPER.

HINT: YOU MAY SUBSTITUTE 1/2 POUND FRESH SHRIMP AND/OR SCALLOPS FOR CRABMEAT.

MINESTRONE BEAN SOUP

PREPARATION TIME: 2 1/2 HOURS *YIELD: 8 SERVINGS*

1 OUNCE PINTO BEANS
1 OUNCE BLACK BEANS
1 OUNCE GREAT NORTHERN BEANS
1 OUNCE RED BEANS
1 OUNCE GARBANZO BEANS
2 QUARTS WATER
1 OUNCE SPLIT PEAS
1 OUNCE BARLEY
1 HAM HOCK
1 CLOVE GARLIC, CRUSHED
1 CUP MINCED ONION
28 OUNCES CANNED TOMATOES
3 OUNCES SPAGHETTI, BROKEN
SALT, TO TASTE

SOAK BEANS OVERNIGHT; DRAIN. ADD WATER, PEAS, BARLEY, HAM HOCK, GARLIC, ONION, AND TOMATOES. BRING TO BOIL; REDUCE HEAT AND SIMMER 2 HOURS OR UNTIL TENDER.

ADD BROKEN SPAGHETTI. COOK UNTIL TENDER. SEASON WITH SALT.

HINT: THE FLAVOR IMPROVES IF MADE AHEAD AND REHEATED.

MELTON'S CAJUN GUMBO 

DELICIOUS AND VERY POPULAR ADDITION TO COCKTAIL BUFFET MENU.

YIELD: 8 SERVINGS *PREPARATION TIME: 4½ HOURS*

2 CUPS CHOPPED ONION
1 CUP CHOPPED CELERY
1 CUP CHOPPED GREEN BELL PEPPER
1 WHOLE BULB GARLIC, MINCED (APPROXIMATELY 8 TO 10 CLOVES)
32 OUNCES CANNED DRAINED TOMATOES (RESERVE JUICE)
20 OUNCES FROZEN CUT OKRA
2 TABLESPOONS WORCESTERSHIRE SAUCE
1 TABLESPOON SALT
1 TABLESPOON FRESHLY GROUND PEPPER
1 TEASPOON CAYENNE PEPPER
2/3 CUP ALL-PURPOSE FLOUR
3/4 CUP VEGETABLE OIL
32 OUNCES CANNED CHICKEN BROTH
2 TO 4 CUPS WATER
2 POUNDS FRESH SHRIMP, PEELED AND DEVEINED
1 POUND LUMP CRABMEAT, CHOPPED
4 CUPS COOKED RICE
3/4 CUP CHOPPED GREEN ONION TOPS
FILÉ POWDER
TABASCO

CHOP ONION, CELERY, BELL PEPPER, GARLIC AND TOMATOES IN FOOD PROCESSOR. TRANSFER TO LARGE SKILLET AND ADD OKRA, WORCESTERSHIRE, SALT, PEPPERS, AND RESERVED TOMATO JUICE. SIMMER OVER LOW HEAT, 1 TO 1½ HOURS, STIRRING OCCASIONALLY.

TO PREPARE ROUX, COOK FLOUR AND OIL IN LARGE IRON SKILLET OVER LOW HEAT, STIRRING CONTINUOUSLY 1¼ HOURS. ADD VEGETABLE MIXTURE AND COOK 3 MINUTES. TRANSFER MIXTURE TO 8 QUART POT. ADD BROTH AND ENOUGH WATER TO FILL POT TWO-THIRDS FULL AND SIMMER ON LOW HEAT 2½ HOURS, STIRRING OCCASIONALLY. ADD SHRIMP AND COOK 20 MINUTES. ADD CRAB AND COOK 10 MINUTES.

TO SERVE PUT ½ CUP COOKED RICE IN EACH BOWL; ADD GUMBO. GARNISH WITH GREEN ONION TOPS. PROVIDE FILÉ POWDER AND TABASCO WITH GUMBO.

HINT: QUICK ROUX: IN HEAVY CAST-IRON SKILLET, HEAT OIL UNTIL SMOKING HOT. QUICKLY WHISK IN SEVERAL TABLESPOONS OF FLOUR, STIRRING CONSTANTLY TO AVOID BURNING MIXTURE. CONTINUE UNTIL ALL FLOUR IS ADDED. AS SOON AS ROUX REACHES DARK RED/BROWN COLOR, REMOVE FROM HEAT; STIR IN VEGETABLE MIXTURE AND CONTINUE STIRRING 3 TO 5 MINUTES. ADD BROTH AND CONTINUE WITH GIVEN METHOD.

HERBED LENTIL SOUP

PREPARATION TIME: 50 MINUTES *YIELD: 8 TO 10 SERVINGS*

8 OUNCES SMOKED, LEAN COUNTRY BACON, COARSELY CHOPPED
2 CUPS DICED ONION
1 CUP DICED CARROT
1/2 CUP PEELED, DICED CELERY ROOT
1 CLOVE GARLIC, MINCED
2 BAY LEAVES
1 1/2 TEASPOONS DRIED MARJORAM, CRUMBLED
1/2 TEASPOON DRIED SAVORY, CRUMBLED
1/4 CUP TOMATO PASTE
2 TABLESPOONS HUNGARIAN SWEET PAPRIKA
1/2 TEASPOON HUNGARIAN HOT PAPRIKA (OR CHILI POWDER)
8 TO 10 CUPS BEEF STOCK
1 CUP LENTILS
SALT AND FRESHLY GROUND PEPPER, TO TASTE
1 1/2 CUPS YOGURT (OR SOUR CREAM)
CRUSHED RED PEPPER FLAKES, TO TASTE

COOK BACON IN 6 QUART SAUCEPAN OVER MEDIUM HEAT UNTIL CRISP, STIRRING OCCASIONALLY. POUR OFF ALL BUT 2 TABLESPOONS FAT. ADD ONION, CARROT, CELERY ROOT, GARLIC, BAY LEAVES, MARJORAM, AND SAVORY. REDUCE HEAT TO MEDIUM-LOW; COVER AND COOK 20 MINUTES OR UNTIL VEGETABLES ARE TENDER, STIRRING OCCASIONALLY.

ADD TOMATO PASTE, SWEET AND HOT PAPRIKA. COOK 3 MINUTES, STIRRING; ADD STOCK. COVER SAUCEPAN PARTIALLY AND SIMMER 1 HOUR. ADD LENTILS; COVER PARTIALLY AND SIMMER 2 1/2 TO 3 HOURS, STIRRING FREQUENTLY. ADD MORE STOCK IF SOUP IS TOO THICK. SEASON WITH SALT AND PEPPER. SERVE HOT, GARNISHED WITH YOGURT AND CRUSHED RED PEPPER FLAKES.

HINT: ADD MORE HOT PAPRIKA; COOK 15 MINUTES LONGER. MAKE UP TO 3 DAYS AHEAD AND REFRIGERATE; DO NOT ADD YOGURT UNTIL READY TO SERVE.

QUICK OYSTER STEW

PREPARATION TIME: 10 MINUTES *YIELD: 4 TO 5 SERVINGS*

16 OUNCES OYSTERS, UNDRAINED
17 OUNCES WHITE CREAMED CORN
1/2 TO 3/4 CUP MILK
PAPRIKA OR GROUND RED PEPPER, TO TASTE
SALT, TO TASTE

PLACE OYSTERS IN 1 QUART SAUCEPAN; BRING TO BOIL. REDUCE HEAT AND SIMMER 1 TO 2 MINUTES. ADD CORN AND HEAT THROUGH. ADD MILK TO THIN AS DESIRED. ADD SEASONINGS; HEAT BUT DO NOT BOIL.

Green Country Market Soup

A quart jar of dry mix is a nice gift.

Yield: 12 servings

Preparation Time: 30 minutes

- 1/3 cup black beans
- 1/3 cup navy beans
- 1/3 cup red kidney beans
- 1/3 cup baby lima beans
- 1/3 cup garbanzo beans
- 1/3 cup pinto beans
- 1/3 cup split peas
- 1/3 cup black-eyed peas
- 1/3 cup lentils
- 1/3 cup pearl barley
- 1 tablespoon salt
- 3 1/2 quarts water
- 1 ham hock
- 1 tablespoon bouquet garni, crumbled
- 1/2 teaspoon ground red pepper
- 32 ounces canned tomatoes, chopped
- 2 cups chopped onion
- 2 cups chopped celery
- 2 cloves garlic, crushed
- 1 pound chicken, skinned, boned and cut into 1 inch pieces
- 1 pound smoked sausage, cut into 1 inch pieces
- Salt, to taste
- 1/4 cup chopped fresh parsley

Combine beans, peas, lentils and barley for dry soup mix. Rinse bean mixture; drain. Cover with water and add salt. Soak overnight. Drain. Add 3 1/2 quarts water, ham hock, and bouquet garni. Cover and simmer 3 hours.

Add red pepper, tomatoes, onion, celery and garlic. Cook 1 1/2 hours. Add chicken and sausage. Simmer until chicken is tender. Add salt. Garnish with parsley. Serve immediately.

POTATO DILL SOUP

PREPARATION TIME: 30 MINUTES

YIELD: 6 TO 8 SERVINGS

- 2 TABLESPOONS BUTTER
- 1/2 CUP CHOPPED ONION
- 3 1/2 CUPS GRATED POTATO, RINSED AND DRAINED
- 1 1/2 CUPS WATER
- 2 CUPS HALF AND HALF
- 1 TEASPOON DRIED DILL WEED
- 2 TABLESPOONS FLOUR
- 1 CUP SOUR CREAM
- CHOPPED FRESH PARSLEY

IN LARGE SAUCEPAN, MELT BUTTER. ADD ONION; COOK 3 MINUTES, STIRRING OCCASIONALLY. ADD POTATO; COOK 2 MINUTES BUT DO NOT BROWN. ADD WATER; BRING TO BOIL. REDUCE HEAT; COVER AND SIMMER 15 MINUTES, OR UNTIL TENDER. ADD HALF AND HALF AND DILL WEED; BRING TO BOIL. STIR FLOUR INTO SOUR CREAM. ADD TO SOUP; WHISK UNTIL BLENDED. HEAT THROUGH. GARNISH WITH PARSLEY.

THREE ONION TOMATO BISQUE

PREPARATION TIME: 30 MINUTES

YIELD: 8 SERVINGS

- 1/2 CUP BUTTER OR MARGARINE
- 1 CUP CHOPPED CELERY
- 1/2 CUP CHOPPED ONION
- 1/2 CUP CHOPPED GREEN ONIONS
- 2 TABLESPOONS CHOPPED SHALLOTS
- 1/2 CUP CHOPPED CARROT
- 1/3 CUP ALL-PURPOSE FLOUR
- 60 OUNCES CANNED TOMATO SAUCE WITH TOMATO BITS
- 2 TEASPOONS SUGAR
- 1 TEASPOON DRIED BASIL, CRUMBLED
- 1 TEASPOON DRIED MARJORAM, CRUMBLED
- 1 BAY LEAF
- 4 CUPS CHICKEN BROTH
- 2 CUPS WHIPPING CREAM
- 1/2 TEASPOON PAPRIKA
- 1/2 TEASPOON CURRY POWDER
- 1/4 TEASPOON WHITE PEPPER
- 1/4 TEASPOON SAVORY, CRUMBLED
- SALT, TO TASTE

MELT BUTTER IN LARGE SAUCEPAN. SAUTÉ CELERY, ONION, GREEN ONIONS, SHALLOTS AND CARROT UNTIL TENDER. STIR IN FLOUR AND COOK 2 MINUTES, STIRRING CONSTANTLY.

ADD TOMATO SAUCE, SUGAR, BASIL, MARJORAM, BAY LEAF AND CHICKEN BROTH. COVER AND SIMMER 30 MINUTES, STIRRING OCCASIONALLY. DISCARD BAY LEAF.

PURÉE ONE-THIRD OF MIXTURE AT A TIME IN BLENDER. RETURN TO SAUCEPAN. ADD CREAM, PAPRIKA, CURRY POWDER, PEPPER, AND SAVORY. STIR TO BLEND; HEAT THROUGH. ADD SALT. SERVE HOT.

PROVENCE TOMATO SOUP WITH CHEVRE

NOT A TOMATO SOUP FAN? THIS MAY CHANGE YOUR MIND!

YIELD: 4 SERVINGS

PREPARATION TIME: 1 HOUR

HEAT OIL IN LARGE SAUCEPAN OVER MEDIUM HEAT. ADD ONION AND SHALLOTS. COOK UNTIL GOLDEN, STIRRING OCCASIONALLY, ABOUT 15 MINUTES. ADD GARLIC AND BOTH HERBS; STIR UNTIL AROMATIC, ABOUT 1 MINUTE. ADD TOMATOES, TOMATO PASTE AND VERMOUTH. SIMMER UNTIL SOUP THICKENS, ABOUT 5 MINUTES. MIX IN STOCK. SIMMER 20 MINUTES, STIRRING FREQUENTLY. ADD CINNAMON, SALT AND PEPPER. LADLE INTO BOWLS; TOP WITH CHEVRE AND SERVE IMMEDIATELY.

SOUP MAY BE PREPARED UP TO 2 DAYS AHEAD AND REFRIGERATED. DO NOT ADD CINNAMON, SALT, PEPPER OR CHEVRE UNTIL SOUP HAS BEEN REHEATED FOR SERVING.

2 TABLESPOONS EXTRA VIRGIN OLIVE OIL
2 CUPS FINELY CHOPPED ONION
2 TABLESPOONS MINCED SHALLOTS
2 LARGE CLOVES GARLIC, MINCED
3/4 TEASPOON HERBES DE PROVENCE, CRUMBLED
1/8 TEASPOON DRIED OREGANO, CRUMBLED
1 1/4 POUNDS TOMATOES, PEELED, SEEDED AND CHOPPED (OR 16 OUNCES CANNED ITALIAN PLUM TOMATOES, CHOPPED)
1/4 CUP TOMATO PASTE
1/4 CUP DRY VERMOUTH
3 1/2 CUPS CHICKEN STOCK
1/8 TEASPOON CINNAMON
SALT AND FRESHLY GROUND PEPPER, TO TASTE
4 OUNCES CHEVRE GOAT CHEESE (SUCH AS MONTRACHET), THINLY SLICED OR CRUMBLED

GAZPACHO

YIELD: 6 TO 8 SERVINGS

PREPARATION TIME: 20 MINUTES

COMBINE VEGETABLES IN LARGE BOWL. ADD SEASONINGS AND VINEGAR. ADD TOMATO JUICE UNTIL DESIRED CONSISTENCY. CHILL SEVERAL HOURS.

1 MEDIUM CUCUMBER, PEELED AND CHOPPED
4 TOMATOES, PEELED, SEEDED AND CHOPPED
2 TABLESPOONS CHOPPED ONION
1 MEDIUM GREEN PEPPER, SEEDED AND CHOPPED
3 CLOVES GARLIC, CHOPPED
1 TEASPOON SALT
FRESHLY GROUND PEPPER, TO TASTE
1/4 CUP VINEGAR
2 TO 4 CUPS TOMATO JUICE

CAJUN DRIP BEEF

HOT AND SPICY SANDWICH WITH OPTIONS.

PREPARATION TIME: 30 MINUTES

YIELD: 10 TO 12 SERVINGS

- 5 POUNDS RUMP ROAST
- 3 TABLESPOONS VEGETABLE OIL
- 1 QUART WATER
- 4 CLOVES GARLIC, CRUSHED
- 2 TEASPOONS SAVORY, CRUMBLED
- 2 TEASPOONS LOWERY'S SEASONED SALT
- 1 TEASPOON CELERY SALT
- 1/2 TEASPOON TABASCO
- 2 TEASPOONS CRACKED PEPPER

BROWN ROAST IN HOT OIL IN LARGE SKILLET OVER MEDIUM-HIGH HEAT. IN CROCKPOT PUT WATER, GARLIC, SAVORY, SEASONED SALT, CELERY SALT, TABASCO AND PEPPER. ADD BROWNED MEAT AND SLOW COOK ALL DAY (8 TO 10 HOURS). SHRED AND SERVE ON HOT FRENCH ROLLS WITH AU JUS.

*VARIATION: **ITALIAN DRIP BEEF:** OMIT BOTH SALTS AND TABASCO. ADD 2 TEASPOONS EACH: OREGANO, ROSEMARY AND 1 BEEF BOUILLON CUBE.*

ZESTY ITALIAN BEEF

PERFECT PICNIC FARE OR GREAT LAZY-DAY MEAL WITH WORK DONE IN ADVANCE.

PREPARATION TIME: 20 MINUTES

YIELD: 10 SERVINGS

- 2 POUNDS COOKED ROAST BEEF
- 3/4 CUP BOTTLED ITALIAN SALAD DRESSING
- 1/3 CUP SLICED GREEN ONIONS
- 1 TABLESPOON PREPARED MUSTARD
- 8 OUNCES RED OR GREEN BELL PEPPER, CUT INTO STRIPS
- 10 OUNCES SWISS CHEESE, CUT INTO 1/4 INCH STRIPS
- 1/3 CUP MAYONNAISE
- 5 LARGE PITA BREAD ROUNDS, CUT IN HALF TO FORM 10 POCKETS
- 10 LARGE LETTUCE LEAVES
- 10 TOMATO SLICES
- 2 CUPS FRESH ALFALFA SPROUTS

CUT BEEF INTO 1/2 INCH STRIPS. COMBINE SALAD DRESSING, GREEN ONIONS AND MUSTARD IN BOWL. ADD ROAST BEEF AND BELL PEPPER; MIX WELL. COVER AND CHILL SEVERAL HOURS OR OVERNIGHT, STIRRING OCCASIONALLY.

IMMEDIATELY BEFORE SERVING DRAIN BEEF; RESERVE DRESSING. ADD CHEESE TO BEEF; TOSS LIGHTLY. COMBINE MAYONNAISE WITH RESERVED DRESSING AND MIX WELL.

LINE PITA POCKETS WITH LETTUCE AND TOMATO. FILL WITH MEAT MIXTURE AND TOP WITH MAYONNAISE DRESSING AND SPROUTS.

CARIBBEAN CHICKEN IN PITA 

YIELD: 10 SERVINGS
PREHEAT OVEN: 350°
PREPARATION TIME: 1 HOUR

COMBINE CHICKEN, SALT, ONION, GARLIC, BAY LEAF, OREGANO AND CAYENNE PEPPER IN HEAVY SAUCEPAN. POUR OIL AND VINEGAR OVER MIXTURE; COVER AND SIMMER OVER LOW HEAT 20 MINUTES, STIRRING FREQUENTLY. TRANSFER CHICKEN TO BOWL.

COOK REMAINING MIXTURE OVER MODERATE HEAT, STIRRING, 5 TO 10 MINUTES OR UNTIL MOST OF LIQUID IS EVAPORATED AND MIXTURE IS THICKENED SLIGHTLY. ADD TO CHICKEN AND CHILL, COVERED, 2 HOURS OR OVERNIGHT. SEASON WITH SALT.

TOSS AVOCADO WITH LEMON JUICE; HEAT PITA HALVES IN FOIL 10 MINUTES. FILL EACH PITA POCKET WITH CHICKEN MIXTURE, ROMAINE, TOMATOES, AVOCADO, OLIVES AND RADISHES.

2 POUNDS CHICKEN BREASTS, SKINNED, BONED, AND CUT INTO 1 INCH PIECES
1/2 TEASPOON SALT
4 CUPS THINLY SLICED ONION
4 CLOVES GARLIC, MINCED
1 BAY LEAF
1 TEASPOON DRIED OREGANO, CRUMBLED
1/4 TEASPOON CAYENNE PEPPER
1/4 CUP EXTRA VIRGIN OLIVE OIL
2 TABLESPOONS WHITE WINE VINEGAR
SALT, TO TASTE
1 1/2 CUPS CUBED AVOCADO
1 TABLESPOON FRESH LEMON JUICE
5 LARGE PITA LOAVES, HALVED TO FORM 10 POCKETS
1 1/2 CUPS SHREDDED ROMAINE HEARTS
1 1/2 CUPS FRESH TOMATOES, PEELED, SEEDED AND CHOPPED
1/2 CUP CHOPPED RIPE OLIVES
8 RADISHES, QUARTERED AND SLICED THIN

HINT: MAY HEAT CHICKEN MIXTURE IN PITA POCKETS FOR HOT SANDWICH. REMOVE FROM OVEN AND ADD VEGETABLES.

CHICKEN AND CHUTNEY SANDWICHES

PREPARATION TIME: 30 MINUTES

YIELD: 4 SERVINGS

- 1/2 CUP MAYONNAISE
- 3/4 TEASPOON MILD CURRY POWDER
- 12 OUNCES COOKED CHICKEN BREAST, FINELY CHOPPED
- 8 SLICES WHOLE GRAIN BREAD
- 4 SLICES WHITE BREAD
- 8 TABLESPOONS CHUTNEY

IN MEDIUM BOWL MIX MAYONNAISE AND CURRY POWDER UNTIL SMOOTH. ADD CHICKEN AND STIR WELL. SPREAD FOUR SLICES OF WHOLE GRAIN BREAD WITH CHICKEN MIXTURE. TOP WITH FOUR SLICES WHITE BREAD. DIVIDE AND SPREAD CHUTNEY ON WHITE BREAD. TOP WITH REMAINING WHOLE GRAIN BREAD. REMOVE CRUSTS. CUT EACH SANDWICH INTO THREE FINGERS.

COVER AND REFRIGERATE UNTIL 20 MINUTES BEFORE SERVING.

TARRAGON CHICKEN SALAD WITH PINE NUTS

PREPARATION TIME: 35 MINUTES

YIELD: 2 SERVINGS

- 1 TABLESPOON RASPBERRY VINEGAR
- 1 TEASPOON DRIED TARRAGON, CRUMBLED
- 1/3 CUP MAYONNAISE
- 1 CUP FINELY CHOPPED, COOKED CHICKEN
- 2 TABLESPOONS TOASTED PINE NUTS, COARSELY CHOPPED
- 2 TABLESPOONS CHOPPED FRESH CHIVES
- SALT AND FRESHLY GROUND PEPPER, TO TASTE
- SLICED BREAD

COMBINE VINEGAR AND TARRAGON IN SMALL SAUCEPAN. BRING TO BOIL. COOK OVER MODERATELY HIGH HEAT, STIRRING, UNTIL VINEGAR IS REDUCED TO ABOUT 1 TEASPOON.

IN BOWL COMBINE TARRAGON MIXTURE, MAYONNAISE, CHICKEN, PINE NUTS AND CHIVES. ADD SALT AND PEPPER. SPREAD ON FAVORITE BREAD.

Creamy Chicken Bake

Yield: 6 servings
Preheat Oven: 325°

Preparation Time: 25 minutes

Cube 2 slices bread and place in bottom of greased 8 inch square baking dish. Combine chicken, vegetables, mayonnaise, stock base, salt and pepper. Spread over cubed bread. Trim crust from remaining bread and place on top of chicken. Combine milk and eggs; pour over bread. Cover and chill overnight.

Spoon undiluted soup over bread; bake 45 minutes. Sprinkle with cheese and continue baking 15 minutes.

- **6 slices white bread (reserve 4)**
- **2 cups diced, cooked chicken**
- **1/2 cup chopped green bell pepper**
- **1/2 cup chopped celery**
- **1/2 cup pimiento**
- **1/2 cup mayonnaise**
- **1 1/2 teaspoons chicken stock base**
- **Salt and freshly ground pepper, to taste**
- **1 1/2 cups milk**
- **2 eggs, beaten well**
- **10 3/4 ounces cream of mushroom soup**
- **1/2 cup shredded sharp cheese**

Mediterranean Tuna Spread

Yield: 6 servings

Preparation Time: 15 minutes

Combine all ingredients except bread. Blend thoroughly. Serve on bread or rolls.

- **6 1/2 ounces light tuna in oil, drained**
- **1/3 cup minced celery**
- **1/3 cup minced roasted red peppers, drained**
- **10 Kalamata olives, pitted and chopped**
- **1/3 cup mayonnaise**
- **2 teaspoons fresh lemon juice**
- **2 tablespoons minced fresh parsley**
- **2 tablespoons chopped red onion**
- **Salt and freshly ground pepper, to taste**
- **Sliced bread or rolls**

Croque Monsieur

Preparation Time: 1 hour

Yield: 6 servings

- **4** slices black rye bread (reserve 2)
- **8** slices Vienna bread (reserve 4)
- **2** tablespoons green pepper mustard
- **1/4** cup mango chutney
- **1/2** pound smoked turkey
- **2** ounces thin sliced Swiss cheese
- **12** ounces country or duck paté
- **4** ounces Petit Montrachet cheese, thinly sliced
- **6** tablespoons butter, room temperature

Lay 2 slices rye bread and 4 slices Vienna bread on counter. Spread mustard on rye bread and chutney on Vienna bread. Place 4 ounces turkey and 1 ounce Swiss cheese on top of each rye bread slice and top with reserved rye slices. Place 3 ounces paté and 1 ounce Montrachet on top of each Vienna bread slice and top with reserved Vienna slices. Butter outside of sandwiches and grill in croque monsieur press until toasted. Alternate light and dark sandwiches (with two light in middle).

Gourmet Ham and Turkey Broil

Preparation Time: 1 hour

Yield: 4 servings
Preheat Oven: Broil

- **1** cup thinly sliced fresh mushrooms
- **2** tablespoons unsalted butter
- **4** thick slices white bread, toasted, crust removed
- **8** slices boiled ham (1/2 pound)
- **8** slices turkey breast (1/2 pound)
- **1/2** cup grated sharp cheddar cheese
- **1/2** cup grated Swiss cheese
- **Sweet paprika, to taste**

In skillet sauté mushrooms in butter over moderately high heat 2 minutes. Set aside. Divide toast among 4 ovenproof serving dishes. Layer with 2 slices each of ham and turkey and top with mushrooms. Prepare sauce and spoon over sandwiches; sprinkle with cheeses and paprika. Broil 3 inches from heat 4 to 5 minutes, or until golden brown.

Sauce:

- **5** tablespoons unsalted butter
- **1/4** cup all-purpose flour
- **1 1/2** cups chicken stock or broth
- **1/2** cup heavy cream, scalded
- **1/2** teaspoon salt
- **2** tablespoons dry sherry

In medium saucepan melt butter; add flour and cook over low heat, stirring, 2 minutes. Remove from heat and gradually whisk in stock. Cook over moderate heat, stirring, 5 minutes. Add cream; stir in salt and sherry.

POPPY SEED HAM AND SWISS

YIELD: 4 SERVINGS
PREHEAT OVEN: 350°
PREPARATION TIME: 30 MINUTES

- **1/2 CUP BUTTER OR MARGARINE, MELTED**
- **1/2 CUP PREPARED MUSTARD**
- **1/4 CUP CHOPPED ONION**
- **1/8 TEASPOON ACCENT**
- **1 TABLESPOON POPPY SEED**
- **4 ROLLS OR BUNS, CUT IN HALF**
- **12 OUNCES THINLY SLICED HAM**
- **8 OUNCES SLICED SWISS CHEESE**

MIX TOGETHER BUTTER, MUSTARD, ONION, ACCENT AND POPPY SEED. SPREAD ON CUT SIDES OF ROLLS OR BUNS. PLACE 3 OUNCES HAM AND 2 OUNCES CHEESE ON EACH SANDWICH. WRAP SANDWICHES IN FOIL AND BAKE 15 MINUTES.

HINT: SANDWICH ALSO WARMS WELL IN MICROWAVE. COVER WITH PAPER TOWEL OR PLASTIC WRAP AND HEAT 1 MINUTE OR LESS.

LOBSTER SALAD IN PHYLLO 

FOR AN IMPRESSIVE LUNCHEON ENTREE THIS ONE IS HARD TO BEAT.

YIELD: 4 SERVINGS
PREHEAT OVEN: 400°
PREPARATION TIME: 45 MINUTES

- **1 1/2 CUPS COOKED LOBSTER, CUT INTO 1/2 INCH PIECES**
- **1/3 CUP MINCED CELERY**
- **1/4 CUP MINCED SHALLOTS**
- **1 TABLESPOON MINCED FRESH PARSLEY**
- **1 SMALL CLOVE GARLIC, MINCED**
- **1/2 CUP MAYONNAISE**
- **2 TEASPOONS FRESH LEMON JUICE**
- **1/2 TEASPOON GRATED LEMON RIND**
- **6 DROPS TABASCO, OR TO TASTE**
- **FRESHLY GROUND PEPPER, TO TASTE**
- **8 SHEETS PHYLLO DOUGH, THAWED**
- **1/2 CUP UNSALTED BUTTER, MELTED**

COMBINE LOBSTER, CELERY, SHALLOTS, PARSLEY AND GARLIC IN MEDIUM BOWL.

IN SMALL BOWL BEAT MAYONNAISE, LEMON JUICE, LEMON RIND, TABASCO AND PEPPER UNTIL WELL BLENDED. ADD TO LOBSTER MIXTURE AND BLEND WELL.

BRUSH 2 SHEETS PHYLLO DOUGH WITH BUTTER. STACK AND FOLD IN HALF. PLACE ONE-FOURTH OF LOBSTER MIXTURE AT CORNER OF PHYLLO, WRAP MIXTURE BY ROLLING AND TUCKING IN ENDS. REPEAT WITH REMAINING PHYLLO AND MIXTURE.

PLACE PHYLLO ROLLS ON PARCHMENT-LINED BAKING SHEET. BAKE 9 TO 12 MINUTES.

HOT SHRIMP AND CRAB CROISSANTS

PREPARATION TIME: 30 MINUTES

YIELD: 4 SERVINGS
PREHEAT OVEN: 425°

4 CROISSANTS
1/4 CUP UNSALTED BUTTER, MELTED (RESERVE 2 TABLESPOONS)
2 TABLESPOONS MINCED SHALLOTS
2 TABLESPOONS MINCED GREEN ONIONS
2 CUPS THINLY SLICED FRESH MUSHROOMS
2 TABLESPOONS ALL-PURPOSE FLOUR
1 CUP HALF AND HALF, SCALDED
1 CUP FRESH CRABMEAT
1 CUP CHOPPED COOKED SHRIMP
2 TABLESPOONS PALE DRY SHERRY
1/2 TEASPOON GRATED LEMON RIND
1/8 TEASPOON CAYENNE PEPPER
2 TABLESPOONS MINCED FRESH PARSLEY
SALT AND FRESHLY GROUND PEPPER, TO TASTE
1/2 CUP GRATED SWISS CHEESE

HALVE CROISSANTS. BRUSH CUT SIDES WITH 2 TABLESPOONS MELTED BUTTER. BAKE CRUST SIDE DOWN 5 MINUTES.

IN MEDIUM SAUCEPAN SAUTÉ SHALLOTS, GREEN ONIONS AND MUSHROOMS IN RESERVED BUTTER OVER MODERATELY HIGH HEAT, STIRRING, 3 MINUTES. ADD FLOUR; REDUCE HEAT TO LOW AND COOK, STIRRING 3 MINUTES. WHISK IN HALF AND HALF IN STREAM. BRING TO BOIL, WHISKING, AND SIMMER 5 MINUTES. STIR IN CRAB, SHRIMP, SHERRY, LEMON RIND, CAYENNE PEPPER AND PARSLEY. COOK 1 MINUTE. ADD SALT AND PEPPER.

HEAT OVEN TO BROIL. FILL BOTTOM HALVES OF CROISSANTS WITH SEAFOOD MIXTURE. TOP WITH CHEESE AND BROIL 6 INCHES FROM HEAT JUST UNTIL CHEESE MELTS (10 TO 20 SECONDS). REPLACE TOP HALVES AND SERVE HOT.

FRUITED CHEESE SPREAD

PREPARATION TIME: 20 MINUTES

YIELD: 4 TO 6 SERVINGS

1 CUP GRATED CHEDDAR CHEESE
3/4 CUP CHOPPED DRIED APPLE
3 TABLESPOONS CHUTNEY
2 TABLESPOONS MAYONNAISE
1 TEASPOON FRESH LEMON JUICE
2 TEASPOONS SNIPPED FRESH CHIVES
2 TABLESPOONS CHOPPED RAISINS
2 SLICES COOKED BACON, CRUMBLED
2 TABLESPOONS WALNUTS, TOASTED AND CHOPPED
4 TO 6 ENGLISH MUFFINS, SPLIT AND TOASTED

IN A MEDIUM BOWL TOSS TOGETHER CHEESE AND APPLE. IN A SMALL BOWL COMBINE CHUTNEY, MAYONNAISE, LEMON JUICE AND CHIVES; STIR INTO CHEESE MIXTURE. ADD RAISINS, BACON AND WALNUTS; MIX WELL. SPREAD MIXTURE ON TOASTED MUFFINS AND SERVE.

MIDDLE EASTERN PITA MEAT PIES

YIELD: 4 SERVINGS
PREHEAT OVEN: 450°

PREPARATION TIME: 35 MINUTES

- **1/2 POUND LEAN GROUND LAMB OR BEEF**
- **1/2 CUP MINCED ONION**
- **3/4 CUP PEELED, SEEDED AND MINCED TOMATO**
- **3 TABLESPOONS MINCED FRESH PARSLEY**
- **2 TABLESPOONS MINCED GREEN BELL PEPPER**
- **1 TABLESPOON TOMATO PASTE**
- **1 TABLESPOON FRESH LEMON JUICE**
- **1 CLOVE GARLIC, MINCED**
- **1 1/2 TEASPOONS MINCED FRESH MINT LEAVES, (OR 1/2 TEASPOON DRIED, CRUMBLED)**
- **1/8 TEASPOON CAYENNE PEPPER**
- **SALT AND FRESHLY GROUND PEPPER, TO TASTE**
- **2 LARGE PITA LOAVES, HALVED HORIZONTALLY TO FORM 4 ROUNDS**
- **3 TABLESPOONS TOASTED PINE NUTS**

COMBINE LAMB, ONION, TOMATO, PARSLEY, BELL PEPPER, TOMATO PASTE, LEMON JUICE, GARLIC, MINT AND CAYENNE PEPPER. ADD SALT AND PEPPER; BLEND WELL.

ARRANGE PITA ROUNDS SMOOTH SIDE DOWN ON UNGREASED BAKING SHEET. SPREAD ROUNDS EVENLY WITH MEAT MIXTURE AND BAKE 10 MINUTES OR UNTIL EDGES ARE BROWNED.

SPRINKLE WITH TOASTED PINE NUTS. SERVE IMMEDIATELY.

HINT: IF MEAT IS NOT LEAN, PARTIALLY COOK AND DRAIN MIXTURE BEFORE SPREADING ON PITA ROUNDS. THIS WILL PREVENT A SOGGY SANDWICH.

PAN BAGNA

THIS IS THE STREET/BEACH SANDWICH SO POPULAR IN NICE, FRANCE.

PREPARATION TIME: 30 MINUTES *YIELD: 4 SERVINGS*

VINAIGRETTE:
2 1/2 TABLESPOONS RED WINE VINEGAR
1 TABLESPOON CAPERS, RINSED, DRAINED AND MINCED
2 OUNCES ANCHOVIES, POUNDED TO PURÉE
1/2 TEASPOON SUGAR
1 TEASPOON DRIED THYME, CRUMBLED
1/2 CUP EXTRA VIRGIN OLIVE OIL
SALT AND FRESHLY GROUND PEPPER, TO TASTE

4 CRUSTY FRENCH BREAD ROLLS
2 LARGE CLOVES GARLIC, HALVED
16 NICOISE OLIVES, PITTED AND FLATTENED
8 TOMATO SLICES, 1/4 INCH THICK
12 1/2 OUNCES WATER PACKED WHITE TUNA, DRAINED
4 RADISHES, SLICED PAPER THIN
4 SLICES RED ONION, 1/8 INCH THICK
12 FRESH BASIL LEAVES (OR 2 TEASPOONS DRIED, CRUMBLED)

COMBINE VINEGAR, CAPERS, ANCHOVIES, SUGAR AND THYME IN SMALL BOWL. WHISK IN OIL IN THIN STREAM. ADD SALT AND PEPPER. HALVE ROLLS; RUB CUT SIDES WITH GARLIC. BRUSH LIGHTLY WITH VINAIGRETTE.

LAYER EACH SANDWICH WITH 4 OLIVES, 1 SLICE TOMATO, DRIZZLE OF VINAIGRETTE, TUNA, RADISHES, ONION, 1 TOMATO SLICE, DRIZZLE OF VINAIGRETTE AND 3 BASIL LEAVES. WEIGHT SANDWICHES WITH HEAVY PLATE 5 MINUTES TO BLEND FLAVORS. SERVE IMMEDIATELY.

HINT: USE LEFTOVER VINAIGRETTE AS SALAD DRESSING.

Techniques

Bread dough may be prepared and refrigerated 1 to 2 hours before rising. Bring dough to room temperature and let rise completely before continuing recipe.

If mixing and kneading dough in food processor, liquid should be very cold. Processor friction can overheat dough and kill yeast if ingredients are warm.

To improve bread texture, give dough "three rises at room temperature" rather than "two rises in a warm place". Allow dough to reach between 2 to 3 times its volume during each rise.

When substituting fresh cake yeast for dry granulated yeast, a 3/5 ounce yeast cake equals 2 tablespoons dry yeast (1 packet).

Salt tempers the growth of yeast and is used not only for flavor but also to control rising.

Use an instant reading thermometer for accuracy in checking the temperature of warm liquids, such as those added to proof yeast.

Bread baked on baking stone or oven rack lined with 1/2-inch thick quarry tiles will have a crisper crust. Preheat stone or tile 30 minutes before baking bread.

Whole-wheat and whole-wheat pastry flour will retain freshness longer if stored in refrigerator.

To test levening power of old baking powder, stir 1 teaspoon into 1/4 cup hot water. If mixture bubbles in few seconds, baking powder is still effective.

To make dry bread crumbs, place bread slices on cookie sheet in 250° oven. Bake until crisp but not browned, approximately 1 hour. Break into pieces and chop in food processor.

It takes 12 ounces of sour cream to make 1 cup.

To make sour milk, add 1 tablespoon lemon juice or vinegar to measuring cup and add milk to make 1 cup.

When testing quick breads for doneness, avoid inserting pick into crack down center. The crack is often wet and may give a false reading.

When braiding long strips of dough, line up ropes 1 inch apart on greased baking sheet. Braid loosely beginning in middle and working towards ends. Pinch ends and tuck under.

ICEBOX ROLLS

SO LIGHT, THEY WILL MELT IN YOUR MOUTH.

YIELD: 4 DOZEN ROLLS
PREHEAT OVEN: 400°

PREPARATION TIME: 2 HOURS

1 CUP SHORTENING
3/4 CUP SUGAR
1 1/2 TEASPOONS SALT
1 CUP BOILING WATER
2 TABLESPOONS ACTIVE DRY YEAST
1/2 CUP WARM WATER (105° TO 115°)
3 EGGS, BEATEN LIGHTLY
7 1/2 CUPS SIFTED ALL-PURPOSE FLOUR
1 CUP COOL WATER
8 TABLESPOONS MELTED BUTTER (RESERVE 6 TABLESPOONS)

COMBINE SHORTENING, SUGAR AND SALT. WITH WOODEN SPOON BEAT UNTIL SMOOTH AND CREAMY. ADD BOILING WATER AND STIR UNTIL SMOOTH; COOL TO LUKEWARM. IN LARGE BOWL SPRINKLE YEAST OVER WARM WATER; STIR UNTIL DISSOLVED. ADD SHORTENING MIXTURE AND EGGS; MIX WELL. ADD FLOUR ALTERNATELY WITH COOL WATER. BEAT UNTIL SMOOTH; GREASE TOP. COVER TIGHTLY WITH FOIL AND REFRIGERATE OVERNIGHT.

TO SHAPE: USING 1/4 OF DOUGH, ON LIGHTLY FLOURED SURFACE, ROLL INTO RECTANGLE 10 × 12 INCHES. BRUSH WITH 2 TABLESPOONS MELTED BUTTER. ROLL UP JELLY-ROLL FASHION FROM LONG END. CUT CROSSWISE INTO 12 PIECES. PLACE, CUT SIDE DOWN, IN GREASED 2 1/2 INCH MUFFIN PAN. REPEAT WITH REMAINING DOUGH. COVER AND LET RISE UNTIL DOUBLED, ABOUT 1 HOUR. BAKE 15 TO 20 MINUTES UNTIL GOLDEN BROWN.

THE GARDEN RESTAURANT

Apple Spice Waffles

Preparation Time: 25 minutes

Yield: 4 large waffles

- 4 eggs, separated
- 2 1/3 cups milk
- 1/2 tablespoon pure vanilla extract
- 3 cups all-purpose flour
- 5 teaspoons baking powder
- 1/2 teaspoon salt
- 2 tablespoons sugar
- 2/3 cup butter, melted and cooled
- 3 1/2 cups peeled, cored and coarsely grated apple
- 1 teaspoon cinnamon

Beat egg whites until stiff; set aside. Beat egg yolks well; add milk and vanilla. Sift together flour, baking powder, salt and sugar. Stir into egg yolk mixture. Blend in butter, apple and cinnamon. Fold in egg whites. Pour batter into waffle iron until it spreads 1 inch from sides; cook until golden.

*Variation: **Blueberry Waffles:** Omit apple and cinnamon. Stir in 1 1/2 cups drained fresh blueberries.*

Butterhorn Rolls

Preparation Time: 3 1/2 hours

Yield: 48 butterhorns
Preheat Oven: 375°

- 2 cups milk
- 1/2 cup butter
- 1/2 cup sugar
- 1 teaspoon salt
- 1 tablespoon active dry yeast
- 2 eggs, beaten well
- 6 1/2 to 7 cups all-purpose flour
- 4 tablespoons butter, melted

In large saucepan, combine milk, butter, sugar and salt; scald. Cool to lukewarm. Add small amount of lukewarm milk to yeast and let stand. Add eggs and yeast to milk. Beat in flour 1 cup at a time. Dough should be sticky but form ball. Turn out onto floured board; knead until smooth and elastic. Place in greased bowl, turning to coat top. Cover and let rise, about 2 hours. Punch down dough. Knead briefly; make rolls immediately or put in refrigerator until needed. Will keep 2 weeks.

To bake rolls, divide dough into 4 parts. Roll each into 12 inch circle. Brush with butter and cut in 12 wedges. Starting at wide ends, roll wedges to points. Place on greased baking sheet. Cover and let rise until double, about 1 hour. Bake 10 minutes.

PECAN HONEY BUNS

YIELD: 40 BUNS
PREHEAT OVEN: 350°

GREASE FOUR 9 INCH ROUND CAKE PANS WITH MELTED BUTTER. BLEND BROWN SUGAR AND HONEY IN SMALL BOWL. SPREAD ONE-FOURTH OF MIXTURE IN EACH PAN. SPRINKLE PECANS ON TOP; SET ASIDE.

TOPPING:
MELTED BUTTER
1 CUP BROWN SUGAR, FIRMLY PACKED
2/3 CUP HONEY
1 1/2 CUPS BROKEN PECANS

WHEN MIXING BUTTERHORN DOUGH, ADD LEMON ZEST WITH EGGS. AFTER DOUGH HAS RISEN IN BOWL, DIVIDE IN HALF. ROLL ONE HALF INTO RECTANGLE 12 INCHES BY 20 INCHES. BRUSH WITH 2 TABLESPOONS MELTED BUTTER.

DOUGH:
USE RECIPE FOR BUTTERHORN ROLLS
1 TABLESPOON LEMON ZEST

COMBINE BROWN SUGAR AND CINNAMON. SPRINKLE HALF OF MIXTURE OVER DOUGH. TOP WITH HALF OF RAISINS. ROLL UP LENGTHWISE LIKE JELLY ROLL; PINCH SEAM TO SEAL. CUT INTO 1/2 INCH SLICES. PLACE CUT SIDE DOWN IN 2 PREPARED PANS ABOUT 1/2 INCH APART. REPEAT WITH REMAINING DOUGH, FILLING AND RAISINS. COVER AND LET RISE UNTIL DOUBLED, ABOUT 45 MINUTES. BAKE UNTIL LIGHT BROWN, ABOUT 15 TO 20 MINUTES. IMMEDIATELY INVERT ON SERVING PLATE. MAY BE FROZEN.

FILLING:
1 CUP BROWN SUGAR, FIRMLY PACKED
2 TEASPOONS CINNAMON
1 CUP RAISINS

VARIATION: **MOLASSES STICKY BUNS:** *FOLLOW PECAN HONEY BUN RECIPE, BUT SUBSTITUTE ORANGE ZEST FOR LEMON, AND USE FOLLOWING TOPPING.*

MIX ALL INGREDIENTS IN SMALL BOWL, AND DIVIDE INTO CAKE PANS AS FOR PECAN HONEY BUNS.

TOPPING:
1 1/2 CUPS SUGAR
3/4 CUP BUTTER, MELTED
3/4 CUP LIGHT MOLASSES
3 TABLESPOONS ORANGE JUICE

Popovers with Variations

Delicious . . . and a real hit.

Preparation Time: 10 minutes

Yield: 8 servings
Preheat Oven: 450°

1 cup all-purpose flour
1/4 teaspoon salt
1 cup milk
2 eggs
1 tablespoon butter, melted

Generously oil popover pans and preheat them. Combine all ingredients (including variation if used) in mixing bowl or blender. Beat just until smooth; do not over beat. Batter should be consistency of heavy cream. Fill pans 1/2 to 2/3 full. Bake 10 minutes. Lower temperature to 350° and bake 15 to 20 minutes more until firm and golden brown. Remove from pans and make slits in bottoms to release steam.

Variations:

Sweet: Add 2 tablespoons sugar

Lemon or Orange: Use sweet variation plus 1 to 2 tablespoons lemon or orange zest

Green onion: Add 1 to 2 tablespoons minced green onions

Herb: Add 1 tablespoon fresh or 1 teaspoon dried herb such as thyme, sage, ground rosemary, basil (or a combination)

Cheese: Add 1/2 cup grated cheddar, Parmesan or Gruyere

Garlic: Add 1 to 2 cloves minced garlic

Cinnamon: Add 2 tablespoons brown sugar and 1/2 teaspoon cinnamon

Miniature: Use 5 ounce tart or muffin pans. Fill 1/2 full and bake at 350° for 20 minutes. (Yield: 30 to 32 mini-popovers)

BRIOCHE AU CITRON 

DELICATE FLAVOR. WORTH THE EFFORT.

YIELD: 12 LARGE BRIOCHES
24 SMALL BRIOCHES
PREHEAT OVEN: 325°

PREPARATION TIME: 2 HOURS

- **1/2 CUP SUGAR**
- **1/2 TEASPOON SALT**
- **2 TABLESPOONS ACTIVE DRY YEAST**
- **4 CUPS ALL-PURPOSE FLOUR (RESERVE 2 1/2 CUPS)**
- **1/2 CUP MILK**
- **2/3 CUP UNSALTED BUTTER**
- **4 EGGS**
- **1 TEASPOON PURE LEMON EXTRACT**
- **1 TEASPOON GRATED LEMON RIND**
- **1 EGG YOLK**
- **1 TABLESPOON WATER**

IN LARGE BOWL COMBINE SUGAR, SALT, YEAST AND 1 1/2 CUPS FLOUR. IN PAN OVER LOW HEAT, COMBINE MILK AND BUTTER UNTIL BUTTER MELTS. ON LOW SPEED GRADUALLY ADD WARM LIQUID IN THIN STREAM TO DRY INGREDIENTS. ON MEDIUM SPEED BEAT 2 MINUTES, OCCASIONALLY SCRAPING BOWL. GRADUALLY BEAT IN EGGS, EXTRACT, RIND AND 1 CUP FLOUR TO MAKE THICK BATTER. CONTINUE BEATING 2 MINUTES. WITH SPOON STIR IN 1 TO 1 1/2 CUPS FLOUR TO MAKE VERY SOFT DOUGH. BEAT 5 MINUTES. PLACE DOUGH IN LARGE, GREASED BOWL. TURN DOUGH TO GREASE TOP. COVER. LET RISE UNTIL DOUBLED, ABOUT 1 HOUR. PUNCH DOWN. COVER BOWL TIGHTLY AND REFRIGERATE OVERNIGHT.

PUNCH DOUGH DOWN; TURN ONTO LIGHTLY FLOURED SURFACE. COVER AND LET REST 15 MINUTES. GREASE 12 LARGE OR 24 SMALL BRIOCHE PANS OR MUFFIN TINS. CUT OFF 1/3 DOUGH; SET ASIDE. CUT REMAINING DOUGH INTO 12 OR 24 PIECES. SHAPE EACH PIECE INTO BALL AND PLACE IN BRIOCHE PANS. CUT RESERVED DOUGH INTO SAME NUMBER OF PIECES AND ROLL INTO SMALL BALLS. WITH FINGER MAKE DEPRESSION IN CENTER OF EACH LARGE BALL. PLACE SMALL BALLS IN DEPRESSIONS. LET REST 10 MINUTES. BEAT EGG YOLK WITH WATER. PAINT BRIOCHE WITH YOLK MIXTURE. BAKE 15 TO 20 MINUTES. COVER TOP KNOTS WITH FOIL IF THEY BROWN TOO QUICKLY. TEST FOR DONENESS WITH WOODEN PICK. TURN ONTO RACK TO COOL.

COUNTRY CLUB MUFFINS

PREPARATION TIME: 20 MINUTES

YIELD: 24 MINI-MUFFINS
PREHEAT OVEN: 300°

- 2 EGGS
- 1 CUP BROWN SUGAR, FIRMLY PACKED
- 1 CUP CHOPPED PECANS
- 1/4 TEASPOON SALT
- 1 TEASPOON PURE VANILLA EXTRACT
- 2 TABLESPOONS BUTTER, MELTED
- 6 TABLESPOONS ALL-PURPOSE FLOUR

IN MEDIUM BOWL BEAT EGGS UNTIL THICK. ADD SUGAR, PECANS, SALT, VANILLA, BUTTER AND FLOUR; COMBINE WELL. HEAVILY GREASE MUFFIN PANS. FILL 3/4 FULL. BAKE 25 TO 30 MINUTES. **PLACE WAXED PAPER BETWEEN LAYERS WHEN STORING AS MUFFINS ARE VERY STICKY.**

LEMONY BLUEBERRY MUFFINS

PREPARATION TIME: 30 MINUTES

YIELD: 12 MUFFINS; 36 MINI-MUFFINS
PREHEAT OVEN: 400°

- 1 CUP SUGAR
- 6 TABLESPOONS UNSALTED BUTTER, SOFTENED
- 2 EGGS
- 1/4 CUP MILK
- 1/2 TEASPOON PURE LEMON EXTRACT
- 1 1/2 CUPS ALL-PURPOSE FLOUR
- 1 1/2 TEASPOONS BAKING POWDER
- 1/4 TEASPOON SALT
- 1/2 TEASPOON GRATED LEMON RIND
- 1/2 CUP FRESH OR DRY PACK FROZEN BLUEBERRIES

IN LARGE MIXING BOWL BEAT SUGAR AND BUTTER UNTIL FLUFFY. ADD EGGS, ONE AT A TIME, BEATING WELL AFTER EACH ADDITION. ADD MILK AND LEMON EXTRACT; SET ASIDE.

IN SMALL BOWL SIFT FLOUR, BAKING POWDER AND SALT. ADD FLOUR MIXTURE AND LEMON RIND TO BUTTER MIXTURE; STIR BY HAND UNTIL FLOUR IS JUST MOISTENED. GENTLY FOLD IN BLUEBERRIES. FILL GREASED MUFFIN TINS 1/2 TO 2/3 FULL AND BAKE 25 MINUTES. PREPARE GLAZE. COOL MUFFINS IN PAN SEVERAL MINUTES. REMOVE TO FOIL LINED COOKIE SHEET AND BRUSH WITH GLAZE. BAKE AN ADDITIONAL 5 MINUTES.

LEMON GLAZE:

- 1 CUP CONFECTIONERS SUGAR
- 2 TABLESPOONS LEMON JUICE
- 1/2 TEASPOON GRATED LEMON RIND

MIX SUGAR, LEMON JUICE AND LEMON RIND UNTIL SMOOTH.

ORANGE SOUR CREAM MUFFINS

YIELD: 24 MUFFINS
PREHEAT OVEN: 425°

PREPARATION TIME: 25 MINUTES

IN LARGE BOWL CREAM BUTTER AND SUGAR. SIFT SODA AND BAKING POWDER WITH FLOUR; ADD TO CREAMED MIXTURE ALTERNATELY WITH EGGS AND SOUR CREAM. ADD ORANGE JUICE, RIND AND VANILLA. DO NOT OVERMIX. FILL GREASED MUFFIN TINS 2/3 FULL AND SPRINKLE WITH SUGAR. BAKE 15 TO 20 MINUTES, OR UNTIL GOLDEN BROWN.

1/2 CUP BUTTER, SOFTENED
1 1/4 CUPS SUGAR
1 TEASPOON BAKING SODA
2 TEASPOONS BAKING POWDER
2 3/4 CUPS ALL-PURPOSE FLOUR
2 EGGS, BEATEN WELL
1 1/2 CUPS SOUR CREAM
1/2 CUP ORANGE JUICE
1 TABLESPOON GRATED ORANGE RIND
1 TEASPOON PURE VANILLA EXTRACT
SUGAR

ZUCCHINI WALNUT MUFFINS

YIELD: 12 LARGE MUFFINS
36 MINI MUFFINS
PREHEAT OVEN: 400°

PREPARATION TIME: 20 MINUTES

SIFT FLOUR, BAKING POWDER, SUGAR, SALT AND BASIL IN LARGE BOWL. STIR IN LEMON RIND. IN SMALL BOWL COMBINE EGG, MILK AND MELTED BUTTER. QUICKLY ADD MILK MIXTURE TO DRY INGREDIENTS AND STIR JUST ENOUGH TO MOISTEN. STIR IN ZUCCHINI AND NUTS. DO NOT OVERMIX. FILL GREASED MUFFIN TINS SLIGHTLY MORE THAN HALF FULL. BAKE 20 TO 25 MINUTES (LESS FOR MINI-MUFFINS). SERVE HOT.

2 CUPS UNBLEACHED ALL-PURPOSE FLOUR
2 TEASPOONS BAKING POWDER
2 TABLESPOONS SUGAR
1/2 TEASPOON SALT
3/4 TEASPOON DRIED BASIL, CRUMBLED
1 TEASPOON GRATED LEMON RIND
1 EGG, BEATEN WELL
1 SCANT CUP MILK
1/4 CUP BUTTER, MELTED
1/2 CUP GRATED ZUCCHINI, SQUEEZED DRY
3/4 CUP CHOPPED WALNUTS

JALAPEÑO CORN BREAD

PREPARATION TIME: 15 MINUTES

YIELD: 6 SERVINGS
PREHEAT OVEN: 450°

- 1 CUP WHITE CORN MEAL
- 2 TABLESPOONS ALL-PURPOSE FLOUR
- 1/2 TEASPOON BAKING SODA
- 2 TEASPOONS BAKING POWDER
- 1/2 TEASPOON SALT
- 1 EGG, BEATEN WELL
- 1 CUP BUTTERMILK
- 2 TABLESPOONS SHORTENING, MELTED (RESERVE 1 TABLESPOON)
- 1 SMALL JALAPEÑO PEPPER, SEEDED AND MINCED
- 1 TABLESPOON DRIED CHOPPED ONION
- 7 1/2 OUNCES CANNED CREAMED CORN

IN MEDIUM BOWL COMBINE DRY INGREDIENTS. ADD EGG AND BUTTERMILK. ADD 1 TABLESPOON SHORTENING, JALAPEÑO, ONION AND CREAMED CORN. HEAT RESERVED TABLESPOON SHORTENING IN 10 INCH IRON SKILLET OVER HIGH HEAT. POUR BATTER INTO SKILLET AND BAKE IN VERY HOT OVEN 18 TO 20 MINUTES. IF CORN BREAD DOES NOT BROWN ON TOP, TURN IT OVER IN PAN LAST 3 MINUTES OF BAKING TIME.

VARIATION: OMIT JALAPEÑO, ONION AND CORN FOR CLASSIC **SOUTHERN CORN BREAD.**

APRICOT-POPPY SEED CARACOIS

PREPARATION TIME: 20 MINUTES

YIELD: 12 SERVINGS
PREHEAT OVEN: 375°

- 16 OUNCES REFRIGERATED CRESCENT ROLLS
- 1/2 CUP FINELY CHOPPED DRIED APRICOTS
- 2 TABLESPOONS SUGAR
- 2 TABLESPOONS POPPY SEED
- 1/4 CUP APRICOT PRESERVES
- 1 TABLESPOON FINELY CHOPPED ALMONDS

SEPARATE CRESCENT DOUGH INTO 4 RECTANGLES; PRESS PERFORATIONS TO SEAL. COMBINE APRICOTS, SUGAR AND POPPY SEED. SPREAD ONE-FOURTH OF MIXTURE EVENLY OVER EACH RECTANGLE. ROLL UP STARTING AT LONG SIDE. PRESS EDGES TO SEAL. WIND DOUGH INTO GREASED 8 INCH CAKE PAN. BEGIN AT OUTER EDGE AND COIL TO CENTER MAKING ONE LARGE SPIRAL. BAKE 20 TO 24 MINUTES OR UNTIL DEEP GOLDEN BROWN.

SPREAD PRESERVES OVER TOP; SPRINKLE WITH ALMONDS. BAKE 2 MINUTES. INVERT BREAD AT ONCE ONTO WIRE RACK, THEN AGAIN ONTO SERVING PLATE.

APPLE STRUDEL

YIELD: 8 SERVINGS
PREHEAT OVEN: 350°
PREPARATION TIME: 45 MINUTES

- **1/2 CUP BUTTER (RESERVE 1/4 CUP)**
- **3 GRANNY SMITH APPLES, PEELED, CORED AND SLICED 1/8 INCH THICK**
- **1/2 TEASPOON CINNAMON**
- **1/4 TEASPOON NUTMEG**
- **3/4 CUP SUGAR**
- **6 SHEETS PHYLLO DOUGH (COVER WITH DAMP CLOTH)**
- **1 TABLESPOON BUTTER, MELTED**
- **SUGAR**

MELT 1/4 CUP BUTTER IN SKILLET. ADD APPLES, CINNAMON, NUTMEG AND SUGAR; COMBINE. COVER; COOK OVER LOW HEAT UNTIL APPLES ARE TENDER. MELT REMAINING BUTTER. BRUSH 1 PHYLLO SHEET WITH MELTED BUTTER. LAY ANOTHER PHYLLO SHEET ON TOP AND BRUSH WITH BUTTER. REPEAT WITH 3RD SHEET. SPOON HALF OF APPLE MIXTURE ALONG SHORT END LEAVING 3 INCH EDGE ON END AND 1 INCH EDGE ON SIDES. FOLD END OVER; THEN FOLD SIDES OVER. ROLL UP ENCLOSING APPLES COMPLETELY. REPEAT PROCESS WITH REST OF PHYLLO AND APPLES. BRUSH TOPS WITH MELTED BUTTER. SPRINKLE WITH SUGAR IF DESIRED. BAKE 20 TO 25 MINUTES OR UNTIL GOLDEN AND CRISP.

BUBBLE COFFEE RING

SO EASY FOR BRUNCH. YOUR GUESTS WILL NEVER GUESS.

YIELD: 1 CAKE
PREPARATION TIME: 15 MINUTES

- **1/2 CUP BROKEN PECANS**
- **24 OUNCES FROZEN WALNUT SIZE DINNER ROLLS**

TOPPING:

- **3/4 CUP BUTTER, MELTED AND COOLED**
- **3/4 CUP BROWN SUGAR, FIRMLY PACKED**
- **1 TEASPOON CINNAMON**
- **1/2 CUP BROKEN PECANS**

GREASE AND FLOUR BUNDT OR ANGEL FOOD CAKE PAN. SPRINKLE PECANS IN BOTTOM OF PAN. ADD FROZEN ROLLS.

MIX BUTTER, BROWN SUGAR, CINNAMON AND PECANS. POUR OVER ROLLS. COVER WITH TOWEL AND LET RISE AT ROOM TEMPERATURE OVERNIGHT. NEXT MORNING PREHEAT OVEN TO 350°; COVER PAN WITH FOIL (TO PREVENT OVERBROWNING) AND BAKE 30 MINUTES. TURN UPSIDE DOWN ON SERVING PLATTER.

Plain Jane Coffee Cake

A tradition on Christmas morning. Cut in fingers and serve warm with butter.

Preparation Time: 3 hours

Yield: 3 cakes
Preheat Oven: 350°

1 cup milk
1/2 cup butter
1 teaspoon salt
2/3 cup sugar
1 tablespoon active dry yeast
4 tablespoons lukewarm water
2 eggs, beaten well
4 to 4 1/2 cups all-purpose flour (reserve 2 1/2 cups)
1 cup raisins
3 tablespoons chilled butter, in bits

In medium saucepan heat milk, butter, salt and sugar until butter melts. Cool. Soak yeast in water 5 minutes. In large bowl combine yeast, eggs and milk mixture. Beat in 2 cups flour. Coat raisins with small amount of reserved flour. Add raisins and remaining flour. Dough will be sticky. Place in greased bowl; cover and let rise until doubled, about 1 1/2 hours, or overnight in refrigerator. To bake, spoon dough into 2 greased 9 × 13 inch pans and one 8 inch square pan. Do not smooth. Dot hollows with bits of butter. Prepare topping and sprinkle on top. Let rise until doubled, about 1 hour. Bake 20 minutes or until golden brown.

Topping:
1/2 cup sugar
1 teaspoon cinnamon
1/2 cup chopped nuts

Mix sugar, cinnamon and nuts.

Quick Coffee Cake

Preparation Time: 15 minutes

Yield: 12 to 15 servings
Preheat Oven: 350°

3 eggs
1 1/2 cups sugar
1 1/2 cups all-purpose flour
1 1/2 teaspoons baking powder
1 1/2 teaspoons cinnamon
3/4 cup milk, scalded
1/4 cup powdered sugar
1 cup finely chopped pecans
1/2 cup butter, melted

Beat eggs until thick; add sugar, flour, baking powder and cinnamon. Mix until blended. Quickly pour in milk and stir well. Spoon into greased 9 × 13 inch baking pan; bake 30 minutes. Punch holes in top of cake; sprinkle with powdered sugar and pecans. Drizzle with butter.

Sour Cream Coffee Cake

Yield: 1 bundt cake
Preheat Oven: 350°
Preparation Time: 25 minutes

Batter:
- **1/2 cup butter, softened**
- **1 cup sugar**
- **2 eggs, beaten well**
- **2 cups all-purpose flour**
- **1 teaspoon baking powder**
- **1 teaspoon baking soda**
- **1/4 teaspoon salt**
- **1 cup sour cream**
- **1 teaspoon pure vanilla extract**

In large bowl, cream butter and sugar thoroughly. Add eggs. Sift flour, baking powder, soda and salt in medium bowl; mix sour cream and vanilla in small bowl. Add dry ingredients to egg mixture alternately with sour cream. Prepare topping. Turn half of batter into greased and floured bundt pan. Sprinkle on half of topping mixture. Add remaining batter and topping mixture. Bake 45 minutes or until toothpick inserted in center comes out clean.

Topping:
- **1/2 cup sugar**
- **1 teaspoon cinnamon**
- **1/2 cup chopped walnuts**

In small bowl, combine sugar, cinnamon and walnuts. Set aside.

HINT: It takes 12 ounces of sour cream to make 1 cup.

Challah 

Yield: 3 loaves
Preheat Oven: 350°
Preparation Time: 1 1/2 hours

- **2 tablespoons active dry yeast**
- **4 teaspoons salt**
- **3/4 cup honey**
- **1 3/4 cups warm water**
- **7 to 8 cups all-purpose flour (reserve 5 to 6 cups)**
- **1 1/4 cups vegetable oil**
- **4 eggs (reserve 1 egg)**
- **1 tablespoon cool water**
- **1 tablespoon poppy seeds**

In large bowl combine yeast, salt, honey and warm water. Add 2 cups flour, oil and 3 eggs. Continue adding flour slowly until dough is stiff enough to pull away from sides of bowl. Divide into 9 pieces. Roll each piece into rope 12 inches long. Take 3 ropes and braid. Repeat with remaining dough. Let rise on greased cookie sheet about 1 hour. Combine water and reserved egg; brush braids with mixture and sprinkle with poppy seeds. Bake 45 minutes. Freezes well.

APRICOT BREAD

PREPARATION TIME: 55 MINUTES

YIELD: 1 LOAF
PREHEAT OVEN: 325°

1 CUP DRIED APRICOTS
1 CUP SUGAR
4 TEASPOONS BUTTER, SOFTENED
1 EGG, BEATEN WELL
1/2 CUP ORANGE JUICE
1/4 CUP WATER
2 CUPS ALL-PURPOSE FLOUR
2 TEASPOONS BAKING POWDER
1/4 TEASPOON BAKING SODA
1 TEASPOON SALT
1/2 CUP CHOPPED PECANS

CUT APRICOTS INTO SMALL PIECES AND SOAK 1/2 HOUR IN WARM WATER. IN LARGE BOWL BLEND SUGAR AND BUTTER. ADD EGG, ORANGE JUICE AND WATER; MIX WELL. SIFT TOGETHER FLOUR, BAKING POWDER, SODA AND SALT IN MEDIUM BOWL. STIR INTO SUGAR MIXTURE. DRAIN APRICOTS AND ADD WITH PECANS TO FLOUR MIXTURE. POUR INTO GREASED AND FLOURED 5×7 INCH LOAF PAN. LET STAND 20 MINUTES. BAKE 1 HOUR. DO NOT OVERBAKE! FREEZES WELL.

CITRUS TEA LOAF

PREPARATION TIME: 1 HOUR

YIELD: 2 LOAVES
PREHEAT OVEN: 350°

8 OUNCES CREAM CHEESE, SOFTENED
1/2 CUP BUTTER, SOFTENED
1 1/4 CUPS SUGAR
2 EGGS, BEATEN WELL
3 TABLESPOONS FRESH LEMON JUICE
1 TABLESPOON GRATED LEMON RIND
1/2 TEASPOON PURE LEMON EXTRACT
1/2 TEASPOON PURE VANILLA EXTRACT
1/2 CUP PLUS 2 TABLESPOONS MILK
2 1/4 CUPS ALL-PURPOSE FLOUR
2 TEASPOONS BAKING POWDER
1 TEASPOON BAKING SODA
2/3 CUP CHOPPED PECANS

IN LARGE BOWL CREAM CHEESE AND BUTTER TOGETHER. ADD SUGAR; BEAT UNTIL FLUFFY. ADD EGGS AND BEAT WELL. MIX LEMON JUICE, RIND AND EXTRACTS WITH MILK. COMBINE DRY INGREDIENTS IN MEDIUM BOWL. ALTERNATELY ADD DRY INGREDIENTS AND MILK TO EGG MIXTURE. STIR IN PECANS. COAT TWO 4 1/2×8 1/2 INCH LOAF PANS WITH VEGETABLE SPRAY. DIVIDE BATTER BETWEEN PANS. BAKE 45 MINUTES. PREPARE GLAZE AND POUR OVER HOT LOAVES WHILE STILL IN PANS. COOL 10 MINUTES. REMOVE FROM PANS TO RACKS AND COOL COMPLETELY.

CITRUS GLAZE:
1 TEASPOON GRATED LEMON RIND
2 TO 3 TABLESPOONS FRESH LEMON JUICE
1/3 CUP CONFECTIONERS SUGAR

COMBINE RIND, LEMON JUICE AND SUGAR.

DATE NUT LOAF

YIELD: 3 LOAVES | *PREPARATION TIME: 30 MINUTES*

IN LARGE BOWL COMBINE EGGS, SUGAR AND OIL; BEAT WELL. COMBINE DRY INGREDIENTS; ADD TO EGG MIXTURE. FOLD IN DATES AND PECANS. GREASE AND FLOUR THREE 3½ × 6 INCH LOAF PANS AND LINE BOTTOMS WITH WAXED PAPER. POUR BATTER INTO PANS. PLACE PANS IN COLD OVEN AND TURN TEMPERATURE TO 300°. BAKE 1 TO 1½ HOURS, OR UNTIL TOOTHPICK INSERTED IN CENTER COMES OUT CLEAN.

4 EGGS, BEATEN WELL
1 CUP SUGAR
½ CUP VEGETABLE OIL
1 CUP ALL-PURPOSE FLOUR
1 TEASPOON SALT
1¾ CUPS CHOPPED DATES
4 CUPS PECANS, COARSELY CHOPPED

RHUBARB BREAD

YIELD: 2 LOAVES
PREHEAT OVEN: 325°
PREPARATION TIME: 20 MINUTES

IN LARGE BOWL COMBINE SUGAR AND OIL. STIR IN EGG, MILK AND VANILLA. COMBINE DRY INGREDIENTS IN MEDIUM BOWL AND ADD TO SUGAR MIXTURE. STIR IN RHUBARB AND NUTS. POUR INTO 2 WELL-GREASED 3½ × 7½ INCH LOAF PANS.

COMBINE SUGAR AND CINNAMON; CUT IN BUTTER. SPRINKLE ON TOP OF LOAVES. BAKE 30 TO 45 MINUTES. FREEZES WELL.

1½ CUPS BROWN SUGAR, FIRMLY PACKED
⅔ CUP VEGETABLE OIL
1 EGG, BEATEN WELL
1 CUP SOUR MILK
1 TEASPOON PURE VANILLA EXTRACT
2½ CUPS ALL-PURPOSE FLOUR
1 TEASPOON SALT
1 TEASPOON BAKING SODA
1½ CUPS FINELY DICED RHUBARB
½ CUP CHOPPED NUTS
½ CUP SUGAR
½ TEASPOON CINNAMON
1 TABLESPOON BUTTER

HINT: SEE TECHNIQUES PAGE OF THIS SECTION FOR INSTRUCTIONS TO PREPARE SOUR MILK.

POPPY SEED BREAD

EXCELLENT FOR COFFEE OR LUNCHEON — VERY MOIST.

PREPARATION TIME: 20 MINUTES

YIELD: 4 MINI LOAVES
PREHEAT OVEN: 350°

- 3 CUPS ALL-PURPOSE FLOUR
- 1/2 TEASPOON SALT
- 1 1/2 TEASPOONS BAKING POWDER
- 3 EGGS
- 1 1/2 CUPS MILK
- 2 1/4 CUPS SUGAR
- 1 1/2 CUPS VEGETABLE OIL
- 1 1/2 TEASPOONS PURE ALMOND EXTRACT
- 1 1/2 TEASPOONS PURE VANILLA EXTRACT
- 1 1/2 TEASPOONS BUTTER FLAVORING
- 1 1/2 TABLESPOONS POPPY SEED

IN MEDIUM BOWL MIX FLOUR, SALT AND BAKING POWDER. SET ASIDE. IN LARGE BOWL BEAT EGGS, MILK, SUGAR AND OIL. ADD EXTRACTS, FLAVORING AND POPPY SEED. COMBINE FLOUR MIXTURE WITH EGG MIXTURE. POUR INTO 4 GREASED AND FLOURED 3 × 5 INCH LOAF PANS. BAKE 45 TO 50 MINUTES.

COOL LOAVES IN PANS ABOUT 10 TO 15 MINUTES. TURN OUT ONTO BAKING RACK PLACED ON COOKIE SHEET. PREPARE GLAZE AND POUR OVER EACH LOAF. COOL THOROUGHLY. SLICE VERY THIN.

GLAZE:

- 1/4 CUP ORANGE JUICE
- 3/4 CUP SUGAR
- 1/2 TEASPOON PURE ALMOND EXTRACT
- 1/2 TEASPOON PURE VANILLA EXTRACT
- 1/2 TEASPOON BUTTER FLAVORING

COMBINE ORANGE JUICE, SUGAR, EXTRACTS AND FLAVORING.

BEER BREAD

BOTH BEGINNERS AND EXPERIENCED COOKS WILL ENJOY THIS.

PREPARATION TIME: 10 MINUTES

YIELD: 1 LOAF
PREHEAT OVEN: 375°

- 3 CUPS SELF-RISING FLOUR
- 1/4 CUP SUGAR
- 12 OUNCES BEER
- 1 EGG

COMBINE FLOUR AND SUGAR IN MIXING BOWL. ADD BEER ALL AT ONCE AND BREAK EGG INTO MIXTURE BEFORE STIRRING. BLEND JUST LONG ENOUGH TO MIX WELL. GREASE 9 × 5 INCH LOAF PAN AND POUR IN BATTER. BAKE 65 TO 70 MINUTES. REMOVE FROM PAN AND COOL ON WIRE RACK.

HERB BREAD

YIELD: 2 LOAVES
PREHEAT OVEN: 325°

PREPARATION TIME: 2 HOURS

- **1 CUP OLD-FASHIONED OATS**
- **2 CUPS BOILING WATER**
- **2 TABLESPOONS ACTIVE DRY YEAST**
- **1/3 CUP WARM WATER**
- **2 TEASPOONS SALT**
- **2 TABLESPOONS HONEY**
- **1/2 CUP BUTTER, MELTED**
- **1/2 TEASPOON DRIED PARSLEY, CRUMBLED**
- **1 TEASPOON DRIED BASIL, CRUMBLED**
- **1/2 TEASPOON ANISEED**
- **2 TEASPOONS SAVORY, CRUMBLED**
- **1/2 TEASPOON GROUND THYME**
- **3 CUPS WHOLE WHEAT FLOUR**
- **3 CUPS UNBLEACHED FLOUR**

PUT OATS IN LARGE BOWL; POUR BOILING WATER OVER. LET STAND 1/2 HOUR. DISSOLVE YEAST IN WARM WATER; SET ASIDE TO PROOF. ADD SALT, HONEY, BUTTER, AND HERBS TO OAT MIXTURE. BLEND; ADD YEAST. STIR IN WHEAT FLOUR; THEN UNBLEACHED FLOUR. KNEAD ON LIGHTLY FLOURED BOARD UNTIL SMOOTH AND ELASTIC. PLACE IN LIGHTLY GREASED BOWL; TURN TO GREASE TOP. COVER; LET RISE UNTIL DOUBLED. PUNCH DOWN; REMOVE AND KNEAD LIGHTLY. DIVIDE IN HALF; PLACE EACH HALF INTO GREASED 5×9 INCH LOAF PAN. COVER; LET RISE UNTIL DOUGH REACHES TOP OF PAN. BAKE 50 MINUTES. TURN ONTO RACK; COOL.

FLORENTINE FRENCH BREAD

GREAT WITH ITALIAN FOOD

YIELD: 1 LOAF
PREHEAT OVEN: 350°

PREPARATION TIME: 30 MINUTES

- **1 LARGE LOAF FRENCH BREAD**
- **20 OUNCES FROZEN CHOPPED SPINACH**
- **1/2 CUP BUTTER, MELTED**
- **1/4 CUP GRATED PARMESAN CHEESE**
- **2 CLOVES GARLIC, CRUSHED**
- **1/4 TEASPOON SEASONED SALT**
- **2 CUPS GRATED MOZZARELLA CHEESE (RESERVE 1 1/2 CUPS)**

CUT BREAD IN HALF LENGTHWISE. SET ASIDE. COOK SPINACH AND SQUEEZE OUT ALL LIQUID. MIX SPINACH WITH BUTTER, PARMESAN CHEESE, GARLIC, SEASONED SALT, AND 1/2 CUP MOZZARELLA. SPREAD ON BREAD. SPRINKLE WITII RESERVED MOZZARELLA. BAKE 5 TO 8 MINUTES OR UNTIL CHEESE MELTS.

PEACH BREAD

PREPARATION TIME: 30 MINUTES

YIELD: 2 LOAVES
PREHEAT OVEN: 350°

- **1/2 CUP BUTTER, SOFTENED**
- **1 CUP SUGAR**
- **3 EGGS**
- **2 3/4 CUPS ALL-PURPOSE FLOUR**
- **1 1/2 TEASPOONS BAKING POWDER**
- **1 TEASPOON SALT**
- **1/2 TEASPOON BAKING SODA**
- **1 1/2 TEASPOONS CINNAMON**
- **1/2 TEASPOON GRATED NUTMEG**
- **2 CUPS THINLY SLICED RIPE PEACHES**
- **3 TABLESPOONS PEACH NECTAR**
- **1 TEASPOON PURE VANILLA EXTRACT**

CREAM BUTTER; GRADUALLY ADD SUGAR, BEATING WELL. ADD EGGS, ONE AT A TIME, BEATING WELL AFTER EACH ADDITION. COMBINE FLOUR, BAKING POWDER, SALT, BAKING SODA, CINNAMON AND NUTMEG. ADD TO BUTTER MIXTURE ALTERNATELY WITH PEACHES, BEGINNING AND ENDING WITH FLOUR. STIR IN NECTAR AND VANILLA. POUR INTO 2 GREASED AND FLOURED 8 1/2 × 4 1/2 INCH LOAF PANS; BAKE 50 MINUTES, OR UNTIL TOOTHPICK INSERTED IN CENTER COMES OUT CLEAN. COOL IN PAN 10 MINUTES; REMOVE AND COOL COMPLETELY ON RACK. FREEZES WELL.

CHEESE BRAID

PREPARATION TIME: 3 HOURS

YIELD: 2 LOAVES
PREHEAT OVEN: 375°

- **5 CUPS ALL-PURPOSE FLOUR (RESERVE 3 CUPS)**
- **1 TABLESPOON ACTIVE DRY YEAST**
- **1 1/2 CUPS MILK**
- **2 TABLESPOONS SUGAR**
- **1 1/2 TEASPOONS SALT**
- **1 EGG**
- **2 CUPS SHREDDED SHARP CHEDDAR CHEESE**

COMBINE FLOUR AND YEAST. HEAT MILK, SUGAR AND SALT UNTIL WARM (115°) AND SUGAR DISSOLVES; ADD TO YEAST MIXTURE. ADD EGG AND CHEESE. BEAT AT LOW SPEED WITH MIXER 30 SECONDS, SCRAPING BOWL. BEAT 3 MINUTES AT HIGH SPEED. STIR IN 2 1/2 TO 3 CUPS RESERVED FLOUR TO MAKE STIFF DOUGH. KNEAD ON FLOURED SURFACE TILL SMOOTH, ABOUT 8 TO 10 MINUTES. SHAPE INTO BALL; PLACE IN GREASED BOWL, TURN TO GREASE TOP. COVER AND LET RISE UNTIL DOUBLE, ABOUT 1 1/2 HOURS.

PUNCH DOWN; DIVIDE INTO 6 PIECES. COVER AND LET REST 10 MINUTES. ROLL EACH PIECE INTO ROPE 15 INCHES LONG. ON GREASED BAKING SHEET, SHAPE INTO 2 BRAIDS, USING 3 ROPES FOR EACH (SEE TECHNIQUES). COVER AND LET RISE UNTIL ALMOST DOUBLE, ABOUT 35 TO 45 MINUTES. BAKE 15 TO 20 MINUTES.

Techniques

To measure 4 ounces of dried spaghetti, tight bundle should be size of a quarter.

When cooking pasta for an entree, cook extra and use a few days later for pasta salad.

Don't break strands of pasta before cooking. If pasta doesn't fit into pan, wait until it softens and push remainder into water.

When cooking with egg yolks, always use non-aluminum pans so there will be no discoloration of food. This also applies to white wine, vinegar, spinach and tomatoes.

A pan with a 7 inch bottom is right for 2 to 3 egg omelette. Depth of egg mass should not be over 1/4 inch.

When poaching eggs, add one tablespoon vinegar to each quart simmering water to speed up coagulation, reduce cooking time and help eggs keep their shape.

To easily separate egg yolks from whites, break into a funnel. The yolk stays in funnel while the white passes through.

Always separate egg whites individually into small bowl; then add to rest of whites. This will ensure no yolks get into bowl of whites. Use a dampened cotton swab or paper towel to remove unwanted egg yolk from separated egg white.

Extra egg whites may be frozen in ice cube trays and placed in plastic bags. Bring to room temperature before using.

Eggs should always be cooked on very gentle heat.

Melt cheese over low heat. High heat makes it tough and stringy.

When adding cheese to sauce, grate, shred or dice first so it melts and blends quickly.

To grate small amount of cheese, use a swivel-bladed vegetable peeler.

Soft cheeses should be served chilled. Other cheeses should be served at room temperature.

To prolong storage of cheese, remove from wrapper and wipe dry. Wrap in paper towel and store in air-tight plastic bag.

Fettuccini Ticino

Yield: 6 to 8 servings *Preparation Time: 20 minutes*

- 1/4 cup butter
- 6 green onions with tops, diced
- 1/2 cup diced ham
- 4 large fresh mushrooms, sliced
- 1 cup frozen green peas, thawed and drained
- 12 ounces fettuccini noodles, cooked and drained
- 8 ounces grated Parmesan cheese
- 1 quart whipping cream
- Salt and freshly ground pepper, to taste
- Chopped fresh parsley

Melt butter; sauté onions over low heat until soft. Add ham, mushrooms and peas; cook 5 minutes. Add fettuccini, cheese and cream. Simmer until cheese has melted, stirring constantly. Add salt and pepper; garnish with parsley. Sauce will thicken as it sets.

The French Hen Restuarant

Capelli Eleganté

Yield: 6 to 8 small servings *Preparation Time: 30 minutes*

- 8 ounces capelli (angel's hair pasta)
- 2 tablespoons vegetable oil
- 2 hard boiled eggs, grated (reserve 3 tablespoons)
- 1/3 cup minced fresh chives (reserve 3 tablespoons)
- 1/4 cup sour cream
- 3 tablespoons fresh lemon juice
- 1 cup heavy whipping cream
- 3 ounces black caviar
- 3 ounces red caviar
- 3 ounces golden caviar

Cook, rinse and drain pasta. Toss with vegetable oil to keep from sticking. Add eggs and chives; toss and set aside. In large bowl blend sour cream, lemon juice and cream. Add pasta; mix gently. Arrange pasta on serving plates. Spoon small amounts of each caviar in center of pasta. Garnish with reserved egg and chives. Serve at room temperature.

James Clary
La Cuisine

Linguini Primavera

"Primavera" means springtime. Use the finest quality and freshest vegetables of the season. Enjoy!

Preparation Time: 30 minutes *Yield: 4 servings*

6 cups chicken stock (reserve 2 cups)
5 cups water
4 tablespoons extra virgin olive oil
1 tablespoon salt
12 ounces linguini
3 ounces fresh snow peas
3 ounces broccoli flowerets
3 ounces zucchini, sliced in 1/2 inch pieces
3 ounces fresh mushrooms, sliced
3 ounces fresh green beans, stemmed and cut in 2 inch pieces
3 cloves garlic, minced
1/2 cup butter
1/2 cup Parmesan cheese
8 cherry tomatoes, halved
Additional Parmesan cheese
Freshly ground pepper, to taste
Chopped fresh parsley

In large stock pot, bring 4 cups stock, water, oil and salt to boil. Add linguini; boil 12 to 14 minutes until just tender. Drain; do not rinse.

Poach vegetables (except tomatoes) and garlic in reserved stock until tender crisp. Add pasta; heat 2 minutes. Remove from heat and add butter. Toss until butter melts; add 1/2 cup Parmesan and tomatoes. Toss to coat. Divide into four portions. Sprinkle with additional Parmesan cheese and pepper; garnish with parsley. Serve immediately.

La Cuisine

Fusilli in Curried Cream and Salmon Sauce

Yield: 8 to 10 servings

Preparation Time: 1 hour

Cook pasta al dente; drain and set aside. In processor or blender, thoroughly blend sour cream, heavy cream, lemon juice, garlic, and curry powder. Transfer to large bowl; stir in salmon, onion and capers. Add fusilli, asparagus, salt and pepper. Toss gently to coat. Serve immediately.

1 pound fusilli pasta (twisted spaghetti)
1½ cups sour cream
½ cup heavy cream
2 tablespoons fresh lemon juice
2 cloves garlic, crushed
1½ teaspoons curry powder
½ pound smoked salmon, cut in julienne strips
2 tablespoons grated onion
¼ cup drained capers
¾ pound fresh asparagus, cut in 1 inch pieces, cooked tender crisp
Salt and freshly ground pepper, to taste

Tortellini with Sauce of Five Cheeses

Yield: 6 servings

Preparation Time: 20 minutes

Cook tortellini according to package directions. Meanwhile in large skillet over medium-low heat, melt butter; add cream, ricotta, mozzarella, provolone, blue cheese, Parmesan and wine. Stirring constantly, cook until cheeses are melted and mixture is blended. Drain tortellini; add to sauce and heat through. Stir in parsley; mix well. Sprinkle with additional Parmesan if desired. Serve immediately.

16 ounces frozen tortellini pasta (meat or cheese filled)
2 tablespoons butter
¾ cup heavy cream
8 ounces ricotta cheese
½ cup shredded mozzarella cheese
½ cup grated provolone cheese
¼ cup crumbled blue cheese
2 tablespoons freshly grated Parmesan cheese
¼ cup dry white wine
¼ cup chopped fresh parsley
Additional Parmesan cheese

JUMBO SHELLS

PREPARATION TIME: 1 HOUR

YIELD: 6 TO 8 SERVINGS
PREHEAT OVEN: 350°

- 2 TABLESPOONS VEGETABLE OIL
- 16 OUNCES JUMBO MACARONI SHELLS (ABOUT 23 SHELLS)
- 4 TABLESPOONS EXTRA VIRGIN OLIVE OIL
- 1 LARGE EGGPLANT, CHOPPED
- 1/2 CUP CHOPPED ONION
- 1/4 CUP CHOPPED SHALLOTS
- 2 LARGE CLOVES GARLIC, CRUSHED
- 2 TABLESPOONS CHOPPED FRESH PARSLEY
- 1 TEASPOON DRIED BASIL, CRUMBLED
- 1/4 TEASPOON DRIED MARJORAM, CRUMBLED
- 1/4 TEASPOON CRUSHED HOT RED PEPPER FLAKES
- SALT, TO TASTE
- 16 OUNCES CANNED TOMATOES, CHOPPED
- 1/2 CUP RICOTTA CHEESE
- 1/2 CUP GRATED MOZZARELLA CHEESE

BRING 4 QUARTS WATER IN LARGE STOCK POT TO BOIL. ADD VEGETABLE OIL AND SHELLS. COOK, STIRRING FREQUENTLY, 8 TO 10 MINUTES UNTIL TENDER. DRAIN. COVER WITH COLD WATER UNTIL READY TO USE.

IN LARGE SKILLET, HEAT OLIVE OIL OVER MEDIUM HEAT. ADD EGGPLANT, ONION, SHALLOTS, GARLIC, PARSLEY, BASIL, MARJORAM, PEPPER AND SALT. COOK OVER LOW HEAT 15 MINUTES UNTIL TENDER. ADD TOMATOES AND COOK UNTIL THICK. COOL; ADD RICOTTA AND SET ASIDE. INVERT SHELLS ON PAPER TOWELING TO DRAIN.

PREPARE SAUCE. SPOON 1 CUP OF SAUCE IN BOTTOM OF LARGE BAKING DISH. FILL SHELLS WITH EGGPLANT MIXTURE AND PLACE IN DISH. SPOON 1/2 TEASPOON OF SAUCE OVER EACH SHELL. BAKE 20 TO 30 MINUTES UNTIL HEATED THROUGH. REMOVE SHELLS TO SERVING PLATES. ADD A LITTLE WATER TO SAUCE IF NEEDED; SPOON AROUND SHELLS. SPRINKLE WITH MOZZARELLA CHEESE.

TOMATO SAUCE:

- 16 OUNCES TOMATO SAUCE WITH TOMATO BITS
- 2 TABLESPOONS EXTRA VIRGIN OLIVE OIL
- 2 TABLESPOONS CHOPPED FRESH PARSLEY
- 1/2 TEASPOON DRIED BASIL, CRUMBLED
- 1/2 TEASPOON DRIED MARJORAM, CRUMBLED
- 1/4 TEASPOON ONION POWDER
- 1/4 TEASPOON GARLIC POWDER
- 2 TABLESPOONS DRY VERMOUTH

IN MEDIUM SKILLET, ADD TOMATO SAUCE, OIL, PARSLEY, BASIL, MARJORAM, ONION POWDER AND GARLIC POWDER. COOK OVER MEDIUM HEAT 5 MINUTES. ADD VERMOUTH; COOK 2 MINUTES OR UNTIL SLIGHTLY THICKENED.

PAN-FRIED RAVIOLI WITH CREAMY TOMATO SAUCE

YIELD: 6 SERVINGS *PREPARATION TIME: 45 MINUTES*

- **24 OUNCES FROZEN LARGE CHEESE RAVIOLI (24 PIECES)**
- **1 LARGE EGG, BEATEN WELL**
- **1 CUP ITALIAN SEASONED BREAD CRUMBS**

DIP FROZEN RAVIOLI IN BEATEN EGG; COAT WELL ON BOTH SIDES WITH CRUMBS. SET ON WAX PAPER TO "DRY".

CREAMY TOMATO SAUCE:

- **3 TABLESPOONS EXTRA VIRGIN OLIVE OIL**
- **3/4 CUP MINCED GREEN BELL PEPPER**
- **3/4 CUP MINCED ONION**
- **1 LARGE CLOVE GARLIC, CRUSHED**
- **1 TABLESPOON ALL-PURPOSE FLOUR**
- **16 OUNCES CANNED TOMATO SAUCE WITH TOMATO BITS**
- **6 OUNCES TOMATO PASTE**
- **1/4 CUP DRY VERMOUTH**
- **1/4 CUP BURGUNDY WINE**
- **1/4 TEASPOON SALT**
- **1/4 TEASPOON DRIED BASIL, CRUMBLED**
- **1/4 TEASPOON DRIED OREGANO, CRUMBLED**
- **1/4 TEASPOON CAYENNE PEPPER**
- **1 TEASPOON SUGAR**
- **3/4 CUP HEAVY CREAM**
- **VEGETABLE OIL**
- **GRATED PARMESAN CHEESE**
- **PARSLEY SPRIGS**

IN MEDIUM SAUCEPAN HEAT OLIVE OIL; ADD BELL PEPPER, ONION AND GARLIC. COOK OVER LOW HEAT UNTIL SOFTENED. ADD FLOUR AND COMBINE. ADD TOMATO SAUCE, TOMATO PASTE, VERMOUTH, WINE, SEASONINGS AND SUGAR. SIMMER 15 MINUTES. STIR IN CREAM AND HEAT THROUGH. (DO NOT BOIL OR IT MAY CURDLE.)

HEAT 1/2 INCH OIL IN 12 INCH SKILLET OVER MEDIUM-HIGH HEAT. ADD RAVIOLI AND COOK 2 MINUTES ON EACH SIDE OR UNTIL GOLDEN. LADLE THREE-FOURTHS OF SAUCE ON PLATES. ARRANGE RAVIOLI OVER SAUCE. SPOON REMAINING SAUCE ON RAVIOLI. SPRINKLE WITH PARMESAN AND GARNISH WITH PARSLEY.

VARIATION: OMIT SAUCE. USE MINI-RAVIOLI AND SERVE WARM WITH HERBED MAYONNAISE (SEE INDEX). GREAT FINGER FOOD.

HINT: PREPARE IN 9×13 INCH CASSEROLE DISH FOR BUFFET.

FLORENTINE LASAGNA ROLLUPS

PREPARATION TIME: 45 MINUTES

YIELD: 6 SERVINGS
PREHEAT OVEN: 350°

12 CURLY LASAGNA NOODLES, COOKED
3/4 CUP CHOPPED ONION
6 TABLESPOONS BUTTER (RESERVE 4 TABLESPOONS)
20 OUNCES FROZEN CHOPPED SPINACH, THAWED AND SQUEEZED DRY
1 1/2 CUPS SHREDDED MOZZARELLA CHEESE
1/2 CUP SOUR CREAM
1 EGG, BEATEN LIGHTLY
1/4 CUP ALL-PURPOSE FLOUR
1 1/2 TEASPOONS INSTANT CHICKEN BOUILLON
1/8 TEASPOON FRESHLY GROUND PEPPER
1/2 CUP HALF AND HALF
1 CUP MILK
1/2 CUP GRATED PARMESAN CHEESE

HOLD NOODLES IMMERSED IN COLD WATER.

SAUTÉ ONION IN 2 TABLESPOONS BUTTER UNTIL TENDER. COMBINE ONION, SPINACH, MOZZARELLA, SOUR CREAM AND EGG. MELT REMAINING BUTTER IN MEDIUM SAUCEPAN. STIR IN FLOUR, BOUILLON AND PEPPER; COOK 1 MINUTE. WHISK IN HALF AND HALF AND MILK. BRING TO BOIL, STIRRING CONSTANTLY; COOK 1 MINUTE. REMOVE NOODLES FROM WATER; PAT DRY.

SPOON SMALL AMOUNT OF SAUCE IN BOTTOM OF BUTTERED 2 QUART RECTANGULAR DISH. SPREAD ABOUT 1/4 CUP SPINACH MIXTURE ON EACH NOODLE. ROLL UP JELLY ROLL FASHION STARTING AT SHORT END. STAND UP IN DISH; SPOON REMAINING SAUCE OVER TOP. SPRINKLE WITH PARMESAN. BAKE 35 MINUTES.

HINT: COOK PASTA IN LARGE AMOUNT OF WATER (ONE QUART OF WATER FOR EVERY 4 OUNCES OF PASTA) SO THAT INDIVIDUAL PIECES FLOAT FREELY.

Athenean Pasta

Yield: 6 servings *Preparation Time: 30 minutes*

Cook, shell and devein shrimp. Set aside. In blender combine lemon juice, parsley, oregano, red pepper and salt. Using medium speed, add oil in steady stream and blend. Rinse, drain and crumble feta.

Combine shrimp, feta, green onions, tomatoes, bell pepper and black olives. Add sauce; let stand at least 1 hour at room temperature. Add pasta to sauce; toss to coat well. Serve immediately.

1 pound fresh medium shrimp
1/4 cup fresh lemon juice
2 tablespoons chopped fresh parsley
1 1/2 teaspoons dried oregano
1/4 teaspoon crushed red pepper flakes
1/4 teaspoon salt
3/4 cup extra virgin olive oil
1 pound milk and brine packed feta cheese
6 green onions, cut into 1/4 inch slices
4 vine ripe tomatoes, peeled, seeded and coarsely chopped
1 cup julienned green bell pepper
1/4 cup black olives, sliced
1 pound medium shell pasta, cooked, rinsed and drained

Baked Omelet

Yield: 6 servings
Preheat Oven: 350°
Preparation Time: 15 minutes

Beat together eggs, sour cream and salt until blended. Stir in cheese. Pour into buttered 1 1/2 quart casserole dish and drizzle with butter. Bake until puffed and set, about 20 minutes. When done tilt dish to distribute butter on top.

8 large eggs
1/2 cup sour cream
1/2 teaspoon salt
1 cup shredded sharp cheddar cheese
2 tablespoons butter, melted

Baked Eggs With Dried Beef

Do-ahead brunch or supper that goes well with hot curried fruit and bran muffins.

Preparation Time: 1 hour | *Yield: 24 servings*

1½ pounds bacon
¼ cup butter
1 pound dried beef
1½ pounds fresh mushrooms, sliced

Cook bacon; drain, crumble and set aside. Pour off grease and wipe out skillet; add butter and melt. Stir in beef and mushrooms. Cook 10 minutes, stirring occasionally. Set aside.

Sauce:
½ cup butter
1 cup all-purpose flour
6 cups milk, scalded
½ cup grated Swiss cheese
10 ounces frozen chopped spinach, thawed and squeezed dry

Melt butter; whisk in flour and cook until smooth and bubbly. Remove from heat. Add half of milk and whisk until smooth. Add remaining milk and cheese. Cook until thick. Add bacon, beef mixture and spinach.

Eggs:
24 eggs
¼ teaspoon salt
12 ounces evaporated milk
¾ cup butter
Parmesan cheese

Combine eggs, salt and milk; beat until smooth. Melt butter in large deep skillet; add egg mixture. Cook over medium heat, stirring, until soft mass forms.

Brush 10×14 or 11×15 inch casserole dish with melted butter. Alternate layers of sauce and egg mixture. Sprinkle with Parmesan cheese. Cover; refrigerate overnight. Bring casserole to room temperature. Preheat oven to 300°. Bake, uncovered, 1 hour or until heated through.

EGGS MORNAY FOR 24 

YIELD: 24 SERVINGS — *PREPARATION TIME: 1 HOUR*

- 1 POUND BACON

COOK BACON OVER LOW HEAT UNTIL GREASE IS RENDERED; DO NOT BROWN. DRAIN THOROUGHLY AND CHOP COARSELY. SET ASIDE.

MORNAY SAUCE:
- 1/2 CUP BUTTER
- 1 CUP ALL PURPOSE FLOUR
- 6 CUPS MILK, SCALDED
- 1 1/2 CUPS FRESHLY GRATED PARMESAN CHEESE
- 1/2 CUP GRATED SWISS CHEESE

MELT BUTTER; WHISK IN FLOUR. COOK OVER LOW HEAT UNTIL SMOOTH AND BUBBLY, STIRRING CONSTANTLY. REMOVE FROM HEAT AND ADD HALF OF MILK, WHISKING UNTIL SMOOTH. RETURN TO MEDIUM HEAT AND ADD REMAINING MILK. COOK AND WHISK CONSTANTLY UNTIL SMOOTH AND THICK. ADD CHEESES AND STIR UNTIL MELTED. SET ASIDE.

EGGS:
- 24 EGGS
- 1 CUP WHIPPING CREAM
- 2 TEASPOONS SALT
- 1/2 TEASPOON FRESHLY GROUND PEPPER
- 1 TEASPOON HERBS DE PROVENCE, CRUMBLED
- 3/4 CUP BUTTER (RESERVE 1/4 CUP)
- 8 TO 10 GREEN ONIONS, CHOPPED
- 1 POUND FRESH MUSHROOMS, SLICED

COMBINE EGGS, CREAM, SALT, PEPPER AND HERBS. BEAT UNTIL SMOOTH. SET ASIDE. MELT 1/2 CUP BUTTER IN LARGE SKILLET; ADD ONIONS AND MUSHROOMS. SAUTÉ SLOWLY UNTIL ALL MOISTURE IS EVAPORATED, ABOUT 5 MINUTES. REMOVE FROM SKILLET. ADD REMAINING 1/4 CUP BUTTER TO SKILLET AND MELT. STIR IN EGG MIXTURE. COOK OVER MODERATE HEAT, STIRRING UNTIL SOFT MASS FORMS; DO NOT OVER COOK. ADD MUSHROOM MIXTURE AND STIR GENTLY. REMOVE FROM HEAT.

PARMESAN CHEESE
CHOPPED FRESH CHIVES
CHOPPED FRESH PARSLEY
FLUTED FRESH MUSHROOMS

BRUSH 10×14 OR 11×15 INCH CASSEROLE DISH WITH MELTED BUTTER AND LAYER INGREDIENTS AS FOLLOWS:
1/3 CUP MORNAY SAUCE; 1/2 EGG MIXTURE; 1/2 BACON; 1/3 MORNAY SAUCE; 1/2 EGG MIXTURE; 1/2 BACON; 1/3 MORNAY SAUCE.

COVER; REFRIGERATE OVERNIGHT. BRING CASSEROLE TO ROOM TEMPERATURE. PREHEAT OVEN TO 300°. BAKE, UNCOVERED, 1 HOUR OR UNTIL THOROUGHLY HEATED. SPRINKLE WITH PARMESAN, CHIVES AND PARSLEY. PLACE MUSHROOMS IN CENTER.

CRAB DEVILED EGGS

PREPARATION TIME: 1 HOUR

YIELD: 12 SERVINGS
PREHEAT OVEN: 300°

12 HARD BOILED EGGS
4 TABLESPOONS MAYONNAISE
1 TEASPOON RED WINE VINEGAR
1 TEASPOON CATSUP
1/4 TEASPOON SALT
1/4 TEASPOON FRESHLY GROUND PEPPER
1/8 TEASPOON CAYENNE PEPPER
2 TEASPOONS DIJON MUSTARD
1 CUP FRESH CRABMEAT

CUT EGGS IN HALF. REMOVE YOLKS AND MASH; MIX IN MAYONNAISE, VINEGAR, CATSUP, SALT, PEPPERS, MUSTARD AND CRABMEAT. FILL EGG WHITES WITH MIXTURE; ARRANGE CUT SIDE UP IN 9 × 13 INCH CASSEROLE DISH. PREPARE SAUCE; POUR OVER EGGS. COVER; BAKE 40 MINUTES OR UNTIL HOT.

SAUCE:
1/4 CUP BUTTER
1/4 CUP ALL-PURPOSE FLOUR
10 3/4 OUNCES CANNED CREAM OF MUSHROOM SOUP
13 OUNCES EVAPORATED MILK
6 OUNCES CANNED SLICED MUSHROOMS, DRAINED
1 CUP GRATED SWISS CHEESE
1 TABLESPOON GRATED ONION
3 TABLESPOONS CHOPPED FRESH PARSLEY
1 CUP FRESH CRABMEAT
14 OUNCES CANNED ARTICHOKE HEARTS, DRAINED AND QUARTERED
1/2 CUP TOASTED ALMONDS

MELT BUTTER IN MEDIUM SAUCEPAN. WHISK IN FLOUR; ADD SOUP AND MILK. STIR CONSTANTLY UNTIL THICKENED. ADD MUSHROOMS, CHEESE, ONION AND PARSLEY. FOLD IN CRABMEAT, ARTICHOKES AND ALMONDS.

HINT: TO KEEP EGGS FROM SLIDING IN DISH, CUT THIN LENGTHWISE SLICE OFF BOTTOM OF EACH EGG HALF.

Cheese Blintz Soufflé

Yield: 6 servings
Preheat Oven: 350°
Preparation Time: 30 minutes

Melt butter in 2 quart glass casserole; place blintzes in single layer. In medium bowl blend eggs, sour cream, sugar, salt, vanilla, orange juice and nutmeg. Pour over blintzes. Bake 45 minutes until just set and lightly browned. Serve with additional sour cream, fresh strawberries or jelly.

- **1/4 pound butter**
- **12 ounces frozen cheese blintzes**
- **4 eggs, beaten well**
- **1 1/2 cups sour cream**
- **1/4 cup sugar**
- **1/2 teaspoon salt**
- **1 teaspoon pure vanilla extract**
- **2 tablespoons orange juice**
- **1 teaspoon nutmeg**
- **Additional sour cream**
- **Fresh strawberries**
- **Jelly**

Jalapeño Grits Soufflé 

Yield: 10 to 12 servings
Preheat Oven: 450°
Preparation Time: 1 hour

Butter 1 1/2 to 2 quart soufflé dish and sprinkle with grated Parmesan cheese.

Combine milk, water and salt in saucepan and bring to boil. Add grits, stirring constantly. Cook 3 to 5 minutes to thicken. Remove from heat. Add butter and pepper, stirring until butter melts. Add yolks and grated cheeses; mix well. Beat egg whites until stiff; add cream of tartar and beat to mix. Using rubber spatula, fold 1/3 of whites into grits. Repeat with remaining whites; pour into dish. Place on cookie sheet in middle shelf of oven. Bake 30 to 35 minutes or until golden brown. Top with bell pepper rings if desired.

- **Grated Parmesan cheese**
- **1 cup milk**
- **1 cup water**
- **1 1/2 teaspoons salt**
- **1 cup quick cooking grits**
- **5 tablespoons unsalted butter**
- **1/4 teaspoon freshly ground pepper**
- **4 egg yolks (reserve whites)**
- **3 ounces sharp Cheddar cheese, grated**
- **3 ounces jalapeño jack cheese, grated**
- **8 egg whites (4 reserved plus 4 additional)**
- **1/4 teaspoon cream of tartar**
- **Red and green bell pepper rings**

PLANTATION BRUNCH CASSEROLE

PREPARATION TIME: 20 MINUTES

YIELD: 10 TO 12 SERVINGS
PREHEAT OVEN: 350°

1 POUND HOT SAUSAGE
1 CUP QUICK GRITS
4 CUPS BOILING WATER
1/2 TEASPOON SALT
1/2 CUP BUTTER
6 OUNCE ROLL KRAFT GARLIC CHEESE, CUBED
1/4 CUP HALF AND HALF
3 EGGS, BEATEN LIGHTLY
6 DASHES TABASCO
1 TABLESPOON DRIED CHOPPED ONION
1/4 TEASPOON GARLIC POWDER
1/2 CUP GRATED CHEDDAR CHEESE
PAPRIKA

FRY SAUSAGE; DRAIN. SLOWLY COOK GRITS IN BOILING SALTED WATER OVER MEDIUM HEAT UNTIL WATER IS ABSORBED, ABOUT 5 MINUTES. ADD BUTTER AND GARLIC CHEESE, STIRRING UNTIL MELTED. REMOVE FROM HEAT. ADD HALF AND HALF, EGGS, TABASCO, ONION AND GARLIC POWDER; MIX WELL. ADD SAUSAGE; COMBINE. POUR INTO 9×13 INCH BUTTERED CASSEROLE DISH. SPRINKLE WITH CHEESE AND PAPRIKA. BAKE 50 TO 60 MINUTES OR UNTIL SET.

CHEESY MUSHROOM AND ONION PIE

PREPARATION TIME: 45 MINUTES

YIELD: 6 SERVINGS
PREHEAT OVEN: 375°

1 9 INCH UNBAKED PIE SHELL
1 EGG WHITE, BEATEN LIGHTLY
1 LARGE ONION, THINLY SLICED
2 TABLESPOONS BUTTER
4 OUNCES CANNED SLICED MUSHROOMS, DRAINED
2 CUPS GRATED SWISS CHEESE
2 EGGS
1 CUP MILK
1/4 TEASPOON SALT
1/4 TEASPOON FRESHLY GROUND PEPPER
1/2 TEASPOON NUTMEG
PAPRIKA

PRICK BOTTOM OF PIE SHELL. BRUSH BOTTOM AND SIDES WITH EGG WHITE. REFRIGERATE 15 MINUTES. BAKE SHELL 5 MINUTES. REDUCE OVEN TEMPERATURE TO 350°.

IN MEDIUM SKILLET OVER LOW HEAT, SAUTÉ ONION IN BUTTER UNTIL TENDER BUT NOT BROWN. ADD MUSHROOMS; COMBINE WELL. SPOON INTO SHELL. ADD HALF OF CHEESE. BEAT EGGS, MILK AND SEASONINGS TOGETHER; POUR INTO SHELL. TOP WITH REMAINING CHEESE. SPRINKLE WITH PAPRIKA. BAKE 35 TO 40 MINUTES. COOL 5 MINUTES BEFORE SERVING.

HINT: BRUSHING PIE SHELL WITH EGG WHITE AND CHILLING WILL HELP KEEP CRUST FLAKY AND PREVENT CUSTARD FILLINGS FROM TURNING IT SOGGY.

HERBED CHEESE TART

YIELD: 6 TO 8 SERVINGS
PREHEAT OVEN: 350°

PREPARATION TIME: 30 MINUTES

CRUST:
- **1 1/4 CUPS FRESH DARK RYE BREADCRUMBS**
- **2 TABLESPOONS SESAME SEED**
- **6 TABLESPOONS BUTTER, MELTED**

MIX BREADCRUMBS, SESAME SEED AND BUTTER. PRESS INTO BOTTOM AND SIDES OF 8 INCH TART PAN OR PIE PLATE. CHILL WHILE PREPARING FILLING.

FILLING:
- **6 OUNCES FETA CHEESE, RINSED AND DRAINED, ROOM TEMPERATURE**
- **8 OUNCES CREAM CHEESE, ROOM TEMPERATURE**
- **1 EGG, BEATEN WELL, ROOM TEMPERATURE**
- **1 TEASPOON FRESH BASIL, MINCED (OR 1/4 TEASPOON DRIED, CRUMBLED)**
- **3/4 TEASPOON FRESH ROSEMARY, MINCED (OR 1/4 TEASPOON DRIED, CRUSHED)**
- **1/2 TEASPOON FINES HERBES, CRUMBLED**
- **1/8 TEASPOON GARLIC SALT**
- **1/4 TEASPOON FRESHLY GROUND PEPPER**
- **1/4 CUP SOUR CREAM, ROOM TEMPERATURE**
- **2 GREEN ONIONS WITH TOPS, FINELY CHOPPED**

IN MEDIUM BOWL CRUMBLE FETA; ADD CREAM CHEESE AND BEAT ON LOW SPEED 4 MINUTES. ADD EGG, BASIL, ROSEMARY, FINES HERBES, GARLIC SALT AND PEPPER. ADD SOUR CREAM; CONTINUE TO BLEND 3 MINUTES. STIR IN GREEN ONIONS. POUR INTO CHILLED CRUST. BAKE 40 TO 45 MINUTES UNTIL CENTER IS SET. COOL ON WIRE RACK. SLICE AND SERVE AT ROOM TEMPERATURE.

HINT: FOR BEST FLAVOR, USE FETA CHEESE PACKED IN JAR WITH MILK AND BRINE.

Zucchinni Quiche

Preparation Time: 20 minutes

Yield: 6 to 8 servings
Preheat Oven: 350°

3 cups thinly sliced zucchini
1/2 cup finely chopped onion
1 cup Bisquick baking mix
1/2 cup grated Parmesan cheese
1/2 teaspoon salt
1/2 teaspoon dried fines herbes, crumbled
1/2 teaspoon freshly ground pepper
1/2 vegetable oil
4 eggs, beaten lightly
1/2 cups grated Swiss cheese

Lightly mix zucchini, onion, baking mix, Parmesan, salt, fines herbes and pepper. Add oil, eggs and Swiss cheese; mix well. Pour into greased 9 inch pie plate. Bake 45 minutes or until set. Serve warm or cold.

Spiedini

Preparation Time: 20 minutes

Yield: 6 servings
Preheat Oven: 300°

12 ounces French bread (baguette)
8 ounces mozzarella cheese
8 ounces provolone cheese
2 tablespoons extra virgin olive oil
2 tablespoons finely chopped oil-packed sun-dried tomatoes, drained

Cut heels from bread; discard. Slice bread into 24 pieces. Cut cheeses into 20 slices (10 each). Alternate bread, mozzarella, bread, provolone, etc. End with bread. Press firmly together; place in shallow baking pan in which it fits tightly. Brush with olive oil. Bake 10 to 15 minutes until cheese begins to melt. Prepare sauce. To serve, place portions of bread on plates; spoon sauce over and sprinkle with tomatoes.

Sauce:
3 anchovy filets
3 tablespoons butter
1 teaspoon cornstarch
2/3 cup milk
1/4 teaspoon freshly ground pepper
1/4 teaspoon garlic powder
2 tablespoons drained capers

Drain and mash anchovies. In small saucepan, melt butter over low heat. Add cornstarch, milk, pepper, garlic and anchovies. Bring to boil, whisking constantly. Boil 1 minute. Reduce heat; stir in capers.

Techniques

Clarified butter is used because it enables food to be fried at higher temperatures without burning. To make clarified butter, cut butter into small pieces and melt completely, without stirring, over low heat. When butter is completely melted, skim foam off top with spoon. Slowly pour clear liquid (clarified butter) into container, being careful not to bring up any milk solids from bottom. Save solids and add to cream sauces for enrichment. Freeze clarified butter for longer storage. One cup butter makes 3/4 cup clarified butter.

Crumble herbs between fingers before adding to release their wonderful flavor.

Add whole, unpeeled cloves of garlic to roast, stew or poultry. After cooking, they develop a sweet flavor that is wonderful squeezed on hot buttered bread.

Enhance flavor of entree sauces by reducing sauce rather than thickening with flour or cornstarch. Boil sauce over medium-high heat until slightly thickened and there is just enough sauce to serve over meat.

Before charcoal grilling steaks, sprinkle generously with soy sauce to add additional flavor and to tenderize.

To easily slice chicken breasts for thin cutlets, place in freezer until just firm.

Cut-up poultry is more perishable than whole bird. If unable to use chicken within day or two of purchase, cook and store in refrigerator or freezer.

Cheese slicer makes an excellent fish scaler. Run wire against grain of scales for easy removal.

When poaching fish, use salted water with a little vinegar. Salt water brings out true flavor of the fish while the vinegar helps it stay firmer and whiter. Poaching liquid should simmer, not boil, so fish does not tear apart. Poach 5 to 8 minutes per pound.

Fish should never be cooked in aluminum pan or stored in aluminum foil. Acid in fish can cause small holes or pits.

When buying fresh fish, look for clear, bright eyes with no redness. Gills should be bright red, and flesh should be firm, pliable and moist.

Fleur De Lis

Yield: 1 serving | *Preparation Time: 45 minutes*

Preheat Oven: 400°

- 2 ounces veal cutlet, pounded thin
- 2 ounces chicken breast, skinned and boned
- 1/4 cup all-purpose flour
- 2 tablespoons butter
- Puff pastry or pie dough for 2 crust pie, prepared and rolled out
- 1 slice lean cooked ham, 1/8 inch thick
- 1 slice Swiss cheese, 1/8 inch thick
- 1 egg yolk
- 1 to 2 tablespoons water
- Vegetable oil
- 1 cup brown sauce
- 2 tablespoons Burgundy wine

Dredge veal and chicken in flour. Melt butter in medium skillet over medium-high heat and sauté veal and chicken until lightly browned and tender; cool.

Cut puff pastry into two 1/8 × 6 inch rounds. On one round place veal, ham, cheese and chicken in layers. Whisk together egg yolk and water. Brush edge of dough with egg wash. Place second round over top and seal edge by pressing with tines of fork or cutter with fluted cutting edge, leaving 1/2 inch edge.

Lightly oil cookie sheet and place pastry in center. Bake 12 to 15 minutes or until pastry is lightly browned.

Meanwhile, in small saucepan, warm brown sauce and wine. Place baked pastry on serving dish and top with sauce.

Donal Weaving, Executive Chef
Southern Hills Country Club

HINT: Decorate pastry tops with cut-outs of dough; attach by brushing with egg wash and placing on pastry.

VEAL SCALLOPINI A LA MARSALA

PREPARATION TIME: 30 MINUTES *YIELD: 4 SERVINGS*

- **1 OUNCE DRIED PORCINI MUSHROOMS**
- **1 CUP WARM WATER**
- **1/2 CUP ALL-PURPOSE FLOUR**
- **1/2 TEASPOON SALT**
- **1/2 TEASPOON FRESHLY GROUND PEPPER**
- **1 POUND VEAL CUTLETS, POUNDED 1/4 INCH THICK**
- **3 TABLESPOONS CLARIFIED BUTTER**
- **1/4 CUP SWEET MARSALA WINE**
- **1 TO 2 TABLESPOONS CONCENTRATED BEEF BOUILLON**

SOAK MUSHROOMS 20 MINUTES IN WARM WATER. REMOVE; RINSE AND DRAIN. STRAIN MUSHROOM LIQUID THROUGH FILTER TO REMOVE GRIT; SET ASIDE. MIX FLOUR, SALT AND PEPPER IN SHALLOW DISH; DREDGE VEAL IN MIXTURE. HEAT BUTTER IN LARGE NON-STICK SKILLET OVER MEDIUM HEAT; SAUTÉ VEAL 1 TO 2 MINUTES ON EACH SIDE. ADD MARSALA; COOK 1 MINUTE OVER MODERATELY HIGH HEAT. REMOVE VEAL; KEEP WARM. ADD BOUILLON AND RESERVED MUSHROOM LIQUID TO PAN, SCRAPE TO LOOSEN PARTICLES. BRING TO BOIL; REDUCE SLIGHTLY AND POUR OVER MEAT. SERVE IMMEDIATELY.

BERNARD RUBENSTEIN
CONDUCTOR

VEAL IN SHALLOT MUSHROOM CREAM

PREPARATION TIME: 45 MINUTES *YIELD: 4 TO 6 SERVINGS*

- **1/2 CUP ALL-PURPOSE FLOUR**
- **1/4 TEASPOON SALT**
- **1/4 TEASPOON FRESHLY GROUND PEPPER**
- **1 POUND VEAL CUTLETS, POUNDED VERY THIN**
- **4 TABLESPOONS CLARIFIED BUTTER**
- **4 TEASPOONS MINCED SHALLOTS**
- **1/2 CUP CHICKEN STOCK**
- **1 CUP RHINE WINE**
- **1 CUP HEAVY CREAM**
- **1 CUP SLICED FRESH MUSHROOMS (RESERVE 1/4 CUP)**

MIX TOGETHER FLOUR, SALT AND PEPPER; DREDGE VEAL IN MIXTURE. IN LARGE NON-STICK SKILLET, MELT BUTTER OVER MEDIUM-HIGH HEAT; SAUTÉ VEAL 2 MINUTES ON EACH SIDE. REMOVE AND SET ASIDE.

REDUCE HEAT AND SAUTÉ SHALLOTS 2 MINUTES OR UNTIL TRANSPARENT. ADD STOCK AND WINE. INCREASE HEAT AND REDUCE TO 1/2 CUP. ADD CREAM; REDUCE TO 1 CUP. ADD CUTLETS; SIMMER 4 MINUTES. ADD 3/4 CUP MUSHROOMS; COOK 1 MINUTE LONGER. TRANSFER CUTLETS TO PLATTER AND COVER WITH SAUCE. SPRINKLE WITH RESERVED MUSHROOMS.

HINT: SAUCE SHOULD BE CONSISTENCY OF VERY THICK CREAM.

VEAL SCALLOPS WITH MUSHROOMS

LEMON JUICE PRODUCES AN ATTRACTIVE GLAZE ON VEAL.

YIELD: 4 SERVINGS
PREHEAT OVEN: 325°

PREPARATION TIME: 40 MINUTES

1/3 CUP ALL-PURPOSE FLOUR
1/2 TEASPOON SALT
1/8 TEASPOON FRESHLY GROUND PEPPER
DASH OF CAYENNE PEPPER
3 TABLESPOONS BUTTER
2 TABLESPOONS VEGETABLE OIL
1 CLOVE GARLIC, PEELED AND HALVED
1 POUND VEAL SCALLOPS, POUNDED TO 1/4 INCH THICK
1 1/4 CUPS SLICED FRESH MUSHROOMS
1 TABLESPOON FRESH LEMON JUICE
1/4 CUP DRY VERMOUTH
1/2 CUP CHICKEN BROTH
1 TABLESPOON FINELY CHOPPED FRESH PARSLEY

MIX TOGETHER FLOUR, SALT AND PEPPERS. IN LARGE SKILLET OVER MEDIUM-HIGH HEAT, MELT BUTTER WITH OIL AND GARLIC. DIP VEAL IN FLOUR MIXTURE; SHAKE OFF EXCESS AND BROWN 2 TO 3 MINUTES ON EACH SIDE. PLACE IN 8 INCH BAKING DISH.

DISCARD GARLIC AND SAUTÉ MUSHROOMS UNTIL SOFTENED. REMOVE MUSHROOMS; ARRANGE ON TOP OF VEAL. ADD LEMON JUICE, VERMOUTH AND BROTH TO SKILLET; BRING TO BOIL, SCRAPING UP BROWN BITS. POUR SAUCE OVER VEAL; BAKE 30 MINUTES. TOP WITH PARSLEY.

FILET IN GARLIC PORT WINE

SIMPLE RECIPE, ELEGANT RESULTS.

YIELD: 4 SERVINGS

PREPARATION TIME: 20 MINUTES

2 TABLESPOONS CLARIFIED BUTTER
1 TO 2 SMALL CLOVES GARLIC, MINCED
8 FILET MIGNON STEAKS, 1/2 TO 3/4 INCH THICK
SEASONED SALT, TO TASTE
3 OUNCES PORT WINE
3 OUNCES WATER

MELT BUTTER OVER MEDIUM HEAT IN LARGE NON-STICK SKILLET; ADD GARLIC. SPRINKLE STEAKS WITH SEASONED SALT ON BOTH SIDES; BROWN UNTIL DESIRED DONENESS. REMOVE STEAKS FROM SKILLET AND KEEP WARM. ADD WINE AND WATER TO SKILLET; BRING TO BOIL OVER MEDIUM-HIGH HEAT, SCRAPING BOTTOM TO RELEASE BITS. REDUCE SLIGHTLY. POUR SAUCE OVER STEAKS.

HINT: A LITTLE CREAM MAY BE ADDED TO SAUCE DURING REDUCTION STAGE.

GARLIC BEEF TENDERLOIN

PREPARATION TIME: 15 MINUTES

YIELD: 3 TO 4 SERVINGS PER POUND
PREHEAT OVEN: 400°

PER POUND OF MEAT, MIX TOGETHER:
- **1 TABLESPOON BUTTER, SOFTENED**
- **1/4 TEASPOON MINCED GARLIC**
- **3/8 TEASPOON SALT**
- **1/8 TEASPOON FRESHLY GROUND PEPPER**

BEEF TENDERLOIN, TRIMMED

MIX TOGETHER BUTTER, GARLIC, SALT AND PEPPER. SPREAD OVER OUTSIDE OF ENTIRE TENDERLOIN. PLACE ON RACK IN ROASTING PAN, TUCKING TAIL END UNDER. ROAST UNTIL DESIRED DONENESS, APPROXIMATELY 45 MINUTES FOR 3 TO 5 POUND TENDERLOIN (MEDIUM RARE).

*HINT: WORKS EQUALLY WELL ON **PORK TENDERLOIN.***

GLAZED BEEF TENDERLOIN

PREPARATION TIME: 15 MINUTES

YIELD: 6 TO 8 SERVINGS
PREHEAT OVEN: 400°

- **4 TO 4 1/2 POUNDS BEEF TENDERLOIN, TRIMMED**
- **1/3 CUP PREPARED MUSTARD**
- **1/3 CUP WORCESTERSHIRE SAUCE**
- **4 TABLESPOONS BUTTER (NO SUBSTITUTIONS)**

WIPE TENDERLOIN WITH DAMP CLOTH. MIX TOGETHER MUSTARD AND WORCESTERSHIRE AND SPREAD OVER ENTIRE TENDERLOIN. PLACE MEAT ON RACK IN ROASTING PAN, TUCKING TAIL END UNDER. BAKE 45 TO 50 MINUTES FOR MEDIUM RARE, OR UNTIL DESIRED DONENESS. REMOVE MEAT AND RACK, PLACE BUTTER IN PAN AND MELT, STIRRING TO RELEASE BROWN BITS. SLICE MEAT AND TOP WITH BUTTER SAUCE.

HINT: IF PAN DRIPPINGS APPEAR TO BE DRYING OUT DURING ROASTING TIME, ADD HOT WATER.

DAVID'S BRISKET

YIELD: 6 TO 8 SERVINGS
PREHEAT OVEN: 300°

PREPARATION TIME: 15 MINUTES

COMBINE CONSOMME, VINEGAR, LIQUID SMOKE, GARLIC, ONION AND CELERY SEED. PLACE BRISKET IN FLAT CASSEROLE, POUR SAUCE OVER BRISKET. COVER WITH FOIL AND REFRIGERATE 12 HOURS OR OVERNIGHT. BAKE 3½ TO 4½ HOURS OR UNTIL TENDER. SLICE AND SERVE WITH BARBEQUE SAUCE.

10¾ OUNCES CANNED BEEF CONSOMME
½ CUP RED WINE VINEGAR
2 TABLESPOONS LIQUID SMOKE
2 TO 3 CLOVES GARLIC, CHOPPED
½ CUP CHOPPED ONION
2 TEASPOONS CELERY SEED
2 TO 4 POUNDS BEEF BRISKET
2 CUPS WARMED BARBEQUE SAUCE

MARINATED FLANK STEAK

THE MARINADE ACTS AS TENDERIZER.

YIELD: 6 SERVINGS

PREPARATION TIME: 15 MINUTES

COMBINE SOY SAUCE, HONEY, OIL, VINEGAR, GARLIC POWDER, GINGER AND GREEN ONIONS. PLACE STEAK IN FLAT CASSEROLE. POUR SAUCE OVER; COVER AND MARINATE OVERNIGHT. GRILL OVER HOT CHARCOAL OR BROIL UNTIL DESIRED DONENESS, APPROXIMATELY 4 TO 6 MINUTES ON EACH SIDE FOR MEDIUM-RARE. SLICE ACROSS GRAIN ON DIAGONAL.

VARIATION: COMBINE ALL INGREDIENTS, MARINATE AND COOK AS DIRECTED ABOVE.

¼ CUP SOY SAUCE
2 TABLESPOONS HONEY
¾ CUP VEGETABLE OIL
2 TABLESPOONS WHITE VINEGAR
1½ TEASPOONS GARLIC POWDER
1½ TEASPOONS GROUND GINGER
2 CHOPPED GREEN ONIONS, TOPS INCLUDED
2½ POUNDS FLANK STEAK

MARINADE II:
12 OUNCES BEER
½ CUP EXTRA VIRGIN OLIVE OIL
3 TABLESPOONS SOY SAUCE
2 TABLESPOONS SUGAR
3 CHOPPED GREEN ONIONS, TOPS INCLUDED
1 TABLESPOON PEELED, GRATED GINGER ROOT
2 LARGE CLOVES GARLIC, MINCED
1 TEASPOON SALT
¼ TEASPOON TABASCO

STEAK LAREDO

PREPARATION TIME: 40 MINUTES

YIELD: 6 TO 8 SERVINGS

4 TABLESPOONS VEGETABLE OIL (RESERVE 2 TABLESPOONS)
2 TO 3 POUNDS BONELESS STEAK, 1/4 INCH THICK
3/4 CUP ALL-PURPOSE FLOUR
4 TABLESPOONS BACON DRIPPINGS
1/2 CUP CHOPPED ONION
1/2 CUP CHOPPED CELERY
1/4 CUP CHOPPED GREEN BELL PEPPER
1 CLOVE GARLIC, CRUSHED
6 TOMATOES, PEELED, SEEDED AND CHOPPED (OR 20 OUNCES CANNED WHOLE TOMATOES)
8 OUNCES TOMATO SAUCE
12 OUNCES HEINZ HOMESTYLE GRAVY
1/4 CUP SHERRY
4 TO 6 DROPS TABASCO
4 OUNCES CHOPPED GREEN CHILES
1/4 TEASPOON THYME, CRUMBLED
1/4 TEASPOON OREGANO, CRUMBLED
1 TEASPOON PURE GROUND MILD CHILI (NOT CHILI BLEND)
1 BAY LEAF
PINCH CRUSHED RED PEPPER

IN LARGE HEAVY DUTCH OVEN OR SKILLET WITH COVER, HEAT 2 TABLESPOONS OIL OVER MEDIUM-HIGH HEAT. CUT STEAK INTO SERVING SIZE PIECES; DREDGE IN FLOUR AND BROWN ON BOTH SIDES. REMOVE AND SET ASIDE. IN SAME PAN, ADD RESERVED OIL AND BACON DRIPPINGS. SAUTÉ ONION, CELERY, BELL PEPPER, AND GARLIC UNTIL SOFT. ADD TOMATOES, TOMATO SAUCE, GRAVY, SHERRY, TABASCO, CHILES AND SEASONINGS. RETURN STEAK TO PAN, COVER AND SIMMER 2 1/2 HOURS OR UNTIL STEAK IS TENDER AND GRAVY THICKENS. ADD WATER IF GRAVY BECOMES TOO THICK. REMOVE BAY LEAF BEFORE SERVING.

FLANK STEAK PINWHEELS

PREPARATION TIME: 40 MINUTES

YIELD: 4 SERVINGS

1 1/2 POUNDS FLANK STEAK
MEAT TENDERIZER
GARLIC POWDER, TO TASTE
LEMON PEPPER, TO TASTE
DRIED PARSLEY, TO TASTE
5 STRIPS BACON, COOKED UNTIL ALMOST DONE
1 CUP BARBEQUE SAUCE

SPRINKLE STEAK WITH TENDERIZER. SCORE AND POUND UNTIL 1/4 INCH THICK. SPRINKLE WITH GARLIC POWDER, LEMON PEPPER AND PARSLEY. LAY BACON STRIPS ON TOP. ROLL UP WITH GRAIN AND CUT ACROSS GRAIN INTO 1/2 INCH SLICES. SECURE EACH WITH TOOTHPICK; BRUSH WITH BARBEQUE SAUCE. CHARCOAL GRILL OR BROIL UNTIL DESIRED DONENESS.

FAJITAS 

YIELD: 6 SERVINGS

PREPARATION TIME: 20 MINUTES

IN SHALLOW DISH COMBINE GARLIC, LIME JUICE, VINEGAR, OIL, CHILES, ONION AND SALT. ADD FLANK STEAK; MARINATE 24 HOURS, TURNING ONCE. GRILL ON BARBEQUE 3 MINUTES ON EACH SIDE FOR MEDIUM RARE, OR TO DESIRED DONENESS. RESERVE 2 TO 3 TABLESPOONS MARINADE.

MEANWHILE, HEAT OIL IN LARGE SKILLET OVER MEDIUM-HIGH HEAT. SAUTÉ BELL PEPPER AND ONION 5 MINUTES OR UNTIL TENDER. ADD RESERVED MARINADE; COOK AN ADDITIONAL 30 SECONDS.

CUT STEAK INTO THIN SLICES; PLACE ON SERVING PLATTER. ARRANGE PEPPER AND ONION MIXTURE OVER STEAK.

TO SERVE, PLACE MEAT AND ONION MIXTURE IN CENTER OF FLOUR TORTILLAS AND TOP WITH LETTUCE, GUACAMOLE, SOUR CREAM, CHEESE, SALSA, GREEN ONIONS, AND TOMATOES. FOLD SIDES OF TORTILLAS OVER CENTER.

VARIATION: BONELESS ***CHICKEN*** *BREASTS OR BONELESS* ***PORK*** *LOIN MAY BE SUBSTITUTED FOR BEEF.*

4 CLOVES GARLIC, CRUSHED
1/2 CUP FRESH LIME JUICE
2 TABLESPOONS RED WINE VINEGAR
1 TABLESPOON VEGETABLE OIL
6 TO 8 PICKLED SERRANOS CHILES
1/3 CUP FINELY CHOPPED ONION
1/2 TEASPOON SALT
2 POUNDS FLANK STEAK
2 TABLESPOONS VEGETABLE OIL
1 LARGE GREEN OR RED BELL PEPPER, CUT IN 1/4 INCH RINGS
1 LARGE ONION, CUT IN 1/4 INCH SLICES AND SEPARATED
12 LARGE FLOUR TORTILLAS
SHREDDED LETTUCE
GUACAMOLE
SOUR CREAM
GRATED CHEDDAR CHEESE
SALSA
CHOPPED GREEN ONIONS
CHOPPED FRESH TOMATOES

HINT: TO PRODUCE SMOKEY FLAVOR, SOAK HICKORY CHIPS IN WATER; ADD TO HOT COALS.

TERIYAKI BEEF

PREPARATION TIME: 45 MINUTES

YIELD: 6 SERVINGS

1½ POUNDS CHUCK OR ROUND STEAK, CUT INTO ¼ INCH STRIPS
MEAT TENDERIZER
¾ CUP PINEAPPLE CHUNKS
1 MEDIUM ONION, CUT INTO WEDGES
8 OUNCES WHOLE WATER CHESTNUTS, DRAINED
½ CUP WHOLE FRESH MUSHROOMS
1 MEDIUM GREEN BELL PEPPER, CUT INTO WEDGES

MARINADE:
½ CUP SOY SAUCE
¼ CUP VEGETABLE OIL
2 TABLESPOONS MOLASSES
2 TABLESPOONS BROWN SUGAR, FIRMLY PACKED
2 TEASPOONS GROUND GINGER
2 TEASPOONS DRY MUSTARD
6 CLOVES GARLIC, MINCED

SPRINKLE MEAT STRIPS WITH TENDERIZER; PLACE IN LARGE FLAT CASSEROLE. PREPARE MARINADE. POUR OVER MEAT; STIR TO COAT. COVER AND REFRIGERATE OVERNIGHT, STIRRING OCCASIONALLY.

LACE MEAT STRIPS ACCORDION STYLE ON SKEWERS, WEAVING PINEAPPLE, ONION, WATER CHESTNUTS, MUSHROOMS, AND BELL PEPPER BETWEEN SECTIONS OF MEAT. CHARCOAL OVER HOT COALS OR BROIL UNTIL DESIRED DONENESS, TURNING AND BASTING FREQUENTLY WITH MARINADE.

COMBINE SOY SAUCE, OIL, MOLASSES, BROWN SUGAR, GINGER, MUSTARD AND GARLIC.

HINT: LOW SODIUM SOY SAUCE WILL REDUCE SALTY TASTE. MEAT MAY BE CUBED TO PROVIDE MORE EVEN COOKING.

ELEGANT FRENCH POT ROAST

PREPARATION TIME: 15 MINUTES

YIELD: 6 TO 8 SERVINGS
PREHEAT OVEN: 300°

3 TO 4 POUND CHUCK OR BOTTOM ROUND ROAST
1 CLOVE GARLIC, CUT INTO SLIVERS
⅓ CUP CHOPPED ONION
24 OUNCES CATSUP
12 OUNCES BEER

MAKE SMALL CUTS IN ROAST AND INSERT GARLIC. BROWN MEAT ON ALL SIDES IN LARGE SKILLET OVER MEDIUM-HIGH HEAT. PLACE IN ROASTING PAN; ADD REMAINING INGREDIENTS. BAKE 1 HOUR. REDUCE HEAT TO 200°; BAKE 5 TO 6 HOURS. SKIM FAT FROM BROTH BEFORE SERVING.

Mexican Fiesta

Yield: 8 servings
Preheat Oven: 350°

Preparation Time: 20 minutes

Cook beef and onion until browned. Drain; set aside. Purée soup and tomatoes in blender. In 3 quart casserole, layer half of tortillas, half of meat mixture, half of beans, half of soup mixture and half of cheese. Repeat layers once more. Bake 30 minutes.

*Variation: **Chicken:** Omit beef and beans; add 3 cups cooked, cubed chicken. To soup mixture, add $10^3/_4$ ounces canned cream of mushroom soup and $^1/_2$ cup chicken broth. Increase cheese to 3 cups. Bake 45 minutes.*

- **1 pound lean ground beef**
- **1 cup chopped onion**
- **$10^3/_4$ ounces canned cream of chicken soup**
- **$10^1/_2$ ounces canned Rotel tomatoes**
- **8 large flour tortillas, torn into pieces**
- **15 ounces canned ranch style beans**
- **1 cup grated Cheddar cheese**

Hunter's Stew

In Poland this dish is called "Bigos."

Yield: 6 servings

Preparation Time: 30 minutes

In Dutch oven, fry bacon until crisp. Remove and drain; set aside. Melt butter in same pan over medium-high heat; add beef and brown well on all sides. Reduce heat to medium; add onion and apple and cook until apple is tender. Add broth, water and salt. Cover; simmer $1^1/_2$ hours. Add carrot and sausage pieces; cook additional 20 minutes. Add cabbage and bacon; simmer until cabbage is crisp-tender, about 10 minutes.

- **4 slices bacon, cut into 1 inch pieces**
- **2 tablespoons butter**
- **1 pound boneless beef, cubed**
- **2 cups finely chopped onion**
- **2 cups finely chopped tart cooking apple, cored**
- **$10^1/_2$ ounces canned beef broth**
- **2 cups water**
- **1 teaspoon salt**
- **2 cups thickly sliced carrot**
- **1 pound Polish sausage, cut into 4 inch pieces**
- **4 cups coarsely shredded cabbage**

OVEN BEEF BURGUNDY

PREPARATION TIME: 30 MINUTES

YIELD: 6 TO 8 SERVINGS
PREHEAT OVEN: 325°

2 POUNDS ROUND STEAK
1 TABLESPOON KITCHEN BOUQUET
2 TABLESPOONS ALL-PURPOSE FLOUR
4 CARROTS, QUARTERED
2 CUPS THINLY SLICED ONION
1 CUP SLICED CELERY
1 CLOVE GARLIC, MINCED
2 TEASPOONS SALT
1/8 TEASPOON FRESHLY GROUND PEPPER
1/8 TEASPOON MARJORAM, CRUMBLED
1/8 TEASPOON THYME, CRUMBLED
1 CUP BURGUNDY WINE
6 OUNCES CANNED MUSHROOMS, UNDRAINED

TRIM FAT FROM MEAT AND CUT INTO 1 1/2 INCH CUBES. PLACE IN 2 1/2 QUART CASSEROLE. SPRINKLE KITCHEN BOUQUET ON MEAT; TOSS TO COAT. STIR IN FLOUR; ADD REMAINING INGREDIENTS. MIX GENTLY, COVER AND BAKE 2 1/2 TO 3 HOURS. STIR EVERY 30 MINUTES.

HINT: FOR EXTRA SAUCE, INCREASE ALL INGREDIENTS EXCEPT MEAT BY ONE-HALF.

CHOP SUEY

PREPARATION TIME: 30 MINUTES

YIELD: 4 TO 5 SERVINGS

VEGETABLE COOKING SPRAY
1 1/2 POUNDS COOKED, CUBED BEEF, CHICKEN OR PORK
1/4 CUP ALL-PURPOSE FLOUR
2 1/2 CUPS BOILING WATER
3 CHICKEN OR BEEF BOUILLON CUBES
2 TABLESPOONS SOY SAUCE
1/8 TEASPOON FRESHLY GROUND PEPPER
1 CUP SLICED CELERY
1 CUP THINLY SLICED ONION
1 CUP SLICED FRESH MUSHROOMS
CHOW MEIN NOODLES OR COOKED RICE

COAT LARGE NON-STICK SKILLET WITH COOKING SPRAY. SAUTÉ MEAT OVER MEDIUM HEAT UNTIL LIGHTLY BROWNED. ADD FLOUR; STIR WELL. STIR IN WATER, BOUILLON, SOY SAUCE, PEPPER, CELERY, ONION AND MUSHROOMS. COVER; SIMMER 20 MINUTES, STIRRING OCCASIONALLY TO PREVENT STICKING. SERVE OVER NOODLES OR RICE.

BEEF TOURNADOES WITH CAPER SAUCE

YIELD: 6 TO 8 SERVINGS

PREPARATION TIME: 20 MINUTES

- 2 POUNDS FILET MIGNON, END CUT
- 1/4 CUP WHITE WINE VINEGAR
- 1/4 CUP FRESH LEMON JUICE
- 1/2 CUP VEGETABLE OIL
- 1/2 CUP EXTRA VIRGIN OLIVE OIL
- 1 TEASPOON DIJON MUSTARD
- 1/4 TEASPOON GARLIC POWDER
- 1 ANCHOVY FILET, MASHED
- 1 CUP SLIVERED RED ONION
- 1/4 CUP DRAINED SMALL CAPERS
- 3 LARGE TOMATOES, CUT IN WEDGES
- BUTTER LETTUCE LEAVES
- MINCED FRESH PARSLEY

GRILL FILET OVER CHARCOAL UNTIL MEDIUM RARE, ABOUT 20 TO 25 MINUTES. REMOVE; SET ASIDE. MEAT WILL CONTINUE TO COOK AS IT STANDS.

IN JAR, COMBINE VINEGAR, LEMON JUICE, BOTH OILS, MUSTARD, GARLIC POWDER AND ANCHOVY. COVER; SHAKE TO BLEND. SET ASIDE.

STARTING AT NARROW END CUT FILET DIAGONALLY INTO 1/2 INCH THICK SLICES. IN SHALLOW DISH COMBINE BEEF, ONION AND CAPERS. ADD DRESSING; TOSS TO COAT. COVER; CHILL 4 HOURS. BRING TO ROOM TEMPERATURE TO SERVE. PLACE BEEF MIXTURE AND TOMATO WEDGES ON LETTUCE-LINED PLATES. DRIZZLE WITH SAUCE; SPRINKLE WITH PARSLEY AND SERVE IMMEDIATELY.

*HINT: **PORK TENDERLOIN** MAY BE SUBSTITUTED FOR FILET MIGNON.*

LAMB CHOPS MADEIRA

YIELD: 2 SERVINGS

PREPARATION TIME: 25 MINUTES

- 1 TO 1 1/2 TABLESPOONS CLARIFIED BUTTER
- 4 LAMB CHOPS, 3/4 INCH THICK
- 2 TABLESPOONS MINCED SHALLOTS
- 1 CLOVE GARLIC, MINCED
- 1/2 CUP RICH BEEF STOCK
- 1/4 TEASPOON GROUND THYME
- 1/4 TEASPOON BASIL, CRUMBLED
- 1/4 TEASPOON ROSEMARY, CRUSHED
- 1/2 CUP SLICED FRESH MUSHROOMS
- 1/2 CUP MADEIRA WINE

MELT BUTTER OVER MEDIUM-HIGH HEAT IN LARGE NON-STICK SKILLET. ADD LAMB AND BROWN ON BOTH SIDES UNTIL DESIRED DONENESS. REMOVE; KEEP WARM. ADD SHALLOTS AND GARLIC; SAUTÉ UNTIL SOFT. ADD STOCK; REDUCE BY HALF. ADD SEASONINGS, MUSHROOMS, WINE AND LAMB; REDUCE BY HALF, TURNING MEAT FREQUENTLY TO WARM THROUGH. SPOON SAUCE OVER LAMB TO SERVE.

HINT: IF RICH BEEF STOCK IS NOT AVAILABLE, REDUCE 1 CUP CANNED BROTH BY HALF.

RACK OF LAMB

PREPARATION TIME: 10 MINUTES

YIELD: 6 SERVINGS
PREHEAT OVEN: 350°

1/4 CUP BUTTER, MELTED
1 TEASPOON GROUND THYME
1/4 TEASPOON GARLIC POWDER
1/4 TEASPOON ONION POWDER
1/2 TEASPOON ROSEMARY, CRUSHED
1/2 CUP BREAD CRUMBS
1 RACK OF LAMB

COMBINE BUTTER, SEASONINGS AND BREAD CRUMBS. PRESS CRUMB MIXTURE ON MEAT SIDE OF RACK. BAKE 40 MINUTES OR UNTIL DESIRED DONENESS.

HINT: FOR ATTRACTIVE DINNER PARTY PRESENTATION, DOUBLE RECIPE; STAND TWO RACKS ON SERVING PLATE, RIBS INTERTWINED. SURROUND WITH VEGETABLES OR RICE PILAF.

LEG OF LAMB

PRODUCES NICE, CRISPY COATING ON LAMB.

PREPARATION TIME: 20 MINUTES

YIELD: 12 TO 15 SERVINGS
PREHEAT OVEN: 325°

5 1/2 TO 6 POUND LEG OF LAMB
1/4 CUP SHORTENING
2 TABLESPOONS FRESH LEMON JUICE
1 1/2 TEASPOONS SALT
1/2 TEASPOON FRESHLY GROUND PEPPER
1/2 TEASPOON MUSTARD
1/2 TEASPOON GROUND GINGER
2 TABLESPOONS ALL-PURPOSE FLOUR

SKIN LAMB; REMOVE MOST OF FAT. MELT SHORTENING; ADD REMAINING INGREDIENTS. SPREAD MIXTURE OVER LAMB. BAKE UNTIL DESIRED DONENESS, APPROXIMATELY 2 1/2 HOURS.

Wine-Braised Pork Loin

Yield: 4 to 6 servings
Preheat Oven: 350°

Preparation Time: 15 minutes

Combine pepper, Italian herbs, garlic powder and onion salt; rub mixture on pork. Wrap in waxed paper; chill several hours. Heat oil in roasting pan; brown pork on all sides and remove. Pour off all but 1 tablespoon of fat. Reduce heat; add shallots and garlic and sauté until translucent, about 2 minutes. Add wine, scraping up brown bits in bottom of pan. Return pork to pan and bring to boil; turn to moisten. Cover; braise 1½ hours or until desired doneness. Remove meat; let stand 10 minutes. Place roasting pan over medium-high heat; reduce pan drippings slightly. Slice meat; spoon sauce over.

- **½ teaspoon freshly ground pepper**
- **1 teaspoon Italian herbs**
- **½ teaspoon garlic powder**
- **½ teaspoon onion salt**
- **2 pounds boneless pork loin, rolled and tied**
- **2 tablespoons vegetable oil**
- **⅓ cup thinly sliced shallots**
- **2 cloves garlic, minced**
- **½ cup white wine**

Curried Pork Chops

Yield: 6 servings
Preheat Oven: 325°

Preparation Time: 20 minutes

Brown chops on both sides in moderately hot skillet. Place in 11 × 7 inch baking dish; sprinkle with salt. Add remaining ingredients to skillet; bring to boil. Pour sauce over chops; cover and bake 1 hour. Uncover; bake 15 minutes longer.

- **6 pork loin chops, ¾ inch thick**
- **Salt, to taste**
- **½ to 2 teaspoons curry powder**
- **1 cup catsup**
- **1 cup water**

CHICKEN FERNAND

YIELD: 8 TO 10 SERVINGS

- 3 TABLESPOONS BUTTER
- 1/2 CUP CHOPPED ONION
- 2 CLOVES GARLIC, CHOPPED
- 2 2 1/3 TO 3 1/2 POUND CHICKENS, CUT INTO SERVING PIECES
- 4 SLICES FRESH PEELED GINGER ROOT
- SALT, TO TASTE
- 6 TABLESPOONS FRESH LEMON JUICE
- 1 CUP WATER
- 4 CUPS FINELY CHOPPED GREEN BELL PEPPER
- PINCH TUMERIC

IN LARGE SKILLET OVER MEDIUM HEAT, MELT BUTTER. ADD ONION AND GARLIC; SAUTÉ UNTIL GOLDEN. ADD CHICKEN PIECES; SAUTÉ UNTIL GOLDEN, TURNING FREQUENTLY. ADD GINGER AND SALT; COVER AND COOK OVER LOW HEAT 15 MINUTES. COMBINE LEMON JUICE AND WATER; POUR OVER CHICKEN. ADD BELL PEPPER AND TUMERIC. COVER; COOK 40 MINUTES MORE, OR UNTIL CHICKEN IS TENDER. SERVE WITH RICE.

EXECUTIVE CHEF FERNAND PAYETTE
TULSA CLUB

SUPREME DE VOLAILLE DONAL

PREPARATION TIME: 30 MINUTES

YIELD: 4 SERVINGS
PREHEAT OVEN: 375°

- 1/2 CUP ALL-PURPOSE FLOUR
- 1 TEASPOON SALT
- 1/2 TEASPOON WHITE PEPPER, (DIVIDED)
- 4 WHOLE CHICKEN BREASTS, SKINNED, BONED AND HALVED
- 3 TABLESPOONS BUTTER
- 3 TABLESPOONS VEGETABLE OIL
- 16 LARGE SHRIMP, COOKED, SHELLED AND DEVEINED
- 1 1/2 CUPS BUTTER, SOFTENED
- 1 TEASPOON GARLIC POWDER
- 2 TABLESPOONS PARSLEY FLAKES
- 1/2 CUP DRY WHITE WINE
- 1 CUP GRATED PARMESAN CHEESE
- 1/4 CUP FRESH BREAD CRUMBS

COMBINE FLOUR, SALT AND 1/4 TEASPOON PEPPER. DREDGE CHICKEN IN MIXTURE. MELT BUTTER AND OIL IN LARGE SKILLET OVER MEDIUM-HIGH HEAT. SAUTÉ CHICKEN UNTIL GOLDEN. REMOVE; PLACE 1 INCH APART IN BUTTERED 2 QUART CASSEROLE. PLACE 4 SHRIMP BETWEEN EACH PAIR OF BREASTS. COMBINE 1 1/2 CUPS BUTTER, RESERVED PEPPER, GARLIC AND PARSLEY. SPREAD OVER CHICKEN BREASTS; POUR WINE OVER ALL. COMBINE PARMESAN AND BREAD CRUMBS; SPRINKLE OVER TOP. BAKE 25 MINUTES OR UNTIL BROWNED.

EXECUTIVE CHEF DONAL WEAVING
SOUTHERN HILLS COUNTRY CLUB

MANDARIN CHICKEN

YIELD: 4 SERVINGS
PREHEAT OVEN: 250°

PREPARATION TIME: 40 MINUTES

2 ORANGES OR TANGERINES
2 EGGS
2 TABLESPOONS CORNSTARCH
8 CHICKEN LEGS, BONED AND CUT IN 1 INCH PIECES
2 CUPS PEANUT OIL
4 TABLESPOONS SOY SAUCE
2 TABLESPOONS VINEGAR
2 TABLESPOONS DRY SHERRY
4 TEASPOONS CORNSTARCH
4 TEASPOONS WATER
2 GREEN ONIONS, SLICED
4 CLOVES GARLIC, SLICED
6 TO 8 SMALL WHOLE DRIED RED PEPPERS
1 CUP SUGAR

PEEL ZEST OF ORANGE AND CUT IN NARROW STRIPS. DRY 30 MINUTES IN OVEN.

COMBINE EGGS WITH CORNSTARCH. ADD CHICKEN; COAT THOROUGHLY. HEAT OIL IN ELECTRIC WOK OR LARGE SKILLET UNTIL VERY HOT. QUICKLY DROP CHICKEN PIECES, ONE BY ONE, INTO OIL. DEEP FRY UNTIL CRISP. REMOVE AND DRAIN; POUR OFF ALL BUT 2 TEASPOONS OIL.

COMBINE SOY SAUCE, VINEGAR, SHERRY, CORNSTARCH AND WATER. IN REMAINING OIL, STIR FRY GREEN ONIONS, GARLIC, PEPPERS AND ORANGE ZEST, STIRRING CONSTANTLY 1 MINUTE. RETURN CHICKEN TO PAN; ADD SOY MIXTURE. STIR UNTIL SAUCE THICKENS. ADD SUGAR AND COOK ON HIGH HEAT, STIRRING CONSTANTLY, UNTIL SUGAR AND SAUCE REDUCE TO GLAZE CHICKEN. REMOVE PEPPERS, IF DESIRED. SERVE WITH, NOT OVER, RICE.

THE WOK
JOHN TSOU, OWNER

HINT: HIGH HEAT ENSURES SUCCESS BUT MUST BE MONITORED THROUGHOUT PREPARATION.

CAJUN BROILED CHICKEN CREOLE

PREPARATION TIME: 1 1/2 HOUR

YIELD: 6 TO 8 SERVINGS
PREHEAT OVEN: 350°

CREOLE SAUCE:
- 1/4 CUP UNSALTED BUTTER
- 1/4 CUP ALL-PURPOSE FLOUR
- 1 1/2 CUPS CHOPPED ONION
- 1 CUP CHOPPED GREEN ONIONS
- 1 CUP CHOPPED CELERY WITH LEAVES
- 1 CUP CHOPPED GREEN BELL PEPPER
- 2 CLOVES GARLIC, MINCED
- 6 OUNCES TOMATO PASTE
- 1 TABLESPOON FRESH LEMON JUICE
- 16 OUNCES CANNED, DICED TOMATOES IN PURÉE
- 8 OUNCES TOMATO SAUCE
- 1 CUP WATER
- 1 TEASPOON WORCESTERSHIRE SAUCE
- 1 TABLESPOON SALT
- 1/2 TEASPOON CHESAPEAKE BAY SEAFOOD SEASONING
- 1 TEASPOON FRESHLY GROUND PEPPER
- 3 BAY LEAVES
- 1 TEASPOON SUGAR

MELT BUTTER IN LARGE CAST IRON SKILLET OR DUTCH OVEN SET OVER MEDIUM HEAT. WHEN BUTTER IS QUITE HOT, ADD FLOUR AND STIR QUICKLY TO BLEND; SMOOTH LUMPS. LOWER HEAT AND COOK, STIRRING CONSTANTLY, UNTIL ROUX IS DARK BROWN AND ACQUIRES NUT-LIKE SMELL, ABOUT 45 MINUTES. IF BROWN FLECKS APPEAR, DISCARD ROUX AS IT IS BURNED.

ADD ONION, GREEN ONIONS, CELERY, BELL PEPPER AND GARLIC. SAUTÉ UNTIL SOFT. ADD TOMATO PASTE AND LEMON JUICE; MIX WELL. ADD TOMATOES, TOMATO SAUCE, WATER, WORCESTERSHIRE, SALT, SEAFOOD SEASONING, PEPPER, BAY LEAVES AND SUGAR. SIMMER 1 HOUR, STIRRING OCCASIONALLY. MAKES 6 CUPS.

- 8 PIECES CHICKEN
- CAYENNE PEPPER
- GARLIC POWDER
- FRESHLY GROUND PEPPER
- HOT COOKED RICE

PLACE CHICKEN ON BROILER RACK, BONE SIDE UP. LIGHTLY DUST WITH CAYENNE PEPPER, GARLIC POWDER AND PEPPER. SET ASIDE 30 MINUTES.

BROIL CHICKEN 10 MINUTES. TURN CHICKEN AND LIGHTLY DUST WITH SPICES. BROIL 10 MINUTES OR UNTIL GOLDEN. PLACE CHICKEN IN FLAT CASSEROLE SET ON BAKING SHEET. COVER WITH 3 CUPS WARM CREOLE SAUCE. COVER WITH FOIL; BAKE 30 MINUTES. SERVE WITH RICE.

RICH JANES
NATIONAL PREPARED FOODS

DEVILED TURKEY

YIELD: 10 SERVINGS
PREHEAT OVEN: 400°

PREPARATION TIME: 1 HOUR

6 TO 7 POUND ROASTED TURKEY

VELOUTE SAUCE:
7 TABLESPOONS BUTTER
7 TABLESPOONS ALL-PURPOSE FLOUR
6 CUPS TURKEY STOCK
1 TABLESPOON ANCHOVY PASTE
1 TABLESPOON SOY SAUCE
2 TABLESPOONS DIJON MUSTARD
4 TABLESPOONS WORCESTERSHIRE SAUCE
2 CUPS HEAVY CREAM
SALT AND FRESHLY GROUND PEPPER, TO TASTE

CARVE TURKEY INTO SERVING SIZE PIECES. MAKE STOCK WITH CARCASS AND BONES.

IN LARGE SAUCEPAN OVER LOW HEAT, MELT BUTTER. WHISK IN FLOUR AND COOK 2 MINUTES, STIRRING CONSTANTLY. GRADUALLY ADD STOCK AND STIR UNTIL THICKENED. STIR IN ANCHOVY PASTE, SOY SAUCE, MUSTARD AND WORCESTERSHIRE. ADD MEAT; COMBINE WELL. OVER MEDIUM HEAT, ADD CREAM AND HEAT THROUGH. SEASON WITH SALT AND PEPPER. POUR INTO CASSEROLE DISH AND BAKE 10 MINUTES.

CHEF GERARD CAMPBELL
BRISTOL CITY RESTAURANT

CHICKEN WITH CHANTERELLE CREAM

YIELD: 6 TO 8 SERVINGS

PREPARATION TIME: 30 MINUTES

1/2 OUNCE DRIED CHANTERELLE MUSHROOMS
1 CUP DRY WHITE WINE
3 TABLESPOONS CLARIFIED BUTTER
4 WHOLE CHICKEN BREASTS, SKINNED, BONED, AND HALVED
1 CUP CHICKEN STOCK
1 CUP HEAVY CREAM
SALT, TO TASTE

SOAK MUSHROOMS IN WINE 30 MINUTES. HEAT BUTTER OVER MEDIUM-HIGH HEAT IN LARGE NON-STICK SKILLET. SAUTÉ CHICKEN, BROWNING BOTH SIDES. ADD WINE WITH MUSHROOMS AND CHICKEN STOCK. BRING TO BOIL. REDUCE HEAT TO LOW; COVER AND COOK 1 HOUR OR UNTIL TENDER. REMOVE CHICKEN TO WARM PLATTER.

REDUCE PAN JUICES TO 1/2 CUP. ADD CREAM; REDUCE, SCRAPING PAN OCCASIONALLY, UNTIL SAUCE THICKLY COATS BACK OF SPOON. TASTE AND ADD SALT, IF DESIRED. SPOON SAUCE OVER CHICKEN AND SERVE.

CHICKEN WELLINGTON

PREPARATION TIME: 20 MINUTES

YIELD: 4 SERVINGS
PREHEAT OVEN: 425°

- 4 TABLESPOONS BUTTER
- 2 WHOLE CHICKEN BREASTS, BONED, SKINNED AND HALVED
- 8 OUNCES REFRIGERATED CRESCENT ROLLS
- 4 THIN SLICES HONEY CURED HAM
- 4 OUNCES HERBED RONDELE CHEESE

IN LARGE SKILLET OVER MEDIUM-HIGH HEAT, MELT BUTTER AND SAUTÉ CHICKEN ABOUT 4 MINUTES ON EACH SIDE. DRAIN AND COOL. SEPARATE CRESCENT ROLLS INTO 4 PIECES; ROLL EACH INTO THIN FLAT SQUARE. PLACE HAM SLICE ON TOP. SPREAD CHEESE ON BOTH SIDES OF CHICKEN; PLACE EACH ON HAM. FOLD CORNERS OF SQUARES TO MIDDLE; PINCH TO SEAL. PLACE SEAM SIDE DOWN ON BUTTERED COOKIE SHEET. (MAY BE REFRIGERATED AT THIS POINT.) BAKE 10 TO 15 MINUTES UNTIL GOLDEN (A FEW MINUTES LONGER IF REFRIGERATED).

HINT: SERVE WITH MUSHROOM BROWN SAUCE FOR EXTRA FLAIR.

CHICKEN AND BROCCOLI CHANTILLY

PREPARATION TIME: 30 MINUTES

YIELD: 6 TO 8 SERVINGS
PREHEAT OVEN: 325°

- 8 CHICKEN BREAST HALVES, SKINNED AND BONED
- 20 OUNCES FROZEN BROCCOLI SPEARS (OR 1½ POUNDS FRESH), COOKED AND DRAINED
- 1.25 OUNCES DRY ONION SOUP MIX (1 ENVELOPE)
- 16 OUNCES SOUR CREAM
- 1 CUP WHIPPING CREAM
- GRATED PARMESAN CHEESE

BOIL CHICKEN UNTIL TENDER. ARRANGE BROCCOLI IN 9 × 13 INCH BUTTERED CASSEROLE. COMBINE SOUP MIX AND SOUR CREAM; SPREAD HALF OF SOUP MIXTURE OVER BROCCOLI. PLACE CHICKEN ON TOP. WHIP CREAM UNTIL STIFF; FOLD INTO REMAINING SOUP MIXTURE. SPREAD OVER CHICKEN BREASTS; SPRINKLE WITH PARMESAN. BAKE 20 TO 30 MINUTES.

SHERRIED CHICKEN WITH ARTICHOKES 

YIELD: 8 SERVINGS
PREHEAT OVEN: 350°
PREPARATION TIME: 30 MINUTES

- 8 CHICKEN BREAST HALVES
- ALL-PURPOSE FLOUR
- 1/2 CUP BUTTER
- 9 OUNCES FROZEN ARTICHOKE HEARTS, THAWED AND DRAINED
- 3/4 POUND FRESH MEDIUM MUSHROOMS
- JUICE OF 1 LEMON
- 1/3 CUP CHOPPED GREEN ONIONS
- 1/3 CUP CHOPPED FRESH PARSLEY
- GARLIC SALT, TO TASTE
- ONION SALT, TO TASTE
- 1/4 TEASPOON THYME, CRUMBLED
- 1/4 TEASPOON ROSEMARY, CRUSHED
- FRESHLY GROUND PEPPER, TO TASTE
- 1 CUP SHERRY
- 3/4 CUP CHICKEN BROTH
- 2 BAY LEAVES
- 1/2 CUP HEAVY CREAM

DREDGE CHICKEN IN FLOUR. IN LARGE SKILLET OVER MEDIUM-HIGH HEAT, SAUTÉ CHICKEN IN BUTTER UNTIL GOLDEN. ARRANGE IN 2 QUART CASSEROLE AND SCATTER ARTICHOKE HEARTS AND MUSHROOMS OVER CHICKEN. SQUEEZE LEMON JUICE OVER ALL AND ADD GREEN ONIONS AND PARSLEY. SPRINKLE WITH GARLIC AND ONION SALTS, THYME, ROSEMARY AND PEPPER. POUR SHERRY AND BROTH OVER AND LAY BAY LEAVES ON TOP. COVER TIGHTLY; BAKE 40 TO 50 MINUTES.

REMOVE CHICKEN TO WARM PLATTER. WHISK CREAM INTO SAUCE; HEAT THROUGH. REMOVE BAY LEAVES; LADLE SAUCE OVER CHICKEN AND SERVE.

*HINT: **VEAL SCALLOPS** MAY BE SUBSTITUTED FOR CHICKEN.*

INSIDE OUT CHICKEN

YIELD: 8 SERVINGS
PREHEAT OVEN: 325°
PREPARATION TIME: 30 MINUTES

- 8 TO 10 PIECES CHICKEN
- 2 CUPS SOUR CREAM
- 3 CUPS HERBED STUFFING MIX

CLEAN CHICKEN; PAT DRY. COAT EACH PIECE THICKLY WITH SOUR CREAM. COVER AND REFRIGERATE OVERNIGHT. CRUSH STUFFING MIX WITH ROLLING PIN. COAT CHICKEN WITH CRUMBS. PLACE IN 9×13 INCH CASSEROLE; REFRIGERATE 2 TO 3 HOURS. BAKE 1 HOUR.

HINT: HANDLE CHICKEN CAREFULLY AFTER COATING WITH SOUR CREAM.

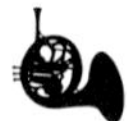

BREAST OF CHICKEN AU CHAMPAGNE

AN EXQUISITE SAUCE CLOAKS EVERY BITE OF THIS ELEGANT DISH.

PREPARATION TIME: 45 MINUTES

YIELD: 4 SERVINGS

- **4 WHOLE CHICKEN BREASTS, SKINNED AND BONED**
- **1/4 CUP ALL-PURPOSE FLOUR**
- **1 TEASPOON SALT**
- **1/2 TEASPOON FRESHLY GROUND PEPPER**
- **1/2 CUP BUTTER**
- **1/2 POUND FRESH MUSHROOMS, SLICED**
- **1 CUP HEAVY CREAM**
- **1/4 CUP DRY CHAMPAGNE**
- **LARGE MUSHROOM CAPS, SAUTÉED IN BUTTER**

FLATTEN CHICKEN SLIGHTLY BETWEEN TWO PIECES OF WAXED PAPER. COMBINE FLOUR, SALT AND PEPPER; DREDGE CHICKEN. SHAKE OFF EXCESS. MELT BUTTER IN LARGE SKILLET OVER MEDIUM-HIGH HEAT; ADD CHICKEN AND SAUTÉ UNTIL GOLDEN. REDUCE HEAT TO LOW; ADD MUSHROOMS. COVER; COOK 10 MINUTES. DRAIN EXCESS BUTTER. ADD CREAM AND SIMMER 10 MINUTES. TRANSFER CHICKEN TO WARM PLATTER. ADD CHAMPAGNE TO SKILLET; BOIL GENTLY UNTIL SAUCE IS REDUCED SLIGHTLY. SPOON OVER CHICKEN; GARNISH WITH MUSHROOM CAPS.

CHICKEN BREASTS ROMANO

PREPARATION TIME: 30 MINUTES

YIELD: 8 SERVINGS
PREHEAT OVEN: 300°

- **1 CUP BUTTER**
- **3 CLOVES GARLIC, MINCED**
- **1 CUP PREPARED CRUMB-STYLE STUFFING MIX**
- **1 CUP GRATED ROMANO CHEESE**
- **1/2 CUP CHOPPED FRESH PARSLEY**
- **1/2 TEASPOON SALT**
- **1/2 TEASPOON FRESHLY GROUND PEPPER**
- **8 CHICKEN BREAST HALVES, SKINNED AND BONED**
- **1 CUP DRY WHITE WINE**

IN MEDIUM SKILLET OVER LOW HEAT MELT BUTTER AND SAUTÉ GARLIC UNTIL TENDER. COMBINE STUFFING, CHEESE, PARSLEY, SALT AND PEPPER. DIP CHICKEN IN GARLIC BUTTER; COAT HEAVILY WITH CHEESE MIXTURE. ARRANGE IN 9×13 INCH CASSEROLE. COVER; BAKE 30 MINUTES. POUR WINE OVER CHICKEN; BAKE, UNCOVERED, 30 MINUTES.

HINT: CAN BE PREPARED AHEAD AND FROZEN. EXTEND BAKING TIME 15 TO 20 MINUTES IF USED DIRECTLY FROM FREEZER.

CHICKEN CALVADOS FLAMBÉ

APPLES AND CHICKEN COMBINE TO PRODUCE A DELICATE, DISTINCTIVE TASTE.

YIELD: 6 SERVINGS
PREHEAT OVEN: 350°
PREPARATION TIME: 45 MINUTES

SALT AND FRESHLY GROUND PEPPER
6 CHICKEN BREAST HALVES, SKINNED AND BONED
ALL-PURPOSE FLOUR
6 TABLESPOONS COLD BUTTER (RESERVE 4 TABLESPOONS, CUT INTO PIECES)
2 TABLESPOONS VEGETABLE OIL
3 GRANNY SMITH APPLES, PEELED, CORED AND SLICED
1/2 CUP DRY WHITE WINE
3/4 CUP APPLE JUICE
3/4 CUP CALVADOS OR APPLE BRANDY
1 1/2 CUPS CHICKEN BROTH
1 CUP HEAVY CREAM
SALT AND WHITE PEPPER, TO TASTE
TOASTED SLIVERED ALMONDS

SALT AND PEPPER CHICKEN BREASTS; DREDGE IN FLOUR. IN LARGE SKILLET OVER MEDIUM-HIGH HEAT, MELT 2 TABLESPOONS BUTTER WITH OIL. BROWN CHICKEN BREASTS ON BOTH SIDES. TRANSFER TO BAKING DISH; BAKE 20 TO 25 MINUTES.

MEANWHILE, ADD APPLES TO SKILLET AND TOSS TO THOROUGHLY COAT. DRAIN EXCESS FAT. ADD WINE; BRING TO BOIL. ADD APPLE JUICE AND BOIL, STIRRING CONSTANTLY; REDUCE BY HALF. ADD CHICKEN TO SKILLET. WARM CALVADOS. POUR OVER CHICKEN; IGNITE. WHEN FLAMES SUBSIDE REMOVE CHICKEN TO SERVING PLATTER; KEEP WARM.

OVER HIGH HEAT, ADD BROTH TO SAUCE. BOIL, STIRRING OCCASIONALLY, UNTIL REDUCED BY HALF. ADD CREAM AND BOIL, STIRRING CONSTANTLY, UNTIL SAUCE THICKLY COATS BACK OF SPOON. WHISK RESERVED COLD BUTTER INTO SAUCE, ONE PIECE AT A TIME. SEASON TO TASTE WITH SALT AND WHITE PEPPER. SPOON SAUCE AND APPLES OVER CHICKEN; TOP WITH TOASTED ALMONDS.

CHICKEN AND CRAB ELEGANTÉ

IMPRESSIVE TASTE—FOR THE OCCASION WHEN IMPRESSION IS EVERYTHING!

PREPARATION TIME: 30 MINUTES

YIELD: 4 SERVINGS
PREHEAT OVEN: 350°

1 POUND COOKED CHICKEN BREASTS, SLICED
3 TABLESPOONS BUTTER
1/2 CUP SLICED FRESH MUSHROOMS
1/4 CUP CHOPPED ONION
3 TABLESPOONS ALL-PURPOSE FLOUR
1/2 TEASPOON SALT
1/8 TEASPOON FRESHLY GROUND PEPPER
1 1/2 CUPS CHICKEN BROTH
1/2 CUP DRY WHITE WINE
2 EGG YOLKS, BEATEN WELL
12 OUNCES FRESH OR FROZEN CRABMEAT, THAWED, DRAINED AND CUT IN 1/2 INCH PIECES
9 OUNCES FROZEN ARTICHOKE HEARTS, THAWED, DRAINED AND QUARTERED
OR
1 CUP COOKED SWEET PEAS
1/2 CUP HEAVY CREAM, WHIPPED
1/4 CUP GRATED PARMESAN CHEESE
PAPRIKA

PLACE CHICKEN SLICES, OVERLAPPING, IN BUTTERED 9 × 13 INCH CASSEROLE. IN MEDIUM SKILLET, MELT BUTTER OVER LOW HEAT AND SAUTÉ MUSHROOMS AND ONION UNTIL SOFT. ADD FLOUR, SALT AND PEPPER. GRADUALLY ADD BROTH AND WINE, STIRRING CONSTANTLY, UNTIL THICKENED.

STIR SMALL AMOUNT OF HOT MIXTURE INTO EGG YOLKS; ADD YOLKS TO SKILLET. COOK 2 MINUTES OVER LOW HEAT. REMOVE FROM HEAT; STIR IN CRAB. ADD EITHER ARTICHOKE HEARTS OR PEAS. GENTLY FOLD IN WHIPPED CREAM.

POUR SAUCE OVER CHICKEN; SPRINKLE WITH PARMESAN AND PAPRIKA. BAKE UNTIL HEATED THROUGH AND LIGHTLY BROWNED; ABOUT 30 MINUTES.

ROAST CHICKEN WITH PISTACHIO RICE

YIELD: 4 TO 6 SERVINGS
PREHEAT OVEN: 375°

PREPARATION TIME: 20 MINUTES

- **4 POUND ROASTING CHICKEN**
- **JUICE OF 1 LEMON (RESERVE 1/2)**
- **SALT**
- **8 TABLESPOONS BUTTER (DIVIDED)**
- **1/2 CUP MINCED ONION**
- **1/2 CUP RAISINS**
- **1/2 CUP CHOPPED PISTACHIOS**
- **1/2 TEASPOON GROUND TUMERIC**
- **1/2 TEASPOON GROUND CUMIN**
- **2 CUPS COOKED RICE**
- **SALT AND FRESHLY GROUND PEPPER, TO TASTE**

RINSE CHICKEN AND BLOT DRY. POUR HALF OF LEMON JUICE INSIDE; SALT LIGHTLY.

IN SMALL SKILLET, MELT 4 TABLESPOONS BUTTER AND SAUTÉ ONION OVER LOW HEAT UNTIL GOLDEN. ADD RAISINS, PISTACHIOS, TUMERIC AND CUMIN. COMBINE ONION MIXTURE WITH RICE; MIX WELL. ADD SALT AND PEPPER.

STUFF CHICKEN WITH RICE MIXTURE; TRUSS. PUT IN ROASTING PAN; SPRINKLE LIGHTLY WITH SALT AND PEPPER. COMBINE RESERVED LEMON JUICE AND REMAINING BUTTER; SPREAD OVER CHICKEN BREAST. ROAST 1 1/2 HOURS, BASTING OCCASIONALLY.

CHICKEN TETRAZZINI

YIELD: 8 SERVINGS
PREHEAT OVEN: 375°

PREPARATION TIME: 45 MINUTES

- **4 CHICKEN BREASTS OR THIGHS, COOKED, SKINNED, BONED AND CUT INTO BITE-SIZE PIECES**
- **1/2 POUND SPAGHETTI, COOKED AND DRAINED**
- **4 OUNCES DICED PIMIENTO, DRAINED**
- **1/2 CUP SLICED FRESH MUSHROOMS**

CHEESE SAUCE:

- **2 TABLESPOONS BUTTER**
- **1 TABLESPOON ALL-PURPOSE FLOUR**
- **1/2 CUP MILK**
- **1/2 CUP CHICKEN BROTH**
- **1/2 POUND VELVEETA CHEESE, CUBED**
- **3 OUNCES GRATED PARMESAN CHEESE**

IN LARGE BOWL, COMBINE CHICKEN, SPAGHETTI, PIMIENTO AND MUSHROOMS; SET ASIDE.

IN MEDIUM SAUCEPAN, MELT BUTTER OVER LOW HEAT. STIR IN FLOUR; COOK 2 MINUTES. ADD MILK AND BROTH, STIRRING CONSTANTLY UNTIL THICKENED. ADD VELVEETA AND PARMESAN; STIR TO MELT.

COMBINE SAUCE WITH CHICKEN MIXTURE; POUR INTO BUTTERED 3 QUART CASSEROLE. BAKE 30 MINUTES, OR UNTIL BUBBLY. DO NOT OVERBAKE.

Chicken Lasagna

Kids love it!

Preparation Time: 45 minutes

Yield: 8 servings
Preheat Oven: 375°

Sauce:
3 tablespoons butter
1/2 cup chopped onion
1/2 cup chopped green bell pepper
1/4 pound fresh mushrooms, sliced (or 3 ounces canned drained mushrooms)
10 1/2 ounces cream of chicken soup
1/3 cup milk
1/4 cup diced pimiento, drained
1/2 teaspoon dried basil, crumbled

Heat butter in large skillet over medium heat. Sauté onion, bell pepper and mushrooms until soft. Add soup, milk, pimiento, and basil. Heat until blended.

8 ounces lasagna noodles, cooked and drained
1 1/2 cups cottage cheese, drained
3 cups cooked, diced chicken
2 cups shredded American or cheddar cheese
1/2 cup grated Parmesan cheese

In buttered 9 × 13 inch casserole, place half of noodles; cover with half of sauce. Top with half of cottage cheese, half of chicken and half of cheeses. Repeat layering second time. Bake 30 minutes or until lightly browned and bubbly.

Oklahoma Rose Chicken

An unusual combination of ingredients results in a splendid sauce.

Preparation Time: 10 minutes

Yield: 4 to 6 servings

1 large chicken (3 1/2 pounds)
12 ounces catsup
6 ounces Coca-Cola

Place all ingredients in 5 quart Dutch oven. Cover and simmer 1 hour. Remove chicken. Cook sauce, uncovered, until reduced by half. Spoon sauce over chicken and serve.

ROSEMARY CHICKEN

YIELD: 4 SERVINGS

PREPARATION TIME: 45 MINUTES

14 TO 20 CLOVES GARLIC, UNPEELED
VEGETABLE COOKING SPRAY
6 PIECES CHICKEN, SKINNED
1 1/2 TEASPOONS ROSEMARY, CRUSHED
1/2 TEASPOON SALT
1/4 TEASPOON FRESHLY GROUND PEPPER
1/2 CUP DRY WHITE WINE
1 CUP BOILING WATER
2 CHICKEN BOUILLON CUBES
2 1/4 TEASPOONS CORNSTARCH

IN PAN OF BOILING WATER, COOK GARLIC 2 TO 3 MINUTES. DRAIN, COOL, PEEL AND SLICE.

COAT LARGE SKILLET WITH COOKING SPRAY. OVER MEDIUM-HIGH HEAT, BROWN CHICKEN LIGHTLY ON BOTH SIDES. ADD 3 TO 4 TABLESPOONS WATER. SPRINKLE WITH ROSEMARY, SALT AND PEPPER. COVER; SIMMER 15 TO 20 MINUTES. TURN CHICKEN AND SPRINKLE WITH GARLIC. ADD MORE WATER, IF NEEDED; COVER AND SIMMER 25 TO 40 MINUTES. CHECK FREQUENTLY, ADDING WATER AS NEEDED.

INCREASE HEAT TO REDUCE LIQUID. BROWN CHICKEN UNTIL GOLDEN; REMOVE TO WARM PLATTER. ADD WINE, SCRAPING TO LOOSEN BROWNED BITS; REDUCE BY HALF. ADD BOILING WATER AND BOUILLON CUBES; BRING TO BOIL. MIX CORNSTARCH WITH ENOUGH WATER TO FORM PASTE; STIR INTO SAUCE UNTIL THICKENED. POUR SAUCE OVER CHICKEN; SERVE.

SNAPPY CHICKEN CASSEROLE

YOUR OVEN DOES PRACTICALLY ALL THE WORK!

YIELD: 6 TO 8 SERVINGS
PREHEAT OVEN: 350°

PREPARATION TIME: 10 MINUTES

2 CUPS LONG GRAIN RICE
1 CUP BUTTER, MELTED
21 OUNCES CANNED BEEF CONSOMMÉ
21 OUNCES CANNED FRENCH ONION SOUP
1 2 1/2 POUND CHICKEN FRYER, CUT UP

COMBINE RICE, BUTTER, CONSOMMÉ AND ONION SOUP; POUR INTO 3 QUART CASSEROLE. LAY CHICKEN ON TOP. COVER AND BAKE 45 MINUTES. REDUCE HEAT TO 325°; BAKE, UNCOVERED, 15 MINUTES OR UNTIL LIQUID IS ABSORBED.

CASSOULET WITH CORNISH HENS

FRENCH BAKED BEANS; C'EST BON!

PREPARATION TIME: 1 1/2 HOURS

YIELD: 8 TO 10 SERVINGS
PREHEAT OVEN: 350°

5 QUARTS WATER
2 POUNDS GREAT NORTHERN WHITE BEANS
1/2 POUND BACON, DICED
1 MEDIUM ONION
6 WHOLE CLOVES
4 CARROTS, PEELED AND COARSELY CHOPPED
5 MEDIUM ONIONS, CHOPPED
3 CUPS CONDENSED CHICKEN BROTH
2 BAY LEAVES
3/4 CUP CHOPPED CELERY LEAVES
4 CLOVES GARLIC, MINCED
2 TEASPOONS DRIED THYME, CRUMBLED
2 TEASPOONS DRIED SAGE, CRUMBLED
1 TEASPOON DRIED MARJORAM, CRUMBLED
1 TEASPOON DRIED ROSEMARY, CRUSHED
1 TEASPOON SALT
4 WHOLE BLACK PEPPERCORNS
4 CORNISH HENS, HALVED
4 TABLESPOONS BUTTER, SOFTENED
3/4 CUP DRY VERMOUTH
28 OUNCES CANNED TOMATOES, UNDRAINED AND CHOPPED
1 POUND POLISH KIELBASA SAUSAGE OR GARLIC SAUSAGE, CUT INTO 1 INCH PIECES
2 CUPS FRESH BREAD CRUMBS
4 TABLESPOONS BUTTER, MELTED

IN LARGE STOCKPOT BRING 5 QUARTS WATER TO BOIL. ADD BEANS; COVER AND BOIL 2 MINUTES. REMOVE FROM HEAT; SOAK 1 HOUR.

FRY BACON UNTIL PARTIALLY COOKED. DRAIN FAT AND ADD BACON TO UNDRAINED BEANS. STUD ONION WITH CLOVES. ADD ONION, CARROTS, CHOPPED ONIONS, BROTH, BAY LEAVES, CELERY LEAVES, GARLIC, THYME, SAGE, MARJORAM, ROSEMARY, SALT AND PEPPERCORNS TO BEANS. BRING TO BOIL; REDUCE HEAT AND SIMMER, COVERED, 1 1/4 HOURS.

MEANWHILE, RUB CORNISH HENS WITH BUTTER; PLACE IN BAKING DISH. ROAST 30 MINUTES. POUR VERMOUTH OVER HENS; COVER AND BAKE 10 MINUTES.

TURN BEANS WITH LIQUID INTO 6 QUART OVEN PROOF CASSEROLE. BAKE UNCOVERED 45 MINUTES. DISCARD WHOLE ONION AND BAY LEAVES. ADD TOMATOES. ARRANGE HEN PIECES OVER BEANS; DRAIN COOKING JUICES FROM ROASTING PAN INTO CASSEROLE. SCATTER SAUSAGE OVER BEANS. COVER TIGHTLY; BAKE 30 MINUTES. COMBINE BREAD CRUMBS AND BUTTER; SPRINKLE OVER BEANS. BAKE, UNCOVERED, 15 TO 20 MINUTES. REFRIGERATING OVERNIGHT GREATLY ENHANCES FLAVOR.

Scherer True Snapper with Watercress Sauce

Yield: 1 serving
Preheat Oven: 375°
Preparation Time: 1 hour

Tarragon Butter:
- **1/2 ounce fresh chopped tarragon (or 1 tablespoon dried, crumbled)**
- **1 tablespoon chopped shallots**
- **1/4 cup tarragon vinegar**
- **1/2 cup white wine**
- **8 ounces butter, softened**
- **Salt and freshly ground pepper, to taste**

In small saucepan combine tarragon, shallots, vinegar and wine. Reduce over high heat until almost dry. Chill 10 minutes. Fold in butter until fully incorporated; add salt and pepper. Chill.

- **3 large Romaine lettuce leaves**
- **Salt and freshly ground pepper, to taste**
- **8 ounces true Red Snapper filet, scored**
- **1 lemon, halved**
- **1 red bell pepper, thinly sliced**
- **1 ounce tarragon butter**
- **1/4 cup white wine**
- **1/4 cup water**
- **2 ounces melted butter**

Steam lettuce 2 to 3 minutes. Lay flat on smooth surface; sprinkle with salt and pepper. Place filet, scored side down, in middle of lettuce and squeeze lemon juice over top. Lay bell pepper on filet and cover with 1 ounce Tarragon butter. Fold lettuce over filet to cover completely. Place seam side down in shallow baking dish. Add wine and water; brush top of lettuce with melted butter. Cover and bake 10 to 15 minutes. Prepare Watercress sauce. Ladle sauce on serving plate. Place fish over sauce; top with ball of tarragon butter.

Watercress Sauce:
- **2 tablespoons butter**
- **2 tablespoons diced shallots**
- **1 tablespoon diced garlic**
- **10 ounces fresh watercress (reserve 1/3 pound)**
- **1 cup white wine**
- **Juice of 1 lemon**
- **6 cups heavy cream**
- **Salt and freshly ground pepper, to taste**

In large skillet melt butter over medium heat. Add shallots, garlic and two-thirds of watercress; sauté 5 minutes or until soft. Add wine and lemon juice; reduce over high heat until almost dry. Add cream; reduce by half. Transfer to blender or food processor; add reserved watercress and purée. Strain back into saucepan. Add salt and pepper; heat through. Makes 3 cups.

Gary Scherer, Executive Chef
Sheraton Kensington, Tulsa

Spicy Skillet Shrimp

Preparation Time: 45 minutes

Yield: 4 to 6 servings

- 1 pound medium fresh shrimp
- 1/2 cup butter
- 4 green onions, chopped
- 1/4 cup diced green bell pepper
- 2 cloves garlic, minced
- 3 tablespoons fresh lemon juice, or to taste
- 1 teaspoon freshly ground pepper
- 1/4 teaspoon crushed red pepper
- 1 teaspoon lemon pepper
- 2 tablespoons chopped fresh parsley
- Salt, to taste

Peel shrimp leaving tails intact; devein. Melt butter in large heavy skillet over medium heat. Add green onions, bell pepper and garlic; sauté 1 minute. Add shrimp, lemon juice, peppers and parsley. Cook over high heat, turning shrimp frequently, until they are pink, curled and slightly golden. Remove to serving dish; drizzle pan juices over. Season with salt.

Nancy Parker Cooking School

Deviled Crab

Preparation Time: 25 minutes

Yield: 6 servings
Preheat Oven: 350°

- 2 cups fresh crabmeat
- 2 hard boiled eggs, finely chopped
- 3 tablespoons mayonnaise
- 1 tablespoon plus 1 teaspoon lemon juice
- 1 teaspoon Worcestershire sauce
- 1 teaspoon dry mustard
- Salt and cayenne pepper, to taste
- 6 tablespoons butter
- 2 tablespoons minced green onions
- 1 1/2 cups fresh bread crumbs (reserve 1/2 cup)
- 1 teaspoon baking powder

Combine crabmeat, eggs, mayonnaise, lemon juice, Worcestershire, mustard, salt and pepper. Mix gently and refrigerate at least 1 hour. Meanwhile, melt butter in medium skillet. Add green onions; sauté over low heat until tender. Stir in 1 cup bread crumbs. When ready to bake stir bread crumb mixture and baking powder into crab mixture, tossing lightly until just mixed. Spoon into baking shells or individual ramekins. Sprinkle with reserved bread crumbs. Bake until golden brown, about 15 minutes.

Stuffed Flounder

Yield: 4 servings
Preheat Oven: 375°

Preparation Time: 30 minutes

8 tablespoons butter, melted (reserve 4 tablespoons)
1 2 to 3 pound whole fresh flounder, boned, or 8 small fresh flounder or sole filets
Salt and freshly ground pepper, to taste

Grease 9 × 13 inch baking dish with 3 tablespoons melted butter. Brush fish with 1 tablespoon butter and season with salt and pepper.

Stuffing:
1/4 cup chopped onion
1/2 cup chopped celery
1/4 cup chopped green onions
2 tablespoons chopped green bell pepper
1 clove garlic, minced
1 tablespoon all-purpose flour
1/2 cup dry white wine
1/2 cup milk
1/2 pound medium fresh shrimp, cooked, peeled, deveined and chopped
1/2 pound fresh or frozen crabmeat, drained and shredded
1/2 cup fresh bread crumbs
2 tablespoons chopped fresh parsley
1 egg, beaten lightly
Salt and freshly ground pepper, to taste
Dash cayenne pepper
Paprika

In medium skillet melt reserved butter over medium-high heat. Add onion, celery, green onions, bell pepper and garlic; sauté until tender. Blend in flour. Add wine and milk; stir until thickened. Remove from heat. Add shrimp, crabmeat, bread crumbs, parsley and egg. Season with salt, pepper and cayenne pepper.

Stuff flounder; press edges together to seal. If using filets, divide and place stuffing over 4 pieces. Top with remaining filets; press edges together. Place in dish. Sprinkle with paprika; bake uncovered 25 minutes. Spoon pan juices over fish and serve.

Lobster Wellington

Preparation Time: 1 hour

Yield: 4 servings
Preheat Oven: 375°

4 tablespoons butter
4 6 ounce whole fresh lobster tails, shelled
2 tablespoons brandy, heated
4 tablespoons butter, softened
1 tablespoon fresh lemon juice
8 phyllo pastry sheets
4 tablespoons butter, melted

Melt 4 tablespoons butter in large skillet over medium heat; add lobster tails. Add 2 tablespoons brandy and ignite, shaking pan until flames subside. Cook lobster until almost done, about 3 minutes. Remove; cool. Reserve cooking liquid.

Whip 4 tablespoons softened butter with 1 tablespoon lemon juice. Spread each lobster tail generously with lemon butter. Brush 1 phyllo sheet with melted butter. Place second sheet on top; brush with butter. Set lobster tail on one end of phyllo; fold up envelope fashion enclosing lobster completely. Repeat with remaining phyllo sheets and lobster tails. Arrange seam side down on baking sheet. Brush tops lightly with melted butter. Bake until golden, about 20 minutes.

Sauce:
Reserved cooking liquid
1 tablespoon butter
1 tablespoon minced shallots
1 cup old fashioned heavy cream
1/4 teaspoon paprika
Salt and white pepper, to taste
4 tablespoons brandy
4 tablespoons cold butter
Fresh lemon juice, to taste

Meanwhile, warm reserved lobster cooking liquid over low heat. Add 1 tablespoon butter and shallots. Cook until translucent. Add cream, paprika, salt and pepper. Stir in brandy; increase heat to high. Cook until sauce is reduced by half and coats wooden spoon thickly. Reduce heat; add butter 1 tablespoon at a time stirring until incorporated. Stir in lemon juice. Arrange lobster on individual plates. Top with sauce; serve immediatley.

HINT: Phyllo dries quickly. Open package only when ready to use. Keep unused portion covered with damp cloth.

Lobster and Veal Chantilly 

Yield: 4 servings *Preparation Time: 20 minutes*

Cut lobster in 3/4 inch slices; set aside. Pound veal very thin. Combine flour, salt and pepper. Heat butter in large non-stick skillet over medium-high heat. Dredge veal in seasoned flour, shaking off excess. Sauté in skillet, a few at a time, about 2 minutes, until browned lightly. Transfer to heated platter; keep warm.

Reduce heat. Add shallots; sauté 2 minutes being careful not to burn. Add cream and vermouth; reduce by one-third. Add tarragon, lobster and green onions; simmer 3 minutes. Add mushrooms; cook 1 minute. Season with cayenne. Spoon over veal and serve.

- **2 medium fresh lobster tails, cooked and shelled**
- **1 pound veal scallops**
- **1/2 cup all-purpose flour**
- **1/2 teaspoon salt**
- **1/4 teaspoon freshly ground pepper**
- **6 tablespoons clarified butter**
- **2 tablespoons minced shallots**
- **1 1/2 cups heavy cream**
- **1/2 cup dry vermouth**
- **1 tablespoon minced fresh tarragon (or 1 teaspoon dried, crumbled)**
- **4 green onions, minced**
- **1 cup sliced fresh mushrooms**
- **Dash cayenne pepper**

Sole with Mushroom Shrimp Sauce 

Yield: 4 servings *Preparation Time: 30 minutes*

Combine flour, salt and pepper; dredge filets in mixture. In large skillet over medium heat melt butter and sauté filets 2 minutes; turn and sauté until fish is done, about 2 to 4 minutes. Transfer to serving platter; keep warm.

Add shallots to skillet and sauté. Add wine and increase heat. Reduce to 1/4 cup liquid. Add green onions and cream and reduce until sauce coats wooden spoon thickly. Add shrimp and mushrooms; cook 1 minute. Pour sauce over filets and serve.

- **1/2 cup all-purpose flour**
- **1/4 teaspoon salt**
- **1/4 teaspoon freshly ground pepper**
- **1 pound fresh sole filets (grey, petrale or lemon)**
- **4 tablespoons clarified butter**
- **2 tablespoons chopped shallots**
- **1 cup Rhine wine**
- **4 tablespoons chopped green onions**
- **1 cup heavy cream**
- **6 ounces medium shrimp, cooked, peeled and deveined**
- **1/2 cup sliced fresh mushrooms**

Halibut Steaks Pecan

Preparation Time: 15 minutes

Yield: 4 servings

- **6 tablespoons clarified butter (reserve 4 tablespoons)**
- **1/2 cup pecan halves, cut lengthwise**
- **1/4 cup all-purpose flour**
- **1/4 teaspoon salt**
- **1/4 teaspoon freshly ground pepper**
- **4 fresh halibut steaks, 1 inch thick (about 1 3/4 pounds)**
- **3 tablespoons vegetable oil**
- **2 ribs celery, cut into 1 1/2 inch strips**
- **1 small red or green bell pepper, cut into 1 1/2 inch strips**
- **1/4 cup slivered red onion**

In medium skillet melt 2 tablespoons butter over medium-low heat; add pecans. Stir until toasted lightly, about 3 minutes. Transfer to small bowl; set aside.

Combine flour, salt and pepper. Dredge halibut in mixture; shake off excess. Over medium-high heat, melt 2 tablespoons butter with oil in large non-stick skillet. Add fish; reduce heat to medium and cook 4 minutes on each side until lightly browned. Transfer to platter; keep warm.

Melt remaining 2 tablespoons butter in medium skillet over low heat. Add celery and cook 2 minutes. Add bell pepper; cook 2 minutes, stirring often. Add onion; cook 2 more minutes until vegetables are just tender. Spoon over fish; sprinkle with pecans and serve immediately.

Orange Roughy Delicious

Light and Lovely!!

Preparation Time: 10 minutes

Yield: 6 servings
Preheat Oven: 350°

- **6 orange roughy filets, rinsed**
- **Garlic powder, to taste**
- **White pepper, to taste**
- **Fresh lemon juice, to taste**
- **1/2 cup dry white wine**
- **1/4 cup butter**
- **2 tablespoons chopped fresh parsley**
- **Lemon slices**

Pat filets with paper towel to dry. Sprinkle each with garlic powder, pepper and lemon juice. Pour wine into broiling pan; place rack in pan. Lay filets on rack; bake 20 to 30 minutes. Meanwhile, melt butter; add chopped parsley. During last 5 minutes of cooking time, drizzle butter over filets. Broil 5 minutes or until lightly browned. Garnish with lemon slices.

Salmon Mousse

Yield: 12 servings *Preparation Time: 45 minutes*

Drain salmon; remove skin and bone. Soften gelatin in cold water; add boiling water, stirring to dissolve. Place half of gelatin mixture, half of salmon and half of onion, mayonnaise, lemon juice, dill weed, paprika, and cream in blender or processor; process until smooth. Remove to bowl. Repeat with remaining ingredients; add to bowl and stir to blend. Pour mixture into lightly oiled 5½ cup fish mold. Chill overnight. Unmold on chilled serving plate. Decorate using olive slices for eyes, pimiento slice for mouth, and parsley sprigs for eyebrows. (Makes 20 appetizer servings.)

15½ ounces canned red salmon
2 envelopes unflavored gelatin
¼ cup cold water
¼ cup boiling water
1 small onion, minced
1 cup mayonnaise
¼ cup fresh lemon juice
1 tablespoon dried dill weed
2 teaspoons paprika
1½ cups heavy cream
Pimiento stuffed olive slices
Pimiento slice
Parsley

Salmon with Tarragon Tomato Sauce

Yield: 2 servings *Preparation Time: 1 hour*

In medium saucepan, melt butter; add shallots and sauté until soft. Add wine; reduce by half. Add tomatoes, tarragon, thyme, salt and pepper. Cook over high heat until thickened. Set aside.

Salt and pepper filets. In non-stick skillet heat oil; add salmon and cook over medium heat 2 minutes. Turn, lower heat and cover; cook 1½ to 2 minutes. Remove salmon to serving plates. Add sauce to pan juices; heat. Spoon over salmon and serve. Serves 4 as an appetizer.

1 tablespoon butter
2 tablespoons chopped shallots
¼ cup Rhine wine
2 large tomatoes, peeled, seeded, and chopped
½ teaspoon tarragon, crumbled
¼ teaspoon thyme, crumbled
½ teaspoon salt
¼ teaspoon freshly ground pepper, to taste
Salt and freshly ground pepper, to taste
2 fresh salmon filets, skin removed (about 1 pound)
1 tablespoon oil

Hint: The salmon is also wonderful prepared this way and served without sauce.

Scalloped Salmon

Preparation Time: 20 minutes

Yield: 4 servings
Preheat Oven: 350°

1 pound fresh salmon filet
1/2 cup water
1/2 cup Rhine wine
5 tablespoons butter, melted (reserve 1 tablespoon)
4 tablespoons chopped onion
2 tablespoons chopped green bell pepper
2 tablespoons all-purpose flour
10 ounces evaporated milk
1/2 teaspoon salt
1/4 teaspoon green peppercorns, crushed
4 tablespoons soft bread crumbs

In medium skillet poach salmon in water and wine over low heat. Remove filet; skin and break into small pieces. Increase heat and reduce liquid in skillet to 2 tablespoons. Add 4 tablespoons butter; lower heat. Stir in onion and bell pepper; sauté until tender. Add flour; cook 1 minute. Whisk in milk; cook 2 minutes. Blend in salmon, salt and peppercorns. Spoon mixture into buttered individual ramekins. Combine bread crumbs with reserved butter. Top salmon with crumb mixture; bake 20 minutes.

HINT: 16 ounces canned salmon or tuna may be substituted for fresh salmon.

Champagne Shrimp

Preparation Time: 30 minutes

Yield: 4 servings

2 tablespoons clarified butter
16 large fresh shrimp, peeled and deveined
2 tablespoons minced shallots
1 1/2 cups dry champagne
3/4 cup heavy cream
1/4 cup sliced mushrooms
2 tablespoons chopped green onions
1/4 teaspoon salt
Freshly ground pepper, to taste
2 cups hot cooked rice
Fresh chervil or parsley sprigs

Heat butter in large skillet over high heat. Add shrimp and shallots; sauté until shrimp turn pink, 2 to 3 minutes. Add champagne; heat to boiling. Remove shrimp with slotted spoon; keep warm. Reduce champagne to 1/2 cup, about 6 to 7 minutes. Add cream; reduce by one-third, about 5 minutes. Add mushrooms and green onions; cook 2 minutes. Remove from heat; add salt and pepper. Arrange shrimp over rice. Pour sauce over; garnish with chervil or parsley.

CHINESE SHRIMP AND VEGETABLES

YIELD: 4 SERVINGS

PREPARATION TIME: 45 MINUTES

- 1 POUND MEDIUM FRESH SHRIMP
- 2 TABLESPOONS SOY SAUCE
- 1/4 TEASPOON SALT
- 1 TEASPOON PEELED, FINELY CHOPPED FRESH GINGER ROOT
- 1 TABLESPOON DRY SHERRY
- 4 TABLESPOONS VEGETABLE OIL (RESERVE 2 TABLESPOONS)
- 1 1/2 CUPS THINLY SLICED ONION
- 3 RIBS CELERY, CUT IN 2 INCH PIECES
- 1/2 CUP SLICED WATER CHESTNUTS

CHOOSE 3 OF THE FOLLOWING:

- 1 CUP FRESH BEAN SPROUTS
- 1/2 POUND FRESH SNOW PEAS
- 1 CUP BROCCOLI FLOWERETS
- 1 CUP SHREDDED GREEN CABBAGE
- 1 CUP SLICED FRESH MUSHROOMS

- 1 TABLESPOON CORNSTARCH
- 1/2 CUP COLD CHICKEN STOCK
- 2 CUPS HOT COOKED RICE

PEEL AND DEVEIN SHRIMP. IN SHALLOW DISH, MARINATE SHRIMP IN MIXTURE OF SOY SAUCE, SALT, GINGER AND SHERRY FOR 1/2 HOUR. HEAT 2 TABLESPOONS OIL IN WOK OR SKILLET. DRAIN SHRIMP AND SAUTÉ 2 MINUTES. REMOVE AND SET ASIDE.

ADD RESERVED OIL TO WOK AND REHEAT. ADD ONION AND CELERY. SAUTÉ 2 MINUTES. ADD WATER CHESTNUTS AND REMAINING VEGETABLES; SAUTÉ 2 MINUTES. ADD SHRIMP.

COMBINE CORNSTARCH AND CHICKEN STOCK IN SMALL BOWL. ADD TO WOK; COOK UNTIL THICKENED, STIRRING CONSTANTLY. SERVE OVER RICE.

BAKED ITALIAN SHRIMP

YIELD: 6 TO 8 SERVINGS
PREHEAT OVEN: 350°

PREPARATION TIME: 15 MINUTES

- 1 1/2 CUPS MARGARINE, MELTED
- 8 TABLESPOONS FRESHLY GROUND PEPPER
- 16 OUNCES BOTTLED ITALIAN SALAD DRESSING
- 1 TABLESPOON WORCESTERSHIRE SAUCE

JUICE OF 2 LEMONS

- 1 TEASPOON SEASONED SALT
- 1 TEASPOON ACCENT SEASONING
- 5 POUNDS FRESH MEDIUM SHRIMP, IN SHELLS

COMBINE MARGARINE, PEPPER, DRESSING, WORCESTERSHIRE, LEMON JUICE, SEASONED SALT AND ACCENT. PLACE SHRIMP IN 9 × 13 INCH BAKING DISH AND POUR DRESSING MIXTURE OVER. STIR TO COMBINE. BAKE 45 MINUTES, STIRRING FREQUENTLY.

CRAWFISH OR SHRIMP ETOUFFEE

PREPARATION TIME: 1 HOUR

YIELD: 8 SERVINGS

4 CUPS BOILED, PEELED, DEVEINED CRAWFISH TAILS, PLUS CRAWFISH FAT (5 POUNDS WHOLE CRAWFISH; RESERVE BODY SHELLS FOR STOCK) OR
2 POUNDS MEDIUM FRESH SHRIMP, PEELED AND DEVEINED (RESERVE SHELLS FOR STOCK)

BASIC SEAFOOD STOCK:
RESERVED SHELLS
4 CUPS WATER
2 RIBS CELERY
1 SMALL ONION, QUARTERED

CREOLE SEASONING MIX:
2 TEASPOONS SALT
1 TEASPOON CAYENNE PEPPER
1/2 TEASPOON FRESHLY GROUND PEPPER
3/4 TEASPOON DRIED THYME, CRUMBLED
3/4 TEASPOON DRIED OREGANO, CRUMBLED
1/2 TEASPOON ONION POWDER
1/2 TEASPOON GARLIC POWDER

1/2 TO 1 TEASPOON CREOLE SEASONING MIX
1/3 CUP CHOPPED CELERY
1/3 CUP CHOPPED ONION
1/3 CUP CHOPPED GREEN BELL PEPPER
1/2 CUP VEGETABLE OIL
1/2 CUP ALL-PURPOSE FLOUR
2 CUPS BASIC SEAFOOD STOCK
4 CUPS COOKED RICE
1/2 CUP CHOPPED GREEN ONIONS
1/2 CUP CHOPPED PARSLEY

FOR BASIC SEAFOOD STOCK: COMBINE SHELLS, WATER, CELERY AND ONION. BOIL UNTIL REDUCED TO 2 CUPS; STRAIN.

FOR CREOLE SEASONING MIX: COMBINE SALT, PEPPERS, THYME, OREGANO, ONION POWDER AND GARLIC POWDER.

IN PROCESSOR, CHOP VERY, VERY FINE CELERY, ONION AND BELL PEPPER. SET ASIDE.

FOR ROUX: PUT OIL IN LARGE HEAVY CAST IRON SKILLET; HEAT. WHEN OIL BEGINS TO SMOKE, ADD FLOUR GRADUALLY; BEGIN WHISKING TO COMBINE. ONCE FLOUR IS ADDED DO NOT STOP STIRRING. ROUX WILL BROWN VERY QUICKLY. COOK UNTIL VERY, VERY DARK REDDISH BROWN. IF BLACK SPECKS APPEAR, IT HAS BURNED. DISCARD AND BEGIN AGAIN. ROUX SHOULD REACH DESIRED COLOR WITHIN 5 MINUTES. IF IT IS DARKENING TOO FAST, REMOVE FROM HEAT; CONTINUE STIRRING UNTIL UNDER CONTROL. WHEN DESIRED COLOR, REMOVE FROM HEAT; IMMEDIATELY ADD VEGETABLE MIXTURE. CONTINUE STIRRING 3 TO 5 MINUTES.

ADD 1/2 TEASPOON CREOLE SEASONING MIX TO SKILLET; COMBINE. ADD STOCK; COOK UNTIL THICKENED. SIMMER 5 MINUTES. ADD CRAWFISH TAILS AND CRAWFISH FAT (OR SHRIMP); SIMMER 5 MINUTES. ADD MORE CREOLE SEASONING MIX, IF DESIRED. REMEMBER MIX IS VERY HOT.

TO SERVE: MOUND RICE IN CENTER OF EACH SERVING PLATE; SPOON ETOUFFEE AROUND IT. SPRINKLE WITH GREEN ONIONS AND PARSLEY.

HINT: CRAWFISH FAT IS YELLOW SUBSTANCE LOCATED BETWEEN TAIL AND BODY. IT IS CONSIDERED A DELICACY AND IS VERY FLAVORFUL.

Gourmet Shrimp

Delicious with spinach salad, hot bread and white wine.

Yield: 4 servings | *Preparation Time: 45 minutes*

Melt butter in large skillet over medium heat. Sauté shrimp, garlic, mushrooms, and green onions until shrimp turn pink. Add basil, salt, wine and Worcestershire. Mix cornstarch with water; add to shrimp mixture. Stir until thickened; cook about 5 minutes. Serve over cooked rice.

- **1/2 cup butter**
- **1 pound medium fresh shrimp, peeled and deveined**
- **1 clove garlic, minced**
- **1/2 pound fresh mushrooms, sliced**
- **3 green onions, chopped**
- **1/2 teaspoon dried basil, crumbled**
- **1 teaspoon salt**
- **1/2 cup dry white wine**
- **1 teaspoon Worcestershire sauce**
- **1 1/2 teaspoons cornstarch**
- **3 tablespoons water**
- **3 cups hot cooked rice**

Sautéed Oysters with Basil

Yield: 2 servings | *Preparation Time: 15 minutes*

Gently pat oysters dry. Dredge in flour and dust off excess. Melt butter in large skillet over medium-high heat. Add oysters and sprinkle with basil. Brown oysters lightly about 2 minutes on each side. Remove oysters to heated serving dish. Add wine to skillet, stirring quickly to deglaze pan. Bring to boil. Spoon sauce over oysters and serve.

- **1/2 pound medium fresh oysters**
- **All purpose flour**
- **3 tablespoons butter**
- **1 teaspoon dried basil, crumbled**
- **1/4 cup dry white wine**

HINT: A little vegetable oil added to butter prevents burning.

Tuna Curry

Preparation Time: 40 minutes

Yield: 4 servings

- $6^1/_2$ ounces canned tuna, drained
- $1^1/_2$ cups medium white sauce
- 2 tablespoons minced onion
- 2 tablespoons chopped green bell pepper
- 2 tablespoons chopped celery
- $^1/_2$ cup ripe olives, sliced
- 2 hard boiled eggs, chopped
- $1^1/_2$ teaspoons curry powder
- 3 cups hot cooked rice
- Pimiento strips

Heat tuna in prepared white sauce. Add onion, bell pepper and celery; cook until vegetables are semi-soft. Add olives and eggs. Blend in curry powder. Serve hot over rice. Garnish with pimiento, if desired.

Sea King Dinner

Preparation Time: 30 minutes

Yield: 8 servings
Preheat Oven: 350°

- $^3/_4$ cup butter (reserve $^1/_4$ cup)
- $^1/_2$ cup chopped green bell pepper
- $^1/_2$ cup chopped celery
- 1 cup chopped green onions
- $^2/_3$ cup all-purpose flour
- $^1/_2$ teaspoon garlic salt
- $^1/_2$ teaspoon salt
- $^1/_4$ teaspoon cayenne pepper
- $^1/_4$ teaspoon paprika
- 2 cups milk
- $10^1/_2$ ounces cream of mushroom soup
- 1 pound fresh or frozen crabmeat, drained
- 1 pound medium fresh shrimp, cooked, peeled and deveined
- 5 ounces canned sliced water chestnuts, drained
- 4 ounces canned sliced mushrooms, drained
- $^1/_2$ cup shredded cheddar cheese
- $^1/_2$ cup bread crumbs

In large skillet melt $^1/_2$ cup butter over medium heat. Add bell pepper, celery and onions; sauté until golden. Add flour, both salts, pepper and paprika. Stirring constantly, cook 2 minutes. Slowly add milk; stir until thickened. Add soup and blend. Add crabmeat, shrimp, water chestnuts and mushrooms; blend well. Pour into buttered 2 quart casserole dish.

Melt remaining butter; combine with cheese and bread crumbs. Sprinkle over casserole; bake 30 minutes. Remove and serve.

Techniques

Use a clean 1 pound coffee can to steam asparagus. Stand asparagus upright in can; place can in deep saucepan. Add water to saucepan to depth of 1 to 2 inches. Steam, covered, to desired tenderness.

To quick soak beans, boil 2 minutes; remove from heat. Cover and soak 1 hour.

To cook corn on grill, pull out excess silk and leave inner husks intact. Stand corn up in bucket; cover with water and let sit overnight. Shake excess water from corn; place on grill rack over hot coals and brown husks on all sides.

Freeze leftover chopped onion in air-tight plastic bags. Add to sauces or soups as needed.

To remove strong-smelling odors (such as onion and garlic) from hands, rub with celery salt, celery seeds or salt; then rinse.

Potatoes will bake faster if first soaked 20 minutes in salt water.

To peel tomato, drop into boiling water 1 minute. Remove peels easily with a sharp knife.

Easily remove membrane from oranges by dropping them, unpeeled, into boiling water. Remove pan from heat and let sit for 2 to 3 minutes. After peeling, easily scrape membrane off with sharp knife. Chill before serving.

Ripen fruit in plastic bag with ripe apple or other fruit. Ripe fruit exudes a natural gas which speeds up ripening process.

Reconstitute dry milk solids with beef, chicken or vegetable broth for more flavorful use in white sauces.

For lump-free gravy, place flour or cornstarch and water in jar with tight-fitting lid. Cover and shake well.

To reduce saltiness of gravy, add dash of brown sugar. Sugar won't sweeten or spoil flavor.

Freeze excess broth or stock in ice cube trays, 2 tablespoons per cube. Place in plastic bag and add to recipes as needed (two cubes equals 1/4 cup).

Place clean, folded dish towel between pan of hot cooked rice and lid. Let sit for 5 minutes. Rice will be fluffy and grains won't stick together.

ASPARAGUS SOUFFLÉ 

YIELD: 6 SERVINGS
PREHEAT OVEN: 350°

PREPARATION TIME: 30 MINUTES

- 1/4 CUP BUTTER OR MARGARINE
- 1/4 CUP ALL-PURPOSE FLOUR
- 1 CUP MILK
- 1/4 TEASPOON SALT
- 1/4 TEASPOON DRY MUSTARD
- 1/8 TEASPOON GROUND RED PEPPER
- 1 CUP GRATED CHEDDAR CHEESE
- 10 1/2 OUNCES CANNED ASPARAGUS, DRAINED AND CHOPPED
- 4 EGG YOLKS
- 4 EGG WHITES, ROOM TEMPERATURE

MELT BUTTER IN HEAVY SAUCEPAN; ADD FLOUR, STIRRING UNTIL SMOOTH. COOK 1 MINUTE. OVER MEDIUM HEAT, GRADUALLY ADD MILK; STIR UNTIL THICKENED AND BUBBLY. ADD SALT, MUSTARD, RED PEPPER AND CHEESE; COOK UNTIL CHEESE MELTS. STIR IN ASPARAGUS; REMOVE FROM HEAT. BEAT EGG YOLKS UNTIL THICK AND LEMON COLORED. GRADUALLY FOLD ONE-FOURTH OF HOT MIXTURE INTO YOLKS. ADD YOLK MIXTURE TO REMAINING SAUCE, STIRRING WELL. BEAT EGG WHITES UNTIL STIFF BUT NOT DRY. GENTLY FOLD INTO SAUCE MIXTURE. SPOON INTO BUTTERED SOUFFLÉ DISH; BAKE 45 MINUTES.

BLOWOUT BAKED BEANS

YIELD: 8 TO 10 SERVINGS
PREHEAT OVEN: 350°

PREPARATION TIME: 20 MINUTES

- 53 OUNCES CANNED PORK AND BEANS
- 1/2 CUP CHOPPED ONION
- 1/2 CUP BROWN SUGAR, FIRMLY PACKED
- 1 TABLESPOON CHILI POWDER
- 2 TABLESPOONS CATSUP
- 1/2 TABLESPOON PREPARED MUSTARD
- 1/2 TEASPOON GARLIC POWDER
- 6 OUNCES BEER (MAY BE FLAT)
- 1/2 TEASPOON TABASCO
- 2 STRIPS BACON

COMBINE ALL INGREDIENTS EXCEPT BACON IN 9 × 13 INCH BAKING DISH. BAKE APPROXIMATELY 1 1/2 HOURS. LAY BACON STRIPS ON TOP AND BAKE 30 MINUTES LONGER. MIXTURE SHOULD BE THICK.

MAY BE PREPARED OUTSIDE IN SLOW COOKER (UP TO 6 HOURS) WHILE BARBEQUEING.

CRAZY BEANS

PREPARATION TIME: 20 MINUTES

YIELD: 8 TO 10 SERVINGS
PREHEAT OVEN: 350°

- **8 SLICES BACON**
- **1 CUP CHOPPED ONION**
- **1/2 TO 1 CUP BROWN SUGAR, FIRMLY PACKED**
- **1/2 TEASPOON SALT**
- **1 TEASPOON DRY MUSTARD**
- **1/2 CUP VINEGAR**
- **30 OUNCES CANNED BUTTER BEANS**
- **15 OUNCES CANNED LIMA BEANS**
- **15 OUNCES CANNED KIDNEY BEANS**
- **30 OUNCES CANNED PORK AND BEANS, UNDRAINED**

FRY BACON; REMOVE, DRAIN AND CRUMBLE. ADD ONION, SUGAR, SALT, MUSTARD AND VINEGAR TO BACON DRIPPINGS. STIR; COVER AND SIMMER 20 MINUTES. DRAIN BUTTER, LIMA, AND KIDNEY BEANS; PLACE IN 2 1/2 QUART CASSEROLE. ADD PORK AND BEANS, BACON AND ONION MIXTURE; COMBINE WELL. COVER AND BAKE ONE HOUR.

GREEN BEANS ROMANOFF

PREPARATION TIME: 25 MINUTES

YIELD: 8 SERVINGS
PREHEAT OVEN: 400°

- **4 TABLESPOONS BUTTER (2 TABLESPOONS RESERVED)**
- **2 TABLESPOONS ALL-PURPOSE FLOUR**
- **1 TEASPOON SALT**
- **1/4 TEASPOON FRESHLY GROUND PEPPER**
- **1 TEASPOON SUGAR**
- **1 TABLESPOON THINLY SLICED GREEN ONIONS**
- **8 OUNCES SOUR CREAM**
- **1/2 POUND SWISS OR EMMENTHAL CHEESE, GRATED**
- **18 OUNCES FRENCH STYLE FROZEN GREEN BEANS, PARTIALLY COOKED**
- **3/4 CUP BREAD CRUMBS**

MELT 2 TABLESPOONS BUTTER IN SKILLET; ADD FLOUR, SALT, PEPPER, SUGAR AND GREEN ONIONS. REMOVE FROM HEAT; ADD SOUR CREAM AND CHEESE. FOLD IN GREEN BEANS. TURN INTO GREASED 2 1/2 QUART CASSEROLE. MELT REMAINING 2 TABLESPOONS BUTTER; MIX WITH BREAD CRUMBS AND SPRINKLE OVER BEANS. BAKE 20 MINUTES.

HINT: EMMENTHAL IS NOT AS STRINGY AS SWISS.

RED BEANS AND RICE

YIELD: 6 SERVINGS

PREPARATION TIME: 1 HOUR

SOAK BEANS OVERNIGHT. DRAIN AND RINSE WELL. IN LARGE DUTCH OVEN, PLACE BEANS, HAM HOCK, WATER, CELERY, ONION, BELL PEPPER AND SEASONINGS. BRING TO BOIL. COVER AND REDUCE HEAT. SIMMER 1 1/2 HOURS. REMOVE HAM HOCK. DISCARD FAT AND BONE; RETURN HAM MEAT TO PAN. CUT SAUSAGE DIAGONALLY INTO 3/4 INCH SLICES AND ADD TO BEANS. CONTINUE SIMMERING BEANS UNTIL TENDER, ABOUT 30 MINUTES. TO SERVE, MOUND 3/4 CUP COOKED RICE IN CENTER OF EACH PLATE. SPOON BEANS AND SAUSAGE AROUND RICE. SPRINKLE WITH PARSLEY AND GREEN ONIONS IF DESIRED.

*AVAILABLE AT SPECIALITY STORES.

1 POUND SMALL RED BEANS*
1 LARGE HAM HOCK
8 CUPS WATER
1/2 CUP FINELY CHOPPED CELERY
1 CUP FINELY CHOPPED ONION
1/2 CUP FINELY CHOPPED GREEN BELL PEPPER
1/2 TEASPOON FRESHLY GROUND PEPPER
1/2 TEASPOON THYME, CRUMBLED
1/2 TEASPOON OREGANO, CRUMBLED
1/2 TEASPOON GARLIC POWDER
1/2 TEASPOON CAYENNE PEPPER, OR TO TASTE
1/2 TEASPOON TABASCO, OR TO TASTE
1 POUND SMOKED SAUSAGE
4 1/2 CUPS HOT COOKED RICE
CHOPPED FRESH PARSLEY
CHOPPED GREEN ONIONS

BROCCOLI STUFFED TOMATOES

COLORFUL AND DELICIOUS DISH ESPECIALLY FESTIVE DURING THE HOLIDAYS.

YIELD: 6 SERVINGS
PREHEAT OVEN: 350°

PREPARATION TIME: 30 MINUTES

CUT OFF TOPS OF TOMATOES AND SCOOP OUT PULP, LEAVING SHELLS INTACT. SPRINKLE CAVITIES WITH SALT AND PEPPER. INVERT ON WIRE RACK; DRAIN 30 MINUTES. COOK BROCCOLI ACCORDING TO PACKAGE DIRECTIONS, OMITTING SALT; DRAIN WELL. COMBINE BROCCOLI, SWISS CHEESE, MAYONNAISE AND ONION. STUFF TOMATOES WITH BROCCOLI MIXTURE; SPRINKLE WITH PARMESAN CHEESE. BAKE 30 MINUTES, GARNISHING WITH BROCCOLI FLOWERETES DURING LAST 5 MINUTES.

6 MEDIUM TOMATOES
SALT AND FRESHLY GROUND PEPPER, TO TASTE
10 OUNCES FROZEN CHOPPED BROCCOLI
1 CUP SHREDDED SWISS CHEESE
1/2 CUP MAYONNAISE
2 TABLESPOONS CHOPPED ONION
2 TABLESPOONS GRATED PARMESAN CHEESE
BROCCOLI FLOWERETS

BROCCOLI WITH BACON AND WALNUTS

THE CRISPNESS OF THE WALNUTS IS A NICE SURPRISE IN THIS SIMPLE BUT DELICIOUS DISH.

PREPARATION TIME: 20 MINUTES *YIELD: 4 SERVINGS*

- **1 POUND BROCCOLI, RINSED, TRIMMED AND CUT INTO PIECES**
- **6 SLICES BACON, DICED**
- **1/4 CUP CHOPPED GREEN ONIONS**
- **3/4 CUP WALNUTS, COARSELY CHOPPED**

STEAM BROCCOLI UNTIL JUST TENDER. MEANWHILE IN SKILLET, COOK BACON UNTIL CRISP; DRAIN. ADD GREEN ONIONS TO SKILLET; COOK 2 MINUTES. ADD WALNUTS; COOK, STIRRING FREQUENTLY, 5 MINUTES OR UNTIL GOLDEN. STIR IN BACON AND BROCCOLI; TOSS AND HEAT THROUGH.

GLAZED BRUSSELS SPROUTS AND ONIONS

PREPARATION TIME: 45 MINUTES *YIELD: 6 SERVINGS*

- **3 CUPS TRIMMED, FRESH BRUSSELS SPROUTS**
- **3 CUPS SMALL WHITE PEELED ONIONS**
- **3 TABLESPOONS BUTTER**
- **2 TEASPOONS SUGAR**
- **1/2 TEASPOON SALT**

CUT DEEP CROSS IN STEM ENDS OF BRUSSELS SPROUTS. PLACE SPROUTS IN SAUCEPAN OF BOILING SALTED WATER. COVER AND COOK OVER MEDIUM HEAT 15 MINUTES; DRAIN. IN SKILLET COVER ONIONS WITH WATER; ADD BUTTER AND SUGAR. BRING TO BOIL; ADD SALT AND COOK, STIRRING OCCASIONALLY, 18 MINUTES OR UNTIL WATER HAS EVAPORATED. ADD SPROUTS; COOK OVER MODERATE HEAT 5 MINUTES, STIRRING UNTIL VEGETABLES ARE GLAZED AND GOLDEN. TRANSFER TO HEATED PLATTER.

HINT: THE KEY TO APPEALING BRUSSELS SPROUTS IS NOT TO OVERCOOK THEM.

CARROTS WITH ARTICHOKES

YIELD: 6 SERVINGS

PREPARATION TIME: 25 MINUTES

- 9 OUNCES FROZEN ARTICHOKE HEARTS
- 1½ POUNDS CARROTS, CUT INTO 1½ INCH PIECES
- 1½ TABLESPOONS BUTTER
- 1 TABLESPOON EXTRA VIRGIN OLIVE OIL
- ½ POUND FRESH MUSHROOMS, QUARTERED
- SALT AND FRESHLY GROUND PEPPER, TO TASTE
- 2 TABLESPOONS CHOPPED GREEN ONIONS
- ½ CUP BEEF STOCK
- 2 TABLSEPOONS MINCED FRESH PARSLEY

COOK ARTICHOKES ACCORDING TO PACKAGE DIRECTIONS, OMITTING SALT. COOK CARROTS UNTIL JUST TENDER. DRAIN ARTICHOKES AND CARROTS; SET ASIDE. MELT BUTTER IN SKILLET. ADD OLIVE OIL; HEAT UNTIL HAZE FORMS. ADD MUSHROOMS; SAUTÉ UNTIL LIGHTLY BROWNED. ADD SALT AND PEPPER. STIR IN GREEN ONIONS AND ARTICHOKE HEARTS; TOSS 2 TO 3 MINUTES OVER MEDIUM HEAT. ADD CARROTS AND BEEF STOCK. COVER; COOK SLOWLY 5 MINUTES. TRANSFER TO SERVING DISH; SPRINKLE WITH PARSLEY.

HINT: ADD 1 TABLESPOON SUGAR PER QUART OF COOKING WATER TO ADD SWEETNESS TO CARROTS.

DEVILED CARROTS

YIELD: 8 SERVINGS

PREPARATION TIME: 30 MINUTES

- 2 POUNDS CARROTS, PEELED AND CUT INTO 1 INCH PIECES
- ½ CUP BUTTER, MELTED
- 3 TABLESPOONS WHITE WINE
- 2 TABLESPOONS SUGAR
- 2 TABLESPOONS BROWN SUGAR, FIRMLY PACKED
- 2 TEASPOONS DRY MUSTARD
- ¼ TEASPOON SALT
- 6 DROPS TABASCO
- 1 TABLESPOON CHOPPED FRESH PARSLEY

SAUTÉ CARROTS IN BUTTER 3 MINUTES; ADD WHITE WINE AND SIMMER 5 MINUTES. ADD SUGARS, MUSTARD, SALT AND TABASCO; COVER AND SIMMER ADDITIONAL 8 TO 10 MINUTES OR UNTIL CARROTS ARE TENDER-CRISP. TRANSFER TO SERVING DISH AND SPRINKLE WITH PARSLEY.

Eggplant Fritters

Preparation Time: 25 minutes — *Yield: 4 to 6 servings*

- 1 cup all-purpose flour
- 1 teaspoon baking powder
- 1/2 teaspoon sugar
- 1/4 teaspoon salt
- 2 cups diced cooked eggplant, drained and mashed
- 1 egg, beaten well
- 3 cups vegetable oil
- 1/2 cup Parmesan cheese

In mixing bowl sift flour, baking powder, sugar and salt. Combine eggplant and egg; add to dry ingredients, mixing thoroughly. Heat oil in 2 quart saucepan or deep fryer to 350°. Drop batter by teaspoons into hot oil. Fry about 3 minutes or until golden brown. Remove with slotted spoon and drain; sprinkle with Parmesan cheese.

HINT: When selecting eggplant look for uniform dark purple or purple-black skin. Skin should be glossy and free from dark spots.

Fresh Mushroom Cutlets with Morney Sauce

Preparation Time: 30 minutes — *Yield: 4 to 6 servings*

- 2 eggs
- 1/2 teaspoon seasoned salt
- 1 cup whole mushrooms, minced
- 2 tablespoons finely chopped green onions
- 1/2 cup bread crumbs
- 3/4 cup grated mild Cheddar cheese
- 1/4 cup butter, melted
- Parmesan cheese

In medium bowl beat eggs and seasoned salt; add mushrooms and green onions. Fold in bread crumbs and cheese until mixed but not mushy. Divide into 8 patties 3/4 inch thick, pressing into shape between sheets of wax paper. Sauté in butter until crispy. Prepare Morney Sauce and spoon over cutlets; sprinkle with Parmesan cheese. Serve immediately. May also be served as an appetizer.

Morney Sauce:

- 2 tablespoons butter
- 2 tablespoons all-purpose flour
- 1 cup milk
- 1/4 cup grated Swiss cheese
- 1/4 teaspoon salt
- 1/4 teaspoon dry mustard
- Freshly ground pepper, to taste

In saucepan melt butter over low heat; stir in flour until blended. Gradually add milk, stirring constantly until smooth. Add Swiss cheese, salt, mustard and pepper. Stir until cheese is melted.

SPECTACULAR SAUTÉED MUSHROOMS

YIELD: 4 SERVINGS

PREPARATION TIME: 10 MINUTES

MELT BUTTER IN LARGE SKILLET AND SAUTÉ GREEN ONIONS UNTIL SOFT. STIR IN REMAINING INGREDIENTS AND COOK, UNCOVERED, OVER LOW HEAT 20 MINUTES OR UNTIL MUSHROOMS ARE TENDER.

1/4 CUP BUTTER OR MARGARINE
3 GREEN ONIONS, CHOPPED
1 POUND FRESH MUSHROOMS
1/4 CUP DRY WHITE WINE
1/4 TEASPOON SALT
1/4 TEASPOON FRESHLY GROUND PEPPER
1/8 TEASPOON GARLIC POWDER
2 TEASPOONS WORCESTERSHIRE SAUCE

HINT: WHEN SHOPPING FOR MUSHROOMS, CHOOSE ONLY OFF WHITE OR CREAM-COLORED MUSHROOMS WITH SMOOTH SURFACE AND TIGHTLY CLOSED CAPS.

OKRA AND TOMATOES

YIELD: 4 TO 6 SERVINGS

PREPARATION TIME: 25 MINUTES

CUT OKRA CROSSWISE IN 1/2 INCH PIECES. IN SAUCEPAN, COMBINE OKRA WITH REMAINING INGREDIENTS. COVER AND COOK OVER LOW HEAT, STIRRING OCCASIONALLY, 10 TO 15 MINUTES OR UNTIL TENDER.

1 POUND FRESH OR FROZEN OKRA (THAWED IF FROZEN)
1 CUP CHOPPED ONION
2 1/2 CUPS PEELED, CUBED TOMATOES
2 TABLESPOONS BUTTER
2 TEASPOONS SALT
FRESHLY GROUND PEPPER, TO TASTE

HINT: BEST WHEN PREPARED WITH GARDEN-FRESH VEGETABLES.

BEST DAMN ONION RINGS EVER!

THE NAME SAYS IT ALL!

PREPARATION TIME: 1 HOUR

YIELD: 6 SERVINGS
PREHEAT OVEN: 200°

12 OUNCES BEER
1 1/2 CUPS ALL-PURPOSE FLOUR
1/4 TEASPOON GARLIC POWDER
1/2 TEASPOON SEASONED SALT
3 TO 4 CUPS VEGETABLE OIL
3 VERY LARGE ONIONS, PEELED, CUT INTO 1/4 INCH SLICES AND SEPARATED INTO RINGS

COMBINE BEER, FLOUR, GARLIC POWDER AND SEASONED SALT. COVER; SET ASIDE AT ROOM TEMPERATURE THREE HOURS. TEN MINUTES BEFORE PREPARATION, PREHEAT OVEN; LINE JELLYROLL PAN WITH PAPER TOWELS. IN ELECTRIC SKILLET AT 375°, HEAT 2 INCHES OIL. USING TONGS, DIP A FEW ONION RINGS INTO BATTER. LET EXCESS BATTER DRIP OFF; CAREFULLY PLACE RINGS IN HOT OIL. (DO NOT ADD TOO MANY AT ONE TIME.) FRY RINGS, TURNING UNTIL LIGHTLY BROWNED. TRANSFER TO JELLYROLL PAN AND PLACE IN OVEN TO KEEP WARM UNTIL ALL HAVE BEEN FRIED. REPEAT WITH REMAINING RINGS.

GARLIC WINTER SQUASH

THE GARLIC IS TRANSFORMED TO A SWEET, DELICATE FLAVOR WHEN COVERED AND COOKED OVER SLOW HEAT.

PREPARATION TIME: 40 MINUTES

YIELD: 4 TO 6 SERVINGS

3 TABLESPOONS UNSALTED BUTTER (RESERVE 2 TABLESPOONS)
2 TABLESPOONS WHITE WINE
10 CLOVES GARLIC, PEELED
1 1/4 POUNDS BUTTERNUT OR OTHER WINTER SQUASH, PEELED, SEEDED AND DICED
SALT AND FRESHLY GROUND PEPPER, TO TASTE
3 TABLESPOONS CHOPPED FRESH PARSLEY

MELT 1 TABLESPOON BUTTER IN HEAVY SKILLET OVER LOW HEAT. ADD WINE AND GARLIC. COVER AND COOK 20 MINUTES, STIRRING OCCASIONALLY. GARLIC WILL BROWN SLIGHTLY BUT SHOULD NOT BURN. WHEN GARLIC IS SOFT, MASH IT; STIR IN REMAINING 2 TABLESPOONS BUTTER AND SQUASH. TOSS THOROUGHLY TO COAT. COVER AND COOK, STIRRING OCCASIONALLY, ABOUT 20 MINUTES OR UNTIL SQUASH IS TENDER. ADD SALT AND PEPPER; SPRINKLE WITH PARSLEY.

LOUISIANA SPANKED POTATOES 

TURNS PLAIN BASIC POTATOES INTO SHOWY SIDE DISH.

YIELD: 8 SERVINGS
PREHEAT OVEN: 400°
PREPARATION TIME: 25 MINUTES

RUB POTATOES WITH OIL AND BAKE UNTIL TENDER. REMOVE FROM OVEN AND CUT IN HALF. WHILE HOT, SCOOP PULP INTO MIXING BOWL. RESERVE POTATO SHELLS. ADD BUTTER AND CREAM; BEAT WELL. ADD CHEESE, GREEN ONIONS, BELL PEPPER, SALT AND CAYENNE PEPPER. COMBINE WELL. SPOON INTO RESERVED POTATO SHELLS. SPRINKLE WITH GRATED CHEESE. MAY BE PREPARED ONE DAY AHEAD AND REFRIGERATED AT THIS POINT. BRING TO ROOM TEMPERATURE. BAKE IN 325° OVEN 20 MINUTES OR UNTIL HEATED THROUGH.

4 LARGE BAKING POTATOES (APPROXIMATELY 3/4 POUND EACH)
VEGETABLE OIL
1/4 CUP BUTTER
1/4 TO 1/2 CUP HEAVY CREAM
1/2 CUP GRATED COLBY CHEESE
1/3 CUP CHOPPED GREEN ONIONS
1/3 CUP CHOPPED GREEN BELL PEPPER
1/2 TEASPOON SALT
1/4 TO 1/2 TEASPOON CAYENNE PEPPER
GRATED CHEESE

TWICE-BAKED SWEET POTATOES

THE BEST THING ABOUT SWEET POTATOES IS THEIR FLAVOR AND THIS RECIPE MAKES THEM EVEN BETTER.

YIELD: 6 SERVINGS
PREHEAT OVEN: 425°
PREPARATION TIME: 30 MINUTES

RUB EACH POTATO WITH SOFTENED BUTTER. BAKE 20 MINUTES. PRICK WITH FORK; CONTINUE BAKING 25 MINUTES. CUT OFF TOP 1/3 OF EACH POTATO. SCRAPE PULP FROM TOPS INTO MIXING BOWL. SCOOP OUT CENTER OF EACH POTATO, LEAVING 1/4 INCH IN SKIN. MASH PULP; ADD BUTTER, CREAM, HONEY, RUM, CARDAMOM AND SALT. BEAT UNTIL FLUFFY. STUFF POTATO SHELLS WITH MIXTURE. SPRINKLE CHOPPED WALNUTS ON TOP AND RETURN TO OVEN. BAKE IN 350° OVEN 20 TO 25 MINUTES.

6 SWEET POTATOES (1/2 POUND EACH)
SOFTENED BUTTER
1/4 CUP BUTTER
1/4 CUP HEAVY CREAM
2 TABLESPOONS HONEY
2 TABLESPOONS DARK RUM
1/2 TABLESPOON GROUND CARDAMOM
1/2 TABLESPOON SALT
1/2 CUP CHOPPED BLACK WALNUTS

SPINACH AND ARTICHOKE CASSEROLE

PREPARATION TIME: 20 MINUTES

YIELD: 8 TO 10 SERVINGS
PREHEAT OVEN: 350°

3/4 CUP BUTTER (RESERVE 1/4 CUP)
8 OUNCES CREAM CHEESE
30 OUNCES COOKED SPINACH, DRAINED WELL
8 OUNCES CANNED SLICED WATER CHESTNUTS, DRAINED
DASH WORCESTERSHIRE SAUCE
DASH TABASCO
SALT AND FRESHLY GROUND PEPPER, TO TASTE
9 OUNCES FROZEN ARTICHOKE HEARTS, THAWED AND DRAINED
3/4 CUP HERBED BREAD CRUMBS

MELT 1/2 CUP BUTTER AND CREAM CHEESE IN LARGE SAUCEPAN. COMBINE WITH SPINACH, WATER CHESTNUTS, WORCESTERSHIRE AND TABASCO. ADD SALT AND PEPPER. IN 9×13 INCH BUTTERED CASSEROLE SPREAD HALF OF SPINACH MIXTURE. LAYER ARTICHOKES ON TOP; SPREAD WITH REMAINING SPINACH MIXTURE. MELT RESERVED BUTTER; TOSS WITH BREAD CRUMBS. SPRINKLE CRUMB MIXTURE OVER TOP OF CASSEROLE; BAKE 30 MINUTES.

HINT: CAN BE PREPARED AHEAD AND REFRIGERATED. BRING TO ROOM TEMPERATURE AND BAKE AS DIRECTED.

SPINACH WITH PINE NUTS AND ALMONDS

PREPARATION TIME: 15 MINUTES

YIELD: 4 SERVINGS

1/4 CUP EXTRA VIRGIN OLIVE OIL
1 LARGE CLOVE GARLIC, PEELED AND HALVED LENGTHWISE
1/4 CUP PINE NUTS
1/4 CUP BLANCHED SLIVERED ALMONDS
1 POUND FRESH COOKED SPINACH, WELL DRAINED AND FINELY CHOPPED
1/4 CUP FINELY DICED SERRANO HAM OR 1 OUNCE PROSCIUTTO HAM
1/2 TEASPOON SALT

IN HEAVY 10 OR 12 INCH SKILLET, HEAT OLIVE OIL UNTIL LIGHT HAZE FORMS. ADD GARLIC AND COOK 1 TO 2 MINUTES, STIRRING CONSTANTLY. REMOVE GARLIC WITH SLOTTED SPOON AND DISCARD. ADD PINE NUTS AND ALMONDS; COOK 2 TO 3 MINUTES, UNTIL SLIGHTLY BROWN. ADD SPINACH, HAM AND SALT; TOSS TOGETHER UNTIL INGREDIENTS ARE THOROUGHLY MIXED AND HEATED THROUGH. ADJUST SEASONING; SERVE IMMEDIATELY.

HINT: 20 OUNCES FROZEN CHOPPED SPINACH, THAWED AND WELL DRAINED MAY BE SUBSTITUTED FOR FRESH SPINACH.

FRIED TOMATOES WITH BASIL

VERY GOOD WITH EGGS FOR BREAKFAST OR WITH BROILED FISH OR CHICKEN.

YIELD: 4 TO 6 SERVINGS

PREPARATION TIME: 15 MINUTES

- **1 TABLESPOON BUTTER**
- **1 TABLESPOON EXTRA VIRGIN OLIVE OIL**
- **4 MEDIUM FIRM RIPE TOMATOES, SLICED THICKLY**
- **3/4 CUP GRATED CHEDDAR OR SWISS CHEESE**
- **1/4 CUP CHOPPED FRESH BASIL**

IN LARGE SKILLET MELT BUTTER OVER MEDIUM HEAT AND ADD OLIVE OIL. ADD TOMATO SLICES; FRY ABOUT 1 MINUTE. TURN; SPRINKLE WITH CHEESE AND BASIL. COVER AND FRY UNTIL CHEESE MELTS, ABOUT 1 MINUTE.

VEGETABLE KA-BOBS

FANTASTIC ON THOSE HOT SUMMER DAYS WHEN COOKING ON GRILL.

YIELD: 6 SERVINGS

PREPARATION TIME: 15 MINUTES

- **2 MEDIUM ZUCCHINI, CUT INTO 2 INCH PIECES**
- **2 MEDIUM YELLOW SQUASH, CUT INTO 2 INCH PIECES**
- **6 SMALL COOKED AND UNPEELED RED POTATOES**
- **6 SMALL BROCCOLI FLOWERETS**
- **6 PEARL ONIONS**
- **6 CHERRY TOMATOES**
- **6 LARGE MUSHROOMS**
- **PARMESAN CHEESE**

PREPARE MARINADE; ADD ALL VEGETABLES, EXCEPT MUSHROOMS AND TOMATOES, AND MARINATE 2 HOURS OR MORE.

ALTERNATE VEGETABLES ON SKEWERS. COOK OVER COALS 10 MINUTES, TURNING ONCE. SERVE WITH ADDITIONAL SAUCE AND SPRINKLE WITH PARMESAN CHEESE.

MARINADE:

- **1 1/3 CUPS WHITE WINE VINEGAR**
- **2/3 CUP VEGETABLE OIL**
- **3 TABLESPOONS SUGAR**
- **2 TEASPOONS SALT**
- **2 TEASPOONS DRIED BASIL, CRUMBLED**

COMBINE ALL INGREDIENTS.

JULIENNE VEGETABLES WITH TARRAGON BUTTER

THE COMBINATION OF STEAMED VEGETABLES AND THE PUNGENT TASTE OF TARRAGON TRULY ENHANCES THIS DISH.

PREPARATION TIME: 30 MINUTES — *YIELD: 6 SERVINGS*

1/2 POUND CARROTS, CUT INTO JULIENNE STRIPS
1/2 POUND PARSNIPS, CUT INTO JULIENNE STRIPS
1/2 POUND ZUCCHINI, CUT INTO JULIENNE STRIPS
1/3 CUP BUTTER
2 TABLESPOONS CHOPPED FRESH TARRAGON
SALT AND FRESHLY GROUND PEPPER, TO TASTE

COVER AND STEAM CARROTS AND PARSNIPS OVER BOILING SALTED WATER 5 MINUTES. ADD ZUCCHINI; STEAM 2 MORE MINUTES. IN LARGE SKILLET, MELT BUTTER AND ADD VEGETABLES. STIR IN TARRAGON AND MIX THOROUGHLY. TRANSFER TO HEATED SERVING DISH AND SEASON WITH SALT AND PEPPER.

VARIATION: YELLOW SQUASH MAY BE SUBSTITUTED FOR PARSNIPS. ADD TO STEAMER WITH ZUCCHINI.

STEAMED VEGETABLES WITH MUSTARD SAUCE

THIS RECIPE IS NOT ELABORATE BUT FLAVORS, TEXTURES AND COLOR PERK UP AN OTHERWISE ORDINARY DISH.

PREPARATION TIME: 30 MINUTES — *YIELD: 4 TO 6 SERVINGS*

1 CUP PEELED AND SLICED CARROT
1 CUP COARSELY CHOPPED YELLOW SQUASH
1 CUP CAULIFLOWERETS
1 CUP FRESH GREEN BEANS, CUT INTO 2 INCH PIECES
1 TABLESPOON SLICED FRESH RED CHILE PEPPER
1 TABLESPOON BUTTER
2 TABLESPOONS ALL-PURPOSE FLOUR
1 CUP BEEF BROTH
1 TEASPOON DIJON MUSTARD
1/4 TEASPOON SALT
2 TABLESPOONS SESAME SEEDS
1/4 CUP GRATED PARMESAN CHEESE

STEAM CARROT, SQUASH, CAULIFLOWERETS, BEANS AND PEPPER 7 MINUTES OR UNTIL JUST TENDER. SPOON VEGETABLES INTO HEATED SERVING DISH. MEANWHILE, MELT BUTTER IN HEAVY SAUCEPAN OVER LOW HEAT; ADD FLOUR, STIRRING UNTIL SMOOTH. ADD BROTH AND COOK 1 MINUTE, STIRRING UNTIL THICKENED. ADD MUSTARD, SALT, AND SESAME SEEDS; SIMMER 1 MINUTE, STIRRING CONSTANTLY. POUR OVER VEGETABLES; SPRINKLE WITH CHEESE.

GREEN PEPPERCORN SAUCE

YIELD: 1 CUP

PREPARATION TIME: 30 MINUTES

- **2 TABLESPOONS GREEN PEPPERCORNS, DRAINED AND RINSED (DIVIDED)**
- **1 TABLESPOON CHOPPED SHALLOTS**
- **2 TABLESPOONS BUTTER, MELTED**
- **3 TABLESPOONS BRANDY**
- **1 PINT HEAVY CREAM**
- **SALT AND WHITE PEPPER, TO TASTE**

COARSELY MASH 1 TABLESPOON PEPPERCORNS. SET ASIDE. IN MEDIUM SKILLET SAUTÉ SHALLOTS IN BUTTER. ADD BRANDY; IGNITE. WHEN FLAMES SUBSIDE, ADD ALL PEPPERCORNS AND CREAM TO SKILLET. REDUCE LIQUID BY TWO-THIRDS OR UNTIL SAUCE COATS WOODEN SPOON. ADD SALT AND PEPPER. SERVE WITH DUCK, CHICKEN OR BEEF.

EXECUTIVE CHEF LOUIS KRUPKA
DOUBLETREE HOTEL, TULSA

BEURRE BLANC 

YIELD: 1 CUP

PREPARATION TIME: 30 MINUTES

- **1/4 CUP SLICED SHALLOTS**
- **1 CUP DRY WHITE WINE**
- **1/4 CUP HEAVY CREAM**
- **2 CUPS COLD UNSALTED BUTTER, CUT INTO 1 INCH PIECES**
- **TABASCO, TO TASTE**
- **SALT AND WHITE PEPPER, TO TASTE**
- **LEMON JUICE, TO TASTE**

IN HEAVY STAINLESS STEEL OR ENAMELED SAUCEPAN, COMBINE SHALLOTS AND WINE; REDUCE TO 2 TABLESPOONS. DISCARD SHALLOTS. ADD CREAM; REDUCE TO 2 TABLESPOONS. WHISK IN BUTTER, ONE PIECE AT A TIME OVER LOW HEAT. ADD EACH PIECE BEFORE PREVIOUS ONE IS COMPLETELY MELTED. LIFT PAN OCCASIONALLY TO COOL MIXTURE SO THAT IT DOES NOT GET HOT ENOUGH TO LIQUIFY. ADD TABASCO, SALT, PEPPER AND LEMON JUICE. SERVE IMMEDIATELY.

VARIATION I:

- **2 TABLESPOONS SLICED SHALLOTS**
- **1/2 CUP WHITE WINE VINEGAR**
- **1/2 CUP COLD UNSALTED BUTTER, CUT INTO 1 INCH PIECES**
- **SALT AND PEPPER, TO TASTE**

FOLLOW DIRECTIONS AS ABOVE OMITTING INSTRUCTIONS FOR CREAM. MAKES 2/3 CUP.

HINT: ADD 1 TABLESPOON MIXED MINCED HERBS SUCH AS PARSLEY, CHIVES, TARRAGON, FINES HERBES OR BASIL FOR BEURRE BLANC AUX HERBS.

VEGETABLE CREAM SAUCE

PREPARATION TIME: 30 MINUTES — *YIELD: 1 CUP*

1 SMALL LEEK
1 TABLESPOON WHITE WINE VINEGAR
1/4 CUP DRY VERMOUTH
1 TABLESPOON MINCED SHALLOTS
1 CLOVE GARLIC, MINCED
6 LARGE MUSHROOM CAPS, CUT IN OVALS AND JULIENNED
SALT AND WHITE PEPPER, TO TASTE
1 CUP WHIPPING CREAM
1 CARROT, PEELED AND CUT INTO JULIENNE STRIPS
1/2 SMALL RIB CELERY, CUT INTO JULIENNE STRIPS

CUT OFF TOP AND ROOT OF LEEK; DISCARD. SLIT REMAINING 3 INCHES LENGTHWISE THROUGH CENTER. RINSE IN COLD WATER TO REMOVE GRIT. CUT INTO THIN STRIPS ABOUT 1 1/2 INCHES LONG. COMBINE VINEGAR, VERMOUTH, SHALLOTS AND GARLIC IN SAUCEPAN AND SIMMER. REDUCE TO 2 TABLESPOONS, STIRRING OFTEN. ADD MUSHROOMS, SALT AND PEPPER; BRING TO BOIL. BLEND IN CREAM; SIMMER, STIRRING OCCASIONALLY, UNTIL SAUCE THICKENS, ABOUT 6 MINUTES. KEEP WARM. BOIL CARROT, LEEK AND CELERY 3 MINUTES; DRAIN WELL. ADD TO SAUCE; HEAT THROUGH. SERVE WITH FISH, SHELLFISH, CHICKEN, EGGS OR FRESH PASTA.

DELICATE CURRY SAUCE

PREPARATION TIME: 20 MINUTES — *YIELD: 3/4 CUP*

4 TABLESPOONS UNSALTED BUTTER (RESERVE 3 TABLESPOONS, CHILLED)
2 1/2 TABLESPOONS FINELY MINCED SHALLOTS
1/4 CUP DRY WHITE WINE
2/3 CUP WHIPPING CREAM
3/4 TEASPOON CURRY POWDER
1 TEASPOON MINCED CHIVES
SALT AND WHITE PEPPER, TO TASTE

MELT 1 TABLESPOON BUTTER IN SAUCEPAN. ADD SHALLOTS; COOK UNTIL TRANSLUCENT, STIRRING OCCASIONALLY. ADD WINE; COOK UNTIL REDUCED TO 2 TABLESPOONS. ADD CREAM AND CURRY POWDER. COOK, STIRRING FREQUENTLY, UNTIL SAUCE THICKENS AND COATS BACK OF SPOON. ADD CHIVES, SALT AND PEPPER; BLEND WELL. REDUCE HEAT AND, WHISKING CONSTANTLY, ADD RESERVED BUTTER 1 TABLESPOON AT A TIME. SERVE IMMEDIATELY WITH CHICKEN, PASTA, CAULIFLOWER, EGGS OR SEAFOOD.

Spiced Cherries In Vinegar

Delectable and so simple.

Yield: 4 cups

Preparation Time: 15 minutes

- 2 **cups white wine vinegar**
- 2 **cups sugar**
- 1 **teaspoon whole allspice, cracked**
- 4 **cloves**
- 2 **cinnamon sticks, broken into pieces**
- 1 **2 inch piece peeled fresh ginger root**
- 4 **cups sour cherries (available frozen)**

Combine vinegar, sugar, allspice, cloves, cinnamon sticks and ginger root in saucepan. Bring to boil. Lower heat; simmer 15 minutes. Stand in cool, dark place overnight, loosely covered. In sterilized canning jars, pack cherries, leaving at least 1/2 inch space at top. Strain vinegar mixture into saucepan; bring to rolling boil. Spoon over cherries, covering completely. Wipe rims; place lids on jars and screw bands on tightly. Place in canner; add hot water to cover 2 inches over tops of jars. Bring to full boil. Cover; process 10 minutes. Remove to towel; cool completely. Test seal by pressing lid with fingertip. If lid does not give, it has sealed properly. Screw bands tightly; store in cool, dark place. Serve with roast pork or game.

Plum Basting Sauce

Yield: 2 cups

Preparation Time: 10 minutes

- 16 **ounces canned, pitted, purple plums, in syrup**
- 1/4 **cup fresh lemon juice**
- 2 **tablespoons dry sherry**
- 3 **tablespoons brown sugar, firmly packed**
- 2 **tablespoons melted butter**
- 1 **tablespoon grated onion**
- 1/4 **teaspoon ground ginger**
- 2 **teaspoons Dijon mustard**
- 1/2 **teaspoon cinnamon**
- **Salt, to taste**

Purée plums with syrup in food processor or blender. In non-aluminum pan combine purée with remaining ingredients. Bring to boil and simmer 10 minutes, stirring constantly. Excellent with chicken, Cornish hens or duck.

BOURBON MARINADE

PREPARATION TIME: 10 MINUTES

YIELD: 1 CUP

- 1/3 CUP BOURBON
- 1/4 CUP SOY SAUCE
- 1/4 CUP LIGHT BROWN SUGAR, FIRMLY PACKED
- 1/2 CUP CHOPPED GREEN ONIONS
- 3 TABLESPOONS DIJON MUSTARD
- 1 TEASPOON WORCESTERSHIRE SAUCE
- 4 DASHES TABASCO

COMBINE ALL INGREDIENTS IN NON-METAL BOWL AND STIR TO MIX. USE TO MARINATE PORK, BEEF OR CHICKEN IN REFRIGERATOR OVERNIGHT, AND AS BASTING MARINADE WHILE GRILLING.

ZESTY GINGER MARINADE

PREPARATION TIME: 30 MINUTES

YIELD: 1 1/2 CUPS

- 3 TABLESPOONS HONEY
- 6 TABLESPOONS PEELED, GRATED FRESH GINGER ROOT
- 3 CLOVES GARLIC, CRUSHED
- 1 CUP SOY SAUCE
- 6 TABLESPOONS FRESH LIME JUICE

COMBINE HONEY, GINGER, GARLIC, SOY SAUCE AND LIME JUICE. USE TO MARINATE MEAT OR FOWL IN REFRIGERATOR OVERNIGHT.

DRAINED CRUSHED PINEAPPLE MAY BE ADDED TO MARINADE.

HERBED MAYONNAISE

PREPARATION TIME: 10 MINUTES

YIELD: 1 PINT

- 2 CUPS BEST QUALITY MAYONNAISE
- 3 EGG YOLKS
- 2 TABLESPOONS EXTRA VIRGIN OLIVE OIL
- 1 TABLESPOON FRESH LEMON JUICE
- 1 1/2 TEASPOONS FINES HERBES, CRUMBLED
- 1/2 TEASPOON GARLIC POWDER

IN BOWL COMBINE MAYONNAISE, YOLKS, OIL, LEMON JUICE, FINES HERBES AND GARLIC POWDER. BEAT WITH MIXER UNTIL SMOOTH. SERVE AS SPREAD ON SANDWICHES OR AS SAUCE FOR VEGETABLES, MEATS, POULTRY OR FISH.

HINT: TO USE AS SAUCE, ADD 2 TABLESPOONS WATER TO THIN SLIGHTLY.

Spicy Apple Holiday Relish

Has the taste and smell of holiday cooking!

Yield: 2 cups

Preparation Time: 20 to 30 minutes

1½ cups cider vinegar
¾ cup brown sugar, firmly packed
1 tablespoon peeled, minced fresh ginger root
¼ teaspoon nutmeg
1 2 inch strip lemon rind
1 3 inch cinnamon stick, broken
6 whole allspice
3 whole cloves
1 large clove garlic, sliced
4 cups peeled, cored, chopped tart apples (about 1½ pounds)
1¼ cups chopped onion
¼ cup coarsely chopped raisins
Fresh lemon juice, to taste
Salt and cayenne pepper, to taste

In non-aluminum pan, combine vinegar, brown sugar, ginger root, nutmeg and lemon rind. Place cinnamon, allspice, cloves and garlic in cheesecloth bag; add to pan. Bring mixture to boil; simmer 5 minutes. Add apples and onion; simmer, stirring occasionally, 20 minutes more. Discard spice bag and lemon rind; stir in raisins and season with lemon juice, salt and cayenne pepper. Spoon relish into non-metal bowl and cool. Cover and chill overnight. May be stored in refrigerator up to 1 week.

Harvest Relish

Lovely at Thanksgiving!

Yield: 4 cups

Preparation Time: 30 minutes

1½ cups cider vinegar
½ cup sugar
1 tablespoon salt
1 teaspoon mustard seed
¼ teaspoon red pepper flakes
2 cloves
1 2 inch cinnamon stick
2 cups peeled, chopped butternut squash
1 cup chopped onion
¼ cup chopped celery
1 cup diced red bell pepper

In non-aluminum pan, combine vinegar, sugar, salt, mustard seed, pepper flakes, cloves and cinnamon stick. Bring to boil, stirring until sugar is dissolved; simmer 5 minutes. Add remaining ingredients; heat to boil. Lower heat and simmer 10 minutes longer. Spoon into non-metal bowl and cool. Cover and refrigerate overnight. May be stored in refrigerator up to 1 week.

Framboise Sorbet

Preparation Time: 20 minutes | *Yield: 12 servings*

- 3 cups water
- $^3/_4$ cup sugar
- 1 750 ml. bottle red wine (such as Zinfandel)
- $1^1/_4$ pounds fresh raspberries (or 20 ounces unsweetened frozen raspberries, thawed)
- $^1/_4$ cup white grape juice
- $^1/_4$ cup fresh lemon juice
- 3 tablespoons Framboise (raspberry liqueur)
- Additional sugar or fresh lemon juice

In saucepan, combine water and sugar. Simmer until sugar dissolves. Bring to boil; cook 5 minutes. Add wine and raspberries; simmer until raspberries are soft, about 10 minutes. Remove from heat; stir in juices and liqueur. Pour into food processor and purée. Strain to remove seeds; cool. Cover and refrigerate overnight.

Taste mixture; add sugar or lemon juice, if needed. Spoon into shallow glass pans; freeze. Return mixture to processor and purée until smooth. Refreeze. Soften slightly before serving.

HINT: Ice cream maker can be used to process sorbet; follow manufacturer's instructions.

Basil Butter

Preparation Time: 30 minutes | *Yield: $^2/_3$ cup*

- 2 unpeeled cloves garlic
- $^1/_2$ cup fresh basil leaves, firmly packed
- $^1/_2$ cup unsalted butter, softened
- 1 teaspoon Dijon mustard
- $^1/_2$ teaspoon grated lemon rind, or to taste
- Salt and white pepper, to taste

In saucepan, boil garlic 10 minutes or until soft. Remove with slotted spoon; cool. Add basil to water; blanch 10 seconds. Drain well and pat dry; mince finely. Peel and mash garlic. Cream garlic, basil, butter, mustard, lemon rind, salt and pepper. Blend well; cover and chill overnight. Serve with fish, grilled meats, steamed vegetables or hot drained pasta.

MAPLE BUTTER

DELICIOUS OVER HOT BISCUITS!

YIELD: 3/4 CUP

PREPARATION TIME: 30 MINUTES

- 1/2 CUP UNSALTED BUTTER, SOFTENED
- 1/2 TEASPOON LEMON ZEST (OR 1 TEASPOON LEMON JUICE)
- 1/2 CUP MAPLE SYRUP
- 1/4 CUP CONFECTIONERS SUGAR

IN FOOD PROCESSOR FITTED WITH STEEL BLADE, COMBINE ALL INGREDIENTS UNTIL SMOOTH, STOPPING ONCE TO SCRAPE DOWN SIDES OF BOWL. TRANSFER TO SERVING DISH. CAN BE PREPARED 1 DAY AHEAD. COVER AND REFRIGERATE; BRING TO ROOM TEMPERATURE BEFORE SERVING.

*VARIATION: **CHERRY BUTTER:** OMIT MAPLE SYRUP AND CONFECTIONERS SUGAR. ADD 1/2 CUP PITTED DARK SWEET CHERRIES, 2 TEASPOONS KIRSCH LIQUEUR AND 1/2 CUP LIGHT BROWN SUGAR, FIRMLY PACKED.*

HINT: BUTTER WILL KEEP, COVERED AND CHILLED, UP TO 2 WEEKS.

PECAN-THYME BUTTER

THESE VERSATILE BUTTERS HAVE ENDLESS USES.

YIELD: 1 CUP

PREPARATION TIME: 30 MINUTES

- 1 CUP BUTTER, SOFTENED
- 4 TABLESPOONS FINELY CHOPPED PECANS
- 2 TABLESPOONS MINCED FRESH THYME (OR 2 TEASPOONS DRIED, CRUMBLED)
- 1 TABLESPOON FRESH LEMON JUICE
- 1 TEASPOON MINCED GARLIC
- 1 TEASPOON WHITE PEPPER

IN BOWL CREAM BUTTER, PECANS, THYME, LEMON JUICE, GARLIC AND PEPPER. CHILL UNTIL FIRM. FORM INTO BALLS; SERVE ON GRILLED FISH SUCH AS HALIBUT OR SOLE.

*VARIATION: **SCALLION BUTTER:** OMIT PECANS, THYME, GARLIC AND PEPPER. ADD 1/4 CUP MINCED GREEN ONIONS, 2 TABLESPOONS CHOPPED FRESH PARSLEY, 1 TEASPOON DIJON MUSTARD, AND TABASCO AND WORCESTERSHIRE SAUCE TO TASTE. SERVE WITH MEAT OR POULTRY.*

Crockpot Apple Butter

Easy to prepare for those short on time!

Preparation Time: 1 hour

Yield: 8 cups

12 to 14 cooking apples (Jonathon or McIntosh)
1 cup apple cider
2 cups sugar
1 teaspoon cinnamon
1/4 to 1/2 teaspoon ground cloves

Core and quarter apples; combine with cider in crockpot. Cover; cook 5 to 6 hours on high or 10 to 12 hours on low, until apples are mushy. Purée in processor or blender in batches. Return to crockpot. Stir in sugar and spices. Cook uncovered 1 to 4 hours until thickened. Will keep several weeks in refrigerator or, if desired, freeze or can.

HINT: Process in boiling water bath 15 minutes if canning.

Freezer Strawberry Jam

Preparation Time: 45 minutes

Yield: 3 pints

3 quarts fresh strawberries, washed, hulled and mashed
1 3/4 ounces fruit pectin
7 cups sugar

Combine strawberries and fruit pectin. Bring to full boil and add sugar. Boil 5 minutes, stirring constantly to prevent sticking. Skim off foam and let stand overnight at room temperature. Place in freezer containers and freeze.

HINT: Excellent served over ice cream.

Lemon Oregano Vinegar

Yield: 4 cups

Preparation Time: 20 minutes

- **2 lemons, quartered**
- **1/2 teaspoon white mustard seed**
- **2 teaspoons white peppercorns**
- **4 whole cloves**
- **1 shallot, thinly sliced**
- **1 cup chopped fresh oregano**
- **4 cups white wine vinegar**
- **Additional sprigs fresh oregano**

In large jar place lemons, mustard seed, peppercorns, cloves, shallot and oregano. Pour vinegar into saucepan; bring to boil. Add to jar; cover and stand at room temperature 2 weeks. Using filter, strain vinegar into decorative jars. Discard lemon mixture. Add sprigs of fresh oregano to each jar. Seal jars tightly.

Variation: ***Basil Garlic Vinegar:*** *Omit lemons, mustard seeds, peppercorns, cloves and oregano. Add 1 cup fresh basil, packed, and 6 cloves garlic, sliced. Add fresh basil sprigs to decorative jars.*

Vinegar of Six Herbs

Savory, tart flavor.

Yield: 4 cups

Preparation Time: 10 minutes

- **1/2 cup chopped fresh rosemary**
- **1/4 cup chopped chive sprigs**
- **1/2 cup chopped fresh thyme**
- **1/4 cup chopped fresh marjoram**
- **1/4 cup chopped fresh oregano**
- **2 tablespoons chopped fresh parsley**
- **4 shallots, thinly sliced**
- **12 peppercorns**
- **4 cups white wine vinegar**
- **Additional sprigs fresh rosemary, thyme, marjoram or oregano**

In large jar place rosemary, chives, thyme, marjoram, oregano, parsley, shallots and peppercorns. Pour vinegar into saucepan; bring to boil. Add to jar; cover and stand at room temperature 2 weeks. Using filter, strain vinegar into decorative jars. Discard herb residue. Add fresh rosemary, thyme, marjoram or oregano sprigs to each jar, if desired. Seal jars tightly.

FUDGE SAUCE

WONDERFUL OVER ICE CREAM.

PREPARATION TIME: 20 MINUTES | *YIELD: 4 TO 6 SERVINGS*

- **3/4 CUP SUGAR**
- **3 TABLESPOONS COCOA POWDER**
- **DASH SALT**
- **2 TABLESPOONS WATER**
- **6 OUNCES EVAPORATED MILK**
- **2 TABLESPOONS MARGARINE**
- **1 TEASPOON PURE VANILLA EXTRACT**

IN SAUCEPAN COMBINE SUGAR, COCOA AND SALT. BLEND IN WATER; STIR UNTIL COCOA IS DISSOLVED. ADD MILK; BRING TO BOIL. BOIL 3 TO 4 MINUTES, STIRRING CONSTANTLY, UNTIL SAUCE BEGINS TO THICKEN. REMOVE FROM HEAT; STIR IN MARGARINE AND VANILLA. COOL SLIGHTLY TO THICKEN. SERVE HOT OR COLD.

VARIATION: ADD 1 TEASPOON BRANDY OR 2 TEASPOONS BANANA LIQUEUR.

BRANDY SAUCE PECAN

PREPARATION TIME: 10 MINUTES | *YIELD: 1 CUP*

- **1 CUP LIGHT BROWN SUGAR, FIRMLY PACKED**
- **1/4 CUP UNSALTED BUTTER**
- **1/4 CUP HEAVY CREAM**
- **2 TABLESPOONS LIGHT CORN SYRUP**
- **1/4 CUP BRANDY**
- **1/4 CUP CHOPPED PECANS**

IN SAUCEPAN COMBINE BROWN SUGAR, BUTTER, CREAM AND CORN SYRUP; BRING TO BOIL, STIRRING CONSTANTLY. REDUCE HEAT TO LOW AND COOK 5 MINUTES, STIRRING FREQUENTLY. STIR IN BRANDY AND PECANS; SIMMER 1 MINUTE. SERVE HOT OVER ICE CREAM.

HINT: MAY BE STORED IN REFRIGERATOR AND REHEATED FOR LATER USE.

Techniques

To prevent meringue from weeping, beat in sugar gradually and be sure it dissolves completely; spread meringue on warm filling. Meringue should be 3/4 to 1 inch thick and bake 6 minutes at 425° or 8 minutes at 400°. Folding in part of sugar at end makes a tender meringue.

Chill bowl and beaters before whipping cream for better results.

Egg whites should be at room temperature before beating for fullest volume.

Lightly sprinkle bottom of cake plate with granulated sugar before placing warm cake on it. The slices will not stick to plate after they are cut.

To keep powdered sugar icings moist and prevent hardening and cracking, add a pinch of baking powder while mixing.

Melt unsweetened and semi-sweet chocolate in the top of a double boiler over hot, not boiling, water. Moisture (even steam) can stiffen chocolate into a solid mass. Speed melting by grating or chopping chocolate first and remove from heat as soon as melted.

If chocolate stiffens, start with 1 teaspoon and add up to 1 tablespoon solid vegetable shortening (not salad oil, butter or margarine which all contain moisture) for each 3 ounces of unsweetened or semi-sweet chocolate. Stir until chocolate liquefies again and becomes smooth.

For light-textured cake, it is important to incorporate air by beating butter until soft and creamy. Add sugar gradually until mixture is about the consistency of whipped cream.

Sugar and acid help poached fruits keep their shape. Wine is often used because of its sugar and acid content.

Store fresh baked cookies in airtight container with two pieces of fresh bread to keep cookies soft.

Use sifted powdered sugar instead of flour when rolling out sweet cookie dough.

Place a piece of plastic wrap over surface of ice cream for frost-free storage.

For a golden brown pie crust, brush with milk before baking.

Powdered sugar and cake flour are very light and pack down easily. Always sift and lightly spoon into measuring container.

GRAND MARNIER SOUFFLÉ

YIELD: 4 SERVINGS

PREHEAT OVEN: 425°

2 TABLESPOONS BUTTER, SOFTENED
3 TABLESPOONS SUGAR
5 EGG YOLKS (RESERVE WHITES)
1/3 CUP SUGAR
1/4 CUP GRAND MARNIER LIQUEUR
1 TABLESPOON FRESHLY GRATED ORANGE PEEL
7 EGG WHITES (RESERVED PLUS 2 EXTRA)
1/4 TEASPOON CREAM OF TARTAR
CONFECTIONERS SUGAR

GREASE BOTTOM AND SIDES OF 1 1/2 QUART SOUFFLÉ DISH WITH BUTTER. SPRINKLE WITH 3 TABLESPOONS SUGAR, TIPPING AND SHAKING DISH TO SPREAD EVENLY. TURN DISH OVER AND KNOCK OUT EXCESS. SET ASIDE.

IN TOP OF DOUBLE BOILER, BEAT EGG YOLKS UNTIL WELL BLENDED. SLOWLY ADD SUGAR; CONTINUE BEATING UNTIL VERY THICK AND PALE YELLOW. SET PAN OVER BARELY SIMMERING WATER; HEAT YOLKS, STIRRING GENTLY AND CONSTANTLY WITH WOODEN SPOON OR RUBBER SPATULA, UNTIL MIXTURE THICKENS AND BECOMES TOO HOT TO TOUCH. STIR IN GRAND MARNIER AND GRATED ORANGE PEEL; TRANSFER TO LARGE BOWL. SET BOWL INTO PAN FILLED WITH ICE AND COLD WATER; STIR MIXTURE UNTIL QUITE COLD. REMOVE BOWL FROM ICE.

IN LARGE MIXING BOWL, BEAT EGG WHITES AND CREAM OF TARTAR UNTIL STIFF. USING RUBBER SPATULA, STIR LARGE SPOONFUL OF BEATEN EGG WHITES INTO EGG YOLK MIXTURE TO LIGHTEN IT. GENTLY FOLD REMAINING EGG WHITES INTO MIXTURE. SPOON SOUFFLÉ INTO BUTTERED DISH, FILLING TO WITHIN 2 INCHES OF TOP. SMOOTH TOP OF SOUFFLÉ WITH SPATULA.

BAKE ON MIDDLE SHELF OF OVEN 2 MINUTES; REDUCE HEAT TO 400°. CONTINUE BAKING 20 TO 30 MINUTES, OR UNTIL SOUFFLÉ HAS RISEN ABOUT 2 INCHES ABOVE TOP OF MOLD AND TOP IS LIGHTLY BROWNED. SPRINKLE WITH CONFECTIONERS SUGAR AND SERVE IMMEDIATELY.

THE SUMMIT CLUB

BREAD PUDDING WITH BOURBON SAUCE

PREPARATION TIME: 15 MINUTES

YIELD: 8 SERVINGS
PREHEAT OVEN: 350°

8 OUNCES FRENCH BREAD, CUT INTO 1 INCH CUBES
5 CUPS MILK
2 CUPS SUGAR
2 TABLESPOONS PURE VANILLA EXTRACT
3 EGGS, BEATEN WELL
1/4 TO 1/2 CUP RAISINS

IN MEDIUM CASSEROLE DISH, SOAK BREAD IN MILK UNTIL SOFT. COMBINE SUGAR, VANILLA, EGGS AND RAISINS IN SMALL BOWL. POUR INTO CASSEROLE DISH; COMBINE WELL. BAKE 1 HOUR, OR UNTIL CONSISTENCY OF PUDDING. PREPARE SAUCE AND SERVE OVER PUDDING.

BOURBON SAUCE:
1/2 CUP UNSALTED BUTTER
1 CUP SUGAR
2 TABLESPOONS BOURBON
1 EGG, BEATEN WELL

MELT BUTTER IN DOUBLE BOILER OVER HOT, NOT BOILING, WATER. ADD SUGAR; COOK UNTIL DISSOLVED. ADD BOURBON AND EGG; MIX WELL. KEEP SAUCE WARM UNTIL READY TO SERVE.

NICOLE'S RESTAURANT

FRESH FRUIT COMPOTE WITH LEMON MOUSSE

YIELD: 5 CUPS

5 CUPS FRESH FRUIT
1/4 CUP SUGAR

PLACE FRUIT (SUCH AS STRAWBERRIES, BLUEBERRIES, PINEAPPLE, AND ORANGES) IN LARGE GLASS BOWL OR COMPOTE. SPRINKLE WITH SUGAR AND SET ASIDE.

LEMON MOUSSE:
5 EGGS, SEPARATED (RESERVE WHITES)
3/4 CUP SUGAR
5 TABLESPOONS FRESH LEMON JUICE
3 TEASPOONS LEMON RIND
1 CUP WHIPPING CREAM
STRAWBERRY SLICES

IN SMALL BOWL, COMBINE EGG YOLKS AND SUGAR; BEAT UNTIL THICK AND LEMON-COLORED. ADD LEMON JUICE. POUR INTO SAUCEPAN; COOK OVER MEDIUM HEAT, STIRRING CONSTANTLY, UNTIL THICKENED. REMOVE FROM HEAT; ADD RIND AND COOL. WHIP CREAM UNTIL STIFF; WHIP EGG WHITES UNTIL STIFF. FOLD EGG WHITES INTO LEMON MIXTURE; FOLD IN WHIPPED CREAM. SPOON OVER FRUIT. GARNISH WITH STRAWBERRY SLICES.

NANCY PARKER COOKING SCHOOL

Apple Strudel Baklava

Yield: 40 pieces
Preheat Oven: 350°

Preparation Time: 1 hour

Keep phyllo sheets covered with damp towel.

Combine apple, walnuts, almonds, sugar, raisins, lemon peel, lemon juice and cinnamon in medium bowl. Set aside.

Heavily butter 15 × 10 inch baking pan. Lay one phyllo sheet in pan; brush with butter. Repeat process with 5 more sheets. Spread half apple mixture over phyllo. Top with 6 more phyllo sheets, buttering each sheet. Spread with remaining apple mixture. Top with remaining phyllo sheets, buttering each sheet. Trim edges; score into diamonds. Bake 35 to 40 minutes. Warm honey; drizzle over baklava. Cool.

3/4 pound phyllo dough (16 × 16 inch sheets)
2 cups peeled, cored and coarsely shredded apple
1 cup chopped walnuts
1 cup chopped, toasted almonds
2/3 cup sugar
1/4 cup raisins
1 teaspoon minced lemon peel
2 tablespoons fresh lemon juice
1 tablespoon cinnamon
1 1/4 cups butter or margarine, melted
1/2 to 3/4 cup honey

Bananas Foster

Yield: 4 to 6 servings

Preparation Time: 15 minutes

Melt butter in flame-proof skillet. Add brown sugar and cinnamon; stir until sugar dissolves, about 3 to 4 minutes. Add bananas; stir to coat. Stir in banana liqueur. Heat rum in small pan over medium-high heat. Pour over bananas; ignite. When flames subside, spoon sauce and bananas over ice cream.

1/4 cup butter
1/4 cup brown sugar, firmly packed
1 1/2 teaspoons cinnamon
4 bananas, split and quartered
3 tablespoons banana liqueur
1/2 cup white rum
Vanilla ice cream

PETITE CHOCOLATE MOUSSE

PREPARATION TIME: 30 MINUTES

YIELD: 40 PETITE CUPS

8 OUNCES HIGH QUALITY DARK BAKING CHOCOLATE, SUCH AS LINDT OR GODIVA
4 TABLESPOONS SUGAR
6 TABLESPOONS OF ONE OF FOLLOWING LIQUEURS: GRAND MARNIER, TIA MARIA, CHAMBORD, FRANGELICO, AMARETTO, OR IRISH MIST
2 CUPS HEAVY CREAM
40 PETITE CHOCOLATE CUPS
CANDIED ORANGE PEEL, CANDIED VIOLETS, CHOPPED ALMONDS, CHOPPED HAZELNUTS OR COFFEE BEAN CANDIES

IN HEAVY SAUCEPAN OR DOUBLE BOILER OVER LOW HEAT, MELT CHOCOLATE WITH SUGAR AND LIQUEUR. COOL. WHIP CREAM UNTIL VERY STIFF. GENTLY BUT THOROUGHLY FOLD CHOCOLATE MIXTURE INTO WHIPPED CREAM.

USING PASTRY BAG FITTED WITH #8 STAR TIP, PIPE MOUSSE INTO CHOCOLATE CUPS. TOP WITH CANDIED ORANGE PEEL, VIOLETS, NUTS OR COFFEE BEAN CANDIES. FOR ELEGANT DINNER PARTY, PIPE INTO CRYSTAL PARFAIT OR WINE GLASSES.

PEACH COBBLER

PREPARATION TIME: 15 MINUTES

YIELD: 6 TO 8 SERVINGS
PREHEAT OVEN: 375°

6 TO 8 PEACHES, PEELED AND SLICED
1¼ CUPS SUGAR (RESERVE ½ CUP)
3 TABLESPOONS BUTTER, SOFTENED
1 TEASPOON BAKING POWDER
¼ TEASPOON SALT
½ CUP MILK
1 CUP ALL-PURPOSE FLOUR
1 TABLESPOON CORNSTARCH
⅔ CUP BOILING WATER

ARRANGE PEACHES IN 11¾×7½ INCH BAKING DISH. MIX TOGETHER ¾ CUP SUGAR, BUTTER, BAKING POWDER, SALT, MILK AND FLOUR; POUR OVER PEACHES. COMBINE RESERVED SUGAR AND CORNSTARCH; SPRINKLE OVER FLOUR MIXTURE. POUR WATER OVER SUGAR MIXTURE. BAKE 45 MINUTES.

HINT: IF PEACHES ARE NOT IN SEASON, FROZEN PEACHES (THAWED) MAY BE SUBSTITUTED.

CREAM PUFFS

YIELD: 12 SERVINGS
PREHEAT OVEN: 425°
PREPARATION TIME: 1½ HOURS

PUFF PASTRY:
1 CUP WATER
½ CUP MARGARINE
1 TABLESPOON SUGAR
½ TEASPOON SALT
1 CUP ALL-PURPOSE FLOUR
4 EGGS

IN LARGE SAUCEPAN OVER MEDIUM-HIGH HEAT, BRING WATER, MARGARINE, SUGAR AND SALT TO BOIL. ADD FLOUR; STIR AND COOK UNTIL BATTER LEAVES SIDE OF PAN AND FOLLOWS SPOON. REMOVE FROM HEAT. ADD EGGS ONE AT A TIME, BEATING WELL WITH MIXER AFTER EACH ADDITION. DROP BY HEAPING TABLESPOONS ONTO GREASED BAKING SHEET TO FORM 12 PUFFS. BAKE 15 MINUTES. REDUCE HEAT TO 350°; BAKE 35 MINUTES LONGER. COOL ON WIRE RACK. CUT OFF TOPS AND REMOVE DOUGH FROM INSIDES. PREPARE PASTRY CREAM. IMMEDIATELY BEFORE SERVING, FILL WITH PASTRY CREAM AND REPLACE TOPS.

PASTRY CREME:
3 CUPS MILK
2 VANILLA BEANS
1 CUP SUGAR
½ CUP ALL-PURPOSE FLOUR
4 EGGS, BEATEN WELL
4 EGG YOLKS

SCALD MILK WITH VANILLA BEANS. DISCARD BEANS. IN DOUBLE BOILER OVER HOT, NOT BOILING, WATER COMBINE SUGAR, FLOUR, EGGS AND YOLKS UNTIL LIGHT AND FLUFFY. GRADUALLY ADD SCALDED MILK; STIR UNTIL WELL BLENDED. COOK UNTIL MIXTURE JUST REACHES BOILING POINT, STIRRING CONSTANTLY. REMOVE FROM HEAT; CONTINUE TO STIR TWO MINUTES. COVER TOP WITH PLASTIC WRAP TO PREVENT SKIN FROM FORMING. COOL COMPLETELY.

RASPBERRY POACHED PEARS

FEATURED IN OUR COVER PHOTOGRAPH.

PREPARATION TIME: 1 HOUR

YIELD: 8 SERVINGS

20 OUNCES FROZEN RASPBERRIES, THAWED AND UNDRAINED
1/2 CUP CHAMBORD LIQUEUR
8 FIRM RIPE PEARS, PEELED WITH STEMS LEFT INTACT

PROCESS RASPBERRIES AND JUICE THROUGH FOOD MILL. STRAIN TO REMOVE ALL SEEDS; ADD CHAMBORD. CORE PEARS FROM BOTTOM AND CUT OFF THIN SLICE TO LEVEL. PLACE IN LARGE SAUCEPAN; POUR PURÉE OVER PEARS. BRING TO SIMMER OVER LOW HEAT; COVER AND SIMMER GENTLY UNTIL TENDER, 20 TO 30 MINUTES. SPOON PURÉE OVER PEARS DURING COOKING. REMOVE PEARS FROM PAN; COOL AND CHILL. PLACE RASPBERRY SAUCE IN SERVING DISHES. TOP WITH PEARS; SPOON ADDITIONAL SAUCE OVER EACH PEAR.

CHOCOLATE MARQUISE

PREPARATION TIME: 30 MINUTES

YIELD: 16 SERVINGS
PREHEAT OVEN: 375°

1 POUND SEMI-SWEET CHOCOLATE
1 CUP BUTTER
3/4 CUP CONFECTIONERS SUGAR, SIFTED
1 TABLESPOON ALL-PURPOSE FLOUR
4 EGGS, SEPARATED
1 TEASPOON PURE VANILLA EXTRACT
8 OUNCES SOUR CREAM
1/2 TEASPOON INSTANT COFFEE GRANULES
1 TEASPOON HOT WATER
1/2 CUP CHOPPED PECANS
WHIPPED CREAM

IN DOUBLE BOILER MELT CHOCOLATE AND BUTTER. COMBINE SUGAR AND FLOUR; GRADUALLY ADD TO CHOCOLATE MIXTURE, STIRRING CONSTANTLY. REMOVE FROM HEAT. WHISK IN YOLKS, ONE AT A TIME, BEATING WELL AFTER EACH ADDITION. STIR IN VANILLA. BEAT EGG WHITES UNTIL STIFF; FOLD INTO CHOCOLATE MIXTURE.

REMOVE 1 CUP MIXTURE; BLEND WITH SOUR CREAM. DISSOLVE COFFEE IN HOT WATER; WHISK INTO SOUR CREAM MIXTURE. ADD PECANS TO REMAINING CHOCOLATE MIXTURE; POUR INTO BUTTERED 8 INCH SQUARE BAKING PAN. TOP WITH SOUR CREAM MIXTURE. BAKE 25 MINUTES (CENTER WILL NOT APPEAR SET). COOL COMPLETELY; COVER AND CHILL 4 HOURS. CUT INTO SQUARES AND TOP WITH WHIPPED CREAM.

STRAWBERRY TORTE

YIELD: 8 TO 10 SERVINGS
PREHEAT OVEN: 350°

PREPARATION TIME: 1 HOUR

- 1 PINT STRAWBERRIES, HULLED AND CRUSHED
- 2 CUPS SUGAR (RESERVE 1½ CUPS)
- 2 TABLESPOONS PLUS 1 TEASPOON CORNSTARCH
- 6 EGG WHITES, ROOM TEMPERATURE
- ¼ TEASPOON CREAM OF TARTAR
- ⅛ TEASPOON SALT
- 1½ TEASPOONS PURE VANILLA EXTRACT
- 1½ CUPS GROUND PECANS
- ¼ CUP CHOPPED PECANS
- ½ CUP BUTTER, SOFTENED
- 1 EGG YOLK
- 1½ CUPS SIFTED CONFECTIONERS SUGAR
- 3 TABLESPOONS GRAND MARNIER LIQUEUR
- 4 CUPS WHIPPED CREAM
- WHOLE STRAWBERRIES
- CONFECTIONERS SUGAR

COMBINE STRAWBERRIES WITH ½ CUP SUGAR IN MEDIUM SAUCEPAN; LET STAND 1 HOUR. ADD CORNSTARCH; COOK OVER MEDIUM HEAT, STIRRING, UNTIL THICKENED AND CLEAR. COOL.

BUTTER BOTTOM AND SIDES OF TWO 9 INCH CAKE PANS. LINE BOTTOMS WITH WAXED OR PARCHMENT PAPER; BUTTER PAPER.

BEAT EGG WHITES, CREAM OF TARTAR AND SALT UNTIL FOAMY. GRADUALLY ADD ¾ CUP SUGAR, 1 TABLESPOON AT A TIME, BEATING UNTIL STIFF PEAKS FORM. ADD VANILLA; BEAT WELL. MIX REMAINING ¾ CUP SUGAR WITH GROUND PECANS; FOLD INTO EGG WHITES UNTIL WELL BLENDED.

SPOON MERINGUE INTO PANS, SPREADING EVENLY. SPRINKLE TOP OF ONE MERINGUE WITH CHOPPED PECANS. BAKE 40 MINUTES. GENTLY LOOSEN LAYERS AROUND EDGES; IMMEDIATELY TURN OUT ON RACKS. REMOVE PAPER; COOL COMPLETELY. (MAY CRUMBLE AROUND EDGES AND HAVE CRACKED APPEARANCE.)

PREPARE BUTTER CREAM BY COMBINING BUTTER, EGG YOLK AND CONFECTIONERS SUGAR. BEAT WITH ELECTRIC MIXER UNTIL SMOOTH. ADD GRAND MARNIER; BLEND WELL.

PLACE PLAIN MERINGUE ON SERVING PLATE. SPREAD TO EDGE WITH BUTTER CREAM. SPOON STRAWBERRY MIXTURE OVER BUTTER CREAM. TOP WITH 2 CUPS WHIPPED CREAM. PLACE REMAINING MERINGUE OVER WHIPPED CREAM, PECAN SIDE UP. FROST SIDES WITH REMAINING WHIPPED CREAM. REFRIGERATE 3 HOURS OR OVERNIGHT. PLACE WHOLE BERRIES AROUND BOTTOM OF TORTE AND SIFT CONFECTIONERS SUGAR OVER TOP.

TULIPS THROUGH THE SNOW

STRAWBERRIES LOOK LIKE TULIPS PUSHING UP THROUGH SNOW.

PREPARATION TIME: 2 HOURS

YIELD: 24 PIECES
PREHEAT OVEN: 400°

- 1/2 CUP BUTTER
- 1 CUP BOILING WATER
- 1 CUP ALL-PURPOSE FLOUR
- 2 TABLESPOONS COCOA POWDER
- 2 TABLESPOONS SUGAR
- 1/4 TEASPOON SALT
- 4 EGGS

IN MEDIUM SAUCEPAN MELT BUTTER IN BOILING WATER. MEANWHILE, STIR TOGETHER FLOUR, COCOA POWDER, SUGAR AND SALT. ADD TO PAN; STIR VIGOROUSLY. COOK AND STIR UNTIL MIXTURE FORMS BALL AND FOLLOWS SPOON. REMOVE FROM HEAT; COOL 10 MINUTES.

ADD EGGS ONE AT A TIME, BEATING WELL AFTER EACH ADDITION. USING PASTRY BAG WITH LARGE STAR TIP (5/8 INCH OPENING), PIPE BATTER INTO 24 SPIRALS 1 3/4 INCHES IN DIAMETER ONTO GREASED BAKING SHEET. (USE ABOUT 2 TABLESPOONS BATTER FOR EACH.)

BAKE 20 TO 25 MINUTES OR UNTIL PUFFED. REMOVE FROM OVEN. COOL ON WIRE RACK. CUT OFF TOPS AND SET ASIDE. REMOVE SOFT DOUGH FROM INSIDE AND DISCARD. SET ASIDE. REDUCE OVEN TEMPERATURE TO 350°.

CHEESECAKE FILLING:

- 16 OUNCES CREAM CHEESE, SOFTENED
- 1/2 CUP PLUS 2 TABLESPOONS SUGAR (RESERVE 2 TABLESPOONS)
- 1 EGG
- 1/2 TEASPOON PURE ALMOND EXTRACT (RESERVE 1/4 TEASPOON)
- 1 CUP WHIPPING CREAM
- 24 LARGE RIPE STRAWBERRIES, HULLED

BEAT CREAM CHEESE, 1/2 CUP SUGAR, EGG AND 1/4 TEASPOON ALMOND EXTRACT JUST UNTIL SMOOTH. FILL BOTTOMS OF PUFFS WITH MIXTURE. PLACE ON UNGREASED BAKING SHEET. BAKE 15 MINUTES OR UNTIL CHEESE MIXTURE IS SET. CHILL. BEAT WHIPPED CREAM TO SOFT PEAKS. ADD RESERVED SUGAR AND ALMOND EXTRACT; BEAT TO STIFF PEAKS. PARTIALLY QUARTER STRAWBERRIES FROM POINTED END TO STEM END (DO NOT CUT THROUGH STEM END). USING PASTRY BAG WITH SAME TIP, PIPE CREAM INTO STRAWBERRIES. PLACE BERRIES ON TOP OF FILLED PUFFS. PLACE RESERVED TOPS ON BERRIES, ANGLING SLIGHTLY. SPRINKLE WITH CONFECTIONERS SUGAR (SNOW).

Frozen Lemon Mousse

A showstopper . . . worth the extra assembly time.

Yield: 12 servings

Preparation Time: 30 minutes

Combine yolks, lemon juice, 1/4 cup sugar and lemon zest in large bowl; blend well. Set aside. In medium bowl beat egg whites until foamy. Add cream of tartar and salt; continue beating until soft peaks form. Gradually add reserved sugar, beating constantly, until stiff but not dry. Gently fold cream and whites into yolk mixture. Cover with foil and freeze overnight.

Soften mousse in refrigerator 30 minutes if too hard. Put piece of macaroon in bottom of clay pot; tamp down. Mound mousse in pot. May be returned to freezer until ready to serve. Place on dessert saucer. Place one flower in middle of each mousse. Serve with Butter Praline Cookies (see index).

- 4 egg yolks
- 1/2 cup fresh lemon juice
- 1 cup sugar (reserve 3/4 cup)
- 1 1/2 tablespoons grated lemon zest (peel)
- 4 egg whites, room temperature
- 1/8 teaspoon cream of tartar
- 1/8 teaspoon salt
- 1 1/2 cups heavy whipping cream
- 1 dozen soft macaroons
- 1 dozen 2 or 3 inch clay flower pots
- 1 bunch small blossomed flowers (daisies or mums), separated into individual flowers with 4 inch stems

Truffles

Do not attempt to roll truffles on very hot day!

Yield: 30 truffles

Preparation Time: 1 hour

In medium bowl whip butter until light and creamy. Combine sugar and cocoa; sift. With mixer running, slowly add half of sugar mixture to butter; add egg and extract. Mix well; slowly add remaining sugar mixture. Refrigerate one hour or longer. Mold into small balls; roll in chocolate sprinkles.

- 1/2 cup unsalted butter, room temperature
- 1 1/2 cups confectioners sugar
- 3/4 cup Dutch cocoa powder
- 1 egg
- 2 teaspoons pure rum extract
- Chocolate sprinkles

Chocolate Fudge Ice Cream

Preparation Time: 1 hour *Yield: 1 gallon*

1/2 gallon milk, scalded
1 cup sugar
12 ounces evaporated milk
14 ounces sweetened condensed milk
6 eggs, beaten well
Dash salt
2 tablespoons pure vanilla extract
4 tablespoons fudge topping
1/4 cup Amaretto liqueur
3 tablespoons Creme de Cacao liqueur

To scalded milk, add sugar; stir until well dissolved. Remove from heat. Add evaporated and condensed milks, eggs, salt and vanilla. Stir in fudge topping, Amaretto and Creme de Cacao. Cool; pour into ice cream freezer. Freeze according to manufacturer's instructions.

HINT: Additional liqueur may be added, to taste.

Chocolate Coquilles

(Chocolate Mint Shell Candies)

Preparation Time: 30 minutes *Yield: 2 dozen mints*

18 ounces semi-sweet chocolate chips
1 1/3 cups sweetened condensed milk
Pinch salt
2 teaspoons peppermint extract

Melt chocolate in double boiler over hot, not boiling, water. Stir until smooth. Remove from heat; add condensed milk, salt and extract. Stir just until smooth. Spread into shell-shaped molds. Place on flat surface in freezer 10 to 15 minutes, until firm to touch. Unmold onto wax paper. Keep candy mixture covered with foil between moldings to prevent drying.

HINT: Substitute flavored liqueur for extract.

MAPLE BOURBON CREAM PRALINES

A TASTE OF HEAVEN FOR PRALINE LOVERS!

YIELD: 24 2-*INCH PRALINES*

PREPARATION TIME: 15 *MINUTES*

- **2 CUPS MAPLE SYRUP**
- **1 CUP HEAVY CREAM**
- **2 TABLESPOONS BOURBON (RESERVE 1 TABLESPOON)**
- **1 TABLESPOON BUTTER**
- **1½ CUPS LIGHTLY TOASTED PECANS, COARSELY CHOPPED**

IN HEAVY 2 QUART SAUCEPAN, COMBINE MAPLE SYRUP, CREAM AND 1 TABLESPOON BOURBON. COOK OVER MEDIUM-HIGH HEAT UNTIL SYRUP REGISTERS 238°F ON CANDY THERMOMETER. REMOVE FROM HEAT AND COOL TO 220°F. ADD BUTTER AND REMAINING BOURBON. BEAT UNTIL MIXTURE IS CREAMY; ADD PECANS. DROP BY TABLESPOONS ONTO BUTTERED BAKING SHEET. COOL. WRAP PRALINES INDIVIDUALLY IN WAX PAPER; STORE IN AIRTIGHT CONTAINER IN COOL, DRY PLACE.

SANTA HOUSE FUDGE

A FAVORITE AT THE TULSA JUNIOR PHILHARMONIC "SANTA HOUSE." OUR THANKS FOR SHARING IT.

YIELD: 3 *POUNDS*

PREPARATION TIME: 30 *MINUTES*

- **12 OUNCES CHOCOLATE CHIPS**
- **½ CUP MARGARINE, SOFTENED**
- **2 TEASPOONS PURE VANILLA EXTRACT**
- **4½ CUPS SUGAR**
- **1½ CUPS EVAPORATED MILK**
- **20 LARGE MARSHMALLOWS**
- **1 CUP CHOPPED NUTS**

COMBINE CHIPS, MARGARINE AND VANILLA; SET ASIDE. IN MEDIUM SAUCEPAN, COMBINE SUGAR, MILK AND MARSHMALLOWS. BRING TO BOIL, STIRRING CONSTANTLY. LOWER HEAT; COOK ADDITIONAL 10 MINUTES (NO VARIATION), STIRRING CONSTANTLY. POUR HOT MIXTURE OVER CHIP MIXTURE. BEAT UNTIL CHIPS ARE MELTED. STIR IN NUTS; POUR INTO BUTTERED 9 × 13 INCH BAKING PAN. COOL; CUT INTO SQUARES.

Favorite Pie Crust

We chose only one — the best!

Preparation Time: 15 minutes

Yield: 2 crusts

- 2 1/4 cups all-purpose flour
- 1/2 teaspoon salt
- 1/4 cup unsalted butter, softened
- 1/2 cup shortening
- 1/3 cup ice water

Sift flour and salt together in large bowl. Cut butter and shortening into flour until mixture resembles pea-size coarse meal. Add water, one tablespoon at a time, and toss to moisten until dough forms ball. Chill in freezer 10 to 15 minutes; roll out on floured surface. Transfer to pie plate; push sides down and crimp edges attractively.

Hint: Too much water in pastry dough will make crust tough.

Best Buttermilk Pie

Preparation Time: 20 minutes

Yield: 8 servings
Preheat Oven: 425°

- 1 1/4 cups sugar
- 3 tablespoons all-purpose flour
- 2 eggs, beaten well
- 1/2 cup butter, melted
- 1 cup buttermilk
- 2 teaspoons pure vanilla extract
- 1/2 teaspoon pure lemon extract
- 1 unbaked 9 inch pie shell

In medium bowl combine sugar and flour; stir in eggs. Add butter and buttermilk; blend well. Stir in vanilla and lemon extracts. Pour into chilled pastry shell; bake 10 minutes. Reduce heat to 350°; bake 35 minutes longer. Do not open oven door during last baking period.

BOURBON PECAN PIE 

YIELD: 8 SERVINGS
PREHEAT OVEN: 350°

PREPARATION TIME: 10 MINUTES

IN MEDIUM BOWL CREAM SUGAR AND BUTTER. ADD FLOUR, EGGS, SALT, LEMON JUICE, VANILLA, BOURBON, CORN SYRUP AND PECANS; MIX WELL. POUR INTO PASTRY SHELL; BAKE 40 TO 50 MINUTES, OR UNTIL GOLDEN BROWN.

VARIATION: OMIT BOURBON AND INCREASE LEMON JUICE TO 1 TABLESPOON.

- 1/4 CUP SUGAR
- 2 TABLESPOONS BUTTER, SOFTENED
- 2 ROUNDED TABLESPOONS ALL-PURPOSE FLOUR
- 2 EGGS, BEATEN WELL
- 1/4 TEASPOON SALT
- 1 TEASPOON FRESH LEMON JUICE
- 1 TEASPOON PURE VANILLA EXTRACT
- 1 1/2 TABLESPOONS BOURBON
- 1 1/2 CUPS LIGHT CORN SYRUP
- 1 1/2 CUPS CHOPPED PECANS
- 1 UNBAKED 9 INCH PIE SHELL

FRENCH LEMON PIE

YIELD: 8 SERVINGS
PREHEAT OVEN: 350°

PREPARATION TIME: 20 MINUTES

IN MEDIUM BOWL BLEND EGGS, CORN SYRUP, LEMON PEEL, LEMON JUICE AND BUTTER. IN SMALL BOWL, COMBINE SUGAR AND FLOUR. STIR INTO EGG MIXTURE; COMBINE WELL. POUR INTO UNBAKED PIE SHELL. BAKE 50 MINUTES. CHILL. WHIP CREAM, SPREAD ONTO CHILLED PIE.

- 4 EGGS, BEATEN WELL
- 1 CUP LIGHT CORN SYRUP
- 1 TEASPOON GRATED LEMON PEEL
- 1/3 CUP FRESH LEMON JUICE
- 2 TABLESPOONS BUTTER, MELTED
- 1/2 CUP SUGAR
- 2 TABLESPOONS ALL-PURPOSE FLOUR
- 1 UNBAKED 9 INCH PIE SHELL
- 1/2 CUP WHIPPING CREAM

LIME PIE

PREPARATION TIME: 1 HOUR

YIELD: 8 SERVINGS
PREHEAT OVEN: 325°

1 1/4 CUPS GRAHAM CRACKER CRUMBS
3 TABLESPOONS SUGAR
1/3 CUP BUTTER, MELTED
14 OUNCES CANNED SWEETENED CONDENSED MILK
2 TABLESPOONS GRATED LIME RIND
1/2 CUP FRESH LIME JUICE
2 EGG YOLKS
GREEN FOOD COLORING
2 EGG WHITES
1/4 TEASPOON CREAM OF TARTAR
3 TABLESPOONS SUGAR
1/2 TEASPOON PURE VANILLA EXTRACT

COMBINE CRUMBS AND SUGAR IN SMALL BOWL. STIR IN BUTTER; MIX WELL. PRESS MIXTURE FIRMLY INTO 9 INCH PIE PLATE, BRINGING CRUMBS EVENLY TO RIM. CHILL 1 HOUR.

IN SMALL BOWL BLEND CONDENSED MILK, RIND, LIME JUICE AND EGG YOLKS. ADD FOOD COLORING, IF DESIRED. POUR FILLING INTO CRUST. CHILL UNTIL FIRM.

BEAT EGG WHITES UNTIL FROTHY. ADD CREAM OF TARTAR; BEAT UNTIL STIFF BUT NOT DRY. BEAT IN SUGAR AND VANILLA. SPREAD OVER CHILLED PIE AND BAKE 10 TO 15 MINUTES UNTIL LIGHTLY BROWNED. CHILL BEFORE SERVING.

PUMPKIN CHIFFON PIES

PREPARATION TIME: 45 MINUTES

YIELD: 16 SERVINGS

2 ENVELOPES UNFLAVORED GELATIN
1/2 CUP COLD WATER
2 1/2 CUPS PUMPKIN
1 CUP MILK
1 TEASPOON GINGER
1 TEASPOON NUTMEG
1 TEASPOON CINNAMON
1 TEASPOON SALT
2 CUPS SUGAR (RESERVE 1 CUP)
4 EGG YOLKS, BEATEN LIGHTLY
4 EGG WHITES, BEATEN STIFFLY
2 BAKED 9 INCH PIE SHELLS
3 TABLESPOONS SUGAR
1 CUP WHIPPING CREAM, WHIPPED

IN SMALL BOWL COMBINE GELATIN AND WATER. COMBINE PUMPKIN, MILK, GINGER, NUTMEG, CINNAMON, SALT, 1 CUP SUGAR AND EGG YOLKS IN TOP OF DOUBLE BOILER. COOK UNTIL SLIGHTLY THICKENED. ADD GELATIN MIXTURE TO HOT PUMPKIN MIXTURE; COOL. ADD RESERVED SUGAR AND EGG WHITES. SPOON INTO PASTRY SHELLS. CHILL. ADD 3 TABLESPOONS SUGAR TO WHIPPED CREAM AND SPREAD OVER PIES.

GOLDEN DELICIOUS PIE PERFECT

YIELD: 8 SERVINGS
PREHEAT OVEN: 450°
PREPARATION TIME: 1 HOUR

PLACE APPLES IN LARGE BOWL AND SPRINKLE WITH LEMON JUICE. COMBINE SUGAR, CINNAMON, NUTMEG, SALT AND FLOUR; TOSS WITH APPLES. STAND TWO HOURS, STIRRING OCCASIONALLY. DRAIN LIQUID INTO SMALL PAN; SET ASIDE. SPOON APPLES INTO PASTRY-LINED PIE PAN. DOT WITH BUTTER. COVER WITH TOP CRUST. SEAL EDGES; FLUTE. MAKE 5 OR 6 LONG OPEN SLITS FOR STEAM TO ESCAPE. BAKE 15 MINUTES. REDUCE HEAT TO 350°; BAKE 40 TO 50 MINUTES OR UNTIL APPLES ARE TENDER. COOK APPLE LIQUID OVER LOW HEAT, STIRRING CONSTANTLY, UNTIL THICKENED. POUR INTO BAKED PIE THROUGH OPEN SLITS. LET STAND 1/2 HOUR BEFORE SERVING.

6 TO 8 GOLDEN DELICIOUS APPLES, PEELED, CORED, AND SLICED 1/8 INCH THICK (7 CUPS)
2 TABLESPOONS FRESH LEMON JUICE
3/4 CUP SUGAR
3/4 TEASPOON CINNAMON
1/4 TEASPOON NUTMEG
1/8 TEASPOON SALT
2 TABLESPOONS ALL-PURPOSE FLOUR
PASTRY FOR 9 INCH DOUBLE CRUST PIE
1 TABLESPOON BUTTER

CHERRY STRAWBERRY PIE

YIELD: 6 TO 8 SERVINGS
PREHEAT OVEN: 425°
PREPARATION TIME: 25 MINUTES

DRAIN FRUIT JUICES INTO SMALL SAUCEPAN. ADD SUGAR, CORNSTARCH AND TAPIOCA. COOK OVER MEDIUM-HIGH HEAT UNTIL CLEAR AND THICKENED. STIR IN FRUITS AND LEMON JUICE. POUR INTO PASTRY-LINED PIE PAN. COVER WITH TOP CRUST; SEAL EDGES AND FLUTE. CUT SEVERAL SLITS IN TOP TO ALLOW STEAM TO ESCAPE. BAKE 25 TO 30 MINUTES.

14 OUNCES CANNED CHERRIES
10 OUNCES FROZEN STRAWBERRIES, THAWED
1 CUP SUGAR
2 TABLESPOONS CORNSTARCH
2 TABLESPOONS QUICK COOKING TAPIOCA
1 TABLESPOON FRESH LEMON JUICE
PASTRY FOR 9 INCH DOUBLE CRUST PIE

CHOCOLATE MOUSSE CAKE

PREPARATION TIME: 1 HOUR

YIELD: 8 TO 10 SERVINGS
PREHEAT OVEN: 325°

- 7 OUNCES SEMI-SWEET CHOCOLATE
- 1/2 CUP UNSALTED BUTTER
- 7 EGGS, SEPARATED
- 1 CUP SUGAR (RESERVE 1/4 CUP)
- 1 TEASPOON PURE VANILLA EXTRACT
- 1/8 TEASPOON CREAM OF TARTAR

CUT PARCHMENT OR WAXED PAPER TO FIT BOTTOM OF 9 INCH SPRING FORM PAN. BUTTER BOTTOM OF PAN; LAY PAPER IN BOTTOM. BUTTER PAPER.

MELT CHOCOLATE AND BUTTER OVER LOW HEAT, STIRRING CONSTANTLY. BEAT EGG YOLKS AND 3/4 CUP SUGAR UNTIL LIGHT AND FLUFFY, ABOUT 5 MINUTES. GRADUALLY BEAT IN CHOCOLATE MIXTURE AND VANILLA. BEAT EGG WHITES WITH CREAM OF TARTAR UNTIL SOFT PEAKS FORM. ADD REMAINING 1/4 CUP SUGAR, 1 TABLESPOON AT A TIME. CONTINUE BEATING UNTIL STIFF. FOLD WHITES CAREFULLY INTO CHOCOLATE MIXTURE. POUR THREE-FOURTHS OF BATTER INTO PAN. COVER REMAINING BATTER; REFRIGERATE. BAKE CAKE 30 TO 35 MINUTES; *DO NOT OVERBAKE.* COOL IN PAN; CAKE WILL DROP AS IT COOLS. REMOVE OUTSIDE RING. INVERT ON PLATE; LOOSEN BOTTOM OF PAN AND REMOVE. PEEL PAPER OFF AND INVERT ONTO PLATTER. TRIM CRUSTY EDGES AWAY. STIR REMAINING BATTER; SPREAD ON TOP OF CAKE. COVER AND REFRIGERATE. PREPARE FROSTING; SPREAD ON CAKE AND REFRIGERATE.

WHIPPED CREAM FROSTING:

- 1 CUP WHIPPING CREAM
- 1/3 CUP CONFECTIONERS SUGAR
- 1 TEASPOON PURE VANILLA EXTRACT

BEAT CREAM IN SMALL BOWL UNTIL SOFT PEAKS FORM. ADD CONFECTIONERS SUGAR AND VANILLA; BEAT UNTIL STIFF.

REPRINTED WITH PERMISSION FROM *COOKERY FOR ENTERTAINING*, H.P. BOOKS, INC.

VARIATION: POUR ALL BATTER IN PAN AND BAKE 45 TO 50 MINUTES. COOL. OMIT FROSTING. SPOON ANGLAISE ON SERVING PLATE. SET SLICE OF CAKE IN MIDDLE; SPOON RASPBERRY PURÉE AROUND CAKE.

(CONTINUED ON NEXT PAGE)

(continued from previous page)

Creme Anglaise:

- 1 cup heavy cream
- 1 cup milk
- 4 egg yolks, room temperature
- 2/3 cup sugar
- 1/8 teaspoon salt
- 1 teaspoon pure vanilla extract

Scald cream and milk in saucepan. Remove; set aside. Whisk yolks and sugar in top of double boiler until thickened and pale yellow; gradually stir in hot cream mixture in thin, steady stream. Cook over simmering water, stirring constantly, until thickened, about 10 minutes. Custard should coat spoon. Remove from heat; stir in salt and vanilla. Cool to room temperature, stirring occasionally.

Raspberry Purée:

- 20 ounces frozen raspberries, thawed
- 1/4 cup sugar
- 1 tablespoon cornstarch

Purée raspberries in food processor. Strain to remove seeds. Combine sugar and cornstarch in saucepan. Add purée; cook until thickened. Cool.

Pumpkin Cake

Yield: 20 servings
Preheat Oven: 350°
Preparation Time: 30 minutes

- 4 eggs, room temperature
- 2 cups sugar
- 1 cup vegetable oil
- 16 ounces canned pumpkin
- 2 cups all-purpose flour
- 2 teaspoons baking soda
- 1 1/2 teaspoons salt
- 1 teaspoon ground cloves
- 2 teaspoons cinnamon
- 1/2 teaspoon ground ginger
- 1/4 teaspoon nutmeg

At high speed, beat eggs with sugar until light and fluffy. Add oil and pumpkin; blend well. Combine flour, soda, salt and spices. Beat flour mixture into pumpkin until combined. Pour into ungreased 10 inch tube pan. Bake 1 hour, or until surface springs back when lightly touched. Cool completely; remove from pan. Prepare frosting; smooth over cake. Cake may be frozen before frosting.

Cream Cheese Frosting:

- 6 ounces cream cheese, softened
- 1 teaspoon pure vanilla extract
- 3 cups confectioners sugar

Beat cheese and vanilla until creamy. Gradually add confectioners sugar and blend well.

MEXICAN CHOCOLATE CAKE

PREPARATION TIME: 1 HOUR

YIELD: 50 PIECES
PREHEAT OVEN: 350°

- 1/2 CUP BUTTER
- 1/2 CUP VEGETABLE OIL
- 2 SQUARES UNSWEETENED CHOCOLATE
- 1 CUP WATER
- 2 CUPS ALL-PURPOSE FLOUR
- 1 TEASPOON BAKING SODA
- 2 CUPS SUGAR
- 1/2 CUP SOUR MILK
- 2 EGGS, BEATEN WELL
- 1 TEASPOON CINNAMON
- 1 TEASPOON PURE VANILLA EXTRACT

IN SAUCEPAN OVER LOW HEAT, COMBINE BUTTER, OIL, CHOCOLATE AND WATER. HEAT UNTIL MELTED; SET ASIDE. IN LARGE BOWL, COMBINE FLOUR, BAKING SODA, SUGAR, MILK, EGGS, CINNAMON AND VANILLA. MIX WELL. ADD CHOCOLATE MIXTURE. POUR INTO GREASED, LIGHTLY FLOURED 18×12 INCH JELLYROLL PAN. BAKE 20 TO 25 MINUTES. PREPARE FROSTING AND SPREAD ON WARM CAKE.

CHOCOLATE PECAN FROSTING:

- 1/2 CUP BUTTER
- 2 SQUARES UNSWEETENED CHOCOLATE
- 5 TABLESPOONS MILK
- 2 1/2 CUPS CONFECTIONERS SUGAR
- 1 TEASPOON PURE VANILLA EXTRACT
- 1/2 CUP CHOPPED PECANS

IN MEDIUM PAN, COMBINE BUTTER, CHOCOLATE AND MILK. HEAT UNTIL BUBBLES FORM AROUND EDGE; REMOVE FROM HEAT. ADD SUGAR AND VANILLA; BEAT WELL. STIR IN PECANS.

HINT: ADD 1 1/2 TEAPOONS VINEGAR TO 1/2 CUP MILK TO MAKE SOUR MILK.

FRUIT CAKE

PREPARATION TIME: 1 HOUR

YIELD: 2 LOAVES
PREHEAT OVEN: 250°

- 4 EGGS
- 1 CUP ALL-PURPOSE FLOUR
- 1 CUP SUGAR
- 1 TABLESPOON PURE VANILLA EXTRACT
- 1 POUND CHOPPED DATES
- 1 POUND CHOPPED PECANS
- 1 POUND CANDIED CHOPPED CHERRIES

BEAT EGGS UNTIL FOAMY. ADD FLOUR AND SUGAR; MIX WELL. ADD REMAINING INGREDIENTS AND STIR TO BLEND. POUR INTO TWO 9×5 INCH GREASED AND FLOURED LOAF PANS. BAKE 3 HOURS, PLACING PAN OF WATER IN OVEN WHILE BAKING. COOL 15 TO 20 MINUTES; REMOVE FROM PANS.

Red Velvet Pound Cake

Rich, luscious velvet!

Yield: 16 servings *Preparation Time: 40 minutes*
Preheat Oven: 325°

Combine butter, shortening and sugar. Cream until light and fluffy. Add eggs, one at a time, beating well after each addition. Stir in vanilla and food coloring. Combine flour and salt. Add to creamed mixture alternately with milk, beating well. Pour into greased and floured 10 inch tube pan. Bake 1 hour and 20 minutes; cool. Prepare frosting and spread on cake.

1 cup butter
1/2 cup shortening
3 cups sugar
7 eggs
2 teaspoons pure vanilla extract
1 ounce red food coloring
3 cups all-purpose flour
1/4 teaspoon salt
1 cup milk

Combine butter and cream cheese; blend until smooth. Stir in vanilla and sugar. Beat until creamy, adding enough milk to make spreadable.

Butter Cream Cheese Frosting:
1/2 cup butter, softened
6 ounces cream cheese, softened
1 teaspoon pure vanilla extract
1 pound confectioners sugar
1 to 2 tablespoons milk

Angel Cake

Yield: 16 servings *Preparation Time: 20 minutes*
Preheat Oven: 325°

With mixer cream margarine and sugar. Add eggs, one at a time, blending well after each addition. Gradually add milk and vanilla; mix well. Stir in wafers, coconut and pecans. Pour in greased and lightly floured 10 inch tube pan. Bake 1 hour and 30 minutes. Cool slightly and remove cake to serving dish.

1 cup margarine, softened
2 cups sugar
6 eggs
1/2 cup milk
1 teaspoon pure vanilla extract
12 ounces vanilla wafers, crushed
7 ounces flaked coconut
1 cup chopped pecans

Blueberry Amaretto Squares

Preparation Time: 45 minutes

Yield: 18 servings
Preheat Oven: 350°

- **1 3/4 cups graham cracker crumbs**
- **1/2 cup sugar**
- **8 tablespoons margarine, softened**
- **2 eggs, beaten lightly**
- **3/4 cup sugar**
- **8 ounces cream cheese, softened**
- **2 1/2 cups milk**
- **5 1/2 ounces instant vanilla pudding (2 small packages)**
- **1/2 cup Amaretto liqueur (divided)**
- **5 cups frozen blueberries, thawed (reserve 4 cups)**
- **1 1/4 cups sugar**
- **1/4 cup cornstarch**

In small bowl combine cracker crumbs, sugar and margarine. Press into bottom of 9 × 13 inch glass dish.

Combine eggs, sugar and cream cheese. Beat until smooth. Spread over crust. Bake 30 minutes. Cool completely.

Combine milk and pudding according to package directions. When thickened, add 1/4 cup Amaretto. Spread over cheese.

In saucepan, mash 1 cup blueberries. Add sugar and cornstarch; cook over medium heat, stirring constantly, until mixture thickens. Add remaining berries and Amaretto. Let mixture cool. Spread evenly over pudding mixture. Refrigerate. To serve, cut into squares.

Heath Bar Cake

Preparation Time: 30 minutes

Yield: 16 servings
Preheat Oven: 350°

- **4 tablespoons butter, softened**
- **2 cups all-purpose flour**
- **1 cup brown sugar, firmly packed**
- **1/2 cup white sugar**
- **1 cup buttermilk**
- **1 teaspoon soda**
- **1 egg, beaten lightly**
- **1 teaspoon pure vanilla extract**
- **6 frozen Heath Bars**
- **1/2 cup chopped pecans**

Combine butter, flour, and sugars in large bowl. Set aside 1/2 cup for topping. Combine buttermilk, soda, egg and vanilla in small bowl. Add to flour mixture. Blend well. Pour into greased and floured 9 × 13 inch cake pan. Break Heath Bars into pieces and chop in blender; mix with reserved butter mixture. Add nuts. Sprinkle over batter; bake 30 minutes.

MINIATURE CHEESECAKES

AN EXQUISITE DESSERT!

YIELD: 24 SERVINGS
PREHEAT OVEN: 300°
PREPARATION TIME: 20 MINUTES

- **24 OUNCES CREAM CHEESE, SOFTENED**
- **1 1/3 CUPS SUGAR (RESERVE 1/3 CUP)**
- **5 EGGS**
- **1 1/2 TEASPOONS PURE VANILLA EXTRACT (RESERVE 1/2 TEASPOON)**
- **2 CUPS SOUR CREAM**
- **FRESH STRAWBERRIES, CHERRIES OR BLUEBERRIES**

BEAT CREAM CHEESE AND 1 CUP SUGAR UNTIL FLUFFY. ADD EGGS, ONE AT A TIME, BEATING WELL AFTER EACH ADDITION. ADD 1 TEASPOON VANILLA; BEAT AGAIN. FILL PAPER-LINED MUFFIN TINS 2/3 FULL; BAKE 35 TO 40 MINUTES. MIX TOGETHER RESERVED SUGAR, RESERVED VANILLA AND SOUR CREAM. SPREAD ON CAKES WHILE WARM AND RETURN TO OVEN 5 MINUTES LONGER. GARNISH WITH FRUIT.

PRIZE CARROT CAKE

YIELD: 16 SERVINGS
PREHEAT OVEN: 350°
PREPARATION TIME: 30 MINUTES

- **1 3/4 CUPS SUGAR**
- **2 CUPS ALL-PURPOSE FLOUR**
- **2 TEASPOONS BAKING POWDER**
- **1/2 TEASPOON BAKING SODA**
- **1 TEASPOON CINNAMON**
- **1/2 TEASPOON GROUND CLOVES**
- **1/2 TEASPOON NUTMEG**
- **1/4 TEASPOON SALT**
- **1 1/2 CUPS VEGETABLE OIL**
- **4 EGGS, BEATEN LIGHTLY**
- **1 1/2 CUPS GRATED CARROT**
- **1/2 CUP FLAKED COCONUT**
- **1/3 CUP FRESH ORANGE JUICE**
- **CONFECTIONERS SUGAR**

IN MEDIUM BOWL, SIFT TOGETHER SUGAR, FLOUR, BAKING POWDER, BAKING SODA, CINNAMON, CLOVES, NUTMEG AND SALT. IN LARGE BOWL, MIX OIL AND EGGS. GRADUALLY ADD DRY INGREDIENTS; BLEND THOROUGHLY. ADD CARROT, COCONUT AND ORANGE JUICE; MIX WELL. GREASE AND FLOUR 10 INCH BUNDT OR TUBE PAN. POUR BATTER IN PAN; BAKE 55 MINUTES. COOL IN PAN ON RACK. EASE ONTO SERVING PLATE; DUST WITH CONFECTIONERS SUGAR.

HINT: IF YOU PREFER A FROSTED CAKE, TRY ONE OF OUR CREAM CHEESE FROSTINGS (SEE INDEX).

BUTTERSCOTCH TEA CAKES

PREPARATION TIME: 20 MINUTES

YIELD: 3 TO 4 DOZEN
PREHEAT OVEN: 350°

- 1/2 CUP BUTTER
- 1 1/2 CUPS BROWN SUGAR, FIRMLY PACKED
- 2 EGGS
- 2 1/2 CUPS ALL-PURPOSE FLOUR
- 1/2 TEASPOON BAKING SODA
- 1/2 TEASPOON SALT
- 1 CUP SOUR CREAM
- 1 TEASPOON PURE VANILLA EXTRACT
- 2/3 CUP CHOPPED WALNUTS

CREAM BUTTER AND SUGAR; ADD EGGS. COMBINE FLOUR, SODA AND SALT; ADD TO BUTTER MIXTURE ALTERNATELY WITH SOUR CREAM. STIR IN VANILLA AND NUTS. CHILL SEVERAL HOURS OR OVERNIGHT. DROP BY WALNUT SIZE TEASPOONS ONTO GREASED COOKIE SHEET. BAKE ABOUT 10 MINUTES; COOL. PREPARE FROSTING AND SPREAD ON CAKES.

BUTTERSCOTCH FROSTING:

- 6 TABLESPOONS BUTTER (NO SUBSTITUTIONS)
- 1 1/2 CUPS CONFECTIONERS SUGAR
- 1 TEASPOON PURE VANILLA EXTRACT
- 2 TABLESPOONS HOT WATER

MELT BUTTER IN SMALL PAN OVER MEDIUM HEAT. COOK UNTIL GOLDEN BROWN; COOL. COMBINE BUTTER, CONFECTIONERS SUGAR AND VANILLA. ADD HOT WATER ONE TABLESPOON AT A TIME UNTIL DESIRED CONSISTENCY. BEAT UNTIL SMOOTH.

PRALINE BARS

PECAN PIE — WITHOUT THE CRUST.

PREPARATION TIME: 1 HOUR 15 MINUTES

YIELD: 3 DOZEN
PREHEAT OVEN: 350°

- 1 18 1/4 OUNCE BOX YELLOW CAKE MIX (RESERVE 2/3 CUP)
- 1/2 CUP BUTTER OR MARGARINE, SOFTENED
- 4 EGGS (RESERVE 3)
- 1/2 CUP BROWN SUGAR, FIRMLY PACKED
- 1 1/2 CUPS DARK CORN SYRUP
- 1 TEASPOON PURE VANILLA EXTRACT
- 1 CUP CHOPPED PECANS

IN MEDIUM BOWL COMBINE CAKE MIX, BUTTER AND 1 EGG; MIX UNTIL CRUMBLY. PRESS INTO 9×13 INCH GREASED CAKE PAN. BAKE 15 TO 20 MINUTES UNTIL LIGHT GOLDEN BROWN. MEANWHILE COMBINE RESERVED CAKE MIX, BROWN SUGAR, CORN SYRUP, VANILLA AND RESERVED EGGS. BEAT AT MEDIUM SPEED 1 TO 2 MINUTES. POUR SECOND MIXTURE OVER CRUST; SPRINKLE WITH PECANS AND BAKE 30 TO 35 MINUTES UNTIL FILLING IS SET. COOL; CUT INTO BARS.

APRICOT SQUARES

YIELD: 2 TO 3 DOZEN
PREHEAT OVEN: 350°

PREPARATION TIME: 20 MINUTES

COMBINE ALL INGREDIENTS EXCEPT PRESERVES. SPREAD ONE-HALF OF MIXTURE IN GREASED 9 INCH PAN. SPREAD PRESERVES OVER CRUMB MIXTURE. COVER WITH REMAINING CRUMB MIXTURE; PAT DOWN. BAKE ABOUT 35 MINUTES OR UNTIL LIGHTLY BROWN. REFRIGERATE. MAY BE FROZEN.

- **1** CUP SUGAR
- **2** CUPS PLUS 1 TABLESPOON ALL-PURPOSE FLOUR
- **1** EGG
- **3/4** CUP MARGARINE, SOFTENED
- **1/4** TEASPOON SALT
- **1** TEASPOON PURE VANILLA EXTRACT
- **1 1/3** CUPS SHREDDED COCONUT
- **1/2** CUP CHOPPED NUTS
- **12** OUNCES APRICOT PRESERVES

BRANDY BROWNIES

YIELD: 3 DOZEN
PREHEAT OVEN: 350°

PREPARATION TIME: 20 TO 30 MINUTES

MELT CHOCOLATE OVER LOW HEAT; COOL AND SET ASIDE. CREAM BUTTER AND SUGAR UNTIL FLUFFY. ADD EGGS; BEAT WELL. MIX TOGETHER CHOCOLATE, CREME DE CACAO, BRANDY AND VANILLA; ADD TO BUTTER MIXTURE. COMBINE FLOUR, BAKING POWDER AND SALT; ADD TO BUTTER MIXTURE. STIR IN PECANS. POUR BATTER INTO GREASED AND FLOURED 9 INCH SQUARE PAN. BAKE 20 TO 25 MINUTES; COOL. PREPARE FROSTING AND SPREAD ON TOP OF BROWNIES. CUT INTO 1 1/2 INCH SQUARES.

- **1** OUNCE UNSWEETENED CHOCOLATE
- **6** TABLESPOONS BUTTER, SOFTENED
- **3/4** CUP SUGAR
- **2** EGGS
- **2** TABLESPOONS CREME DE CACAO LIQUEUR
- **1 1/2** TABLESPOONS BRANDY
- **1** TEASPOON PURE VANILLA EXTRACT
- **2/3** CUP ALL-PURPOSE FLOUR
- **1/2** TEASPOON BAKING POWDER
- **1/4** TEASPOON SALT
- **1/2** CUP CHOPPED PECANS

CHOCOLATE BRANDY FROSTING:

SIFT CONFECTIONERS SUGAR IF LUMPY. ADD CREME DE CACAO, VANILLA AND BRANDY; BLEND WELL. ADD BUTTER; BEAT UNTIL SMOOTH.

- **1** CUP CONFECTIONERS SUGAR
- **1** TABLESPOON CREME DE CACAO LIQUEUR
- **1** TEASPOON PURE VANILLA EXTRACT
- **1 1/2** TABLESPOONS BRANDY
- **2** TABLESPOONS BUTTER, SOFTENED

MINT BROWNIES

VERY SPECIAL CHRISTMAS COOKIES.

PREPARATION TIME: 30 MINUTES

YIELD: 2 TO 3 DOZEN
PREHEAT OVEN: 350°

COOKIE LAYER:
- **1/2 CUP BUTTER**
- **2 OUNCES UNSWEETENED CHOCOLATE**
- **3/4 CUP ALL-PURPOSE FLOUR**
- **1 CUP SUGAR**
- **2 EGGS, BEATEN LIGHTLY**
- **1 TEASPOON PURE VANILLA EXTRACT**

IN SMALL PAN MELT BUTTER AND CHOCOLATE OVER LOW HEAT. COMBINE FLOUR AND SUGAR IN MEDIUM BOWL; ADD CHOCOLATE MIXTURE AND STIR TO BLEND. ADD EGGS AND VANILLA; BLEND WELL. POUR INTO GREASED 9×9 INCH PAN. BAKE 20 MINUTES.

MINT CREAM:
- **1 1/2 CUPS CONFECTIONERS SUGAR, SIFTED**
- **2 TABLESPOONS BUTTER, SOFTENED**
- **2 TABLESPOONS HEAVY CREAM**
- **3/4 TEASPOON PEPPERMINT FLAVORING**
- **GREEN FOOD COLORING**

COMBINE ALL INGREDIENTS; BEAT UNTIL SMOOTH. SPREAD OVER COOKIE LAYER; CHILL UNTIL FIRM.

CHOCOLATE GLAZE:
- **4 OUNCES GERMAN'S SWEET CHOCOLATE**
- **2 1/2 TABLESPOONS BUTTER**
- **1 1/4 TEASPOONS PURE VANILLA EXTRACT**

IN SMALL PAN MELT CHOCOLATE AND BUTTER OVER LOW HEAT. ADD VANILLA; POUR OVER BROWNIES. COOL AND CUT INTO SMALL SQUARES.

PECAN OATMEAL COOKIES

VERY DIFFERENT — CHILDREN REALLY LIKE THEM.

YIELD: 4 TO 5 DOZEN
PREHEAT OVEN: 350°
PREPARATION TIME: 30 MINUTES

- 1 CUP MARGARINE, SOFTENED
- 1½ CUPS SUGAR
- 2 EGGS (ROOM TEMPERATURE)
- 1 TEASPOON PURE VANILLA EXTRACT
- 2 CUPS ALL-PURPOSE FLOUR
- 1 TEASPOON BAKING SODA
- ½ TEASPOON SALT
- 2 CUPS QUICK OATS
- ½ CUP CHOPPED PECANS
- 1 CUP PECAN HALVES

IN LARGE BOWL, CREAM MARGARINE AND SUGAR. ADD EGGS AND VANILLA; BEAT. SIFT TOGETHER FLOUR, SODA AND SALT IN SMALL BOWL; ADD ONE-THIRD AT A TIME TO BUTTER MIXTURE. STIR IN OATS AND CHOPPED PECANS; MIX WELL. SHAPE INTO WALNUT SIZE BALLS. PLACE ON GREASED COOKIE SHEETS 2 INCHES APART; FLATTEN. PRESS PECAN HALF INTO CENTER OF EACH COOKIE. BAKE 15 TO 18 MINUTES OR UNTIL GOLDEN BROWN.

HINT: COOKIES KEEP WELL IN AIRTIGHT CONTAINER; FREEZE WELL, TOO.

OATMEAL CHEWS

YIELD: 5 DOZEN
PREHEAT OVEN: 350°
PREPARATION TIME: 45 MINUTES

- 1 CUP BUTTER
- 1 CUP SUGAR
- 1 CUP BROWN SUGAR, FIRMLY PACKED
- 2 EGGS
- 1 TEASPOON PURE VANILLA EXTRACT
- 2 CUPS ALL-PURPOSE FLOUR
- 2 TEASPOONS BAKING SODA
- ½ TEASPOON BAKING POWDER
- 1½ CUPS OLD FASHIONED OATS
- ½ CUP CHOPPED PECANS
- ½ CUP CHOCOLATE CHIPS
- 1½ CUPS FLAKED COCONUT

IN LARGE BOWL CREAM BUTTER WITH BOTH SUGARS. ADD EGGS AND VANILLA; MIX WELL. IN SMALL BOWL COMBINE FLOUR, SODA AND BAKING POWDER; ADD TO BUTTER MIXTURE. STIR IN OATS, PECANS AND CHOCOLATE CHIPS. REFRIGERATE ONE HOUR. ROLL INTO WALNUT SIZE BALLS; ROLL LIGHTLY IN COCONUT. PLACE ON LIGHTLY BUTTERED COOKIE SHEET; FLATTEN WITH FORK. BAKE 8 MINUTES. FOR BEST RESULTS, BAKE ONE SHEET OF COOKIES AT A TIME ON CENTER RACK OF OVEN.

HINT: FOR VARIETY, SUBSTITUTE RAISINS FOR THE CHOCOLATE CHIPS.

PRALINE BUTTER COOKIES

PREPARATION TIME: 20 MINUTES

YIELD: 4 DOZEN
PREHEAT OVEN: 300°

- 1 CUP BUTTER, SOFTENED (NO SUBSTITUTIONS)
- 1 CUP SUGAR
- 2 EGG YOLKS
- 1/2 TEASPOON PURE VANILLA EXTRACT
- 2 TABLESPOONS PRALINE LIQUEUR
- 2 CUPS ALL-PURPOSE FLOUR
- 1 TEASPOON BAKING POWDER
- 1/4 TEASPOON SALT
- 1 CUP PECAN HALVES (APPROXIMATELY)

IN MEDIUM BOWL CREAM BUTTER; GRADUALLY ADD SUGAR, BEATING UNTIL LIGHT AND FLUFFY. ADD EGG YOLKS, ONE AT A TIME, BEATING WELL AFTER EACH ADDITION. ADD VANILLA AND PRALINE LIQUEUR. COMBINE FLOUR, BAKING POWDER AND SALT. ADD TO CREAMED MIXTURE AND BEAT WELL. ROLL DOUGH INTO 1 INCH BALLS; PLACE ABOUT 2 INCHES APART ON UNGREASED COOKIE SHEETS. PRESS PECAN HALF INTO CENTER OF EACH COOKIE AND FLATTEN. BAKE 20 MINUTES OR UNTIL LIGHTLY GOLDEN. COOL ON WIRE RACKS.

HINT: *MAY SUBSTITUTE 1 TABLESPOON BOURBON FOR PRALINE LIQUEUR. DOUGH MAY BE CHILLED BEFORE BALLS ARE MADE.*

SNOWBALLS

SENT TO SOLDIERS DURING WWII — STAYED FRESH FOR MONTHS.

PREPARATION TIME: 30 MINUTES

YIELD: 4 TO 5 DOZEN
PREHEAT OVEN: 250°

- 1 CUP BUTTER, SOFTENED
- 4 TABLESPOONS CONFECTIONERS SUGAR
- 2 TEASPOONS PURE VANILLA EXTRACT
- 2 CUPS ALL-PURPOSE FLOUR
- DASH SALT
- 2 CUPS CHOPPED PECANS
- CONFECTIONERS SUGAR

CREAM BUTTER, SUGAR AND VANILLA IN MEDIUM BOWL. ADD FLOUR AND SALT; COMBINE WELL. ADD PECANS. ROLL DOUGH INTO SMALL BALLS AND PLACE VERY CLOSE TOGETHER ON UNGREASED COOKIE SHEET. BAKE 35 TO 40 MINUTES. DO NOT BROWN. *IMMEDIATELY* ROLL COOKIES IN POWDERED SUGAR; *IMMEDIATELY* ROLL AGAIN UNTIL HEAVILY COATED.

ALMOND CHRISTMAS COOKIES

YIELD: 4 DOZEN
PREHEAT OVEN: 325°

PREPARATION TIME: 20 MINUTES

CREAM BUTTER, VANILLA AND SUGAR IN LARGE BOWL. ADD FLOUR AND ALMONDS; MIX AND KNEAD DOUGH WITH HANDS UNTIL WELL COMBINED. ROLL DOUGH A TEASPOON AT A TIME INTO SMALL BALLS. PLACE ON UNGREASED COOKIE SHEET; PRESS CHERRY INTO EACH BALL. BAKE 20 TO 30 MINUTES OR UNTIL LIGHT BROWN. REMOVE FROM SHEET AND DUST WARM COOKIES WITH CONFECTIONERS SUGAR.

1 CUP BUTTER, SOFTENED
1 TEASPOON PURE VANILLA EXTRACT
1/2 CUP CONFECTIONERS SUGAR
2 CUPS ALL-PURPOSE FLOUR
1 CUP GROUND ALMONDS
1/2 TO 1 POUND WHOLE CANDIED CHERRIES (GREEN OR RED)
ADDITIONAL CONFECTIONERS SUGAR FOR DUSTING

HINT: THESE KEEP WELL IN COOKIE TIN AND CAN BE STORED SEVERAL WEEKS.

APPLE JACKS

FUN TO MAKE AND EAT.

YIELD: 3 DOZEN
PREHEAT OVEN: 375°

PREPARATION TIME: 30 MINUTES

IN LARGE BOWL, CREAM SHORTENING AND SUGAR. BEAT IN EGG. SIFT DRY INGREDIENTS INTO CREAMED MIXTURE AND BLEND WELL. FOLD IN APPLES. SHAPE INTO SMALL BALLS AND PLACE ON GREASED COOKIE SHEET. BAKE 10 TO 12 MINUTES. REMOVE FROM OVEN AND SPRINKLE EACH COOKIE WITH 4 TO 5 DROPS OF RUM.

1/2 CUP SHORTENING
1 CUP LIGHT BROWN SUGAR, FIRMLY PACKED
1 EGG
1 1/2 CUPS ALL-PURPOSE FLOUR
1/2 TEASPOON SALT
1 TEASPOON FRESHLY GRATED NUTMEG
1 CUP CORED, CHOPPED UNPEELED APPLES
RUM

HINT: FREEZES WELL.

CHOCOLATE KRINKLE MACAROONS

PREPARATION TIME: 40 MINUTES

YIELD: 6 TO 7 DOZEN
PREHEAT OVEN: 350°

1/2 CUP VEGETABLE OIL
4 SQUARES UNSWEETENED CHOCOLATE, MELTED
2 CUPS SUGAR
4 EGGS
2 TEASPOONS PURE VANILLA EXTRACT
2 CUPS ALL-PURPOSE FLOUR
2 TEASPOONS BAKING POWDER
1 CUP CONFECTIONERS SUGAR

COMBINE OIL, CHOCOLATE AND SUGAR. BEAT IN EGGS, ONE AT A TIME; MIX WELL. ADD VANILLA. COMBINE FLOUR AND BAKING POWDER AND ADD TO CHOCOLATE MIXTURE; BLEND WELL. CHILL SEVERAL HOURS OR OVERNIGHT. ROLL DOUGH INTO SMALL BALLS AND ROLL IN CONFECTIONERS SUGAR. PLACE ABOUT 2 INCHES APART ON GREASED BAKING SHEET. BAKE 10 TO 12 MINUTES. DO NOT OVERBAKE. COOL ON SHEET 5 TO 10 MINUTES BEFORE REMOVING.

HINT: DOUGH CAN BE KEPT IN REFRIGERATOR SEVERAL DAYS BEFORE BAKING.

ESKIMO COOKIES

A NO-BAKE COOKIE; STORE IN THE REFRIGERATOR.

PREPARATION TIME: 40 MINUTES

YIELD: 2 1/2 TO 3 DOZEN

3/4 CUP BUTTER BLEND MARGARINE
3/4 CUP SUGAR
1 TEASPOON WATER
1 TEASPOON PURE VANILLA EXTRACT
3 TABLESPOONS COCOA POWDER
2 CUPS OLD-FASHIONED OATS
1 CUP CONFECTIONERS SUGAR

IN LARGE BOWL CREAM BUTTER AND SUGAR UNTIL WELL BLENDED. ADD WATER, VANILLA AND COCOA; MIX WELL. STIR IN OATS; COVER AND REFRIGERATE SEVERAL HOURS OR OVERNIGHT. POUR CONFECTIONERS SUGAR INTO SMALL BOWL. FORM DOUGH INTO 1 INCH BALLS; ROLL IN CONFECTIONERS SUGAR. PLACE COOKIES IN CONTAINER; REFRIGERATE.

MOCHA CHOCOLATE CHIP COOKIES 

YIELD: 7 DOZEN
PREHEAT OVEN: 350°

PREPARATION TIME: 30 MINUTES

- 3 CUPS SEMI-SWEET CHOCOLATE CHIPS (RESERVE 1½ CUPS)
- ½ CUP BUTTER
- 4 OUNCES UNSWEETENED CHOCOLATE
- ½ CUP ALL-PURPOSE FLOUR
- ½ TEASPOON BAKING POWDER
- ½ TEASPOON SALT
- 4 EGGS, ROOM TEMPERATURE
- 1½ CUPS SUGAR
- 1 TABLESPOON INSTANT COFFEE POWDER
- 1 TEASPOON CINNAMON
- 2 TEASPOONS PURE VANILLA EXTRACT
- ½ CUP CHOPPED PECANS

MELT 1½ CUPS CHOCOLATE CHIPS, BUTTER AND UNSWEETENED CHOCOLATE IN TOP OF DOUBLE BOILER OVER HOT, NOT BOILING, WATER. STIR UNTIL MELTED AND SMOOTH. REMOVE FROM HEAT; SET ASIDE. COMBINE FLOUR, BAKING POWDER AND SALT; SET ASIDE. IN LARGE BOWL COMBINE EGGS, SUGAR, COFFEE POWDER, CINNAMON AND VANILLA; BEAT 2 MINUTES. ADD CHOCOLATE MIXTURE; COMBINE. ADD FLOUR MIXTURE; COMBINE. STIR IN RESERVED CHOCOLATE CHIPS AND PECANS.

LINE BAKING SHEETS WITH PARCHMENT PAPER. DROP BATTER ONTO PREPARED SHEETS BY TEASPOONS. BAKE UNTIL COOKIES ARE CRACKED AND SHINY ON SURFACE, ABOUT 8 MINUTES. *DO NOT OVERBAKE.* COOL COMPLETELY BEFORE REMOVING FROM SHEETS. STORE IN AIR-TIGHT CONTAINER.

CHRISTMAS JEWEL COOKIES

YIELD: 4 DOZEN
PREHEAT OVEN: 375°

PREPARATION TIME: 1 HOUR

- 1 CUP BUTTER, SOFTENED (NO SUBSTITUTIONS)
- 1¼ CUPS SUGAR
- 1 EGG, BEATEN WELL
- 1 TEASPOON PURE VANILLA EXTRACT
- 2½ CUPS ALL-PURPOSE FLOUR (RESERVE ½ CUP)
- 1½ TEASPOONS BAKING SODA
- ¼ TEASPOON SALT
- 4 OUNCES CANDIED PINEAPPLE, CHOPPED
- 2 OUNCES EACH RED AND GREEN CANDIED CHERRIES, CHOPPED
- ½ CUP WHITE RAISINS
- 1 CUP CHOPPED PECANS

WITH MIXER CREAM BUTTER AND SUGAR. ADD EGG AND VANILLA; COMBINE WELL. SIFT TOGETHER 2 CUPS FLOUR, SODA AND SALT; ADD TO BUTTER MIXTURE, BEATING WELL. COMBINE RESERVED FLOUR WITH REMAINING INGREDIENTS; STIR INTO DOUGH. COVER AND REFRIGERATE SEVERAL HOURS. FORM DOUGH INTO 6 ROLLS, 1 INCH IN DIAMETER. COVER AND REFRIGERATE UNTIL FIRM. SLICE DOUGH AND PLACE ON UNGREASED BAKING SHEET. BAKE 10 MINUTES. REMOVE COOKIES AND COOL.

SPICY GINGER SNAPS

PREPARATION TIME: 30 MINUTES

YIELD: 3 TO 4 DOZEN
PREHEAT OVEN: 375°

- 3/4 CUP SHORTENING
- 1 CUP BROWN SUGAR, FIRMLY PACKED
- 1/4 CUP MOLASSES
- 1 EGG
- 2 1/4 CUPS ALL-PURPOSE FLOUR
- 1/2 TEASPOON SALT
- 1 TEASPOON GINGER
- 1 TEASPOON CINNAMON
- 1/2 TEASPOON GROUND CLOVES
- GRANULATED SUGAR

IN LARGE BOWL CREAM SHORTENING, SUGAR, MOLASSES AND EGG UNTIL LIGHT. COMBINE DRY INGREDIENTS IN SMALL BOWL; GRADUALLY ADD TO CREAMED MIXTURE. FORM INTO SMALL BALLS AND ROLL IN SUGAR. PLACE ON UNGREASED COOKIE SHEET AND BAKE 10 MINUTES. DOUGH MAY BE CHILLED AND BAKED AT A LATER TIME.

HINT: THESE IMPROVE WITH AGE AND CAN BE KEPT IN COOKIE TIN 3 TO 4 WEEKS.

MERINGUE COOKIES

PREPARATION TIME: 15 MINUTES

YIELD: 3 DOZEN
PREHEAT OVEN: 275°

- 2 EGG WHITES
- 1 TEASPOON PURE VANILLA EXTRACT
- 1/4 TEASPOON SALT
- 1/2 CUP SUGAR
- ONE OR MORE OF FOLLOWING:
- 1 CUP FLAKED COCONUT
- 1 CUP CHOPPED NUTS
- 1 CUP CHOPPED DATES
- 1 CUP CHOCOLATE CHIPS
- 1 CUP BUTTERSCOTCH CHIPS
- 1 CUP RAISINS

IN MEDIUM BOWL BEAT EGG WHITES UNTIL FOAMY. ADD VANILLA AND SALT; BEAT UNTIL STIFF, BUT NOT DRY. CONTINUE BEATING WHILE GRADUALLY ADDING SUGAR. MIX THOROUGHLY. FOLD IN COCONUT, NUTS, DATES, CHIPS OR RAISINS. DROP BY TEASPOONS ONTO WELL BUTTERED COOKIE SHEET. BAKE 30 MINUTES. REMOVE IMMEDIATELY.

HINT: THIS COOKIE DOES NOT FREEZE WELL.

Techniques

For low-cal soda prepare frozen juice concentrate as directed on package. Fill glass half full with juice and add club soda.

For quick salad, marinate choice of vegetables in low calorie dressing.

When eating salad with dressing, place dressing in small dish beside the salad. By lightly dipping forkfuls into dressing, you will use less and thus save calories.

Make meaty soups and sauces day ahead, refrigerate overnight and skim off fat that has risen to top and hardened. It saves 100 calories per tablespoon.

When making stock, toss in onion skins to give golden color. Strain before using.

For lighter pancakes and waffles, substitute club soda, sparkling mineral water or seltzer for amount of liquid called for in batter.

Toasted wheat germ, raw unprocessed bran and whole wheat flours may be kept in freezer several months. Thawing is not necessary before using.

An empty clean lemon juice or other plastic squeeze bottle is ideal for sprinkling oil sparingly into skillets or on baking pans.

To easily remove skin from uncooked chicken, use paper towels to get a firmer grip.

Baste fish with white wine instead of butter when broiling. Alcohol burns off and adds no calories.

Thicken with cornstarch instead of flour. While both have about the same calories per tablespoon, less cornstarch is needed.

Use whipped butter instead of regular (except in baking). It looks like more, spreads more easily and you save 10 calories per teaspoon.

To season vegetables or rice without butter, add 1 bouillon cube to liquid. No additional salt is needed.

Prepare low calorie whipped topping by beating very ripe banana with an egg white until stiff and banana completely dissolves, about 4 minutes.

Neufchatel cheese may be substituted for cream cheese in most recipes. It contains lower fat and fewer calories.

Disclaimer

THE NUTRITIONAL INFORMATION INCLUDED IN THIS SECTION IS APPROXIMATE AND SHOULD BE USED ONLY AS A GENERAL GUIDE.

Spinach Dip

Yield: 2 1/2 cups

Preparation Time: 20 minutes

- **1 cup low-fat cottage cheese**
- **1/2 cup reduced-calorie mayonnaise**
- **1/2 cup chopped green onions**
- **1/2 cup chopped fresh parsley**
- **1 tablespoon dried dill weed**
- **10 ounces frozen spinach, thawed and squeezed dry**
- **1/4 teaspoon Tabasco**
- **1/2 small carrot, chopped**

Combine all ingredients in food processor or blender 1 to 2 minutes or until smooth. Chill mixture overnight. Serve with fresh vegetables such as cucumber, celery, carrots, zucchini or broccoli.

HINT: Be sure all moisture is removed from spinach.

NUTRITIONAL INFORMATION: 14 calories per tablespoon

Low-Calorie Onion Dip

Tastes just like regular onion dip.

Yield: 2 1/2 cups

Preparation Time: 5 minutes

- **1/2 cup skim milk (or low-fat)**
- **2 cups low-fat cottage cheese**
- **1.25 ounces dry onion soup mix**

Combine milk and cottage cheese in blender or food processor until smooth. Stir in soup mix; chill two hours. Serve with fresh vegetables.

NUTRITIONAL INFORMATION PER SERVING: 13 calories per tablespoon

TORTILLA BEEF APPETIZERS

PREPARATION TIME: 20 MINUTES

YIELD: 40 APPETIZERS

4 10-INCH FLOUR TORTILLAS
8 OUNCES BACON-HORSERADISH DIP
10 OUNCES *THINLY SLICED* COOKED ROAST BEEF

COVER EACH TORTILLA WITH 2 TABLESPOONS HORSERADISH DIP. TOP WITH ONE-FOURTH OF BEEF. SPREAD WITH ANOTHER 2 TABLESPOONS DIP. ROLL TORTILLAS UP JELLY-ROLL STYLE. PLACE SEAM SIDE DOWN ON PLATTER. FREEZE 4 HOURS; REMOVE. USING SHARP KNIFE, SLICE INTO 1 INCH PIECES. THAW; SECURE WITH TOOTHPICKS.

HINT: 7½ OUNCES (3 PACKAGES) SLICED SMOKED OR DRIED BEEF MAY BE SUBSTITUTED FOR ROAST BEEF.

NUTRITIONAL INFORMATION: 45 CALORIES EACH

SESAME PITA CHIPS

LOW SODIUM SNACK ALTERNATIVE TO POTATO CHIPS.

PREPARATION TIME: 10 MINUTES

YIELD: 48 CHIPS
PREHEAT OVEN: 350°

2 TABLESPOONS VEGETABLE OIL
1 TABLESPOON GRATED PARMESAN CHEESE
1 TEASPOON SESAME SEED
¼ TEASPOON DRIED BASIL, CRUMBLED
⅛ TEASPOON GROUND RED PEPPER
3 PITA BREAD ROUNDS

IN LARGE BOWL, COMBINE OIL, CHEESE, SESAME SEED AND SEASONINGS. CUT PITA ROUNDS INTO EIGHTHS; SEPARATE LAYERS TO MAKE 16 CHIPS FROM EACH ROUND. TOSS CHIPS IN OIL MIXTURE UNTIL WELL COATED. PLACE IN SINGLE LAYER ON UNGREASED BAKING SHEET AND BAKE 10 TO 12 MINUTES UNTIL CRISP AND GOLDEN.

NUTRITIONAL INFORMATION PER SERVING: 9 CALORIES PER CHIP

ZUCCHINI SQUARES

YIELD: 24 SQUARES
PREHEAT OVEN: 325°

PREPARATION TIME: 45 MINUTES

IN LARGE SKILLET OVER MEDIUM HEAT, SAUTÉ ONION AND GARLIC IN MARGARINE UNTIL GOLDEN. ADD ZUCCHINI AND COOK, STIRRING, ABOUT 2 MINUTES OR UNTIL TENDER-CRISP. REMOVE FROM HEAT AND SET ASIDE.

COMBINE EGGS, CHEESE, CORNMEAL, SEASONINGS AND ZUCCHINI MIXTURE IN LARGE BOWL. POUR INTO GREASED 8 INCH SQUARE BAKING PAN. BAKE 20 TO 25 MINUTES OR UNTIL SET. CUT IN BITE-SIZE SQUARES AND SERVE HOT.

- 2 TABLESPOONS MINCED ONION
- 1 CLOVE GARLIC, MINCED
- 1 TABLESPOON MARGARINE
- 1½ CUPS COARSELY GRATED ZUCCHINI
- 3 EGGS, BEATEN LIGHTLY
- 1½ CUPS SHREDDED MONTEREY JACK CHEESE
- 3 TABLESPOONS CORNMEAL
- ¼ TEASPOON DRIED THYME, CRUMBLED
- ¼ TEASPOON CUMIN SEED, CRUSHED
- ¼ TEASPOON DRIED OREGANO, CRUMBLED
- DASH NUTMEG

NUTRITIONAL INFORMATION PER SERVING: 40 CALORIES

CHESAPEAKE CRAB

TART, TANGY, TERRIFIC TASTING.

YIELD: 1½ CUPS

PREPARATION TIME: 10 MINUTES

COMBINE ALL INGREDIENTS EXCEPT YOGURT; MIX WELL. FOLD IN YOGURT. COVER; CHILL SEVERAL HOURS. SERVE ON TOAST ROUNDS OR SMALL SLICES OF SWISS CHEESE.

- 1 CUP FRESH CRABMEAT, FLAKED
- 1 TEASPOON HORSERADISH
- ¼ TEASPOON DRIED BASIL, CRUMBLED
- ¼ TEASPOON DRIED THYME, CRUMBLED
- ⅛ TEASPOON SALT
- DASH GROUND RED PEPPER
- ½ CUP PLAIN LOW-FAT YOGURT
- TOAST ROUNDS OR SWISS CHEESE

NUTRITIONAL INFORMATION: 10 CALORIES PER TABLESPOON.

Mushroom Caps with Seasoned Stuffing

Preparation Time: 30 minutes

Yield: 24
Preheat Oven: 350°

- 24 medium fresh mushrooms
- 1/2 cup soft breadcrumbs
- 1/3 cup grated Parmesan cheese
- 1/4 cup extra virgin olive oil
- 1/4 cup minced onion
- 2 tablespoons minced fresh parsley
- 1 clove garlic, minced
- 1/4 teaspoon dried oregano, crumbled
- 1/4 teaspoon dried basil, crumbled
- 1/4 teaspoon freshly ground pepper

Remove mushroom stems; mince. Set caps aside. In small bowl combine stems with remaining ingredients; mix well. Press mixture into caps. Place caps on jelly roll pan; add 1/4 cup water to bottom of pan. Bake 25 to 30 minutes. Serve hot. May also be served as vegetable side dish.

Nutritional Information: 38 calories each

Mocha Cocoa

Preparation Time: 15 minutes

Yield: 7 cups

- 3 tablespoons sugar
- 3 tablespoons cocoa powder
- 3 tablespoons instant coffee granules
- 1/4 teaspoon nutmeg
- 1/2 cup water
- 1 3 inch cinnamon stick
- 6 1/2 cups skim milk
- 1 1/2 teaspoons pure vanilla extract

In large saucepan combine sugar, cocoa, coffee, nutmeg, water and cinnamon. Heat, stirring constantly, until liquid boils. Lower heat; add milk and vanilla and simmer until thoroughly heated. Discard cinnamon stick; pour into mugs.

Hint: Add cinnamon stick to each mug as flavorful garnish.

Nutritional Information per Serving: 116 calories

Grapeberry Holiday Punch

Yield: 50 4-ounce servings

Preparation Time: 15 minutes

24 ounces frozen grape juice, thawed and undiluted
6 ounces frozen cranberry juice, thawed and undiluted
4 cups unsweetened orange juice, chilled
Ice cubes
4 liters diet lemon-lime soda, chilled
Orange and lemon slices

Combine grape, cranberry and orange juices in large pitcher. Chill. To serve, pour juice mixture into large punch bowl; add ice and soda. Float orange and lemon slices in punch.

HINT: For smaller crowd, halve ingredients and serve from pitcher.

NUTRITIONAL INFORMATION PER SERVING: 20 calories

Sea Breeze Tomato Cocktail

Yield: 7¼ cups

Preparation Time: 10 minutes

4 cups clam and tomato juice
2 cups tomato juice
10 ounces Snap • E • Tom tomato and chili cocktail
1 tablespoon fresh lemon juice
1 teaspoon Worcestershire sauce
¾ teaspoon celery seeds, crushed
½ teaspoon freshly ground pepper
½ teaspoon Tabasco
Leafy celery sticks

Combine all ingredients except celery, mixing well. Chill several hours before serving. Garnish with leafy celery sticks.

HINT: Leafy celery sticks add color and make tasty swizzle sticks.

NUTRITIONAL INFORMATION PER SERVING: 45 calories

Fruited Iced Teas

Preparation Time: 5 minutes

Yield: 8 cups

- 2 cups boiling water
- 4 tea bags
- 6 cups unsweetened apple juice
- Orange slices

Pour boiling water over tea bags; steep 4 minutes. Remove tea bags; chill. Combine with apple juice; blend. Serve over ice; garnish with orange slices.

Variation: Omit apple juice. Add 1 cup orange juice, 1/4 cup fresh lemon juice and 2 tablespoons sugar.

Nutritional Information per Serving: 60 calories

Cran-Orange Blender Drink

Preparation Time: 15 minutes

Yield: 5 cups

- 3 cups cranapple juice
- 1 1/2 cups orange juice
- 1 banana, sliced
- 1/4 teaspoon pure vanilla extract

Combine juices, banana and vanilla in blender. Mix until frothy. Serve immediately.

Nutritional Information per Serving: 128 calories

Strawberry Shake

Preparation Time: 10 minutes

Yield: 6 servings

- 3 cups frozen whole strawberries
- 1 1/2 cups skim milk
- 2 tablespoons plain low-fat yogurt
- 1/2 banana, sliced
- 1 tablespoon sugar
- 1 teaspoon pure vanilla extract

Mix all ingredients in blender until smooth. Serve immediately.

Nutritional Information per Serving: 55 calories

CHICKEN SALAD INDIENNE

YIELD: 4 SERVINGS

PREPARATION TIME: 20 MINUTES

- 2 CUPS COLD COOKED RICE
- 2 CUPS COOKED, DICED CHICKEN
- 1 CUP FRESH ORANGE SECTIONS
- 1/3 CUP CHOPPED CELERY
- 1/4 CUP REDUCED-CALORIE MAYONNAISE
- 1/4 CUP LOW-FAT PLAIN YOGURT
- 1 TABLESPOON CHOPPED GREEN ONIONS
- 1 TABLESPOON GOLDEN RAISINS
- 1 TEASPOON CURRY POWDER
- 1/4 TEASPOON GROUND NUTMEG
- 1/4 TEASPOON THYME, CRUMBLED
- SHREDDED LETTUCE OR TOMATO WEDGES
- SLICED ALMONDS

COMBINE RICE, CHICKEN, ORANGE SECTIONS, CELERY, MAYONNAISE, YOGURT, GREEN ONIONS, RAISINS, CURRY POWDER, NUTMEG AND THYME IN LARGE BOWL; MIX THOROUGHLY. COVER AND CHILL SEVERAL HOURS. SERVE ON SHREDDED LETTUCE OR OVER TOMATO WEDGES. GARNISH WITH ALMONDS.

NUTRITIONAL INFORMATION PER SERVING: 259 CALORIES

SAN FRANCISCO PASTA SALAD

YIELD: 6 SERVINGS

PREPARATION TIME: 30 MINUTES

- 4 CUPS COOKED PASTA (SUCH AS SPAGHETTI, BROKEN INTO 2 INCH PIECES, OR MACARONI)
- 1 TABLESPOON VEGETABLE OIL
- 1 TABLESPOON FRESH LEMON JUICE
- 2 TABLESPOONS DICED CELERY
- 2 TABLESPOONS CHOPPED GREEN ONIONS
- 2 TABLESPOONS CHOPPED FRESH PARSLEY
- 1/2 CUP REDUCED-CALORIE MAYONNAISE
- 2 1/2 CUPS FRESH CRABMEAT, FLAKED

TOSS WARM PASTA WITH OIL AND LEMON JUICE. IN LARGE BOWL, COMBINE PASTA AND REMAINING INGREDIENTS EXCEPT CRAB AND MIX WELL. ADD CRAB AND TOSS GENTLY. COVER; CHILL SEVERAL HOURS BEFORE SERVING.

NUTRITIONAL INFORMATION PER SERVING: 160 CALORIES

Cotillion Chicken Salad

Preparation Time: 20 minutes — *Yield: 4 to 6 servings*

- 4 cups cooked, cubed chicken
- 1 cup thinly sliced celery
- 1 tablespoon chopped green onions
- 1/4 cup coarsely chopped pecans
- 1/4 teaspoon salt
- 1/3 cup reduced-calorie mayonnaise
- 1 teaspoon fresh lemon juice
- 1/2 teaspoon Dijon mustard
- 1 cup peeled, cubed Kiwi fruit

In large bowl, combine chicken, celery, green onions, pecans and salt. Set aside. Combine mayonnaise, lemon juice and mustard in small bowl; pour over chicken mixture and toss gently. Cover and chill to meld flavors. Just before serving, stir in Kiwi.

Nutritional Information per 3/4 cup serving: 141 calories

Marinated Shrimp Salad

Preparation Time: 30 minutes — *Yield: 6 servings*

- 2 1/2 pounds medium fresh shrimp, cooked, peeled and deveined
- 1/2 cup diagonally sliced celery
- 1/2 cup chopped green bell pepper
- 1/3 cup slivered red onion
- 1/2 cup unpeeled chopped cucumber
- 2 ounces diced pimiento, drained
- 1 cup unsweetened apple juice
- 2/3 cup cider vinegar
- 1/2 teaspoon Tabasco
- 1/4 teaspoon paprika
- 1/3 pound fresh snow peas

Combine shrimp, celery, bell pepper, onion, cucumber and pimiento in large non-aluminum shallow dish. Mix apple juice, vinegar, Tabasco and paprika; pour over shrimp mixture. Cover and refrigerate overnight. Stir occasionally.

Steam snow peas 3 to 5 minutes or until tender-crisp. Chill.

Fan snow peas around edge of serving platter and mound shrimp mixture in center. Serve immediately.

Nutritional Information per serving: 154 calories

Asparagus Spears Vinaigrette

Simple but sensational.

Yield: 4 servings *Preparation Time: 10 minutes*

Cook asparagus until just tender; drain and chill. Combine oil, vinegar, parsley, onion and seasonings; chill 1 hour.

Arrange lettuce leaves on each salad plate and top with asparagus. Spoon dressing over and garnish with pimiento strips.

- **10 ounces frozen asparagus spears**
- **1/4 cup vegetable oil**
- **3 tablespoons vinegar**
- **1 tablespoon minced fresh parsley**
- **1 teaspoon finely chopped red onion**
- **1/4 teaspoon dried basil, crumbled**
- **1/4 teaspoon salt**
- **1/8 teaspoon freshly ground pepper**
- **Red leaf lettuce leaves**
- **Pimiento strips**

NUTRITIONAL INFORMATION PER SERVING: 28 calories

Calico Slaw

Colorful with zesty flavor.

Yield: 8 servings *Preparation Time: 20 minutes*

Combine all ingredients and toss well. Chill 1 hour or overnight to blend flavors.

- **3 cups shredded green cabbage**
- **1 1/2 cups shredded red cabbage**
- **1/2 cup shredded carrot**
- **1/2 cup chopped celery**
- **1/4 cup chopped green onions**
- **2 tablespoons chopped green bell pepper**
- **3/4 cup reduced-calorie coleslaw or cucumber dressing**

NUTRITIONAL INFORMATION: High fiber

CITRUS SPINACH SALAD

PREPARATION TIME: 15 MINUTES

YIELD: 4 TO 6 SERVINGS

1 POUND FRESH SPINACH
1 CUP FRESH GRAPEFRUIT SEGMENTS
1 CUP FRESH ORANGE SEGMENTS
1 RED ONION, THINLY SLICED AND SEPARATED INTO RINGS
SEEDS OF 1 POMEGRANATE

REMOVE STEMS FROM SPINACH AND TEAR INTO BITE-SIZE PIECES. COMBINE SPINACH, FRUIT AND ONION. PREPARE DRESSING AND POUR OVER SPINACH MIXTURE; TOSS UNTIL THOROUGHLY MIXED. SPRINKLE POMEGRANATE SEEDS OVER TOP.

DIJON SALAD DRESSING:
1/3 CUP CORN OIL
2 TABLESPOONS VINEGAR
2 TABLESPOONS FRESH LEMON JUICE
1/2 TEASPOON DIJON MUSTARD
1/2 TEASPOON DRIED BASIL, CRUMBLED

MIX ALL INGREDIENTS IN JAR WITH TIGHT FITTING LID. REFRIGERATE AT LEAST 1 HOUR BEFORE USING. SHAKE VIGOROUSLY TO RECOMBINE BEFORE ADDING TO SALAD.

HINT: POMEGRANATE SEEDS ARE A CRUNCHY, COLORFUL ACCENT. IF UNAVAILABLE, SUBSTITUTE 2 TABLESPOONS SUNFLOWER SEEDS.

NUTRITIONAL INFORMATION: HIGH IN FIBER AND VITAMIN C

SAUCE VINAIGRETTE

PREPARATION TIME: 8 MINUTES

YIELD: 5 TABLESPOONS

SALT, TO TASTE
1 TABLESPOON RED WINE VINEGAR
1 1/2 TEASPOONS DIJON MUSTARD
3 TABLESPOONS SAFFLOWER OIL
FRESHLY GROUND PEPPER, TO TASTE

IN SMALL BOWL, COMBINE SALT, VINEGAR AND MUSTARD THOROUGHLY. ADD OIL, MIX WELL. ADD PEPPER AND BLEND.

USE 1 TABLESPOON ON SMALL SALAD FOR 2 OR 3 SERVINGS. TOSS WELL.

HINT: DOUBLE RECIPE AND STORE EXTRA IN REFRIGERATOR.

NUTRITIONAL INFORMATION: 76 CALORIES PER TABLESPOON

Sesame Seed-Honey Dressing

Yield: 6 1/2 tablespoons — *Preparation Time: 5 minutes*

Place all ingredients in blender and mix 40 seconds. Refrigerate.

- **3 tablespoons vegetable stock**
- **1 1/2 tablespoons sesame seeds**
- **1 tablespoon fresh lemon juice**
- **2 teaspoons honey**
- **1 teaspoon safflower oil**
- **2 drops Tabasco**
- **Dash curry powder**

Nutritional Information: 26 calories per tablespoon

Blue Cheese Dressing

Yield: 1 1/2 cups — *Preparation Time: 10 minutes*

Combine cheeses, milk and mustard in blender or processor. Add garlic and process 25 seconds (blue cheese should be chunky). May be refrigerated up to one week in tighty covered jar.

- **1 1/4 cups low-fat cottage cheese**
- **2 tablespoons (rounded) crumbled blue cheese**
- **2 tablespoons skim milk**
- **1/2 teaspoon Dijon mustard**
- **1 clove garlic, minced**

Nutritional Information: 10 calories per tablespoon

Akin's Vegetarian Chili

"You'd swear there was meat in it!"

Preparation Time: 1 hour | *Yield: 6 to 8 servings*

1½ tablespoons safflower oil
3 cups chopped fresh mushrooms
3 cups chopped onion
1 cup chopped carrot
1 cup chopped celery
4 cloves garlic, minced
28 ounces canned tomatoes, chopped
13 ounces tomato juice
10 ounces canned Rotel tomatoes with green chiles
½ pound pinto beans, cooked, undrained (or 30 ounces canned pinto beans, undrained)
3 tablespoons chili powder
1½ teaspoons ground cumin
1 teaspoon dried oregano, crumbled
½ teaspoon ground coriander
Salt and freshly ground pepper, to taste

In large pan heat oil and sauté mushrooms, onion, carrot, celery and garlic about 5 minutes. Add tomatoes, tomato juice, Rotel tomatoes and pinto beans. Simmer 15 minutes over medium heat. Add chili powder, cumin, oregano, coriander, salt and pepper. Simmer additional 10 minutes; serve immediately.

Akin's Special Foods

NUTRITIONAL INFORMATION: Meatless Entre

Chiffon Consommé

Simple, but delicious with delicate flavor.

Preparation Time: 25 minutes | *Yield: 4 servings*

3 cups chicken broth
1½ cups finely grated zucchini
1 teaspoon fresh lemon juice

Combine broth and zucchini in large saucepan. Heat to boil; reduce heat to low and simmer 12 to 15 minutes. Stir in lemon juice and serve.

NUTRITIONAL INFORMATION PER SERVING: 44 calories

Peppery Chicken Consommé

Yield: 6 1/2 cup servings *Preparation Time: 10 minutes*

Combine stock, peppercorns, red pepper, garlic and lemon juice in saucepan. Bring to boil; simmer 20 minutes. Strain and return to pan. Add salt, if desired; heat through. Add green onions and mushrooms. Ladle into bowls and serve immediately.

- **4 cups clarified chicken stock**
- **1 teaspoon black peppercorns**
- **1/4 teaspoon dried red pepper flakes**
- **1 clove garlic, sliced**
- **3 tablespoons fresh lemon juice**
- **Salt, to taste**
- **2 tablespoons chopped green onions**
- **1/2 cup sliced fresh mushrooms**

Nutritional Information per serving: 11 calories

Spicy Mexican Tomato Soup

Yield: 16 5 ounce servings *Preparation Time: 15 minutes*

Pureé tomatoes in blender or food processor. In large saucepan, heat oil; add onion, green chiles, and garlic powder. Simmer 2 to 3 minutes. Add flour and cook 1 minute. Gradually stir in tomatoes and chicken broth. Add spices, salt, pepper, and sugar; bring to boil. Reduce heat; simmer 15 to 20 minutes, stirring often. Cool; cover and refrigerate 3 hours. Stir in sour cream; cover and refrigerate 2 to 48 hours. Ladle into clear mugs or wine glasses. Garnish with parsley and lemon slices.

- **2 pounds ripe tomatoes, peeled and seeded (or 28 ounces canned Italian plum tomatoes)**
- **2 tablespoons extra virgin olive oil**
- **1/2 cup minced onion**
- **4 ounces canned chopped green chiles, drained**
- **1/2 teaspoon garlic powder**
- **3 tablespoons flour**
- **3 cups chicken broth**
- **1/4 teaspoon ground cumin**
- **1/4 teaspoon ground coriander**
- **1/4 teaspoon salt**
- **1/4 teaspoon white pepper**
- **1 teaspoon sugar**
- **1/2 cup sour cream**
- **Chopped fresh parsley**
- **Fresh lemon slices**

Nutritional Information per serving: 55 calories

OYSTER SPINACH SOUP

PREPARATION TIME: 30 MINUTES *YIELD: 6 SERVINGS*

2 CUPS CHICKEN BROTH
10 OUNCES FROZEN CHOPPED SPINACH, THAWED
2 TABLESPOONS MINCED ONION
10 TO 12 FRESH OYSTERS, WITH OYSTER LIQUOR
1/8 TEASPOON ALLSPICE
1 CUP PLAIN LOW-FAT YOGURT

IN LARGE SAUCEPAN HEAT BROTH TO BOIL; ADD SPINACH. LOWER HEAT; SIMMER 3 MINUTES. REMOVE FROM HEAT AND SET ASIDE. IN MEDIUM SKILLET COMBINE ONION, OYSTERS AND OYSTER LIQUOR. COOK OVER LOW HEAT JUST UNTIL EDGES OF OYSTERS CURL, ABOUT 4 MINUTES. CHOP FOUR OYSTERS; RESERVE. PUREÉ SPINACH MIXTURE AND REMAINING OYSTER MIXTURE IN BLENDER OR FOOD PROCESSOR IN BATCHES UNTIL SMOOTH. RETURN TO PAN; BRING TO BOIL. LOWER HEAT; STIR IN RESERVED CHOPPED OYSTERS, ALLSPICE AND YOGURT. HEAT THROUGH, ABOUT 3 MINUTES; SERVE IMMEDIATELY.

NUTRITIONAL INFORMATION PER SERVING: 58 CALORIES

PITA POCKETS

PREPARATION TIME: 20 MINUTES *YIELD: 4 SERVINGS*

1 LARGE FRESH TOMATO
2 SMALL WHOLE WHEAT PITA BREAD ROUNDS
4 OUNCES COOKED, DICED CHICKEN
1 1/3 CUPS DICED CUCUMBER
1 LARGE HARD-BOILED EGG, MINCED
1 CUP ALFALFA SPROUTS
4 OUNCES REDUCED-CALORIE ITALIAN DRESSING

CUT TOMATO IN 8 THIN SLICES. SET ASIDE. CUT PITA BREAD ROUNDS IN HALF TO FORM 4 POCKETS. STUFF EACH HALF WITH ONE-FOURTH OF CHICKEN, TOMATO, CUCUMBER, EGG, SPROUTS AND DRESSING. SERVE IMMEDIATELY.

NUTRITIONAL INFORMATION PER SERVING: 125 CALORIES

Handsome Ham Sandwiches (open faced)

A great company treat after theatre or a sporting event.

Yield: 6 servings

Preparation Time: 25 minutes

10 ounces frozen asparagus spears, cooked without salt
Lettuce leaves
6 slices whole grain bread, toasted
12 thin slices lean cooked turkey-ham
6 thin slices Monterey Jack cheese
1/3 cup plain low-fat yogurt
1/3 cup reduced-calorie mayonnaise
1 1/2 teaspoons fresh lemon juice
1/2 teaspoon Dijon mustard
Pimiento strips

Pat asparagus dry. Place lettuce on each toast slice; top each with 2 ham slices, 1 cheese slice, and 3 asparagus spears. In small saucepan combine yogurt, mayonnaise, lemon juice and mustard. Cook over medium heat, stirring constantly until heated (do not boil). Spoon sauce over sandwiches. Garnish with pimiento strips.

NUTRITIONAL INFORMATION PER SERVING: 265 calories

Irish Reuben

Yield: 4 servings
Preheat Oven: Broil

Preparation Time: 20 minutes

4 slices whole-grain bread
Reduced calorie creamy Italian dressing
2 cups shredded cabbage
4 strips lean cooked bacon
4 slices Monterey Jack cheese

Toast bread lightly; place on broiler pan. Spread each slice with dressing. Layer with cabbage, bacon and cheese. Place under broiler just until cheese melts. Serve hot.

HINT: Use leftover pieces of roast beef or chicken in place of bacon.

NUTRITIONAL INFORMATION PER SERVING: 320 calories; High fiber

Apple Muffins

Preparation Time: 25 minutes

Yield: 24 2 inch muffins
Preheat Oven: 350°

- 2 cups whole wheat pastry flour
- 1 cup unprocessed bran flakes
- 1/3 cup wheat germ
- 1/2 teaspoon salt
- 1 1/4 teaspoons baking soda
- 1/2 teaspoon nutmeg
- 1 tablespoon grated orange rind
- 1 1/2 cups cored unpeeled chopped apple
- 1/2 cup chopped nuts
- 1 egg, beaten well
- 1/2 cup molasses
- 2 tablespoons safflower oil
- 1 1/2 to 1 2/3 cups buttermilk
- Juice of one orange

Combine flour, bran flakes, wheat germ, salt, soda and nutmeg. Stir in orange rind, apple, and nuts. Combine egg, molasses and oil in small bowl. Add buttermilk to orange juice to make 2 cups and combine with egg mixture. Stir into dry ingredients. Pour into greased muffin tins, filling 2/3 full; bake 25 minutes.

NUTRITIONAL INFORMATION: High fiber

Corn Muffins

Preparation Time: 20 minutes

Yield: 1 dozen
Preheat Oven: 375°

- 3/4 cup plus 2 tablespoons skimmed milk
- 1/4 cup low fat plain yogurt
- 4 tablespoons honey
- 2 eggs
- 1 cup whole wheat pastry flour
- 3/4 cup corn meal
- 1/2 teaspoon baking soda
- Vegetable cooking spray

Combine milk, yogurt, honey and eggs; blend well. Mix together flour, corn meal and baking soda. Add to liquid ingredients and mix well. Spray muffin pan with cooking spray; spoon batter into cups, filling 2/3 full. Bake 15 to 20 minutes. Cool on wire rack.

NUTRITIONAL INFORMATION: 52 calories each

BANANA HONEY BRAN BREAD

YIELD: 2 LOAVES
PREHEAT OVEN: 350°

PREPARATION TIME: 45 MINUTES

- 2 CUPS MASHED RIPE BANANAS
- 3½ CUPS WHOLE WHEAT PASTRY FLOUR
- 2½ TEASPOONS BAKING POWDER
- ⅔ TEASPOON BAKING SODA
- 1 TEASPOON SALT
- ⅓ CUP TOASTED WHEAT GERM
- ¼ CUP UNPROCESSED BRAN FLAKES
- ⅔ CUP MARGARINE, SOFTENED
- 1¼ CUPS HONEY
- 4 EGGS

SET BANANAS ASIDE TO LIQUEFY. GREASE TWO 8½ × 4½ INCH LOAF PANS. SIFT TOGETHER FLOUR, BAKING POWDER, SODA, AND SALT. LIGHTLY MIX IN WHEAT GERM AND BRAN. PLACE MARGARINE AND HONEY IN LARGE BOWL; BEAT WITH MIXER. ADD EGGS; BEAT 3 MINUTES. BEAT IN FLOUR MIXTURE ALTERNATELY WITH BANANAS UNTIL SMOOTH. TURN INTO PANS; BAKE 1 HOUR OR UNTIL PICK INSERTED IN CENTER COMES OUT CLEAN. COOL 10 MINUTES. REMOVE TO WIRE RACK. MAY BE FROZEN 3 TO 4 MONTHS.

NUTRITIONAL INFORMATION: WHOLE GRAIN; HIGH FIBER

WHOLE WHEAT BISCUITS

YIELD: 1½ DOZEN

PREPARATION TIME: 30 MINUTES

- 2 CUPS WHOLE WHEAT PASTRY FLOUR
- 1 TABLESPOON SUGAR
- 1 TEASPOON BAKING POWDER
- ½ TEASPOON BAKING SODA
- ¼ TEASPOON SALT
- 3 TABLESPOONS UNSALTED BUTTER-BLEND MARGARINE, SOFTENED
- 1 ROUNDED TABLESPOON DRY ACTIVE YEAST (1 PACKAGE)
- ¼ CUP WARM WATER (105°-115°)
- ⅔ CUP BUTTERMILK
- VEGETABLE COOKING SPRAY

COMBINE FLOUR, SUGAR, BAKING POWDER, SODA AND SALT. CUT IN MARGARINE UNTIL MIXTURE RESEMBLES COARSE MEAL. DISSOLVE YEAST IN WARM WATER; ADD BUTTERMILK. ADD TO FLOUR MIXTURE; BLEND UNTIL MOISTENED. COVER; REFRIGERATE OVERNIGHT. (MAY BE KEPT IN REFRIGERATOR 3 TO 4 DAYS.) PREHEAT OVEN TO 425°. TURN DOUGH ONTO LIGHTLY FLOURED SURFACE; KNEAD 1 MINUTE. ROLL DOUGH ½ INCH THICK; CUT INTO 2 INCH ROUNDS. PLACE ON BAKING SHEET COATED WITH COOKING SPRAY. BAKE 12 MINUTES OR UNTIL GOLDEN.

NUTRITIONAL INFORMATION: 72 CALORIES EACH

Zucchini Walnut Bread

Preparation Time: 30 minutes

Yield: 2 loaves
Preheat Oven: 325°

- 1¾ cups grated zucchini, drained
- 3¾ cups whole wheat pastry flour
- 1 teaspoon baking powder
- 1 teaspoon ground cloves
- 1 teaspoon ground allspice
- ½ teaspoon baking soda
- ¼ teaspoon cinnamon
- 1⅓ cups vegetable oil
- 1 cup honey
- 2 eggs
- 2 tablespoons plain low-fat yogurt
- 1½ tablespoons grated lemon peel
- 1 cup chopped walnuts
- 2 tablespoons unprocessed bran flakes

Set zucchini aside to soften until needed. Line bottoms of two 9 × 5 inch loaf pans with waxed paper. Sift together all dry ingredients. In large bowl blend oil, honey and eggs with electric mixer. Add yogurt and lemon peel; mix lightly. Gradually mix in dry ingredients. Stir in zucchini and walnuts. Pour batter into prepared pans. Sprinkle tops with bran. Bake about 1 hour or until tester inserted in center comes out clean. Cool bread in pans 10 minutes. Remove to wire racks; cool completely. May be frozen up to 4 months.

NUTRITIONAL INFORMATION: Whole grain; high fiber

Blender Pancakes

Preparation Time: 20 minutes

Yield: 12 to 15 three inch servings

- 1 cup low-fat milk
- 1 tablespoon cider vinegar
- 1 egg
- 1 cup whole wheat pastry flour, sifted
- 1 teaspoon baking soda
- 1 tablespoon wheat germ
- Butter-flavored vegetable cooking spray

Combine milk and vinegar; set aside 5 minutes. Combine milk and egg in blender; add flour, baking soda and wheat germ. Blend until moistened. Coat cold griddle with cooking spray and heat. For each pancake pour ¼ cup batter on hot griddle. Cook 2 minutes; turn and cook 2 minutes until golden. Serve with Apple Fruit or Peach-Berry Sauce (see index).

NUTRITIONAL INFORMATION: 50 calories each

Fusilli with Zucchini Sauce

Mahvelous, Mahvelous—Absolutely Mahvelous!!!

Yield: 4 servings

Preparation Time: 45 minutes

- **1/2 pound fusilli (rotelle or corkscrew pasta)**
- **2 tablespoons butter (reserve 1 tablespoon)**
- **1/4 cup finely chopped shallots**
- **1/4 cup finely chopped onion**
- **2 cloves garlic, minced**
- **1/2 cup chicken broth**
- **1 tablespoon chopped fresh parsley**
- **1/2 teaspoon fines herbes, crumbled**
- **1/8 teaspoon nutmeg**
- **1/8 teaspoon freshly ground pepper**
- **3/4 cup skim-milk ricotta cheese**
- **1 pound zucchini, grated**
- **1/3 cup Parmesan cheese**

In large saucepan cook pasta; drain. Return to pan; toss with 1 tablespoon butter. Set aside.

In large skillet melt remaining tablespoon butter. Add shallots, onion, and garlic. Sauté over low heat until transparent. Add broth, parsley, fines herbes, nutmeg and pepper. Bring to boil; reduce heat and stir in ricotta until smooth. Add zucchini and heat 2 minutes. Add pasta; heat through. Spoon into serving dish; sprinkle with Parmesan.

Nutritional Information per Serving: 395 calories; 160 mg. calcium

Stuffed Shells Rockefeller

Preparation Time: 30 minutes

Yield: 4 servings
Preheat Oven: 350°

- **8 jumbo shells, cooked, rinsed and drained**
- **1 tablespoon vegetable oil**
- **1 tablespoon fresh lemon juice**
- **1 egg, beaten lightly**
- **1½ cups low-fat cottage cheese**
- **10 ounces frozen chopped spinach, thawed and squeezed dry**
- **2 tablespoons chopped green onions**
- **¼ teaspoon dried basil, crumbled**
- **¼ teaspoon dried thyme, crumbled**
- **Dash ground allspice**
- **2 tablespoons Parmesan cheese**

Toss warm shells with oil and lemon juice. Set aside. Prepare tomato sauce. While sauce is cooking, combine egg, cottage cheese, spinach, green onions, basil, thyme, and allspice in large bowl. Mix well. Stuff shells with spinach mixture.

Spread tomato sauce in bottom of 1½ quart baking dish. Place stuffed shells on sauce. Sprinkle with Parmesan cheese; cover. Bake 30 minutes until heated through. Transfer to warm plates; spoon band of sauce over shells.

Delightful Tomato Sauce:

- **8 ounces canned tomato sauce**
- **1 cup peeled chopped tomato**
- **¼ teaspoon poultry seasoning**
- **¼ teaspoon dried basil, crumbled**
- **⅛ teaspoon ground allspice**

Combine all ingredients in large skillet; simmer 15 minutes.

HINT: Cook several extra shells to replace any broken during preparation.

NUTRITIONAL INFORMATION PER SERVING: 230 calories

Fettucine Al Luce 

Easy, economical, with gourmet results.

Yield: 4 servings
Preheat Oven: 325°
Preparation Time: 30 minutes

- 1 cup low-fat plain yogurt
- 1/2 cup low-fat cottage cheese
- 1/3 cup grated Parmesan cheese
- 4 egg whites
- 4 tablespoons chopped fresh parsley
- 1 teaspoon onion powder
- 1/4 teaspoon freshly ground pepper
- 8 ounces fettucine noodles, cooked, rinsed and drained

In large bowl combine all ingredients except noodles. Add noodles; toss gently until well mixed. Spoon into greased 9 inch square baking pan. Bake 15 to 20 minutes. Serve warm.

Nutritional Information Per Serving: 330 calories

Egg in a Cup with Broiled Grapefruit

Yield: 4 servings
Preparation Time: 10 minutes

- 4 eggs
- 4 large fresh mushrooms, sliced (divided)
- 4 teaspoons chopped green onions (divided)
- 4 tablespoons grated Monterey Jack cheese (divided)
- 2 medium grapefruit, halved, seeded and sections loosened
- 2 teaspoons brown sugar, firmly packed (divided)

Place 1 egg in custard cup. Add 1 sliced mushroom, 1 teaspoon green onions and 1 tablespoon cheese. Repeat with remaining eggs, vegetables and cheese. Heat water in large skillet; place cups in water. Cover; steam 15 to 20 minutes until eggs are set.

Meanwhile place grapefruit in broiler pan. Sprinkle each with 1/2 teaspoon sugar; broil 6 inches from heat 2 to 3 minutes until sugar is bubbly. Place 1 egg and 1 grapefruit on each plate; serve immediately.

Spa recipe from Judy Stout

Nutritional Information Per Serving: 158 calories

Scrambled Eggs Aztec

Preparation Time: 20 minutes

Yield: 6 servings
Preheat Oven: 300°

- 6 flour tortillas
- 8 eggs
- 1/4 cup water
- 2 tablespoons chopped green chiles
- 2 tablespoons taco sauce
- 1 tablespoon chopped fresh cilantro or parsley
- Vegetable cooking spray
- 3/4 cup taco sauce (divided)
- 9 tablespoons grated Cheddar cheese (divided)

Wrap tortillas in foil; bake 7 minutes. Set aside and keep warm. Combine eggs, water, green chiles, taco sauce, and cilantro; whisk well. Spray non-stick skillet with cooking spray; heat. Add egg mixture; cook over medium heat, stirring gently until just set and moist. Divide and spoon eggs onto each tortilla. Top each with 1 tablespoon taco sauce and 1 tablespoon cheese; fold sides over. Garnish each with 1 tablespoon sauce and 1/2 tablespoon cheese.

Nutritional Information Per Serving: 246 calories

Scrambled Eggs Seville

Preparation Time: 25 minutes

Yield: 6 servings

- Vegetable cooking spray
- 1/2 cup chopped green bell pepper
- 1/2 cup finely chopped green onions, with tops
- 6 eggs
- 1/4 cup skim milk
- 1/4 teaspoon freshly ground pepper
- 1/4 teaspoon Tabasco
- 1/2 cup chopped tomato
- 1/4 cup grated Colby cheese
- Pimiento strips
- Fresh parsley

Coat large non-stick skillet with cooking spray; add bell pepper and green onions. Cook over medium-low heat until soft, stirring occasionally. Remove from skillet; set aside.

Combine eggs, milk, pepper and Tabasco, beating well. If needed, respray skillet; heat. Add egg mixture; cook over low heat, stirring gently, until just set and still moist. Stir in sautéed vegetables and tomato; heat through. Sprinkle with cheese; garnish with pimiento and parsley.

Nutritional Information Per Serving: 109 calories

Crustless Spinach Quiche

Yield: 6 servings
Preheat Oven: 350°
Preparation Time: 10 minutes

- **3 eggs, beaten well**
- **6 drops Tabasco**
- **10 ounces frozen chopped spinach, thawed and well drained**
- **2 cups low-fat cottage cheese**
- **1/4 cup grated Parmesan cheese**
- **4 tablespoons grated Swiss cheese**
- **1 teaspoon Dijon mustard**
- **1/2 teaspoon dried minced onion**
- **1/8 teaspoon cayenne pepper**
- **1/8 teaspoon salt**
- **Vegetable cooking spray**

Combine eggs, Tabasco, spinach, all cheeses, mustard, onion, pepper and salt; mix well. Coat 8 inch square pan with cooking spray; add spinach mixture. Bake 35 to 40 minutes or until just set and still moist.

Nutritional Information Per Serving: 135 calories

French Loaf Puff

An easy make ahead dish for the busy cook.

Yield: 8 servings
Preparation Time: 1 hour

- **Vegetable cooking spray**
- **10 ounces French bread**
- **8 large eggs**
- **3 cups skim milk**
- **1 tablespoon sugar**
- **1 teaspoon apple-pie spice**
- **3/4 teaspoon salt**
- **1 1/2 tablespoons pure vanilla extract**
- **2 tablespoons unsalted butter-blend margarine**

Lightly spray 9×13 inch pan with cooking spray. Cut bread in 1 inch slices; layer in pan. Beat eggs, milk, sugar, seasonings and vanilla. Pour mixture over bread; cover and refrigerate 4 hours or overnight. To bake, uncover and dot with margarine; put in cold oven. Turn oven temperature to 350°; bake 45 to 50 minutes until golden and puffed. Let stand 5 minutes before serving.

Nutritional Information Per Serving: 285 calories; 11 grams fat

Filet Southhampton-Lite

Preparation Time: 45 minutes *Yield: 4 servings*

- 1/2 cup margarine
- 1/2 cup soy sauce
- 7 ounces lean beef filet, cut into 1 inch slices
- 1/4 pound fresh spinach, washed and stems removed
- 1 cup bay shrimp
- 1 cup sliced fresh mushrooms
- 1/2 teaspoon chopped shallots
- 1/4 teaspoon minced garlic
- 1/4 cup Marsala wine

In medium skillet heat margarine and soy sauce until simmering. Add filets; brown about 3 minutes on each side until medium-rare. Remove to serving platter covered with bed of fresh spinach.

To remaining sauce in skillet, add shrimp, mushrooms, shallots, garlic and wine. Cook until shrimp are heated through, stirring constantly. Pour sauce over filets and serve.

Charlie Mitchell's

Nutritional Information per serving: 375 calories

Moroccan Lamb

Preparation Time: 30 minutes *Yield: 4 servings*

- 1 pound lean boneless lamb, cut into 1 inch cubes
- 1 teaspoon vegetable oil
- 1/2 cup small fresh mushrooms
- 1/2 cup chopped onion
- 1/2 cup raisins
- 1/2 cup slivered almonds
- 16 ounces canned stewed tomatoes, chopped
- 1 teaspoon sugar
- 1 teaspoon salt
- 1/2 teaspoon cinnamon
- 1/4 teaspoon allspice
- 1/4 teaspoon ground cloves
- 2 teaspoons fresh lemon juice
- 1 teaspoon cornstarch

Place lamb cubes in large cold non-stick skillet. Over medium-low heat brown meat slowly on all sides; remove from pan. Add oil; heat. Add mushrooms and onion; brown briefly. Stir in raisins, almonds, tomatoes, sugar, salt, cinnamon, allspice and cloves. Simmer 5 minutes. Add lamb; bring to boil. Cover and simmer one hour.

Mix together lemon juice and cornstarch; add to skillet. Boil 1 minute, stirring, and serve.

Valhalla Health Retreat
Deer Valley, Utah

Nutritional Information per serving: 300 calories; 9 grams of fat

BRAN' NEW MEATLOAF

YIELD: 8 SERVINGS
PREHEAT OVEN: 350°

PREPARATION TIME: 20 MINUTES

- 2 EGGS, BEATEN LIGHTLY
- 2 POUNDS LEAN GROUND BEEF
- 1 CUP TOMATO SAUCE
- 1/2 CUP CHOPPED ONION
- 1/4 CUP UNPROCESSED BRAN FLAKES
- 1/4 CUP WHEAT GERM
- 2 TABLESPOONS DRIED PARSLEY FLAKES, CRUMBLED
- 1 TEASPOON DIJON MUSTARD
- 1/2 TEASPOON SALT
- 1/2 TEASPOON POULTRY SEASONING
- 2 SLICES WHOLE-GRAIN BREAD, CRUMBLED

IN LARGE BOWL, COMBINE ALL INGREDIENTS. FORM INTO LOAF; PLACE ON RACK OF BROILER PAN TO DRAIN FAT. BAKE ONE HOUR OR UNTIL LOAF IS FIRM.

NUTRITIONAL INFORMATION PER SERVING: REDUCED FAT; ADDED FIBER.

MANDARIN STIR-FRY

YIELD: 4 SERVINGS

PREPARATION TIME: 30 MINUTES

- 2 TABLESPOONS VEGETABLE OIL
- 1 CUP SLIVERED BEEF, CHICKEN OR PORK
- 2 CUPS CHOPPED VEGETABLES SUCH AS: ONION, CELERY, SNOW PEA PODS, BROCCOLI, BEAN SPROUTS, SQUASH, MUSHROOMS
- 3 CUPS SHREDDED LETTUCE
- 2 CUPS HOT COOKED RICE
- LOW-SODIUM SOY SAUCE

IN LARGE SKILLET, HEAT OIL OVER MEDIUM HEAT; SAUTÉ MEAT UNTIL BROWNED. ADD VEGETABLES; STIR-FRY UNTIL CRISP-TENDER, ADDING WATER IF NECESSARY. ADD LETTUCE TO SKILLET; STEAM 1 MINUTE OR JUST UNTIL WILTED. PLACE MIXTURE IN SERVING BOWL; TOSS THOROUGHLY. SERVE OVER RICE WITH SOY SAUCE.

HINT: TO ADD VISUAL APPEAL TO VEGETABLES, CUT INTO VARIOUS SHAPES.

NUTRITIONAL INFORMATION PER SERVING: LOW FAT; HIGH FIBER

Burgundy Beef Kabobs

Preparation Time: 25 minutes *Yield: 6 servings*

- 1½ pounds lean boneless sirloin steak, cut into 1½ inch pieces
- 1 large red onion, cut into 6 wedges
- 1 medium green bell pepper, cut into 1 inch squares
- 1 medium red bell pepper, cut into 1 inch squares
- 8 ounces reduced-calorie Italian salad dressing
- ⅓ cup Burgundy wine
- 8 ounces juice pack pineapple chunks, drained (reserve juice)
- 3 cups hot cooked rice

Place meat and vegetables in 9×13 inch baking dish. Combine salad dressing, wine and reserved pineapple juice; pour over meat mixture. Cover; refrigerate several hours or overnight, stirring occasionally. Strain mixture, reserving marinade. Thread meat, pineapple chunks, and vegetables on 6 skewers. Grill over medium-hot coals 15 to 20 minutes, or until cooked as desired. Turn and baste frequently with marinade. Serve with rice.

Nutritional Information Per Serving: 300 calories

Spicy Orange Pork

Preparation Time: 20 minutes *Yield: 6 servings*

- Vegetable cooking spray
- 1½ pounds lean pork loin, cut into 1 inch cubes
- 1 medium onion, sliced
- 2 cloves garlic, crushed
- 1½ cups orange juice
- 2 tablespoons Dijon mustard
- ⅛ teaspoon salt
- ¼ teaspoon allspice
- 1½ cups sliced carrot
- 2 cups shredded cabbage

Coat large non-stick skillet with cooking spray; heat over medium heat. Add pork; brown 15 minutes. Add onion and garlic. Cook, stirring frequently, until onion is soft.

Combine orange juice, mustard, salt and allspice; add to skillet. Add carrot and cabbage. Cover; cook over medium heat 30 minutes. Uncover; simmer 10 minutes. Serve immediately.

Nutritional Information Per Serving: 253 calories; 9 grams of fat

CHICKEN A LÁ LEMON

LEMON ADDS A PIQUANT FLAVOR.

YIELD: 4 SERVINGS *PREPARATION TIME: 15 MINUTES*

- **1 EGG, BEATEN LIGHTLY**
- **DASH GROUND RED PEPPER**
- **4 CHICKEN BREAST HALVES, SKINNED AND BONED**
- **1/2 CUP WHEAT GERM**
- **1 TABLESPOON MARGARINE**
- **3 TABLESPOONS FRESH LEMON JUICE**
- **1 TABLESPOON WATER**
- **1 TEASPOON DRIED TARRAGON, CRUMBLED**
- **LEMON SLICES**
- **PARSLEY SPRIGS**

IN LARGE SHALLOW BOWL COMBINE EGG AND GROUND RED PEPPER. FLATTEN CHICKEN BREASTS TO 1/2 INCH THICK. DIP CHICKEN IN EGG MIXTURE; COAT WITH WHEAT GERM. IN LARGE NON-STICK SKILLET MELT MARGARINE OVER MEDIUM-HIGH HEAT. ADD CHICKEN; COOK 3 TO 4 MINUTES PER SIDE. REMOVE TO PLATTER. ADD LEMON JUICE, WATER, AND TARRAGON TO SKILLET; COOK OVER HIGH HEAT 1 MINUTE, STIRRING. POUR OVER CHICKEN; GARNISH WITH LEMON SLICES AND PARSLEY SPRIGS. SERVE IMMEDIATELY.

NUTRITIONAL INFORMATION PER SERVING: 240 CALORIES

CHICKEN CACCIATORE

SUPER-EASY FAMILY SUPPER!

YIELD: 3 SERVINGS *PREPARATION TIME: 15 MINUTES*

- **3 CHICKEN BREAST HALVES**
- **VEGETABLE COOKING SPRAY**
- **3/4 CUP TOMATO JUICE**
- **2 OUNCES CANNED SLICED MUSHROOMS**
- **2 TEASPOONS MINCED ONION FLAKES**
- **1 TEASPOON DRIED PARSLEY FLAKES, CRUMBLED**
- **1/2 TEASPOON SALT**
- **1/2 TEASPOON DRIED BASIL, CRUMBLED**
- **1/8 TEASPOON GARLIC POWDER**

SKIN AND BONE CHICKEN BREASTS. COAT MEDIUM SKILLET WITH COOKING SPRAY AND BROWN CHICKEN ON BOTH SIDES OVER MEDIUM HEAT. ADD REMAINING INGREDIENTS; COVER AND SIMMER 1 HOUR. SPOON SAUCE OVER CHICKEN; SERVE.

NUTRITIONAL INFORMATION PER SERVING: LOW CALORIE; LOW FAT

Chicken Breast Duxelles

Preparation Time: 25 minutes

Yield: 4 servings
Preheat Oven: 325°

- 1/2 cup diced celery
- 1/2 cup diced carrot
- 1 tablespoon minced onion
- 1 clove garlic, minced
- 1/4 teaspoon dried basil, crumbled
- 1/4 teaspoon ground sage
- 1/8 teaspoon freshly ground pepper
- 1 1/2 cups chicken broth (reserve 1 cup)
- 2 egg whites
- 2 slices whole-grain bread, diced
- 1 tablespoon chopped fresh parsley
- 4 chicken breast halves, skinned and boned
- Dash paprika
- 1 tablespoon cornstarch
- Dash ground red pepper
- 1/2 teaspoon fresh lemon juice
- 1/2 cup sliced fresh mushrooms

Combine celery, carrot, onion, garlic, basil, sage, pepper and 1/2 cup broth in medium skillet. Simmer over low heat until tender-crisp, about 5 minutes. In large bowl, whisk egg whites until frothy; stir in vegetable mixture, bread and parsley. Mix well. Flatten chicken breasts to 1/4 inch thick. Place one fourth of stuffing on each chicken breast; roll up and place seam side down in shallow baking dish. Sprinkle with paprika; cover and bake 25 to 30 minutes until done.

To prepare sauce, combine cornstarch, pepper, lemon juice and reserved cup of broth in saucepan. Cook over medium heat until thickened. Add mushrooms and heat through. Remove chicken to warm platter and spoon sauce over.

HINT: Fluted mushroom caps are a natural garnish for this dish.

NUTRITIONAL INFORMATION PER SERVING: 180 calories; 10 grams carbohydrates

ORIENTAL CHICKEN WITH VEGETABLES

YIELD: 4 SERVINGS | *PREPARATION TIME: 30 MINUTES*

SKIN AND BONE CHICKEN BREASTS. CUT INTO 1 INCH PIECES AND SET ASIDE. HEAT 1/3 CUP WATER IN LARGE NON-STICK SKILLET. ADD ONION; SAUTÉ OVER MEDIUM HEAT UNTIL TRANSPARENT. ADD CHICKEN AND BROWN. ADD CELERY AND CARROT. IN SMALL SAUCEPAN DISSOLVE BOUILLON CUBE IN WATER. ADD TO CHICKEN; COVER AND SIMMER 10 TO 12 MINUTES. ADD LEMON SLICES, PEPPER, GARLIC POWDER AND BROCCOLI. SIMMER 10 TO 12 MINUTES LONGER. REMOVE 1/2 CUP LIQUID FROM SKILLET AND ADD TO ARROWROOT; RETURN MIXTURE TO SKILLET. ADD SOY SAUCE AND CASHEWS. ADD PEPPER MIX AND ADDITIONAL SOY SAUCE TO TASTE. SERVE IMMEDIATELY OVER HOT RICE. GARNISH WITH FRESH ORANGE SLICES.

1 1/2 POUNDS CHICKEN BREASTS
1/3 CUP WATER
1 SMALL ONION, FINELY CHOPPED
1 RIB CELERY, SLICED DIAGONALLY
1 CARROT, SLICED DIAGONALLY
1 LOW-SODIUM CHICKEN BOUILLON CUBE
1 1/2 CUPS BOILING WATER
2 THIN SLICES LEMON
1/4 TEASPOON WHITE PEPPER
1/4 TEASPOON GARLIC POWDER
4 LARGE FRESH BROCCOLI FLOWERETS, SLICED LENGTHWISE
1/2 TEASPOON ARROWROOT
2 TEASPOONS LOW-SODIUM SOY SAUCE
1/2 CUP DRY ROASTED CASHEWS
SEASONED PEPPER MIX
FRESH ORANGE SLICES

NUTRITIONAL INFORMATION: LOW FAT; HIGH FIBER.

BAVARIAN BAKED CHICKEN

YIELD: 4 TO 6 SERVINGS | *PREPARATION TIME: 15 MINUTES*
PREHEAT OVEN: 425°

RUB PAPRIKA INTO CHICKEN. PLACE IN BAKING PAN; BAKE 30 MINUTES. TRANSFER CHICKEN TO PLATTER. WIPE OUT PAN; LAYER CABBAGE, ONION AND APPLE IN BOTTOM. SPRINKLE WITH SEASONINGS; POUR IN JUICE. TOP WITH CHICKEN, COVER WITH FOIL AND BAKE 30 MINUTES LONGER OR UNTIL CHICKEN IS TENDER.

1 TABLESPOON PAPRIKA
2 1/2 POUNDS CHICKEN PIECES, SKINNED
4 CUPS SHREDDED CABBAGE
1 MEDIUM ONION, THINLY SLICED
1 RED APPLE, CORED AND SLICED INTO THIN WEDGES
1/4 TEASPOON SALT
1/2 TEASPOON ALL-PURPOSE SEASONING
1/2 CUP APPLE JUICE

NUTRITIONAL INFORMATION: LOW FAT; HIGH FIBER

TURKEY VEGETABLE POT PIE

THIS HAS AN EXCEPTIONAL FLAVOR.

YIELD: 6 SERVINGS
PREHEAT OVEN: 400°

PASTRY SHELL:

- **1 CUP WHOLE WHEAT PASTRY FLOUR (OR UNBLEACHED ALL-PURPOSE FLOUR)**
- **1/2 TEASPOON SALT**
- **1/4 CUP VEGETABLE OIL**
- **2 TABLESPOONS ICE WATER**

IN MEDIUM BOWL COMBINE FLOUR AND SALT. BLEND IN OIL WITH FORK. SPRINKLE WATER OVER MIXTURE; MIX WELL. SHAPE INTO BALL; CHILL 1 HOUR.

FILLING:

- **3 CARROTS, CUT INTO 1 INCH PIECES**
- **2 LARGE ONIONS, CHOPPED**
- **3 TABLESPOONS LIGHT MARGARINE**
- **1/4 CUP ALL-PURPOSE FLOUR**
- **1/2 TEASPOON SALT**
- **1/4 TEASPOON DRIED THYME, CRUMBLED**
- **1/4 TEASPOON FRESHLY GROUND PEPPER**
- **2 CUPS CHICKEN BOUILLON**
- **1/2 CUP FROZEN PEAS**
- **2 CUPS CHOPPED, COOKED TURKEY OR CHICKEN**

COOK CARROTS AND ONIONS IN WATER IN MEDIUM PAN UNTIL TENDER-CRISP, ABOUT 10 MINUTES. DRAIN; SET ASIDE. IN SAME PAN, MELT MARGARINE OVER LOW HEAT. BLEND IN FLOUR, SALT, THYME AND PEPPER; COOK 1 MINUTE, STIRRING. GRADUALLY ADD BOUILLON, STIRRING CONSTANTLY, UNTIL SAUCE IS THICK. SET ASIDE.

IN 2 QUART CASSEROLE, COMBINE CARROT MIXTURE, SAUCE, PEAS AND TURKEY; MIX WELL.

ROLL DOUGH OUT BETWEEN 2 PIECES OF WAX PAPER. REMOVE TOP LAYER OF PAPER; INVERT PASTRY OVER TOP OF CASSEROLE. REMOVE PAPER; SEAL PASTRY AROUND DISH. CUT SLITS IN TOP FOR STEAM TO ESCAPE. BAKE 30 MINUTES OR UNTIL PASTRY IS GOLDEN BROWN.

HINT: IF PREBAKED PIE SHELL IS NEEDED FOR ANOTHER USE, BAKE IN PREHEATED 450° OVEN 10 TO 12 MINUTES. YIELDS 6 SERVINGS; 156 CALORIES PER SERVING.

NUTRITIONAL INFORMATION PER SERVING: 485 CALORIES

ENCHILADAS SOUTHWEST

YIELD: 8 SERVINGS *PREPARATION TIME: 45 MINUTES*
PREHEAT OVEN: 400°

IN LARGE NON-STICK SKILLET, HEAT 1 TABLESPOON OIL. ADD 3/4 CUP GREEN ONIONS, TOMATO, BELL PEPPER AND GARLIC; SAUTÉ OVER LOW HEAT UNTIL SOFT. ADD ENCHILADA AND TOMATO SAUCE; BRING TO BOIL. LOWER HEAT; SIMMER 10 MINUTES.

MEANWHILE, IN ANOTHER LARGE SKILLET HEAT REMAINING OIL OVER MEDIUM HEAT. ADD GROUND TURKEY AND COOK UNTIL NO LONGER PINK. ADD CHILES, RESERVED GREEN ONIONS, WATER, CORIANDER AND SALT; SIMMER 5 MINUTES. COMBINE CHEESES; SET ASIDE.

TO SOFTEN TORTILLAS, COAT EACH WITH COOKING SPRAY. PLACE ON COOKIE SHEETS, BAKE 2 MINUTES; TURN AND BAKE 1 MORE MINUTE.

ARRANGE 4 TORTILLAS ON BAKING SHEET. SPREAD 1/3 CUP TURKEY MIXTURE ON EACH. SPRINKLE EACH WITH 1/4 CUP CHEESE AND 3 TABLESPOONS SAUCE. REPEAT LAYERS WITH SECOND TORTILLA, CHEESE AND SAUCE. TOP WITH THIRD TORTILLA AND 1 TABLESPOON SAUCE. BAKE 10 MINUTES. TOP WITH LETTUCE, TOMATO AND REMAINING SAUCE. CUT IN HALF TO SERVE.

2 TABLESPOONS VEGETABLE OIL (DIVIDED)
1 CUP CHOPPED GREEN ONIONS WITH TOPS (RESERVE 1/4 CUP)
1 MEDIUM TOMATO, PEELED, SEEDED AND CHOPPED
1/2 CUP CHOPPED GREEN BELL PEPPER
2 CLOVES GARLIC, MINCED
20 OUNCES CANNED ENCHILADA SAUCE
16 OUNCES CANNED TOMATO SAUCE
1 POUND GROUND TURKEY (THAWED, IF FROZEN)
4 OUNCES CHOPPED GREEN CHILES, DRAINED
1/4 CUP WATER
1 TEASPOON GROUND CORIANDER
1/2 TEASPOON SALT
1 CUP GRATED SWISS CHEESE (4 OUNCES)
1 CUP SHREDDED PART-SKIM MOZZARELLA CHEESE (4 OUNCES)
12 CORN TORTILLAS
VEGETABLE COOKING SPRAY
SHREDDED LETTUCE
DICED TOMATO

HINT: GROUND TURKEY IS AVAILABLE IN FROZEN ROLL.

NUTRITIONAL INFORMATION PER SERVING: 318 CALORIES; 10 GMS. FAT

Easy Chicken Packets

Preparation Time: 15 minutes

Yield: 4 servings
Preheat Oven: 450°

- **1** medium onion, sliced and separated into rings
- **4** chicken breast halves, skinned and boned
- **2** teaspoons dried basil, crumbled
- **2** teaspoons sweet paprika
- **2** medium carrots, cut into julienne strips
- **1** cup sliced zucchini
- **1** cup sliced yellow squash
- **16** fresh mushrooms, sliced
- **4** tablespoons water
- **Salt and freshly ground pepper to taste**

Divide onion rings among four 12 × 18 inch sheets of heavy duty foil. Place chicken breasts on top of onions and sprinkle each with 1/4 teaspoon basil and 1/4 teaspoon paprika. Top each with one-fourth of carrots, zucchini, squash, mushrooms and water. Sprinkle each remaining basil, paprika, salt and pepper. Fold edges of foil sheets together; seal tightly. Place packets on baking sheet; bake 40 minutes. Remove from foil to serving plates.

NUTRITIONAL INFORMATION: Low fat

Savory Chicken Bake

Preparation Time: 20 minutes

Yield: 6 servings
Preheat Oven: 400°

- **3** pounds cut-up chicken, skinned
- **3** tablespoons mixed dried seasonings (reserve 1 tablespoon)
- **1/3** cup diced green bell pepper
- **3** tablespoons instant minced onion
- **2** cups tomato juice
- **16** ounces canned French-style green beans, drained

Place chicken in 9 × 13 inch glass baking dish. Sprinkle with 2 tablespoons seasoning mixture (blend of oregano, fines herbes, thyme, sage, allspice and pepper). Combine bell pepper, onion and 1 tablespoon seasoning mixture with tomato juice. Pour over chicken. Cover dish with foil; bake 1 hour. Remove cover; top with green beans and bake uncovered 15 minutes more.

NUTRITIONAL INFORMATION: Low fat

Flounder Creole

Yield: 4 servings | *Preparation Time: 15 minutes*

In large skillet over low heat sauté onion and bell pepper in butter until soft. Add remaining ingredients, except flounder, and cook 10 minutes over low heat. Add filets and cook, covered, 10 minutes longer or until fish flakes and is opaque. Place filets on individual plates; spoon sauce over and serve.

- **1/4 cup chopped onion**
- **1/4 cup chopped green bell pepper**
- **2 tablespoons butter**
- **8 ounces fresh mushrooms, sliced**
- **16 ounces canned tomatoes, chopped**
- **1 bay leaf**
- **1/4 teaspoon tarragon, crumbled**
- **2 tablespoons fresh lemon juice**
- **1/2 teaspoon salt**
- **Freshly ground pepper, to taste**
- **1 pound fresh flounder filets**

Nutritional Information Per Serving: 175 calories

Baked Dill Salmon

Yield: 6 servings | *Preparation Time: 20 minutes*
Preheat Oven: 375°

Cut 6 pieces foil in 12 inch squares. Place one salmon filet on each. Cover each with 3 cucumber slices, 1 lemon slice, 1/4 teaspoon dill weed, one parsley sprig, and one shrimp. Fold edges of foil together; seal tightly. Place in baking dish and bake 20 minutes. Remove from foil to individual plates; drizzle juices over fish. Serve immediately.

- **6 4 ounce salmon filets, skin removed (1 1/2 pounds)**
- **18 cucumber slices, peeled and cut 1/4 inch thick**
- **6 lemon slices, peeled**
- **1 1/2 teaspoons dried dill weed**
- **6 parsley sprigs**
- **6 large fresh shrimp, peeled and deveined**

Nutritional Information Per Serving: 156 calories

Polynesian Filet of Sole

Be prepared to serve "seconds".

Preparation Time: 15 minutes

Yield: 8 servings
Preheat Oven: 450°

- 1 medium onion, thinly sliced
- 1 medium green bell pepper, seeded and chopped
- 1 rib celery, finely chopped
- 8 ounces canned small carrots, drained
- 1/8 teaspoon garlic salt
- 2 pounds fresh or frozen sole or flounder filets (thawed, if frozen)
- 16 ounces canned tomato sauce
- 1 cup juice pack crushed pineapple, drained

Spread onion, bell pepper, celery, and carrots in bottom of 9 × 13 inch baking pan. Sprinkle with garlic salt. Place fish on top of vegetables. Combine tomato sauce with pineapple and pour over fish. Bake 20 minutes, basting frequently. Fish is done when it flakes easily and most of liquid has evaporated to form thick sauce. Serve immediately.

NUTRITIONAL INFORMATION PER SERVING: 140 calories

Orange Roughy Filets with Julienne Vegetables

Preparation Time: 20 minutes

Yield: 4 servings

- 2 ribs celery
- 2 medium zucchini
- 2 medium carrots
- 4 Orange Roughy filets
- 1/2 cup chopped onion
- 2 tablespoons chopped fresh parsley
- 2 tablespoons fresh lemon juice
- 1/4 teaspoon freshly ground pepper
- 1 medium red bell pepper, cut into thin strips

Cut celery, zucchini and carrots in thin julienne strips. Place fish filets in microwave dish. Combine vegetables, onion, parsley, lemon juice and pepper; spoon over fish. Top with bell pepper. Cover with waxed paper. Microwave on medium power 5 minutes. Turn dish; cook additional 10 minutes or until fish flakes with fork. Let stand 2 to 3 minutes before serving.

NUTRITIONAL INFORMATION PER SERVING: 145 calories

SOLE WITH SHRIMP STUFFING

YIELD: 4 SERVINGS
PREHEAT OVEN: 350°

PREPARATION TIME: 30 MINUTES

COOK, PEEL AND DEVEIN SHRIMP. CHOP AND SET ASIDE. DICE BREAD. IN LARGE SKILLET SAUTÉ GARLIC AND ONION IN 2 TABLESPOONS MARGARINE UNTIL GOLDEN. REMOVE FROM HEAT. ADD SHRIMP, BREAD, MINCED CELERY, PARSLEY AND SEASONINGS; MIX WELL. COAT BAKING PAN WITH COOKING SPRAY; SCATTER CHOPPED CELERY IN PAN. SPREAD SHRIMP MIXTURE OVER FILETS; ROLL UP AND PLACE ON CELERY, SEAM SIDE DOWN. DOT WITH REMAINING MARGARINE. BAKE 25 TO 30 MINUTES. GARNISH WITH LEMON SLICES AND PARSLEY SPRIGS.

- 8 MEDIUM FRESH SHRIMP
- 2 SLICES WHOLE GRAIN BREAD
- 1 CLOVE GARLIC, MINCED
- 2 TABLESPOONS MINCED ONION
- 4 TABLESPOONS MARGARINE (DIVIDED)
- 1 TABLESPOON MINCED CELERY
- 1 TABLESPOON CHOPPED FRESH PARSLEY
- 1/2 TEASPOON HARMONY SEASONING (SEE INDEX)
- SALT AND FRESHLY GROUND PEPPER, TO TASTE
- VEGETABLE COOKING SPRAY
- 1 CUP CHOPPED CELERY
- 4 SOLE FILETS
- LEMON SLICES
- PARSLEY SPRIGS

NUTRITIONAL INFORMATION PER SERVING: 264 CALORIES

SWEET AND SOUR SHRIMP

YIELD: 4 SERVINGS

PREPARATION TIME: 30 MINUTES

PEEL AND DEVEIN SHRIMP; SET ASIDE. IN LARGE SKILLET COMBINE CORNSTARCH, JUICE AND BROTH. BOIL OVER MEDIUM HEAT, STIRRING, UNTIL THICKENED. ADD VINEGAR AND SHERRY. STIR AND COOK 1 MINUTE. ADD BELL PEPPER AND ONION; COOK 1 MINUTE. ADD SHRIMP AND PINEAPPLE; COOK 4 MINUTES UNTIL TENDER. SPOON OVER HOT RICE; SERVE IMMEDIATELY.

- 12 OUNCES MEDIUM FRESH SHRIMP
- 2 TABLESPOONS CORNSTARCH
- 1 CUP UNSWEETENED PINEAPPLE JUICE
- 1/2 CUP NO-FAT CHICKEN BROTH
- 1/3 CUP RED WINE VINEGAR
- 1/4 CUP DRY SHERRY
- 1 GREEN BELL PEPPER, CUT IN 1 × 1/2 INCH PIECES
- 1 TABLESPOON CHOPPED ONION
- 1/4 CUP CANNED PINEAPPLE TIDBITS, DRAINED
- 2 CUPS HOT COOKED RICE

NUTRITIONAL INFORMATION PER SERVING: 280 CALORIES; 40 GMS. CARBOHYDRATES

Sherried Shrimp and Scallops

Preparation Time: 20 minutes

Yield: 4 to 6 servings

- 1/2 pound fresh scallops
- 1/2 pound fresh shrimp
- 1 tablespoon margarine
- 1/2 cup dry sherry
- 1 tablespoon chopped fresh parsley
- 1/2 teaspoon dried basil, crumbled
- 1/2 teaspoon dried thyme, crumbled
- 1/8 teaspoon Tabasco
- 12 ounces canned artichoke hearts, drained and halved

Drain scallops and pat dry. Peel and devein shrimp. Set aside. Melt margarine in large skillet over medium heat; stir in sherry and seasonings. Add scallops and artichoke hearts; simmer 3 minutes. Add shrimp; simmer 3 minutes longer. Remove to warm platter. Increase heat to high and reduce liquid in skillet to 1/2 cup. Spoon over scallop mixture and serve.

NUTRITIONAL INFORMATION PER SERVING: 125 calories; 298 mg. sodium

Scrumptious Shrimp

Preparation Time: 15 minutes

Yield: 12 servings

- 10 peppercorns
- 6 whole cloves
- 4 bay leaves
- 1/2 teaspoon nutmeg
- 1/2 teaspoon dried oregano
- 1/2 teaspoon dried basil
- 1/2 teaspoon mustard seed
- 1/2 teaspoon crushed red pepper flakes
- 1/4 teaspoon thyme
- 1/2 teaspoon salt
- 2 ribs celery with leafy tops, cut into 3 inch pieces
- 1/2 lemon
- 1/2 lime
- 1 clove garlic, sliced
- 3 pounds medium to large fresh shrimp, in shells

In square of cheesecloth combine all herbs and spices. Gather ends of cloth; tie into bag. In large stockpot bring 6 quarts water to boil; add spice bag and remaining ingredients. Simmer just until shrimp turn pink, 3 to 5 minutes. Drain shrimp; rinse and chill. Peel and devein shrimp, or heap unpeeled in bowl for Peel-Your-Own Party.

NUTRITIONAL INFORMATION: High protein; low calorie

Lemony Asparagus

Fancy with gourmet flair.

Yield: 8 servings — *Preparation Time: 20 minutes*

- 2 pounds fresh asparagus
- Vegetable cooking spray
- 1/2 cup thinly sliced celery
- 1/2 cup chopped green onions
- 2 tablespoons fresh lemon juice
- 1/2 teaspoon grated lemon rind
- 1/8 teaspoon garlic powder
- 1 cup sliced water chestnuts
- 1/4 cup diced pimiento

Snap tough ends off asparagus and cook, covered, in boiling water 6 minutes or until crisp-tender. Drain; arrange on serving platter and keep warm. Prepare large skillet with cooking spray. Sauté celery, green onions, lemon juice, lemon rind and garlic powder until celery is crisp-tender. Add water chestnuts and pimiento; heat thoroughly. Spoon mixture over asparagus and serve.

Nutritional Information Per Serving: 35 calories

Zesty Broccoli

Tasty and easy to prepare.

Yield: 6 servings — *Preparation Time: 10 minutes*

- 1 1/2 pounds fresh broccoli spears
- 1/3 cup plain low-fat yogurt
- 1/3 cup reduced-calorie mayonnaise
- 1 1/2 teaspoons Dijon mustard
- 3/4 teaspoon prepared horseradish

Steam broccoli until tender-crisp. Arrange broccoli on serving platter. Keep warm. Combine remaining ingredients in small saucepan and simmer until warm, stirring constantly. Ladle sauce over broccoli spears; serve immediately.

Nutritional Information Per Serving: 70 calories

Carrots Caribbean

Preparation Time: 30 minutes

Yield: 4 servings

- 2 cups julienned carrot (3 × 1/4 inch strips)
- 1/2 cup water
- 3/4 cup canned juice pack pineapple tidbits, undrained
- 2 teaspoons cornstarch
- 1/4 teaspoon ground ginger
- 1/8 teaspoon garlic powder
- 1/8 teaspoon allspice

In medium skillet, combine carrot and water. Cover; cook over medium heat until crisp-tender. Drain and return to skillet. In small bowl, combine pineapple, cornstarch, ginger, garlic powder, and allspice. Add to skillet. Cook over low heat, stirring constantly until thickened.

Nutritional Information per serving: 60 calories

Baked Potato with Special Toppings

Quick, filling snack or meal.

Preparation Time: 20 minutes

Yield: 2 servings
Preheat Oven: 425°

- 2 medium baking potatoes

Primavera Topping:

- 2 tablespoons broccoli flowerets
- 1 tablespoon chopped green onions
- 2 teaspoons chopped fresh parsley
- 1/4 cup shredded Monterey Jack cheese

Mexicana Topping:

- 1/4 cup shredded lettuce
- 2 tablespoons diced tomato
- 1 tablespoon chopped green onions
- 1/4 cup shredded Cheddar cheese
- 2 teaspoons picante sauce

Prick potatoes with fork. Bake 45 minutes or until tender. Make crosscut in top of potatoes. Squeeze to open; fluff up with fork. Add desired toppings and return to oven several minutes until cheese melts. Serve hot.

Nutritional Information per serving: Primavera: 160 calories, Mexicana: 180 calories

SLIM SIMMERED ZUCCHINI

YIELD: 4 SERVINGS

PREPARATION TIME: 10 MINUTES

- **1** POUND SLICED ZUCCHINI
- **16** OUNCES CANNED TOMATOES, CHOPPED
- **1/2** CUP CHOPPED ONION
- **1/2** TABLESPOON CHOPPED FRESH PARSLEY
- **1/8** TEASPOON GARLIC POWDER
- **1/8** TEASPOON WHITE PEPPER

COMBINE ALL INGREDIENTS IN MEDIUM SKILLET AND SIMMER OVER LOW HEAT UNTIL ZUCCHINI IS TENDER-CRISP, ABOUT 10 TO 15 MINUTES.

VARIATION: JUST BEFORE SERVING, ADD 1/3 CUP GRATED LOW-MOISTURE, PART-SKIM MOZZARELLA CHEESE. THIS WILL ADD 20 CALORIES PER SERVING.

NUTRITIONAL INFORMATION PER SERVING: 40 CALORIES

TOMATOES BRITTANY

YIELD: 6 SERVINGS

PREPARATION TIME: 20 MINUTES

- **6** MEDIUM TOMATOES
- **20** OUNCES FROZEN FRENCH-STYLE GREEN BEANS
- **1/2** CUP SLICED FRESH MUSHROOMS
- **1/3** CUP REDUCED-CALORIE ITALIAN DRESSING
- **1/4** CUP CHOPPED GREEN ONIONS
- **1/4** TEASPOON DRIED BASIL, CRUMBLED
- **1/4** TEASPOON DRIED THYME, CRUMBLED
- **1/8** TEASPOON FRESHLY GROUND PEPPER

SLICE TOP OFF EACH TOMATO; SCOOP OUT PULP. INVERT SHELLS TO DRAIN. COOK AND DRAIN BEANS; COMBINE WITH REMAINING INGREDIENTS. COVER; CHILL 3 HOURS. FILL TOMATO SHELLS WITH BEAN MIXTURE AND SERVE.

HINT: MARINATED BEAN MIXTURE CAN BE SERVED AS SALAD OR VEGETABLE.

NUTRITIONAL INFORMATION PER SERVING: 40 CALORIES

Fabulous Rice

Preparation Time: 5 minutes *Yield: 8 servings*

- **2½ cups water**
- **½ teaspoon instant beef bouillon granules**
- **1¼ cups uncooked converted rice**
- **¼ teaspoon garlic powder**
- **¼ teaspoon freshly ground pepper**
- **1½ tablespoons chopped fresh parsley**

In medium saucepan bring water to boil; stir in bouillon granules. Add rice, garlic powder and pepper. Lower heat; cover and simmer until rice is tender and water is absorbed, about 20 to 25 minutes. Remove from heat; add parsley and stir.

Nutritional Information per Serving: 105 calories

No Sugar Barbeque Sauce

Preparation Time: 30 minutes *Yield: 2 cups*

- **1 tablespoon margarine**
- **1¼ cups finely chopped onion**
- **2 cups tomato sauce**
- **1 tablespoon Worcestershire sauce**
- **1 tablespoon vinegar**
- **1 tablespoon fresh lemon juice**
- **¼ teaspoon salt**
- **¼ teaspoon dry mustard**
- **¼ teaspoon curry powder**
- **¼ teaspoon Tabasco**
- **⅛ teaspoon freshly ground pepper**
- **½ teaspoon liquid smoke**

In medium saucepan melt margarine over low heat. Add onion and sauté until transparent; stir in remaining ingredients and simmer 15 minutes. Cool; pour into glass jar with lid. Refrigerate. Use to baste chicken or as topping on fish.

Nutritional Information: 11 calories per tablespoon

Marinara Sauce 

Real Italian taste, with no sugar, no added salt!

Yield: 4 1/2 cups *Preparation Time: 30 minutes*

In large skillet over medium heat, sauté garlic and onion in oil until golden. Add remaining ingredients; simmer 30 to 45 minutes, or until sauce is thickened.

- **2 teaspoons minced fresh garlic**
- **1 tablespoon minced onion**
- **2 tablespoons extra virgin olive or safflower oil**
- **24 ounces canned plum tomatoes, undrained and chopped**
- **2 cups peeled, chopped tomato**
- **1/2 cup chopped fresh parsley**
- **1 1/4 teaspoons dried basil, crumbled**
- **1/4 teaspoon crushed red pepper flakes**
- **1/4 teaspoon allspice**
- **Freshly ground pepper, to taste**

Nutritional Information per 1/2 cup: 110 calories

Apple Fruit Sauce

Wonderful added to plain yogurt or served over ice milk.

Yield: 2 cups *Preparation Time: 15 minutes*

Combine 1 1/2 cups apple juice, cinnamon and allspice. Bring to boil; reduce heat to low. Combine cornstarch and reserved juice in jar with tight fitting lid; shake to dissolve. Whisk into juice mixture. Cook until thickened and smooth, stirring constantly. Serve warm over pancakes.

- **2 cups apple juice (reserve 1/2 cup)**
- **1 1/4 teaspoons cinnamon**
- **1/2 teaspoon allspice**
- **2 tablespoons cornstarch**

Nutritional Information: 10 calories per tablespoon

Peach-Berry Fruit Sauce

Preparation Time: 15 minutes *Yield: 1½ cups*

- **1 cup sliced fresh peaches (divided)**
- **1 cup fresh blueberries (divided)**
- **½ cup apple juice**
- **⅛ teaspoon allspice**

In medium saucepan combine ½ cup peaches, ½ cup blueberries and remaining ingredients. Bring to boil; reduce heat and simmer, uncovered, 15 minutes. Add remaining fruit, stirring well. Serve warm.

HINT: When fresh fruit is out of season substitute frozen, unsweetened fruit.

NUTRITIONAL INFORMATION: 13 calories per tablespoon

Harmony Seasoning

Natural all-purpose seasoning; no salt, no sugar.

Preparation Time: 10 minutes *Yield: 13½ teaspoons*

- **2 teaspoons dried parsley**
- **2 teaspoons ground allspice**
- **1½ teaspoons ground coriander**
- **1 teaspoon rosemary**
- **1 teaspoon freshly ground pepper**
- **1 teaspoon dried basil**
- **1 teaspoon marjoram**
- **1 teaspoon dried mustard**
- **1 teaspoon ground sage**
- **½ teaspoon garlic powder**
- **½ teaspoon onion powder**
- **½ teaspoon dried savory**
- **½ teaspoon ground thyme**

Combine all spices and herbs in large bowl; mix thoroughly. Store in jar or air-tight plastic bag. Use within 4 months.

deLIGHTful Sour Cream

Creamy and versatile.

Yield: 1 cup *Preparation Time: 5 minutes*

Process cottage cheese and milk in blender or food processor until smooth. Stir in lemon juice.

- **1 cup low-fat cottage cheese**
- **1 tablespoon skim milk**
- **1 tablespoon fresh lemon juice**

Nutritional Information: 15 calories per tablespoon

deLIGHTful Hollandaise

Delicately flavored.

Yield: 1½ cups *Preparation Time: 20 minutes*

Melt margarine over low heat; add cottage cheese, stir until warm. Add dry mustard. In blender, process yolks slightly; gradually add cottage cheese mixture. Blend until smooth. Pour into bowl; stir in pepper and lemon juice.

- **3 tablespoons margarine**
- **1 cup low-fat cottage cheese, drained**
- **¼ teaspoon dry mustard**
- **2 egg yolks**
- **Dash ground red pepper**
- **1 tablespoon fresh lemon juice**

Nutritional Information: 22 calories; 12 mg. calcium per tablespoon

Akin's Carrot Cake

Preparation Time: 30 minutes

Yield: 12 servings
Preheat Oven: 350°

- 2 cups whole wheat pastry flour
- 1 cup oat flour
- 2 teaspoons baking soda
- 2 teaspoons cinnamon
- 1 teaspoon salt
- 3/4 cup unsalted butter, softened
- 1 1/2 cups honey
- 4 eggs
- 1/2 cup plain low-fat yogurt
- 3 cups grated carrot
- 1 cup chopped walnuts

Sift flours, soda, cinnamon and salt together in small bowl. Set aside.

With electric mixer, cream butter and honey until light. Blend in eggs and yogurt. Add flour mixture; beat well. Stir in carrot and nuts; pour into greased 9 × 13 inch pan. Bake 40 to 45 minutes or until tester inserted in center of cake comes out clean; cool. Prepare frosting and spread over cake.

Honey Cheese Frosting:

- 8 ounces cream cheese, softened
- 1/3 cup honey
- 1 tablespoon fresh lemon juice
- 1/2 teaspoon pure vanilla extract

Combine all ingredients and beat until smooth.

Akin's Special Foods

Nutritional Information: high fiber, no refined sugar

Golden Apple Rings

Preparation Time: 20 minutes

Yield: 4 servings

- 1 tablespoon grated orange rind
- 1/2 teaspoon grated lemon rind
- 3/4 cup unsweetened apple juice
- 1/4 cup golden raisins
- 2 large Golden Delicious apples, cored and sliced crosswise into rings

In large skillet combine rinds, juice and raisins; bring to boil. Add apple rings; lower heat and cover. Simmer 6 to 8 minutes or until apples are tender. Uncover and reduce liquid if needed.

Nutritional Information per Serving: 105 calories

Fruit 'N' Raisin Bread Pudding

Yield: 8 servings — *Preparation Time: 25 minutes*
Preheat Oven: 325°

Cut 2 apricots into 1/2 inch cubes. In greased 8 inch square baking dish, combine bread with cubed apricots. Mash remaining apricots. Whisk in milk, sugar, extract and eggs until blended. Pour over bread mixture. Set dish in roasting pan on oven shelf. Pour boiling water into pan halfway up side of baking dish. Bake 1 hour 20 minutes, or until knife inserted in center comes out clean. Serve with whipped cream, if desired.

- **4 medium ripe apricots (or equivalent canned, rinsed and drained), divided**
- **8 ounces cinnamon raisin bread, cut into 1 inch squares**
- **1 cup low-fat milk**
- **1/2 cup sugar**
- **3/4 teaspoon pure almond extract**
- **3 eggs, beaten well**
- **Whipped cream**

Nutritional Information: 185 calories

Refreshing Strawberry Whip

Cool dessert for a hot summer day.

Yield: 8 servings — *Preparation Time: 30 minutes*

Thaw strawberries 10 to 15 minutes. In large bowl combine 16 ounces strawberries with egg whites, sugar, almond extract and lemon juice. Beat on high speed of electric mixer until stiff peaks form (about 10 to 12 minutes). Add whipped topping; beat until smooth. Spoon into 8 individual serving dishes and freeze until firm.

Crush remaining strawberries and spoon over dessert to serve.

- **24 ounces frozen whole unsweetened strawberries (reserve 8 ounces)**
- **2 egg whites**
- **1/4 cup sugar**
- **1/2 teaspoon pure almond extract**
- **1 tablespoon fresh lemon juice**
- **1 cup frozen non-dairy whipped topping, thawed**

Nutritional Information per serving: 110 calories

deLIGHTful Eclairs

Preparation Time: 1½ hour

Yield: 9 servings
Preheat Oven: 375°

Puff Pastry:
½ cup water
2 tablespoons vegetable oil
½ cup sifted all-purpose flour
½ teaspoon salt
2 large eggs

In medium saucepan, heat water and oil to boiling. With wooden spoon, beat in flour and salt. Remove from heat. Add eggs, one at a time, beating well after each addition. Spoon mixture into nine 1×3 inch strips on lightly greased baking sheet. Allow room for spreading. Bake 40 to 45 minutes. Cool.

Prepare Custard Filling and cool. Slit eclairs, remove dough from inside and fill with custard. Prepare glaze and drizzle over tops.

Custard Filling:
1½ cups skim milk
1½ tablespoons cornstarch
4 tablespoons sugar
2 egg yolks, beaten well
1 teaspoon pure vanilla extract

In medium pan heat milk over moderate heat. Combine cornstarch and sugar and add to milk. Mix well; remove from heat and slowly whisk in egg yolks. Cook over low heat until thick, stirring constantly. Remove from heat; stir in vanilla and cool.

Mocha Glaze:
2 teaspoons cocoa powder
5 tablespoons confectioners sugar
1 to 1½ tablespoons brewed coffee

Mix cocoa and sugar. Beat in enough coffee to make a thin glaze.

Nutritional Information Per Serving: 155 calories

APPLE BERRY CRUNCH

YIELD: 6 SERVINGS *PREPARATION TIME: 20 MINUTES*
PREHEAT OVEN: 375°

- 3 CUPS CORED, THINLY SLICED TART APPLES
- $1\frac{1}{2}$ CUPS FRESH CRANBERRIES
- 3 TABLESPOONS ORANGE JUICE
- 1 TABLESPOON GRATED ORANGE RIND
- 3 TABLESPOONS UNBLEACHED ALL-PURPOSE FLOUR
- 1/4 CUP QUICK OATS
- 1/4 CUP CHOPPED PECANS
- 1/4 CUP DARK BROWN SUGAR, FIRMLY PACKED
- 1 TEASPOON CINNAMON
- 1/2 TEASPOON NUTMEG
- 1/8 TEASPOON ALLSPICE
- 2 TABLESPOONS VEGETABLE OIL

COMBINE APPLES, CRANBERRIES, JUICE AND RIND. PLACE IN $1\frac{1}{2}$ QUART SHALLOW BAKING DISH. COMBINE REMAINING INGREDIENTS; TOSS UNTIL CRUMBLY. SPOON OVER APPLE MIXTURE. BAKE 25 TO 30 MINUTES OR UNTIL TOPPING IS GOLDEN.

NUTRITIONAL INFORMATION PER SERVING: 193 CALORIES; 8.5 GRAMS FAT

LEMON MOUSSE

YIELD: 10 SERVINGS *PREPARATION TIME: 20 MINUTES*

- 1 CUP SUGAR (RESERVE 1/4 CUP)
- 1/2 CUP CORNSTARCH
- 3 CUPS SKIM MILK
- $1\frac{1}{2}$ TEASPOONS GRATED LEMON RIND
- 1/2 CUP FRESH LEMON JUICE
- 4 EGG WHITES
- $2\frac{1}{2}$ CUPS SLICED FRESH STRAWBERRIES, CHILLED

COMBINE 3/4 CUP SUGAR AND CORNSTARCH IN MEDIUM SAUCEPAN; ADD MILK. COOK OVER MEDIUM HEAT, STIRRING CONSTANTLY, UNTIL THICKENED. REMOVE FROM HEAT; ADD RIND AND JUICE. COOL, STIRRING OCCASIONALLY. BEAT EGG WHITES UNTIL FOAMY. GRADUALLY ADD RESERVED SUGAR, ONE TABLESPOON AT A TIME, BEATING UNTIL SOFT PEAKS FORM. FOLD INTO LEMON MIXTURE. SPOON INTO SERVING DISHES; CHILL. TOP EACH SERVING WITH 1/4 CUP STRAWBERRIES.

NUTRITIONAL INFORMATION PER SERVING: 153 CALORIES; LOW CHOLESTEROL

Pears Melba

Preparation Time: 30 minutes

Yield: 4 servings

- 3 cups water
- 1 3 inch cinnamon stick
- 1 teaspoon pure vanilla extract
- 1½ tablespoons fresh lemon juice (reserve ½ teaspoon)
- Lemon rind, cut into 1 × 3 inch piece
- 4 large fresh pears, stems intact, peeled, halved and cored
- 1 tablespoon cornstarch
- 10 ounces frozen raspberries, thawed, drained (reserve juice)
- 1 cup low-fat cottage cheese
- 2 teaspoons sugar
- Mint leaves

In large skillet combine water, cinnamon stick, vanilla, 1 tablespoon lemon juice and rind. Bring water to high simmer; add pears and poach, covered, 10 minutes. (Can be prepared up to this point, covered and chilled overnight.) Add cornstarch to reserved raspberry juice; heat until slightly thickened. Add berries; cool.

Purée cottage cheese, reserved lemon juice and sugar until smooth and creamy. Matching halves, fill each pear half with 2 tablespoons cheese mixture; stand upright on plate and press halves together. Level bottom, if necessary, by cutting off thin slice. Spoon 2 tablespoons raspberry sauce over each pear. Place mint leaf at each stem. May be chilled several hours.

HINT: If fresh pears are not available, canned pear halves can be substituted.

NUTRITIONAL INFORMATION PER SERVING: 148 calories

Peach Strawberry Compote

Preparation Time: 15 minutes

Yield: 6 servings

- 1½ teaspoons cornstarch
- 2 tablespoons white grape juice or apple juice
- 1½ cups frozen sliced strawberries, thawed and drained (reserve juice)
- 1 tablespoon orange-flavored liqueur
- 24 fresh or frozen peach slices (no sugar added)

In medium saucepan combine cornstarch, grape juice and reserved strawberry juice. Stir over low heat until mixture is smooth and thickened. Remove from heat and add strawberries, liqueur and peaches. Chill.

NUTRITIONAL INFORMATION PER SERVING: 112 calories

MINTED PINEAPPLE

YIELD: 8 SERVINGS

PREPARATION TIME: 30 MINUTES

1 LARGE RIPE PINEAPPLE
1 TEASPOON SUGAR
1 TEASPOON PURE MINT EXTRACT
1 QUART LEMON SHERBET
1/4 CUP GREEN CREME DE MENTHE
FRESH MINT LEAVES

CUT PINEAPPLE IN HALF LENGTHWISE, THROUGH TOP LEAVES. LOOSEN AND REMOVE FRUIT FROM SHELL. RESERVE SHELLS AND CHILL. TRIM OFF WOODY CORE OF PINEAPPLE; CUT FRUIT INTO BITE-SIZE CHUNKS. COMBINE PINEAPPLE, SUGAR AND MINT EXTRACT IN MEDIUM BOWL; COVER AND CHILL 4 TO 5 HOURS. SCOOP SHERBET INTO BALLS; PLACE ON COOKIE SHEET AND STORE IN FREEZER. WHEN READY TO ASSEMBLE, FILL SHELLS WITH PINEAPPLE MIXTURE; TOP WITH SHERBET BALLS AND SPRINKLE WITH CREME DE MENTHE. GARNISH WITH MINT LEAVES. SPOON INTO INDIVIDUAL DESSERT BOWLS TO SERVE.

HINT: FOR VARIATION, USE PINEAPPLE SHERBET OR FROZEN VANILLA YOGURT.

NUTRITIONAL INFORMATION PER SERVING: 136 CALORIES

KIWI SORBET

YIELD: 8 SERVINGS

PREPARATION TIME: 10 MINUTES

1 CUP PEELED AND CHOPPED KIWI (APPROXIMATELY 3)
1 CUP UNSWEETENED APPLE JUICE
3/4 CUP WHITE GRAPE JUICE
1 TABLESPOON FRESH LIME JUICE
1/2 TEASPOON GRATED LIME RIND

COMBINE KIWI AND JUICES IN BLENDER; PURÉE. STIR IN RIND. POUR MIXTURE INTO 8 INCH SHALLOW GLASS PAN; FREEZE UNTIL NEARLY SOLID. TURN ICY MIXTURE INTO BOWL OF ELECTRIC MIXER; BEAT UNTIL FOAMY. RETURN MIXTURE TO PAN; FREEZE UNTIL FIRM.

HINT: SORBET WILL BE EASIER TO SERVE IF REMOVED FROM FREEZER AND ALLOWED TO STAND 10 MINUTES.

NUTRITIONAL INFORMATION PER SERVING: 52 CALORIES

Tarte Aux Fruites (Fresh Fruit Tart)

Beautiful, colorful presentation. Great for summer party!

Preparation Time: 1 hour

Yield: 10 servings
Preheat Oven: 400°

Citrus Glaze:
- 1 tablespoon cornstarch
- 1/3 cup water
- 3/4 cup fresh orange juice
- 1 tablespoon fresh lemon juice
- 1/2 teaspoon grated lemon rind

Combine cornstarch, water and orange juice in small saucepan. Bring to boil; cook over medium heat 1 minute, stirring constantly. Remove from heat; stir in lemon juice and rind. Place wax paper or plastic wrap on surface; cool. Can be made ahead. Makes 1 cup.

Pastry:
- 1 cup whole wheat pastry flour (or unbleached all-purpose flour)
- 1/4 cup cornstarch
- 1/4 cup sugar
- 1/3 cup margarine
- 1 egg, beaten lightly
- Vegetable cooking spray

Mix together flour, cornstarch and sugar; cut in margarine with pastry blender until mixture resembles coarse meal. Add egg; stir with fork until moistened. Shape dough into ball; chill.

Spray 12 × 14 1/2 inch flat cookie sheet with cooking spray. Put dough directly on sheet. Roll pastry into 10 1/2 inch circle; trim edges. Bake 12 to 15 minutes, or until lightly browned. Cool on baking sheet 10 minutes; carefully remove to wire rack to cool completely. Place pastry on serving platter.

Fruit:
- 1 cup sliced fresh strawberries
- 1 cup sliced fresh nectarines or peaches
- 1/2 cup seedless green grapes, halved
- 1/4 cup fresh or unsweetened, frozen blueberries (thawed and drained, if frozen)

Arrange fruit attractively over top of pastry in pinwheel or concentric circles. Spoon citrus glaze evenly over fruit. Refrigerate tarte at least one hour before serving.

Nutritional Information Per Serving: 170 calories

SUPER COOKIES

YIELD: 5 TO 6 DOZEN
PREHEAT OVEN: 300°

PREPARATION TIME: 30 MINUTES

2 EGGS, BEATEN LIGHTLY
1 CUP HONEY
1/2 CUP SAFFLOWER OIL
3 TEASPOONS CINNAMON
1/3 CUP SUGAR
1 CUP WHOLE WHEAT PASTRY FLOUR
2 TABLESPOONS POWDERED MILK
2 CUPS OLD-FASHIONED OATS
1/3 CUP WHEAT GERM
1/2 CUP SUNFLOWER SEEDS
1/3 CUP SESAME SEED
1/2 CUP CHOPPED CASHEWS
2 TEASPOONS PURE VANILLA EXTRACT
VEGETABLE COOKING SPRAY

COMBINE EGGS, HONEY AND OIL IN LARGE BOWL. SET ASIDE. IN MEDIUM BOWL COMBINE ALL DRY INGREDIENTS. ADD TO EGG MIXTURE WITH VANILLA AND COMBINE WELL. COAT COOKIE SHEET WITH COOKING SPRAY. DROP DOUGH BY ROUNDED TEASPOONS ONTO SHEET AND FLATTEN WITH FORK. BAKE 25 MINUTES OR UNTIL GOLDEN. COOL ON WIRE RACK AND STORE IN AIR-TIGHT CONTAINER.

NUTRITIONAL INFORMATION: WHOLE WHEAT; HIGH FIBER

Freezer Date Cookies

Preparation Time: 45 minutes

Yield: 4 1/2 dozen
Preheat Oven: 350°

- 1/2 cup unsalted butter or margarine, softened
- 1 egg
- 1 teaspoon pure vanilla extract
- 1 cup less 2 tablespoons unbleached all-purpose flour
- 1 teaspoon baking powder
- 1/4 teaspoon salt
- 1 cup chopped pitted dates
- 1 cup shredded coconut
- 1 cup chopped walnuts or pecans
- Vegetable cooking spray

In large bowl cream butter, egg, and vanilla with mixer until smooth. In separate bowl combine 1 cup less 2 tablespoons flour, baking powder and salt. Gradually add flour mixture to butter mixture until well blended. Spread 2 tablespoons flour on chopping board. Chop dates on board, coating knife with flour to prevent sticking. Combine dates, coconut and nuts. Stir into flour mixture. Form dough into two 1 1/2 inch rolls and wrap in wax paper or foil. Chill in freezer until firm enough to slice, about 2 hours. With sharp knife, cut rolls into 3/8 inch slices. Place on cookie sheet coated with cooking spray; bake about 12 minutes or until golden.

Loosen cookies with spatula immediately after removing from oven. Cool on cookie sheet 5 minutes before removing to wire rack.

NUTRITIONAL INFORMATION: 55 calories per cookie

Sounds Delicious *Testers*

Caroline Abbot
Felice Abels
Jacqueline Abraham
Judy Acklin
Jackie Adams
Le Akers
Jean Akin
Maxine Alexander
B. Allen
Ginger Anderson
Lili Anderson
Madeline Argenbright
Sally Armstrong
Elizabeth Ashley
Mary Atkinson
Susan Bailey
Beverly Baker
Sandy Bakke
Pam Bandy
Connie Barton
Polly Batchelor
Gertrude Baulis
Betty Baumer
Nora Berard
Betsy Berkemeyer
Judy Bernham
Terry Bevins
Judith Bianchi
Sue Biasiolli
Margaret Bloomberg
Loretta Boerger
Lois Bonnell
Joyce Bowman
Maureen Brady
Loretta Brewer
Shelley Briggs
Doris Brooks
Judie Brown
Natalie Brundred
Monica Bryant
Pat Bryant
Lori Buntz
Anne Burlingame
Carthel Burt
Patti Burton
Sharon Butler
Geralann Caldwell
K. Caldwell
Frances Campbell
Karla Campbell
Jane Camporeale
Bonnie Canada
Carolyn Carlton
Jerry Carroll
Nancy Caudill
Edna Cheatham
Marilyn Chenoweth
Judy Cherry
Jean Childs
June Chittom
Susan Coats
Geralann Coldwell
Beth Colpitts
Maggie Confer
Sharon Conley
Pat Connery
Liz Copeland
Kathy Craft
Ann Crawley
Nannette Creamer
Donna Cropper
Fran Crosby
Ann Culver
Katherine Cunningham
Betty Daggs
Phyllis Dammen
Beverley D'Angelo
Mary Lou Daniel
Melonnie Dauben
Grace Davis
Kathy Dawes
Carol DeBiase
Margaret Dean
Kristi DeNoya
Debbie Dill
Helen Dillon
Mary Beth Dolan
Keryl Doss
Desma Downs
Sue Doyle
Sara Duncan
Marti Dunham
Betty Dupree
Elizabeth Easton
Anne Ebeling
Janine Eggers
Martha English
Charlene Ernst
Dorothy Estill
Clara Etter
Nancy Evans
Joan Ewing
Elizabeth Failing
Katy Farris
Cleo Fenwick
Joanna Fidler
Ann Fields
Lois Finley
Laurie Fiocchi
Jean Fisk
Pat Ford
Jackie France
Karen Fraser
Mary Freeland
Ruth Freeman
Patty Freese
Mary Jane Friend
Janis Fritz
Randy Gamel
Jean Gannon
Franne Gathright
Catherine Gawey
Charlene Gibson
Sue Gilmore
Susan Gingrich
Linda Goldsmith
Jackie Graham
May Graham
Bernice Grandpre
Jane Green
Danna Gresham
Jane Grimshaw
Linda Grimshaw
Paula Gulley
Sue Gulley
Betty Guthrie
Molly Guzan
Valerie Gwyn
Jimmie Haggard
Lisa Haglam
Janice Hall
Polly Hamilton
Pat Hanley
Mariann Harms
Jane Ann Harper
Carolyn Steele Hastings
Gretchan Haugh
June Hause
Kathy Hayes
Gretchen Heatherington
Bee Helgeson
Betty Henry
Janice Henry
Lowana Henshaw
Chris Herrmann
Doris Hewitt
Allen Hocker
Jeanne Honeywell
Marjorie Hooker
Virginia Hooper
Judy Hopkins
Elizabeth Horne
Barbara Houghton
Debbie Hughes
Mary Hyatt
Ella May Ingraham
Ellen Ingram
Zena Ingram
Ginni Jacobs
Marie Jett
Jewel Jobe
Julie Jobe
Lydia Johns
Dianna Johnson
Jeannie Johnson
Kathy Johnson
Lucille Johnson
Mary Jane Johnson
Terri Johnson
Jan Jones
Sandi Jones
Barbara Katapodis
Cindy Keeling
Judith Keil
Amy Kelly
Dianne Kesinger
Cindy Kilkenny
Elizabeth Kindred
Kay King
Rosemary Kittle
Judi Klein
Caroline Kline

Deanna Kline
Judy Knorpp
Cathy kranz
Bobbie Kristinik
Lydia Kronfield
Marsha Krummel
Dorothy Kugler
Joy Laden
Helen Laughlin
Loma Lavell
Jo Ann Lawrence
Nancy Leatzow
Barbara Lee
Julia Lee
Sayde LeVine
Pam Liggett
Mell Littlefield
Sandi Livingston
Lee Lobeck
Nevin Loerke
Joyce Lohrenz
Phyllis Kent Long
Christie Lord
Katherine Louros
Marguerite Lovell
Gertrude Lovoi
Helen Lowry
Ellen Luke
Lisa Lutz
Linda Lynch
Bonita Maddox
Brenda Magoon
Lee Major
Diana Mallonee
Linda Malone
Ruth Manley
Janie Manning
Alexa Maples
Nancy Jo Marsden
Mary Ann Martin
Shara Mattern
Barbara McCrary
Teri McDonald
Carla McGill
Doris McGrath
Debbie McHattie
Zara McKinney
Kathy McLaughlin
Judith McQuay
Libby Meyer
Margaret Meyer
Susan Middlebrooks
Judy Miller
Millie Millspaugh
Pat Minielly
Carol Minshall
Fae Mitchell
Genne Mitchell
Karel Moore
Paula Moore
Betty Moses
Claire Mueller
Donna Muscovalley
Lucille Musgrove
Barbara Naugle
Nicole Nauman
Sylvia Nay
Nancy Neale
Betty Neeley
Romney Nesbitt
Ann Nolen
Almeta Norfleet
Jan Nunn
Marilyn Olsen
Mary Ann Orr
Peggy Orr
Kathy O'Brien
Lynn O'Sullivan
Janet Pagano
Beth Palmer
Suzanne Palmer
Kristi Pape
Lorraine Patchett
Phyllis Patton
Pat Payton
Patty Payton
Jenifer Perigo
Pat Perry
Teri Peters
Jane Philips
Helen Pickett
Sandi Pitman
Linda Pond
Fritzie Prather
Maxine Province
Jonene Pruitt
Teka Regnier
Lynn Reilly
Jan Reinhart
Dianne Renkes
Kathryn Rheam
Marilyn Rhodes
Jean Risser
Nancy Roach
Dale Roberson
Audrey Robinson
Laura Roe
Dee Dee Rogers
Julia Rogers
Marcella Rollins
Joyce Roodman
Betty Rose
Margaret Rose
Anna Running
Marge Rush
Martha Rusko
Margaret S. Rutter
Betty Sample
Carolyn Savage
Beverly Schafer
Carol Schwake
Joyce Scroggins
Karen Selby
Doris Shelton
Jean Shields
Dean Sigle
Doreen Sigle
Karen Simpson
Claudia Sloan
Leona Sloan
Betty Jane Smith
Connie Smith
Linda Smith
Lonnie Snyder
Carol Southard
Pat Spears
Rhonda Spears
Linda Sproule-Jones
Alice Sprouse
Pat Stamper
Charlene Stamps
Anne Steelman
Jan Steffensen
Sadie Stephens
Nan Stevens
Lois Stratton
Iris Studenny
Judie Suess
Ann Sullivan
Juanita Sunderman
Rosann Sundvahl
Florence Swabb
Cathy Swadener
Jayne Swartz
Susan Swartz
Marilyn Sylvan
Lona Symour
Judy Taylor
Beth Teel
Dorothy Thomas
Debbie Thornberry
Donna Tidwell
Jeanette Todd
Catherine Tolin
Elizabeth Lord Tooman
Tina Townsend
Fran Treacy
Genie Tumilty
Mary Turkal
Debbie Turner
Betty Vemt
Nadine Vickery
Cinda Viles
Frank Walters
Nora Walworth
Virginia Watkins
Peggy Welch
Nancy Wells
Peggy Wentworth
Katie Wertz
Midge West
Rusty Wilcox
Judy Wiley
Daphne Wilkerson
Cathy Wilson
Debra Wilson
Julie Wilson
Faye Wink
Freda Winsett
Kathy Winslow
Sandy Wood
Virginia Wood
Jean Wortham
Lee Ann Wortham
Earline Wyman
Louise Zelifs
Ruth Zetik
Debbie Zinke

INDEX

C

D

E

F

Q

R

S

T

V

W

Z

PAN SIZES AND SUBSTITUTIONS

Pan Size	Capacity	Substitution
Two 8 inch round layers	4 cups each	Two thin 8 × 8 × 2 inch squares
		18 to 24 cupcakes
One 7 × 3 × 2 inch loaf pan	4 cups	
One 8 inch pie plate	3 cups level	
	4 to 4½ cups mounded	
Three 8 inch round layers	4 cups each	Two 9 × 9 × 2 inch squares
One 9 inch pie plate	4 cups level	
	5 to 6 cups mounded	
Two 9 inch round layers	6 cups each	Two 8 × 8 × 2 inch squares
		One 15 × 10 × 1 inch jelly roll pan
		30 cupcakes
One 8 × 3½ × 2½ inch loaf pan	6 cups	
One 10 inch pie plate	6 cups level	
	6½ to 7 cups mounded	
One 10 × 4 inch bundt pan	6 cups	
Two 8 × 8 × 2 inch squares	8 cups each	One 13 × 9 × 2 inch rectangle
		Two 9 inch round layers
One 9 × 5 × 3 inch loaf pan	8 cups	One 9 × 9 × 2 inch square
		24 to 30 cupcakes
One 9 × 9 × 2 inch square pan	10 cups	Two thin 8 inch round layers
One 15 × 10 × 1 inch jelly roll pan	10 cups	Two 9 inch round layers
One 10 × 4 inch tube pan	12 cups	Two 9 × 5 × 3 inch loaves
		One 13 × 9 × 2 inch rectangle
		One 15 × 10 × 1 inch rectangle
One 13 × 9 × 2 inch rectangle	12 cups	Two 8 × 8 × 2 inch squares
		Two 9 inch round layers
One 13 × 9 × 3 inch roasting pan	16 cups	Two 15 × 10 × 1 inch jelly roll pans

MEASUREMENTS FOR BEFORE AND AFTER

(Measurements are approximate and are provided only as a guide.)

Crumbs		
Bread	1 slice	1/2 to 3/4 cup soft 1/4 to 1/3 cup fine dry
Cookies, Chocolate Wafers	19 wafers	1 cup finely crushed
Vanilla wafers	22 wafers	1 cup finely crushed
Crackers, Graham	14 squares	1 cup finely crushed
rich round	24 crackers	1 cup finely crushed
Saltine	28 crackers	1 cup finely crushed
Potato chips	4 ounces	2 cups coarsely crushed
Dairy		
Eggs	5 to 6 large	1 cup
	12 to 14 yolks	1 cup
	8 to 10 whites	1 cup
Cheese, cream	3 ounces	6 tablespoons
Fruits		
Apples	1 medium	1 cup sliced or diced
Apricots, whole	8 to 12 (1 pound)	2 1/2 cups halved or sliced
Avocados	1 medium	1 1/4 cups sliced
Bananas	1 medium	1/3 to 1/2 cup mashed
		3/4 cup sliced
Cherries	1 pound	2 cuts pitted
Cranberries	4 cups (1 pound)	3 to 4 cups sauce
Dates, pitted	1 pound	2 to 3 cups chopped
Grapes	1 pound	2 cups seeded
Lemons	1 medium	3 tablespoons juice
		1 to 2 tablespoons grated rind
Limes	1 medium	1 1/2 to 2 tablespoons juice
		1 to 1 1/2 teaspoons grated rind
Oranges	1 medium	1/3 to 1/2 cup juice
		2 to 3 tablespoons grated rind
		3/4 cup sections
Peaches, pears	1 medium	1/2 cup sliced
Rhubarb, cut	1 pound	2 cups cooked
Strawberries	1 quart	4 cups sliced

Meats and Seafood		
Bacon	8 slices cooked	1/2 cup crumbled
Crab, in shell	1 pound	3/4 to 1 cup flaked
Meat, boneless raw	1 pound	2 cups cooked, chopped
cooked	1 pound	3 cups chopped
Shrimp, raw in shell	1 1/2 pounds	2 cups cleaned, cooked
Miscellaneous		
Chocolate	1 ounce	4 tablespoons grated
Ginger root	1 tablespoon fresh	1 teaspoon powdered
Herbs	1 tablespoon fresh	1 teaspoon dried
Nuts		
Almonds, in shell	1 pound	3/4 to 1 cup shelled
shelled	1 pound	3 to 3 1/4 cups
Pecans, in shell	1 pound	1 3/4 to 2 cup shelled
shelled	1 pound	4 1/4 to 5 cups halves
Walnuts, in shell	1 pound	1 1/2 to 1 3/4 cups shelled
shelled	1 pound	4 cups chopped
Vegetables		
Beans, dried kidney, lima, navy	2 1/2 cups (1 pound)	6 to 7 cups cooked
Cabbage	1 small (1 pound)	4 1/2 to 5 cups shredded
Carrots, without tops	1 pound	3 cups shredded
Celery	8 ribs	2 3/4 cups chopped
Corn	2 medium ears	1 cups kernels
Green beans, cut up	3 cups (1 pound)	2 1/2 cups cooked
Green bell pepper	1 large	1 cup chopped or diced
Green onions, with tops	1 bunch	1 cup sliced
without tops		1/3 cup sliced
Lettuce	1 pound head	6 to 6 1/2 cups torn
Mushrooms	1 pound	5 cups sliced
		1 1/2 to 2 cups sliced, cooked
Onions	1 medium	1/2 cup chopped
Peas, in pods	1 pound	1 cup shelled
dried	2 cups (1 pound)	4 1/2 to 5 cups cooked
Potatoes	1 pound	3 1/2 to 4 cups sliced or diced
		2 cups mashed
Spinach	1 pound	1 1/2 cups cooked
Tomatoes	1 medium	1/2 cup cooked
Zucchini	1 medium	3/4 cup sliced or 1 cup grated

ROASTING TIMETABLE
(APPROXIMATE TIMES)

VARIETY AND CUT OF MEAT	APPROXIMATE WEIGHT (POUNDS)	°F OVEN TEMPERATURE	INTERNAL TEMPERATURE OF MEAT*	MINUTES PER POUND ROASTING TIME
BEEF				
RIB ROAST	4 TO 8	325°	140° (RARE)	25 – 30
			160° (MEDIUM)	30 – 35
RIB EYE ROAST	4 TO 6	325°	140° (RARE)	25 – 30
			160° (MEDIUM)	30 – 35
TENDERLOIN	4 TO 6	400°	140° (RARE)	12 – 14
TOP SIRLOIN ROAST	3 TO 6	325°	140° (RARE)	25 – 30
			160° (MEDIUM)	30 – 35
RUMP ROAST	5 TO 7	325°	150–170°	25 – 30
PORK				
FRESH				
CENTER LOIN	3 TO 5	325°	170°	30 – 35
LOIN, BONELESS	8 TO 10	325°	170°	30 – 35
HAM	10 TO 16	325°	170°	25 – 35
PICNIC SHOULDER	5 TO 8	325°	170°	30 – 35
SHOULDER BLADE ROAST	4 TO 6	325°	170°	30 – 40
CURED				
HAM, HALF (COOKED)	5 TO 7	325°	140°	18 – 24
WHOLE (COOKED)	10 TO 14	325°	140°	15 – 18
PICNIC SHOULDER (COOK-BEFORE-EATING)	5 TO 8	325°	170°	30 – 35
LAMB				
LEG, WHOLE	5 TO 9	325°	140° (RARE)	25 – 30
			160° (MEDIUM)	30 – 35
			170° (WELL)	35 – 40
SHOULDER, BONELESS	3½ TO 5	325°	160° (MEDIUM)	35 – 40
			170° (WELL)	40 – 45
CROWN ROAST	2½ TO 4	325°	140° (RARE)	30 – 35
			160° (MEDIUM)	35 – 40
			170° (WELL)	40 – 45
VEAL				
LEG, HALF	3 TO 5	325°	170°	40 – 50
RIB ROAST	3 TO 5	325°	170°	40 – 45
SHOULDER ROAST, BONELESS	4 TO 6	325°	170°	40 – 45
POULTRY				
CHICKEN, FRYER	2½ TO 3½	375°	185°	20 – 24
CHICKEN, ROASTING	4 TO 6	375°	185°	20 – 25

Cornish Hen	1 to 1½	375°	180–185°	45 - 55
Duck	4 to 6	350°	185°	20 - 25
Turkey, Unstuffed	8 to 12	325°	180–185°	20 - 22
	12 to 16	325°	180–185°	18 - 20
	16 to 20	325°	180–185°	16 - 18
	20 to 24	325°	180–185°	14 - 16

*Insert tip of meat thermometer in thickest part of roast. Tip should not touch bone, fat or gristle. Remove meat from oven when thermometer reads 5° below internal temperature shown in chart, as cooking continues after removal. Allow meat to stand 10 to 15 minutes before carving.

Substitution Chart

Baking powder	1 teaspoon equals 1/3 teaspoon baking soda plus 1/2 teaspoon cream of tartar
Butter	1 cup equals 7/8 cup oil; substitute only if recipe calls for melting butter
Chocolate, semisweet	6 ounces equals 6 tablespoons cocoa plus 7 tablespoons sugar and 1/4 cup shortening
Chocolate, sweetened	4 ounces equals 3 tablespoons cocoa, 1/4 cup plus 1½ teaspoons sugar and 2 tablespoons plus 2 teaspoons shortening
Chocolate, unsweetened	1 ounce equals 3 tablespoons cocoa plus 1 tablespoon butter, margarine or vegetable oil or 3 tablespoons carob powder plus 2 tablespoons water
Cornstarch, as thickener	1 tablespoon equals 2 tablespoons all-purpose flour
Cream, heavy	1 cup equals 3/4 cup milk plus 1/3 cup butter (will not whip)
Cream, light	1 cups equals 7/8 cup milk plus 3 tablespoons butter
Cream, sour	In baking, 1 cup equals 7/8 cup buttermilk, sour milk or yogurt plus 3 tablespoons butter; for dips, 1 cup equals 1 cup cottage cheese puréed with 1/4 cup yogurt or buttermilk or 6 ounces cream cheese plus enough milk to make 1 cup
Crumbs, bread	1 cup equals 3/4 cup cracker crumbs
Milk, sour	1 cup equals 1 cup minus 1 tablespoon milk plus 1 tablespoon lemon juice or white vinegar; let sit 5 minutes
Mushrooms, canned	6 ounces drained equals 1/2 pound fresh
Mushrooms, dried	3 ounces equals 1 pound fresh
Mustard, dried	1 teaspoon equals 1 tablespoon prepared
Soy sauce	1/4 cup equals 3 tablespoons Worcestershire sauce plus 1 tablespoon water
Tomatoes, fresh	1⅓ cups chopped, cooked equals 1 cup canned
Tomato, purée	1 cup equals 1/2 cup tomato paste plus 1/2 cup water
Worcestershire sauce	1 teaspoon equals 1 tablespoon soy sauce plus dash of hot pepper sauce

MEASUREMENTS

All Foods

Measurement	Equals	To Halve Recipe
1 pinch (Dry measure only)	1/8 teaspoon or less	1/16 teaspoon
1/2 tablespoon	1 1/2 teaspoons	3/4 teaspoon
1 tablespoon	3 teaspoons	1 1/2 teaspoons
1/6 cup	2 tablespoons + 2 teaspoons	1 tablespoon + 1 teaspoon
1/4 cup	4 tablespoons	2 tablespoons
1/3 cup	5 tablespoons + 1 teaspoon	2 tablespoons + 2 teaspoons
3/8 cup	1/4 cup + 2 tablespoons	3 tablespoons
1/2 cup	8 tablespoons	1/4 cup
5/8 cup	1/2 cup + 2 tablespoons	1/4 cup + 1 tablespoon
2/3 cup	10 tablespoons + 2 teaspoons	1/3 cup
3/4 cup	12 tablespoons	3/8 cup
7/8 cup	3/4 cup + 2 tablespoons	1/4 cup + 3 tablespoons
1 cup (1/2 pint)	16 tablespoons	1/2 cup
1 pint	2 cups	1 cup
1 quart	4 cups	2 cups
1 gallon	4 quarts (16 cups)	8 cups

Liquid

Measurement	Equals	To Halve Recipe
1 dash	4 to 6 drops	2 to 3 drops
1/4 teaspoon	24 drops	12 drops (1/8 teaspoon
1/2 tablespoon	1/4 fluid ounce	3/4 teaspoon
1 tablespoon	1/2 fluid ounce	1/2 tablespoon
2 tablespoons	1 fluid ounce	1 tablespoon
1 jigger	1 1/2 fluid ounces	4 1/2 teaspoons
1/2 cup	4 fluid ounces	2 fluid ounces
1/2 pint (1 cup)	8 fluid ounces	4 fluid ounces
1 pint (2 cups)	16 fluid ounces	8 fluid ounces
2 pints (1 quart)	32 fluid ounces	16 fluid ounces
2 quarts (1/2 gallon)	64 fluid ounces	32 fluid ounces
4 quarts (1 gallon)	128 fluid ounces	64 fluid ounces

VOLUNTEER COUNCIL OF THE TULSA PHILHARMONIC SOCIETY, INC.
8177 S. HARVARD
SUITE 431
TULSA, OKLAHOMA 74137

NAME ________________________________

ADDRESS ________________________________

CITY ____________________ STATE __________ ZIP ______

PLEASE SEND ME ______ COPIES OF SOUNDS DELICIOUS @ $14.95 ______

POSTAGE AND HANDLING @ $2.00 EACH ______

OKLAHOMA RESIDENTS PLEASE ADD $.94 SALES TAX PER COPY ______

TOTAL ______

CHECKS PAYABLE TO VOLUNTEER COUNCIL OF THE TULSA PHILHARMONIC SOCIETY, INC.

PLEASE CHARGE TO MY: ☐ **VISA** ☐ **MASTERCARD**

CARD NO. ☐☐☐☐☐☐☐☐☐☐☐☐☐☐☐☐

EXPIRATION DATE ______________

SIGNATURE OF CARD HOLDER ________________________________

- -

Sounds Delicious!

VOLUNTEER COUNCIL OF THE TULSA PHILHARMONIC SOCIETY, INC.
8177 S. HARVARD
SUITE 431
TULSA, OKLAHOMA 74137

NAME ________________________________

ADDRESS ________________________________

CITY ____________________ STATE __________ ZIP ______

PLEASE SEND ME ______ COPIES OF SOUNDS DELICIOUS @ $14.95 ______

POSTAGE AND HANDLING @ $2.00 EACH ______

OKLAHOMA RESIDENTS PLEASE ADD $.94 SALES TAX PER COPY ______

TOTAL ______

CHECKS PAYABLE TO VOLUNTEER COUNCIL OF THE TULSA PHILHARMONIC SOCIETY, INC.

PLEASE CHARGE TO MY: ☐ **VISA** ☐ **MASTERCARD**

CARD NO. ☐☐☐☐☐☐☐☐☐☐☐☐☐☐☐☐

EXPIRATION DATE ______________

SIGNATURE OF CARD HOLDER ________________________________

VOLUNTEER COUNCIL OF THE TULSA PHILHARMONIC SOCIETY, INC.
8177 S. HARVARD
SUITE 431
TULSA, OKLAHOMA 74137

NAME ____________________

ADDRESS ____________________

CITY ____________________ STATE __________ ZIP ________

PLEASE SEND ME ________ COPIES OF SOUNDS DELICIOUS @ $14.95 ________

POSTAGE AND HANDLING @ $2.00 EACH ________

OKLAHOMA RESIDENTS PLEASE ADD $.94 SALES TAX PER COPY ________

TOTAL ________

CHECKS PAYABLE TO VOLUNTEER COUNCIL OF THE TULSA PHILHARMONIC SOCIETY, INC.

PLEASE CHARGE TO MY: ☐ **VISA** ☐ **MASTERCARD**

CARD NO. ☐☐☐☐☐☐☐☐☐☐☐☐☐☐☐☐

EXPIRATION DATE ____________

SIGNATURE OF CARD HOLDER ____________________

VOLUNTEER COUNCIL OF THE TULSA PHILHARMONIC SOCIETY, INC.
8177 S. HARVARD
SUITE 431
TULSA, OKLAHOMA 74137

NAME ____________________

ADDRESS ____________________

CITY ____________________ STATE __________ ZIP ________

PLEASE SEND ME ________ COPIES OF SOUNDS DELICIOUS @ $14.95 ________

POSTAGE AND HANDLING @ $2.00 EACH ________

OKLAHOMA RESIDENTS PLEASE ADD $.94 SALES TAX PER COPY ________

TOTAL ________

CHECKS PAYABLE TO VOLUNTEER COUNCIL OF THE TULSA PHILHARMONIC SOCIETY, INC.

PLEASE CHARGE TO MY: ☐ **VISA** ☐ **MASTERCARD**

CARD NO. ☐☐☐☐☐☐☐☐☐☐☐☐☐☐☐☐

EXPIRATION DATE ____________

SIGNATURE OF CARD HOLDER ____________________